A READER'S GUIDE TO CANADIAN HISTORY

2
CONFEDERATION TO THE PRESENT

EDITED BY J.L. GRANATSTEIN
AND PAUL STEVENS

A Reader's Guide to Canadian History

2
CONFEDERATION TO THE PRESENT

13724-2 c.2

UNIVERSITY OF TORONTO PRESS
Toronto Buffalo London

© University of Toronto Press 1982
Toronto Buffalo London
Printed in Canada

ISBN 0-8020-6490-6

Canadian Cataloguing in Publication Data

Main entry under title:
A Reader's guide to Canadian history

Vol. 2 previously published as: Canada since 1867:
a bibliographical guide.
Contents: v. 1. Beginnings to Confederation / edited
by D.A. Muise – v. 2. Confederation to the present /
edited by J.L. Granatstein and Paul Stevens.
ISBN 0-8020-6442-6 (v. 1). – ISBN 0-8020-6490-6 (v. 2).

1. Canada History – To 1763 (New France) – Bibliography*.
2. Canada – History – 1763-1867 – Bibliography.
3. Canada – History – 1867- – Bibliography.
I. Muise, D.A. (Delphin Andrew), 1941-   II. Granatstein, J.L., 1939-   III. Stevens, Paul 1938-
IV. Title: Canada since 1867.

Z1382.R42   016.971   C82-094447-5

Publication of this book has been assisted by the Canada Council and
the Ontario Arts Council under their block grant programmes.

Contents

ix Contents

x Contents

Abbreviations

In the text abbreviations have been used for certain places, publishers, and journals as follows:

PLACE OF PUBLICATION

H Halifax
L London
M Montreal
NY New York
O Ottawa

Q Quebec City
T Toronto
TR Trois-Rivières
V Vancouver

PUBLISHERS

BE Le Boréal Express
CC Copp Clark
CI Clarke, Irwin
CIIA Canadian Institute of International Affairs
CS Champlain Society
HMH Editions Hurtubise – HMH
HRW Holt, Rinehart & Winston
KP/QP King's Printer/Queen's Printer
MAC Macmillan
MHR McGraw-Hill Ryerson

MQUP McGill-Queen's University Press
M&S McClelland and Stewart
OUP Oxford University Press
PAC Public Archives of Canada
PH Prentice-Hall
PUL Les Presses de l'université Laval
PUM Les Presses de l'Université de Montréal
PUQ Les Presses de l'Université du Québec
UBCP University of British Columbia Press
UTP University of Toronto Press

JOURNALS

BCS *BC Studies*
CCHAR Canadian Catholic Historical Association *Report*
CHAR Canadian Historical Association *Report*
(*Historical Papers* after 1972)
CHR *Canadian Historical Review*
CJEPS *Canadian Journal of Economics and Political Science*
DR *Dalhousie Review*
JCS *Journal of Canadian Studies*
NSHS Nova Scotia Historical Society (*Collections*)
OH *Ontario History*
QQ *Queen's Quarterly*
RHAF *Revue d'histoire de l'Amérique française*
SH *Social History*
TRSC *Transactions of the Royal Society of Canada*
UHR *Urban History Review*

A READER'S GUIDE TO CANADIAN HISTORY

2
CONFEDERATION TO THE PRESENT

J.L. GRANATSTEIN AND PAUL STEVENS

National politics

Political history has dominated the writing of Canadian historians since the turn of the century. Excessively national in scope, too heavily biographical in approach, overly episodic, based on an insufficient understanding of the country's social and economic development, and lacking in the application of the tools and methodologies historians elsewhere have begun to make use of, it can yet be easily justified. In a country artificially created to expedite the economic exploitation of an otherwise inaccessible transcontinental expanse, persistently differentiated in the racial and religious composition of its dominant components, politics has been the core of its historical development. Politics in Canada has provided the milieu in which the deepest passions of religion, race, and economic ambition have been harmonized and adjusted without resort to the destructive agencies of civil war and revolution which at different times have disrupted the political development of the three nations from which Canada has derived her national heritage.

INTRODUCTION

The political history of Canada has not lacked distinguished interpreters and annalists. Although there are no general studies of the historical development of the political party system, there are a number of texts where the student can begin his study. Edgar McInnis, *Canada: A Political and Social History* (T: HRW 1959), is an objective and well-balanced history from the founding of New France to the Conservatives' victory in March 1958. *Canada: A Story of Challenge* (Cambridge: Cambridge UP 1953), by J.M.S. Careless, is the second volume in the British Commonwealth series, intended 'to tell young students in each part of the Commonwealth about the history of the other parts.' Written in a clear and simple style, it fulfils its purpose extremely well, without indulging in patriotic excesses. A.R.M. Lower, *Colony to Nation: A History of Canada* (T: Longmans 1946), is an interesting study, the old story of the development of dominion status. More provocative, however, is Donald Creighton, *Dominion of the North: A History of Canada* (T: MAC 1944). Elaborating on the thesis conceived by Harold Innis and developed in his earlier study, *The Commercial Empire of the St. Lawrence*, 1760-1850 (T: Ryerson 1937), Creighton looks at Canada as the gradual expansion of the commercial empire based on the economic system of the St Lawrence region, and argues that the success of this system was the primary factor in the survival of Canada, both French and British. His 'The Decline and Fall of the Empire of the St. Lawrence,' CHAR, 1969, and *Canada's First Century* (T: MAC 1970), supplement the text, and the conclusions he comes to are somewhat foreboding. The most comprehensive single-volume history of Canada yet published, however, is W.L. Morton, *The Kingdom of Canada: A General History from Earliest Times* (T: M&S 1963). Although he was critical of the Laurentian historians in his earliest writing, Morton accepts almost completely the main lines of their thesis in this book.

There are some other texts as well which might be consulted. The best is *Canada: A Modern Study*, by Ramsay Cook with John Saywell and John Ricker (T: CI 1964). Kenneth McNaught concentrates on economic expansion, national unity, and Canadian-American relations in *The Pelican History of Canada* (T: Longmans 1969). Three other texts incorporate some of the themes and conclusions of more recent scholarship: Paul Cornell, Jean Hamelin, Fernand Ouellet, and Marcel Trudel, *Canada: Unity in Diversity* (T: HRW 1967); D.M.L. Farr and J.S. Moir, *The Canadian Experience* (T: Ryerson 1968); and J.L. Finlay and D.N. Sprague, *The Structure of Canadian*

5 National politics

History (Scarborough: PH 1979). June Callwood's *Portrait of Canada* (Garden City, NY: Doubleday 1981) is completely unreliable. Also useful as an introduction to the field are the volumes published in the Canadian Centenary series. In *The Critical Years: The Union of British North America, 1857-1873* (T: M&S 1964), W.L. Morton describes the events of the decade of ferment leading up to Confederation, and carries the narrative down to the defeat of the Macdonald government, the weakest chapters in the book. Peter Waite's *Canada 1874-1896: Arduous Destiny* (T: M&S 1971) is a sound, rather conventional political history, providing numerous fresh anecdotes, but little in the way of new interpretations. The colourful story of Canadian expansion into the northern frontiers is told in Morris Zaslow, *The Opening of the Canadian North, 1870-1914* (T: M&S 1971). The most valuable book in this important series is R.C. Brown and Ramsay Cook, *Canada 1896-1921: A Nation Transformed* (T: M&S 1974). Based on a wide range of primary and secondary sources, it is an impressive synthesis of the major themes in the years between the election of Wilfrid Laurier and the resignation of Robert Borden. In *Canada 1939-1957: The Forked Road* (T: M&S 1976) Donald Creighton once again pounds home the argument that Canada 'simply exchanged the free and equal association of the Commonwealth for an increasing economic and military dependence on the United States' during World War II and in the years that followed.

A number of interpretive essays and surveys should also be mentioned. Although they vary in quality, the chapters surveying each of the decades since 1860 in J.M.S. Careless and R.C. Brown, eds., *The Canadians 1867-1967* (T: MAC 1967), are extremely valuable as an introduction to the post-Confederation period, particularly the chapters on the 1890s and the 1900s. F.H. Underhill's *The Image of Confederation* (T: CBC 1964), a series of six half-hour radio lectures broadcast as the third series of the Massey Lectures, contains some brilliant insights into some of the major controversies about Canada's national purposes and goals, as does his *In Search of Canadian Liberalism* (T: MAC 1960). Another valuable study is W.L. Morton, *The Canadian Identity* (T: UTP 1961), an historian's attempt to define the character of Canadian nationhood. Indispensable to the student of Canadian history, as well, are two collections of essays by Ramsay Cook, *Canada and the French-Canadian Question* (T: MAC 1966), in which Cook writes of the relations between French and English Canadians, and *The Maple Leaf Forever: Essays on Nationalism and Politics in Canada* (T: MAC 1971), an attempt to view Canadian nationality in terms of the distinction between a nationalist state and the nation state. Murray Beck's *Pendulum of Power: Canada's Federal Elections* (T: PH 1968) provides brief sketches of each of Canada's federal election campaigns from 1867 to 1968 and a wealth of statistics to supplement the text. Another important book is Robert Presthus, *Elite Accommodation in Canadian Politics* (T: MAC 1973). Based on 1123 interviews with federal and provincial legislators, senior civil servants, and interest group leaders, the author concludes that public policy in Canada is largely shaped by accommodation among these three political elites, 'motivated essentially by a managerial ethic, rather more than by ideological commitment,' with little participation by back-benchers and citizens. The result, he contends, is the survival of Canada, despite its deepseated cleavages of regionalism, ethnicity, and religion. Although there is little that is new in this interpretation of Canadian politics, it is the first major systematic attempt at interpretation supported by survey data. A companion volume, *Elites in the Policy Process* (T: MAC 1974), provides a comparative analysis of policy-making in Canada and the United States.

Three other studies of French-Canadian history are also important. The first is Robert Rumilly's 41-volume *Histoire de la province de Québec* (M: Fides 1940-69). The earlier volumes are based heavily upon newspaper sources, while the later volumes use information gathered from the author's personal interviews with leading public figures in the province of Quebec. Rumilly also had access to a number of private archives and collections in the preparation of the *Histoire*. Mason Wade's *The French Canadians 1760-1945* (T: MAC 1955) is the most complete study in English of French-Canadian history for this period, but it contains little that is original. A more recent study is Paul-André Linteau, René Durocher, and Jean-Claude Robert, *Histoire du Québec contemporain: De la Confédération à la crise (1867-1929)* (M: BE 1979; trans. T: Lorimer 1982).

This is a well-written synthesis by a group of young, Montreal historians, solidly based on recent scholarship in the field, and written thematically with separate sections on the social, economic, and political history of the province.

THE POLITICS OF NATION BUILDING

It was a fragile union which the politicians of the sixties had pieced carefully together. And the predominant figure, whose task was to preside over its destiny, was Sir John A. Macdonald. The most important book in the immediate post-Confederation period is the second volume of Donald Creighton's biography of Macdonald, *John A. Macdonald: The Old Chieftain* (T: MAC 1955). Beginning in 1867 and ending with Macdonald's death in 1891, there are few aspects of Canadian life in the intervening years which Professor Creighton does not cover. It is based primarily on the Macdonald Papers, but Creighton had also used the wide range of sources which were available to him in the Canadian and British archives. And it is written with the clarity and charm which has characterized most of his work. The most controversial aspect is his treatment of Louis Riel. The Métis leader stood in the way of Macdonald's plans for the opening of the West, and Creighton treated him with scorn and contempt. Still valuable, as well, is the official biography of Macdonald by his former secretary and literary executor, Joseph Pope, *The Memoirs of Sir John A. Macdonald*, 2 vols. (O: 1894). Sympathetic, sound, and solidly based on the Macdonald Papers, it was written too close to the events it described, and consists primarily of extracts from Sir John's personal correspondence strung together in a loose narrative form. A more popular biography, P.B. Waite, *Macdonald: His Life and World* (T: MHR 1975), follows the general lines of interpretation laid down by Creighton. An important primary source is Pope's *Correspondence of Sir John Macdonald 1840-1891* (T: OUP 1921), and Sir John Willison's review, 'The Correspondence of Sir John A. Macdonald,' DR, 1922.

There are some other studies of Macdonald which should also be consulted: A.L. Burt, 'Peter Mitchell on John A. Macdonald,' CHR, 1961; J.A. Roy, 'John A. Macdonald, Barrister and Solicitor,' *Cana-*

dian Bar Review, 1945; T.W.L. MacDermot, 'The Political Ideas of John A. Macdonald,' CHR, 1933; and two articles by Peter Waite, 'The Political Ideas of John A. Macdonald,' in Marcel Hamelin, ed., *The Political Ideas of the Prime Ministers of Canada* (O: University of Ottawa Press 1969), and 'Sir John A. Macdonald, the Man,' in H.L. Dyck and H.P. Krosby, eds., *Empire and Nations: Essays in Honour of F.H. Soward* (T: UTP 1969). Keith Johnson has written an important essay on Macdonald's political career during the Union period in J.M.S. Careless, ed., *The Pre-Confederation Premiers: Ontario Government Leaders, 1841-1867* (T: UTP 1980). It was Macdonald who set the tone for political debate in the new Confederation and who drew up the rules by which the game would be played, and Johnson deals with these questions skilfully and effectively. Donald Creighton has also written a number of essays on Macdonald, most of which he completed while preparing his biography. Particularly useful are 'Sir John Macdonald and Kingston,' CHR, 1950, and 'Sir John A. Macdonald and Canadian Historians,' CHR, 1948.

Macdonald's Conservative colleagues have been less adequately dealt with. E.M. Saunders, *The Life and Letters of Sir Charles Tupper*, 2 vols. (NY: 1916); J. Castell Hopkins, *Life and Work of Sir John Thompson* (T: 1895); O.D. Skelton, *The Life and Times of Sir A.T. Galt* (T: OUP 1920); and John Boyd, *Sir George-Etienne Cartier, Bart.: His Life and Times* (T: MAC 1914), are not without value, but each of these figures deserves more scholarly treatment based on the sources now available. More interest has been shown in recent years in the activities of Macdonald's associates in Quebec. Alastair Sweeney's *George-Etienne Cartier: A Biography* (T: M&S 1976) suffers from a lack of Cartier Papers, but it is the most thorough study of Macdonald's Quebec lieutenant. More useful, however, is Brian Young's analysis of his role as spokesman for the Montreal bourgeoisie, *George-Etienne Cartier: Montreal Bourgeois* (M: MQUP 1981). Barbara Fraser, 'The Political Career of Sir Hector Langevin,' CHR, 1961, is a fine article on Sir John's principal lieutenant, while Andrée Désilets, *Hector-Louis Langevin: Un père de la confédération canadienne 1826-1906* (Q: PUL 1969), is a comprehensive survey of his political career. Langevin's rival in Quebec for political influence in the Conservative caucus, J.A. Chapleau, has been studied in an excellent article by H.B. Neatby and J.T. Saywell, 'Chapleau and the Conservative Party in Quebec,' CHR, 1956. Also useful are Jacques Gouin, 'Histoire d'une amitié: correspondence intime entre Chapleau et De Celles, 1875-1898,' RHAF, 1964, and F. Ouellet, 'Lettres de J.A. Chapleau, 1870-1896,' *Rapport de l'Archiviste de la province de Québec, 1959-1960*. The most important study of Israël Tarte is an unpublished PHD dissertation, Laurier Lapierre's 'Politics, Race and Religion in French Canada: Joseph Israël Tarte,' (University of Toronto 1962). Also useful are two articles by Lapierre, 'Joseph Israël Tarte: Relations between the French-Canadian Episcopacy and a French-Canadian Politician, 1874-1896,' CCHAR, 1958, and 'Joseph Israël Tarte and the McGreevy-Langevin Scandal,' CHAR, 1961. The most immediate problem confronting the new prime minister was the formation of a cabinet, and two articles by W.L. Morton fill in many of the details: 'The Formation of the First Federal Cabinet,' CHR, 1955, and 'The Cabinet of 1867,' in F.W. Gibson, ed., *Cabinet Formation and Bi-Cultural Relations: Seven Case Studies, vol. 6: Studies of the Royal Commission on Bilingualism and Biculturalism* (O: QP 1970). The agitation for repeal of the Confederation agreement in Nova Scotia has prompted a number of studies: L.J. Burpee, 'Joseph Howe and the Anti-Confederation League,' TRSC, 1916; D.C. Harvey, 'Incidents of the Repeal Agitation in Nova Scotia,' CHR, 1934; and two articles by J.M. Beck, 'Joseph Howe: Opportunist or Empire Builder?' CHR, 1960, and 'Joseph Howe and Confederation: Myth and Fact,' TRSC, 1964. More comprehensive, however, is Kenneth Pryke, *Nova Scotia and Confederation 1864-74* (T: UTP 1979). Morton's work on Manitoba and the Riel resistance is extremely important for an understanding of the problems involved in that province's joining Confederation. His brilliant analysis of the Red River Rebellion in the introduction to *Alexander Begg's Red River Journal* (T: CS 1956), in *Manitoba: A History* (T: UTP 1957), and in *The Birth of a Province* (Altona, Man.: Records of the Manitoba Historical Society 1970) tell the story with considerable skill. Also of use are George Stanley, *The Birth of Western Canada* (1936; T: UTP 1960); D.F. Warner, 'Drang nach Norden – The United States and the Riel Rebellion,' *Mississippi Valley Historical Review*, 1953; and

A.C. Gluek, *Minnesota and the Manifest Destiny of the Canadian Northwest* (T: UTP 1966). The best study on British Columbia and its entry into Confederation is to be found in Margaret Ormsby's *British Columbia: A History* (T: MAC 1958), while F.W.P. Bolger, *Prince Edward Island and Confederation* (Charlottetown: St Dunstan's UP 1964), provides a thorough account of the debate on the Island. Macdonald also had considerable dealings with the American government during his first term of office and particularly useful are Goldwin Smith, *The Treaty of Washington: A Study in Imperial History* (Ithaca: Cornell UP 1941); R.S. Longley, 'Peter Mitchell, Guardian of the North Atlantic Fisheries, 1867-1871,' CHR, 1941; C.P. Stacey, 'Britain's Withdrawal from North America,' CHR, 1955; and M.M. Robson, 'The Alabama Claims and Anglo-American Reconciliation, 1865-1871,' CHR, 1961.

There are other studies as well which should be considered to understand tne nature of Macdonald conservatism in the first years of Confederation. The most important, perhaps, is Donald Creighton's 'Conservatism and National Unity,' in R. Flenley, ed., *Essays in Canadian History presented to George M. Wrong* (T: MAC 1939), in which he attempts to distinguish conservative doctrines from those of the other parties. Also useful are the articles by A.D. Lockhart, 'The Contribution of Macdonald Conservatism to National Unity 1854-78,' CHAR, 1939, and J.I. Cooper, 'The Political Ideas of George-Etienne Cartier,' CHR, 1942. An important study on the development of the Canadian political party system is F.H. Underhill, 'The Development of National Political Parties in Canada,' CHR, 1935. Underhill's conclusions about the nature of the party system in Canada have been largely accepted by historians and much of their work has been written within the conceptual framework he laid down. Another useful essay is Escott Reid's 'The Rise of National Parties in Canada,' *Papers and Proceedings of the Canadian Political Science Association*, 1932, in which he describes the fragility of political parties at Confederation and the lack of sophistication in their organizational techniques.

The Liberal party had little success against the wily Macdonald and the biographies of its leaders tell part of the story. The basic book on George Brown after Confederation is J.M.S. Careless,

Brown of the Globe, vol. II: *Statesman of Confederation, 1860-1880* (T: MAC 1963). Not only does it present a thorough and well-balanced study of mid nineteenth-century politics, it illustrates Careless's views about the contribution of British ideas to Canadian liberalism and about the growing influence of Toronto over its metropolitan hinterlands. Dale Thomson's *Alexander Mackenzie: Clear Grit* (T: MAC 1960) tells the story of Brown's successor in the leadership of the Liberal party. Although Thomson fails to probe the reasons for the party's political collapse in 1878 after five years in office, and particularly the responsibility Mackenzie may have borne for it, the book is a well-written account of the Liberal leader and of his prime ministership from 1873 to 1878. Joseph Schull's two-volume biography, *Edward Blake: The Man of the Other Way* (T: MAC 1975), and *Edward Blake: Leader in Exile* (T: MAC 1976), are interesting portraits of the intellectually brilliant but politically unsophisticated Ontario lawyer who became the party's leader in 1880. More penetrating in analysis are two fine essays by F.H. Underhill: 'Edward Blake,' in C.T. Bissell, ed., *Our Living Tradition*, First Series (T: UTP 1957), and 'Edward Blake and Canadian Liberal Nationalism,' in Flenley, ed., *Essays in Canadian History Presented to George M. Wrong*. J.D. Livermore, 'The Personal Agonies of Edward Blake,' CHR, 1975, examines some of the physical and emotional problems which contributed to his erratic behavior as a political leader.

There are a number of books and articles which supplement these studies and throw further light on the development of Canadian liberalism during the later part of the nineteenth century. Of primary importance are W.R. Graham, 'Liberal Nationalism in the 1870's,' CHAR, 1946; W.S. Wallace, ed., 'Edward Blake's Aurora Speech,' CHR, 1921; and two articles by Underhill, 'Political Ideas of the Upper Canadian Reformers, 1867-1878,' CHAR, 1942, and 'Edward Blake, the Supreme Court Act and the Appeal to the Privy Council 1875-1876,' CHR, 1938. Sister T.A. Burke describes Mackenzie's difficulties in forming his cabinet in 'Mackenzie and his Cabinet, 1873-1878,' CHR, 1960, while Margaret Ormsby tells the story of his dealings with British Columbia in 'Prime Minister Mackenzie, the Liberal party and the Bargain with British Columbia,' CHR, 1945.

Another important source for the railway question is C.W. de Kiewiet and F.H. Underhill, eds., *The Dufferin-Carnarvon Correspondence, 1874-1878* (T: CS 1955). M. Ayearst, 'The Parti Rouge and the Clergy,' CHR, 1934, describes some of the problems faced by the Liberals in Quebec, but Jean-Paul Bernard, *Les Rouges: Libéralisme, nationalisme et anti-cléricalisme au milieu du XIXe siècle* (M: PUQ 1971), is a fuller and more valuable study. Also important in providing a context for the dilemma in which the Liberals found themselves are Denis Monière, *Le développement des idéologies au Québec: Des origines à nos jours* (M: Québec/Amérique 1977; trans. T: UTP 1981), essentially a synthesis of secondary literature in the field, provocative in its analysis, though unconvincing in its application of neo-Marxist models and rhetoric to Quebec; and Nadia Eid, *Le clergé et le pouvoir politique au Québec: Une analyse de l'idéologie ultramontaine au milieu du XIXe siècle* (M: HMH 1978), a thoughtful, though somewhat narrowly conceived analysis, in which Mme Eid argues the clergy made use of the ultramontane ideology to further its own interests against the rising middle-class in the province; Nive Voisin, *Louis-François LaFlèche* (TR: Eaisem 1980), a well-researched biography of the influential bishop of Three Rivers; and two articles by Roberto Perin, 'Troppo Ardenti Sacerdoti: The Conroy Mission Revisited,' CHR, 1980, and 'St-Bourget, évêque et martyr,' JCS, 1980-1, in which the author argues that apostolic delegates came to Quebec, not to deal equitably with the various parties involved in fifteen years of controversy, but to strike down Archbishop Bourget's faction within the Catholic church. One explanation for the defeat of the Liberals in the general election of 1878, based on the papers of the party's Ontario organizer, is provided in D. Lee, 'Dominion General Election of 1878 in Ontario,' OH, 1959.

There are numerous studies on the economic background to the origins and development of the National Policy. Particularly important are Donald Creighton, *British North America at Confederation* (O: KP 1939), and W.A. Mackintosh, *The Economic Background of Dominion-Provincial Relations* (O: KP 1939), both appendices to *The Report of the Royal Commission on Dominion-Provincial Relations*. O.J. Firestone, *Canadian Economic Development* (L: Bowes & Bowes 1953), and O.J. MacDiarmid, *Commercial Policy in the Canadian*

Economy (Cambridge: Harvard UP 1946), are also helpful. The leading critic of the National Policy is John Dales. In 'Canada's National Policies,' in his *The Protective Tariff in Canada's Development* (T: UTP 1966), Dales challenges the assumption that the policy was of general benefit to the country. Another critic of the policy of tariff protection is Michael Bliss, 'Canadianizing American Business: The Roots of the Branch Plant,' in Ian Lumsden, ed., *Close the 49th Parallel etc: The Americanization of Canada* (T: UTP 1970). Also important are two articles by Creighton, 'Economic Nationalism and Confederation,' CHAR, 1942, and 'George Brown, Sir John Macdonald and the Workingman,' CHR, 1943; Bernard Ostry's 'Conservatives, Liberal, and Labour in the 1870's,' CHR, 1960, and 'Conservatives, Liberals and Labour in the 1880s,' CJEPS, 1961; R.C. Brown, 'The Nationalism of the National Policy,' in Peter Russell, *Nationalism in Canada* (T: McGraw-Hill 1966); Benjamin Forster, 'The Coming of the National Policy: Business, Government and the Tariff, 1876-1879,' JCS, 1979; K. Norrie, 'The National Policy and the Rate of Prairie Settlement,' JCS, 1979; and T.W. Acheson, 'The National Policy and Industrialization of the Maritimes,' *Acadiensis*, 1972.

The building of the Canadian Pacific Railway has been written about several times. Although he concentrates heavily on the financial aspects of the line, the best account is still H.A. Innis, *A History of the Canadian Pacific Railway* (L: P.S. King & Son 1923). G.P. de T. Glazebrook, *A History of Transportation in Canada* (T: Ryerson 1938), traces the story of transportation through Canadian history, describing the methods and relating them to the rise of Canadian civilization. J.M. Gibbon, *The Romantic History of the Canadian Pacific: The Northwest Passage of To-day* (NY: Tudor 1937), is also useful. A good biography of George Stephen, through whose financial genius the railway was achieved, is Heather Gilbert's *Awakening Continent: The Life of Mount Stephen*, vol. I (Aberdeen: Aberdeen UP 1965). L.B. Irwin, *Pacific Railways and Nationalism in the Canadian-American Northwest, 1845-1873* (1939; NY: Greenwood Press 1968), tells the early story of the Canadian Pacific and Northern Pacific railways and describes their influence on the political history of the northwest before the panic of 1873. The most recent and widely publicized books on the question are Pierre Berton, *The National Dream: The Great Railway, 1871-1881* (T: M&S 1970) and *The Last Spike: The Great Railway, 1881-1885* (T: M&S 1971). In a colourful narrative account, Berton mistakenly assumes that there was no feasible alternative to the expensive line and that the national interest was identical with the interests of central Canada. Indeed, one of the most striking features of Canadian politics during the decade of the 1880s was the reappearance and growth of regional and particularist feeling. The background to the discontent is described in the *Report of the Royal Commission on Dominion-Provincial Relations: Book 1* (O: KP 1940), while J.A. Maxwell, *Federal Subsidies to the Provincial Governments in Canada* (Cambridge: Harvard UP 1937), provides a well-balanced account of federal-provincial financial relations. The best study of the rise of the provincial rights movement in Ontario is J.A. Morrison, 'Oliver Mowat and the Development of Provincial Rights in Ontario,' in *Three History Theses* (T: Ontario Department of Public Records and Archives 1961). This should now be read in conjunction with Christopher Armstrong, *The Politics of Federalism: Ontario's Relations with the Federal Government, 1867-1942* (T: UTP 1981). Armstrong argues that the province's struggle with the federal government over the terms of Confederation and the right to exploit resources has been intensified by private interests playing one level of government off against the other and by competing bureaucrats who resisted any loss of authority. As well, he questions the conventional view that the provincial rights movement, usually led by Ontario, is to be blamed for the emergence of a weak and decentralized union of co-ordinate sovereignties, despite Macdonald's plan that the provinces should possess little more power than large municipalities. Robert Rumilly's *Mercier* (M: Zodiaque 1936) picks up the story in Quebec, but much fuller accounts may be found in Ramsay Cook, *Provincial Autonomy: Minority Rights and the Compact Theory, 1867-1921* (O: QP 1969), an analysis of the origins, development, and uses of the idea that Confederation represented a compact of provinces or cultures, and in Arthur Silver, *The French-Canadian Idea of Confederation, 1864-1900* (T: UTP 1982), a study of the ways in which French Quebeckers changed their view of Confederation from one in which the future of Quebec was virtually their only concern to one in which the French-speaking minorities outside the province were of equal concern in what was essentially a bicultural country. Unrest in the Maritime provinces is described in S.A. Saunders, *The Economic History of the Maritime Provinces: A Study prepared for the Royal Commission on Dominion-Provincial Relations* (O: KP 1939); Murray Beck, *The Government of Nova Scotia* (T: UTP 1957); and Beck, *History of Maritime Union: A Study of Frustrations* (Fredericton: QP 1969). In addition to Morton's *Manitoba*, J.A. Maxwell, 'Financial Relations between Manitoba and the Dominion, 1870-1886,' CHR, 1934, is important for the movement in Manitoba, as is Douglas Owram, *Promise of Eden: The Canadian Expansionist Movement and the Idea of the West 1856-1900* (T: UTP 1980), a valuable study outlining the emergence of a western regional consciousness. Students should also consult John Saywell's first-rate analysis in *The Office of Lieutenant-Governor* (T: UTP 1957); Eugene Forsey, 'Disallowance of Provincial Acts, Reservation of Provincial Acts, Reservation of Provincial Bills, and Refusal of Assent by Lieutenant-Governors since 1867,' CJEPS, 1938, and Bruce W. Hodgins, Don Wright, and W.H. Heick, eds., *Federalism in Canada and Australia: The Early Years* (Waterloo: Wilfrid Laurier UP 1978).

Unrest in the West took another form and brought into question the cultural *modus vivendi* worked out by the Fathers of Confederation. George Stanley's *The Birth of Western Canada* and his *Louis Riel* (T: Ryerson 1963) tell the story well. In contrast to Creighton, Stanley views Riel as a tragic hero of the frontier West rather than the fanatical half-breed rebel embodying the nationalism of the Métis. In Thomas Flanagan's *Louis 'David' Riel: Prophet of the New World* (T: UTP 1979), together with *The Diaries of Louis Riel* (Edmonton: Hurtig 1976) which Flanagan has edited as well, Riel emerges not as the calculating politician, but as a man obsessed with religious messianism, regarding himself as the chosen instrument of God. To Quebec, Riel was the defender of the French and Catholic tradition in the West, and R.E. Lamb, *Thunder in the North: Conflict over the Riel Risings, 1870-1885* (NY: Pageant Press 1957), and Rumilly's *Mercier* and his *Mgr Laflèche et son temps* (M: Zodiaque 1938) describe the *nationaliste* response in 'la belle province.' Arthur

Silver's 'French Quebec and the Métis Question, 1869-1883,' in C.
Berger and R. Cook, eds., *The West and the Nation: Essays in Honour
of W.L. Morton* (T: M&S 1976), should also be consulted. In *The
Jesuits' Estates Question, 1760-1888: A Study of the Background for the
Agitation of 1889* (T: UTP 1968), Roy Dalton explores the origins of
another issue which aggravated the relations between the French
and the English. J.R. Miller completes the story in *Equal Rights: The
Jesuits' Estates Act Controversy* (M: MQUP 1979). Although he under-
estimates the role of D'Alton McCarthy and the Equal Rights
movement in the schools controversy which followed, he points out
once more that the Jesuits' Estates question symbolized a defensive
nationalism in Quebec, triggering the emergence of the ERA in
Ontario, both movements symptomatic of the breakdown of the cultural settlement of Confederation. In addition to the books by Cook
and Silver referred to above, there are three articles which should
also be consulted, all of which place the problem in a somewhat
larger context: W.L. Morton, 'The Conservative Principle in Confederation,' QQ, 1965; Donald Creighton, 'John A. Macdonald,
Confederation and the Canadian West,' *Transactions of the Historical
and Scientific Society of Manitoba, 1966-7*; and Ralph Heintzman,
'The Spirit of Confederation: Professor Creighton, Biculturalism,
and the Use of History,' CHR, 1971.

   The reciprocity issue and the question of Canada's commercial
relations with the United States represented another challenge to
the basic foundations of Confederation. The standard source is still
C.C. Tansill, *Canadian-American Relations, 1875-1911* (New Haven:
Yale UP 1943), but it must now be supplemented by Craig Brown's
excellent study, *Canada's National Policy, 1883-1900: A Study in
Canadian-American Relations* (Princeton: Princeton UP 1964). Based
primarily on Canadian sources, Brown emphasizes the major impact
of Canadian politics on Canadian-American diplomacy. D.F. Warner,
*The Idea of Continental Union: Agitation for the Annexation of Canada
to the United States 1849-1893* (Lexington: University of Kentucky
Press 1960), surveys the movements for the annexation of Canada
to the United States from the manifesto of 1849 to the election of
1891, but it is episodic in approach and uneven in its research. A
more satisfactory treatment of the ideas of at least one continentalist

is Ian Grant, 'Erastus Wiman: A Continentalist Replies to Canadian Imperialism,' CHR, 1972. The origins of the movement for commercial union are discussed in R.C. Brown, 'The Commercial Unionists in Canada and the United States,' CHAR, 1963, while W.R. Graham, 'Sir Richard Cartwright, Wilfrid Laurier and the Liberal Party Trade Policy, 1887,' CHR, 1952, looks at the Liberal party's decision to adopt reciprocity as an issue. Three articles by F.H. Underhill are also important: 'Edward Blake, the Liberal Party and Unrestricted Reciprocity,' CHAR, 1939; 'Laurier and Blake, 1882-1891,' CHR, 1939; and 'Laurier and Blake 1891-1892,' CHR, 1943. Students should also take a look at one contemporary source: Goldwin Smith, *Canada and the Canadian Question* (T: 1891; ed. C. Berger, T: UTP 1971).

For some time historians have realized the critical nature of the 1890s and the subtle and complex interrelationship of forces that shaped the decade. Imperialism and nationalism, racism and nativism, continentalism and anti-Americanism battled for supremacy, though the alliances were often strange and the generalship uncertain. The Manitoba Schools question brought many of these forces into play, and one of the best treatments of the problem is John Saywell's introduction to the *Canadian Journal of Lady Aberdeen 1893-1898* (T: CS 1960). Saywell and H.B. Neatby's earlier article, 'Chapleau and the Conservative Party in Quebec,' CHR, 1956; Saywell's 'The Crown and the Politicians: The Canadian Succession Question,' CHR, 1956; Barbara Fraser's 'The Political Career of Sir Hector Louis Langevin,' CHR, 1961, together with Brian Young's *Promoters and Politicians: The North-Shore Railways in the History of Quebec 1854-85* (T: UTP 1978) detail the breakdown of the Conservative party, particularly in Quebec, at a time when leadership and party unity were of critical importance. Lovell Clark, *The Manitoba School Question: Majority Rule or Minority Rights?* (T: CC 1968), is a useful compendium of documents, while his 'The Conservative Party in the 1890's,' CHAR, 1961, and 'Macdonald's Conservative Successors, 1891-1896,' in John Moir, ed., *Character and Circumstance: Essays in Honour of Donald Grant Creighton* (T: MAC 1970), examine the decline of the Conservative party after the death of Macdonald. Also important is Paul Crunican, *Priests and Politicians: Manitoba Schools and the Election of 1896* (T: UTP 1974), a study solidly based upon the rich resources of the ecclesiastical archives and the private papers of the politicians involved. It also adds another dimension to the historiographical controversy surrounding the election of 1896. While confirming Saywell and Neatby's earlier hypothesis that the Conservatives lost Quebec because of divisions in the party and a lack of leadership in the province, Crunican argues that the clergy played a pivotal role in the outcome of the campaign. Division within the hierarchy of the Quebec bishops and the resulting weakness of their *mandement* allowed Laurier to convince enough voters that the gap between what the bishops were demanding and what the Liberals were promising was not as wide as Bishop Laflèche and the Conservatives were implying. Also of use for the politics of the early 1890s are J.T. Watt, 'Anti-Catholic nativism in Canada: The Protestant Protective Association,' CHR, 1967; J.W. Lederle, 'The Liberal Convention of 1893,' CJEPS, 1950; and R. Stamp, 'J.D. Edgar and the Liberal Party: 1867-1896,' CHR, 1964.

THE POLITICS OF NATIONAL UNITY

The Laurier years were of critical importance in the development of Canada. During this period, in which the destinies of the country were, for the first time, presided over by a member of the minority race, the national economic expansion, optimistically promised by the Fathers of Confederation to have followed immediately upon the creation of the union, finally took place. In both its domestic and external affairs, Canada arrived at a cross-roads as well. Confronting the Canadian people and their political representatives were two closely-related problems: What was the exact nature of the connection between Canada and Great Britain? And was the maintenance of this connection compatible with the existence of a bicultural state?

The starting-point for any examination of Laurier's career must still be the official biography by Professor O.D. Skelton, the *Life and Letters of Sir Wilfrid Laurier*, 2 vols. (T: OUP 1921). This was 'official biography' in every sense of the word; it was undertaken at Laurier's request and was solidly based on the vast mass of the Laurier

Papers and long talks with Sir Wilfrid on the important aspects of his career. For the 1920s it was a fine book. But Skelton was much too close to the subject of his study and too restricted in the sources he was able to use to produce anything other than a partisan work. In his determination that Laurier should emerge as a symbol of national unity and racial harmony, he overlooked important aspects of both the man and his career. There is more than one instance when his objectivity must be questioned as well. On some occasions he has rearranged quotations to make Laurier's views appear more coherent; on other occasions he has simply left out controversial sentences. Skelton's sympathy for Laurier also led him to minimize Sir Wilfrid's responsibility for some of the important decisions taken by his government. And he has virtually ignored Laurier's relationship with the Roman Catholic church, despite an abundance of material in the Laurier correspondence.

Other biographies have also been published. But they are incomplete in their research and, with the exception of John Dafoe's analytical essay, *Laurier: A Study* (T: 1922), have followed the lines of interpretation laid down by Skelton. J.S. Willison's *Sir Wilfrid Laurier and the Liberal Party*, 2 vols. (T: Morang 1903), was written in the aftermath of the federal election of 1900, in which the Liberal party suffered humiliating losses in the province of Ontario, and was an attempt to demonstrate that English-speaking voters had been unfair to Laurier and that he should be viewed in the light of his efforts to unify and consolidate Confederation. Joseph Schull's more recent study, *Laurier: The First Canadian* (T: MAC 1965), develops a similar theme. In an effort to show that Sir Wilfrid embodied the spirit of Canada more completely and satisfactorily than any of his predecessors, he drew a sympathetic picture of the Liberal leader, more boldly sketched and more dramatically presented than that of Skelton's, but basically the same Laurier. And nowhere does Schull question the achievements of his subject, nor the tactics he used.

Only recently have other historians begun to fill in the picture. Although he has accepted many of Skelton's conclusions, H.B. Neatby looked at Laurier's management of the Liberal party in the province of Quebec in *Laurier and a Liberal Quebec: A Study in Politi-*

cal Management (T: M&S 1973). Developing the theme in an essay entitled 'Wilfrid Laurier: Politician,' in Hamelin, ed., *The Political Ideas of the Prime Ministers of Canada*, Paul Stevens argued that Laurier's statesmanship was dependent upon his success as a politician, and he began to analyse the approaches and techniques the Liberal leader developed. And in *Laurier: His Life and World* (T: MHR 1979), Richard Clippingdale suggests that he may have learned the lessons of Canadian statecraft in the later nineteenth century so well that he could not respond adequately to the problems of the twentieth. In each of these studies the authors quote with approval Dafoe's conclusion that the final appraisal would show Laurier 'an abler man, but one not quite so preternaturally good; a man who had affinities with Machiavelli as well as with Sir Galahad.' An article by Marc La Terreur, 'Correspondence Laurier-Mme Joseph Lavergne, 1891-1893,' CHAR, 1964, provides one insight at least into Laurier's personal life.

There are surprisingly few biographies of Laurier's political associates to supplement these studies. John Dafoe's *Clifford Sifton in relation to his Times* (T: MAC 1931), together with David Hall's *Clifford Sifton*, I: *The Young Napoleon 1861-1900* (V: UBCP 1981), are the most useful, while A.H.U. Colquhoun, *Press, Politics and People: The Life and Letters of Sir John Willison* (T: MAC 1935), and Willison's *Reminiscences, Political and Personal* (T: M&S 1919) provide some interesting insights into the politics of the era. No examination of the development of labour policy could be written without placing William Lyon Mackenzie King in a central role, and in *'An Impartial Umpire': Industrial Relations and the Canadian State 1900-1911* (T: UTP 1980) Paul Craven carries out this task with skill and care. But C.B. Fergusson's biography of Laurier's minister of finance, W.S. Fielding, *Mr Minister of Finance* (Windsor, NS: Lancelot Press 1971), is disappointing, particularly in view of the important role he played throughout the period, though it must be pointed out that the Fielding Papers for the period during which he was minister are of little value. Laurier's one-time protégé, Henri Bourassa, has been the subject of a number of studies: Robert Rumilly, *Henri Bourassa* (M: Chantecler 1953); Casey Murrow, *Henri Bourassa and French Canadian Nationalism* (M: Harvest House 1968); Joseph

Levitt, *Henri Bourassa and the Golden Calf: The Social Program of the Nationalists of Quebec, 1900-1914* (O: University of Ottawa Press 1969); and Martin O'Connell, 'The Ideas of Henri Bourassa,' CJEPS, 1953. But the most revealing work is a sensitive and subtle essay by André Laurendeau in R.L. McDougall, ed., *Our Living Tradition*, Fourth Series (T: UTP 1962).

The dominant issue confronting Laurier and his colleagues was the question of imperialism. At the turn of the century Canada looked out upon a world feverishly pursuing the myths of imperial grandeur. Canadian historians have focused considerable attention upon the different aspects of the problem. The most comprehensive account is Charles Stacey, *Canada and the Age of Conflict: A History of Canadian External Policies*, I: *1867-1921* (T: MAC 1977), a judicious, well-balanced study, solidly based on the author's primary research. Much of the writing about Canada's relations with the British empire has emphasized political and diplomatic developments. R.M. Dawson, *The Development of Dominion Status 1900-1936* (L: OUP 1937), details the paper-strewn path to national status, concentrating on Colonial Office dispatches, the records of Imperial conferences, and the centralizing tendencies of the British government. In *Canada and Imperialism, 1896-1899* (T: UTP 1965), Norman Penlington took another tack. Rejecting the argument that Canada's participation in the Boer War was the result of Downing Street influence, Penlington argued that there were powerful forces within Canadian society which demanded involvement. Anti-Americanism, he concluded, was largely responsible for the enthusiasm for imperial unity and was the outlet for a form of jingoism that closely resembled that in the United States and Great Britain. Carl Berger, *The Scene of Power: Studies in the Ideas of Canadian Imperialism 1867-1914* (T: UTP 1970), maintained that the problem was even more complex. In a brilliant analysis of the nature of Canadian imperialism, Berger contended that some Canadian imperialists saw nothing inconsistent between Canadian nationalism and closer relations with Great Britain, and believed that Canada could best achieve national status within a transformed empire. Ramsay Cook's 'Stephen Leacock and the Age of Plutocracy, 1903-1921,' in Moir, *Character and Circumstance: Essays in Honour of Donald Grant Creigh-*

ton; Richard Clippingdale, 'J.S. Willison and Canadian Nationalism, 1886-1902,' CHAR, 1969; Douglas Cole, 'John S. Ewart and Canadian Nationalism,' CHAR, 1969; and Robert Page, 'Canada and the Imperial Idea in the Boer War,' JCS, 1975, provide further insights into the meaning of nationalism and imperialism at the turn of the century.

The complexity of these ideas was something Laurier did not fully understand at the outset of his prime ministership. As a result, the government's response to the Boer War crisis in 1899 was seen by many in English-speaking Canada as that of a subordinate colony, rather than that of country approaching nationhood, and was bitterly resented. In their introduction to *Lord Minto's Canadian Papers: A Selection of the Public and Private Papers of the Fourth Earl of Minto* (T: CS 1981), Paul Stevens and John Saywell maintain that the evidence strongly suggests that the Colonial Office deliberately tried to force Laurier's hand. What mattered, however, was not what Downing Street was trying to do, but that it had to do anything at all. Stevens and Saywell also contend that Minto's determination to press issues connected with the imperial relationship to a conclusion actually aided the movement for Canadianization, leading as it did to a definition of Canada's relationship with the empire which denied any role for the governor general other than a purely formal one, and that a constitutional crisis was averted largely because of Laurier's political adroitness. Carman Miller presents a more sympathetic account of Minto's Canadian experience in his *The Canadian Career of the Fourth Earl of Minto: The Education of a Viceroy* (Waterloo: Wilfrid Laurier UP 1980), a well-documented analysis which dispells the conventional assumption that Rideau Hall and Downing Street worked completely in tandem.

There are a number of studies of other aspects of Canada's imperial relations which students should consult. In 'Sir Wilfrid Laurier and the British Preferential Tariff System,' CHAR, 1955, James Colvin examines the background to the preferential tariff of 1897. Exhaustive treatments of the question of imperial defence are D.C. Gordon, *The Dominion Partnership in Imperial Defense, 1870-1914* (Baltimore: Johns Hopkins UP 1965), and R.A. Preston, *Canada and 'Imperial Defense': A Study of the Origins of the British Commonwealth's Defense Organization, 1867-1919* (Durham: Duke UP 1967).

Desmond Morton, *Ministers and Generals: Politics and the Canadian Militia, 1868-1904* (T: UTP 1970), analyses the conflicts between the British general officers commanding the Canadian militia and their political superiors, and describes the process by which Canadians assumed the responsibility for framing their own policies. Anglo-American diplomacy leading to the settlement of the Alaska Boundary dispute is dealt with in Charles S. Campbell, *Anglo-American Understanding 1898-1903* (Baltimore: Johns Hopkins UP 1957); A.E. Campbell, *Great Britain and the United States, 1895-1903* (L: Longmans 1960); Norman Penlington, *The Alaska Boundary Dispute: A Critical Reappraisal* (T: MHR 1972); and F.W. Gibson, 'The Alaska Boundary Dispute,' CHAR, 1945. On the debate over naval defence G.N. Tucker, *The Naval Service of Canada* (Ottawa: KP 1952), is particularly useful. Also of interest are H.B. Neatby, 'Laurier and Imperialism,' CHAR, 1955; R.C. Brown, 'Goldwin Smith and Anti-Imperialism,' CHR, 1962; H.P. Gundy, 'Sir Wilfrid Laurier and Lord Minto,' CHAR, 1952; two articles by Carman Miller, 'English-Canadian Opposition to the South African Wars as seen through the Press,' CHR, 1974, and 'Sir Frederick William Borden and Military Reform, 1896-1911,' CHR, 1969; and James Eayrs, 'The Round Table Movement in Canada, 1909-1920,' CHR, 1957.

The problem of education in Canada and the relationship between the English-speaking majority and the French-speaking minority was a complex one as well. W.L. Morton, 'Manitoba Schools and Canadian Nationality, 1890-1923,' CHAR, 1951, and Ramsay Cook, 'Church, Schools, and Politics in Manitoba, 1903-1912,' CHR, 1958, describe the resolution of the Manitoba Schools question. The most detailed study of the school question in Alberta and Saskatchewan is Manoly R. Lupul, *The Roman Catholic Church and the North-West School Question: A Study in Church-State Relations in Western Canada, 1875-1905* (T: UTP 1974). The author's careful research in the ecclesiastical and clerical archives is impressive. But on the critical question of the educational clauses in the Autonomy bills, his conclusion that Laurier was guilty of nothing worse than carelessness in its drafting is open to question, as Evelyn Eager, 'Separate Schools and the Cabinet Crisis of 1905,' *Lakehead University Review*, 1969, and D.J. Hall, 'A Divergence of Principle: Clifford Sifton, Sir Wilfrid Laurier and the North-West Autonomy Bills, 1905,' *Laurentian University Review*, 1974, have begun to suggest. Still useful as well is C.C. Lingard, *Territorial Government in Canada: The Autonomy Question in the Old North-West Territories* (T: UTP 1946). Based largely on newspaper sources and personal interviews with the territorial premier, Sir Frederick Haultain, it is a sympathetic presentation of the case for provincial rights and a vindication of their champion. Also interesting is Lupul, 'The Campaign for a French Catholic School Inspector in the North-West Territories, 1898-1903,' CHR, 1967, a study of the Roman Catholic hierarchy's attempts to secure a French-language school inspector for the denominational schools in the Territories. Franklin Walker, *Catholic Education and Politics in Ontario: A Documentary Study* (T: Nelson 1964); Margaret Prang, 'Clerics, Politicians, and the Bilingual Schools Issue in Ontario, 1910-1917,' CHR, 1960; Marilyn Barber, 'The Ontario Bilingual Schools Issue: Sources of Conflict,' CHR, 1966; and Peter Oliver, 'Regulation 17: Resolution of the Ontario Bilingual Crisis, 1916-27,' in his *Public and Private Persons* (T: CI 1975), describe the controversy in Ontario over bilingual schools. Although it is essentially a study of the conflict between Irish- and French-Canadian Catholics in Ontario, Robert Choquette's *Language and Religion: A History of English-French Conflict in Ontario* (O: University of Ottawa Press 1975) argues that Regulation 17 was largely a consequence of that controversy. His research, however, is mainly from Roman Catholic sources, and the conclusions he draws, therefore, about the Anglo-Protestant majority are open to question.

The defeat of the Laurier government in 1911 has aroused considerable interest on the part of the historians as well. Still the most comprehensive survey of the reciprocity question is L.E. Ellis, *Reciprocity, 1911: A Study in Canadian-American Relations* (New Haven: Yale UP 1939). Although he emphasized the role of the business and financial interests which implanted fears of annexation in the minds of many Canadians, Ellis accepted the view of most of his colleagues in the profession that reciprocity was the issue that broke the government's back. More recent research, however, has added another dimension to the question. In 'The Conservative Party Machine and the Election of 1911 in Ontario,' OH, 1965, Robert Cuff maintained that the Conservative party's organization in Ontario was sufficiently strong that the results would not have been much different whatever issue had emerged in the campaign. Looking at the Liberals, Paul Stevens, 'Laurier, Aylesworth, and the Decline of the Liberal Party in Ontario,' CHAR, 1968, argued that the party was in considerable difficulty even before reciprocity became the centre of political controversy. Lack of leadership and party division, he contended, seriously undermined the Liberal campaign to sell reciprocity and forced valuable ground to be yielded to the opposition as the debate unfolded. Stevens has also assembled the important primary and secondary sources on the election campaign in his *The 1911 General Election: A Study in Canadian Politics* (T: CC 1970).

The study of the political career of Robert Borden should begin with R.C. Brown, *Robert Laird Borden: A Biography*, 2 vols. (T: MAC 1975, 1980). Essentially a political biography, this is an excellent study, solidly researched, judicious and objective in its historical analysis, and written with clarity and precision. Although he is generally sympathetic towards the Conservative leader, noting in particular the progressive character of much of his early thought and the role which he played in setting up of the mechanisms to deal with the demands of the First World War, he repeatedly points out that Borden was lacking in tact and warmth, that he had no comprehension of Quebec, and that he is to be rebuked for the passage of the Wartime Elections Act. Important as well, as a supplement to the biography, are two of Brown's articles: 'The Political Ideas of Robert Borden,' in Hamelin, ed., *The Political Ideas of the Prime Ministers of Canada*; and ' "Whither are we being shoved"? Political Leadership in Canada during World War I,' in J.L. Granatstein and R.D. Cuff, eds., *War and Society in North America* (T: Nelson 1971). Borden's memoirs have also been published, Henry Borden, ed., *Robert Laird Borden: His Memoirs* (T: MAC 1938), but they are largely unanalytical and unreflective, based as they are on Borden's equally unanalytical and unreflective personal diaries. John English's *The Decline of Politics: The Conservatives and the Party System* (T: UTP 1977), however, is essential reading. Less sympathetic to Borden than is his recent biographer, English maintains that one of the Conservative leader's objectives was to usher in a new and more creative political system, but that in the final analysis the results of his labours were disappointing. W.S. Wallace, *The Memoirs of the Rt. Hon. Sir George Foster* (T: MAC 1933), provides some material on one of Borden's principal colleagues, as does J.W. Dafoe, 'The Political Career of Sir George Foster,' CHR, 1934, a review article of Wallace's book. But of much greater importance is W.R. Graham's *Arthur Meighen, I: The Door of Opportunity* (T: CI 1960). A sympathetic treatment, Graham makes no attempt to conceal his conclusion that Meighen was an intellectual giant among political pygmies. Although he sees issues and personalities through the eyes of Meighen and adopts most of the conclusions reached by his subject, it is a well-written account of Meighen's early career. Equally important is Margaret Prang's *N.W. Rowell: Ontario Nationalist* (T: UTP 1975), a massive study of the Ontario Liberal leader who entered Borden's coalition in 1917. The book is a steady, reliable guide to the politics of the period, but it fails to provide much insight into the motivation of Rowell and his powerful and wealthy Methodist friends.

W.R. Graham, 'The Cabinet of 1911,' in Gibson, ed., *Cabinet Formation and Bi-cultural Relations*, is an interesting account of the problems Borden confronted in forming his cabinet. But most of the studies of the Borden administration revolve around the conscription issue. The most complete work on the subject is J.L. Granatstein and J.M. Hitsman, *Broken Promises: A History of Conscription in Canada* (T: OUP 1977), a study very critical of the government's handling of the issue during the First World War. Still valuable, however, is Elizabeth Armstrong, *The Crisis of Quebec, 1914-1918* (NY: Columbia UP 1937), an analysis of French-Canadian opinion during the period. The issue was profoundly important in western Canada as well, as John H. Thompson makes clear in *The Harvest of War: The Prairie West* (T: M&S 1978). There are a number of good articles on the subject. The most suggestive, perhaps, is one by A.M. Willms, 'Conscription 1917: A Brief for the Defence,' CHR, 1956, in which the author argues that conscription was militarily necessary and politically unpopular. Others include Ramsay Cook, 'Dafoe, Laurier, and the Formation of Union Government,' CHR, 1961; J.M. Bliss, 'The Methodist Church and World War I,' CHR,

1968; Martin Robin, 'Registration, Conscription, and Independent Labour Politics, 1916-1917,' CHR, 1966; W.R. Young, 'Conscription, Rural Depopulation, and the Farmers of Ontario, 1917-1919,' CHR, 1972; and two articles by R.M. Bray, 'Fighting as an Ally: The English Canadian Patriotic Response to the Great War,' CHR, 1980, and 'A Conflict of Nationalisms: The Win-the-War and National Unity Convention 1917,' JCS, 1980-1. The complexities of the government's railway policies are partially unravelled in T.D. Regehr, *The Canadian Northern Railway: Pioneer Road of the Northern Prairies 1895-1918* (T: MAC 1976), and John A. Eagle, 'Monopoly or Competition: The Nationalization of the Grand Trunk Railway,' CHR, 1981, both of which suggest that the nationalization of these roads appears to have been a positive decision towards the establishment of a nationalized and integrated railway network, rather than, as in the conventional view, a makeshift solution in response to circumstances over which it had but little control. Labour unrest following the end of the war and the government's response to it has drawn the attention of historians as well. D.C. Masters, *The Winnipeg General Strike* (T: UTP 1950), has been supplanted as the standard source for the notorious strike by David Bercuson's well-done *Confrontation at Winnipeg* (M: MQUP 1974) and by Bercuson and Kenneth McNaught, *The Winnipeg Strike: 1919* (T: James Lewis and Samuel 1973), an account of the strike, prepared by the strikers' defence committee.

AFTER THE GREAT WAR

The political and social ferment of Canada after the Great War was unprecedented in its intensity. The war had left Laurier's Liberals in tatters and the reactionary policies of the Union government had tarnished all who served with Borden. The situation was tailor-made for the rise of a new political movement, and the farmers, long feeling left out of the profits and progress of the boom years, seized their chance.

The basic book on the subject is *The Progressive Party of Canada* (T: UTP 1950) by W.L. Morton. For more than thirty years this well-researched and well-written volume has effectively dominated the field, and no one has yet tried to revise Morton in a fundamental way, though Richard Allen's *The Social Passion: Religion and Social Reform in Canada 1914-28* (T: UTP 1971) shows that any study of reform is incomplete without generous reference to the Social Gospel. Studies of the farmers' movement are surprisingly scarce (the best may still be W.K. Rolph, *Henry Wise Wood of Alberta* (T: UTP 1950), and historians generally seem to have devoted themselves to essays, collected in a number of edited books: Richard Allen, ed., *A Region of the Mind* (Regina: University of Saskatchewan 1973); H.C. Klassen, ed., *The Canadian West* (Calgary: University of Calgary 1977); L.H. Thomas, ed., *Essays on Western History* (Edmonton: University of Alberta Press 1976); Carl Berger and Ramsay Cook, eds., *The West and the Nation* (T: M&S 1976); D.P. Gagan, ed., *Prairie Perspectives* (T: HRW 1970); A.W. Rasporich and H.C. Klassen, eds., *Prairie Perspectives 2* (T: HRW 1973); D. Francis and H. Ganzevoort, eds., *The Dirty Thirties in Prairie Canada* (V: Tantalus 1980); H. Palmer and D. Smith, eds., *The New Provinces: Alberta and Saskatchewan, 1905-80* (V: Tantalus 1980); H. Palmer, ed., *The Settlement of the West* (Calgary: University of Calgary 1977); and perhaps the best ones, Susan Trofimenkoff, ed., *The Twenties in Western Canada* (O: National Museum 1972); D.J. Bercuson, ed., *Canada and the Burden of Unity* (T: MAC 1977); and Bercuson and P.A. Buckner, eds., *Eastern and Western Perspectives* (T: UTP 1981). The last two, as their titles suggest, treat the Maritimes as well as the West.

Among still useful contemporary books are two by William Irvine, one of the Progressive leaders, *Cooperative Government* (O: 1929), and *The Farmers in Politics* (T: 1920). Another is L.A. Wood, *A History of Farmers Movements in Canada* (1924; reprinted with an introduction by F.J.K. Griezic, T: UTP 1975). There is valuable material in Vernon C. Fowke, *Canadian Agricultural Policy: The Historical Pattern* (1946; reprinted T: UTP 1978) and *The National Policy and the Wheat Economy* (T: UTP 1957, 1973); and in C.F. Wilson's massive and sprawling volume, *A Century of Canadian Grain: Government Policy to 1951* (Saskatoon: Western Producer Prairie Books 1978), there is enough material to stimulate a dozen researchers.

Paul F. Sharp, *The Agrarian Revolt in Western Canada* (Minneapolis: University of Minnesota Press 1948), deliberately attempted to draw American parallels to the Prairie west and largely succeeded. There is readily available primary source material in Ramsay Cook, ed., *The Dafoe-Sifton Correspondence* (Altona, Man.: Manitoba Record Society 1966), and much of value in Rolph's *Henry Wise Wood of Alberta*, still the only study of the United Farmers' leader. For Ontario Progressives, students may use E.C. Drury, *Farmer Premier* (T: M&S 1966), and W.C. Good, *Farmer Citizen* (T: Ryerson 1958), neither of which is very analytical. The best source for the Ontario farmers may well be Peter Oliver's splendidly researched *G. Howard Ferguson: Ontario Tory* (T: UTP 1977), even though this study approaches the Progressives from the viewpoint of the man who did them in. Not to be forgotten, however, is the book produced by the party's educational secretary, M.H. Staples, *The Challenge of Agriculture: The Story of the United Farmers of Ontario* (T: 1921). Manitoba farmers can be studied through John Kendle's able and exhaustive *John Bracken: A Political Biography* (T: UTP 1979) and the weaknesses of those in the East can be followed in E.R. Forbes, *Maritime Rights: The Maritime Rights Movement, 1919-27* (M: MQUP 1979).

Politics in Ottawa in the 1920s were dominated by the battles between Arthur Meighen and Mackenzie King. The brilliant, lucid Meighen fought against King's puffy platitudes and won all the individual combats only to lose all the wars. Meighen's biography by Roger Graham, particularly *Arthur Meighen*, II: *And Fortune Fled* (T: CI 1963), is also brilliant and lucid, employing Meighen's Papers to build an effective portrait of the Tory chief, one that almost invariably accepts Meighen's versions of events and espouses his position. Graham's essay, 'Some Political Ideas of Arthur Meighen' in Hamelin, ed., *The Political Ideas of the Prime Ministers of Canada*, is also helpful. Meighen's speeches are collected in the characteristically titled *Unrevised and Unrepented* (T: CI 1949), and while they convey the spirit of the man, Meighen at his vitriolic best should be read in House of Commons *Debates*.

Only dedicated researchers should try to read Mackenzie King in *Hansard*. It is much more rewarding to turn to the official biography, *William Lyon Mackenzie King*, where King's exercises in circumlocution have been sorted out in workmanlike fashion. The first volume, covering the period from 1874 to 1923, is by R. Mac-Gregor Dawson; the second, 1924-32, and the third, 1932-9, are by H. Blair Neatby (T: UTP 1958, 1963, 1976). The biographers are generally sympathetic to King, Dawson more so than Neatby, but there is no real attempt to hide Mr King's many warts. Neatby's accounts of King's tactics during the constitutional crisis of 1926 or of his waffling during the 1930s are admirably fair, although both have been the subject of polemics in the past. The three volumes show appreciation for King's political skills and his sensitivity to the national, or regional, mood, and form the best foundation for the revisionist looks at King that are now underway.

Charles Stacey's *A Very Double Life: The Private World of Mackenzie King* (T: MAC 1976) is one of those revisionist studies, a rather prying examination of King's sex life and his recourse to the spirit worlds. Stacey's version was roundly and effectively denounced by Joy Esberey in *Knight of the Holy Spirit* (T: UTP 1980), a book that is eminently fair in its treatment of Mackenzie King's tortured psyche but less than sound in relating the psyche to King's policies. Another book not to be missed is Craven's *'An Impartial Umpire': Industrial Relations and the Canadian State 1900-1911* which, despite its title, is one of the best examinations of King we have. There is a good debate on King in *Labour*, with Reginald Whitaker examining 'The Liberal Corporatist Ideas of Mackenzie King' (1977) and Craven attacking them in 'King and Context: A Reply to Whitaker' (1979). Other views, revisionist and traditional, can be found in John English and John Stubbs, eds., *Mackenzie King: Widening the Debate* (T: MAC 1978), and in the picture book by J.L. Granatstein, *Mackenzie King: His Life and World* (T: MHR 1977). Additional material on King can be found in Bruce Hutchison's *The Incredible Canadian* (T: Longmans 1952); in Harry Ferns and B. Ostry's *The Age of Mackenzie King: The Rise of the Leader* (1955; T: Lorimer 1976), an out-and-out hatchet job; and in the book by King's long-time secretary, F.A. MacGregor, *The Fall and Rise of Mackenzie King: 1911-1919* (T: MAC 1962).

To understand King, as most of the recent writers fully realize, recourse must be had to his massive diaries. The entire diary, 1932-50 – except for some spiritualism sections that were destroyed by the executors of the King estate – is available in a microfiche edition from the University of Toronto Press (1980). A published version for the period from 1939 to 1948, *The Mackenzie King Record*, vols. I-IV (T: UTP 1960-70), has been edited by J.W. Pickersgill (assisted on the latter three volumes by D.F. Forster). The *Record* is useful for all work on the years it covers, a good, reliable account of events from King's perspective. Some essays on King include Jean Dryden's 'The Mackenzie King Papers: An Archival Odyssey,' *Archivaria*, 1978, a fascinating account of how King's diaries (or most of them) came to be preserved despite his will's instructions to destroy them; Pickersgill's 'Mackenzie King's Speeches,' QQ, 1950; articles by Esberey and John Courtney on 'Prime Ministerial Character,' CJPS, 1975; and assaults on King launched by Eugene Forsey, many of which are collected in Forsey's *Freedom and Order* (T: M&S 1974).

Much additional useful material on the politics of the 1920s is available, although this decade still requires more work before historians can unplug their word processors. *Les mémoires du Senateur Raoul Dandurand (1861-1942)* (Q: PUL 1967) unfortunately adds little, but no student should miss the brilliant essays by F.H. Underhill, many of which are collected in his *In Search of Canadian Liberalism*. Many of the Underhill pieces first appeared in the *Canadian Forum*, and the backfiles of that small intellectual and leftist journal are rich in left-centre comment throughout the interwar years. Ramsay Cook's *The Politics of J.W. Dafoe and the Free Press* (T: UTP 1963) offers an excellent look at the influential Winnipeg editor, but as James H. Gray's memoir of his time on the newspaper, *Troublemaker* (T: MAC 1978), makes clear, Dafoe should not be idealized. James Eayrs's *In Defence of Canada*, I: *From the Great War to the Great Depression* (T: UTP 1964), remains the solitary study of defence policy in the 1920s. There is no history of the Liberal or Conservative parties during this period (or for most of the rest of post-Confederation history), but the Communists have been studied effectively in William Rodney's *Soldiers of the International: A History of the Communist Party of Canada 1919-29* (T: UTP 1968), which is based on excellent research and may be contrasted with Ivan Avakumovic's *The Communist Party in Canada: A History* (T: M&S 1975).

32 J.L. Granatstein and Paul Stevens

THE DEPRESSION

The easy prosperity of the 1920s, never uniformly spread across the land, disappeared almost completely with stunning suddenness as the twenties ended and the thirties began. There are no detailed, solid histories of Canada and Canadians during the Great Depression, but students should be aware of H. Blair Neatby's *The Politics of Chaos: Canada in the Thirties* (T: MAC 1972), a collection of TV lectures that provide a helpful overview of the decade. Also enjoyable and good browsing is Michiel Horn's *The Dirty Thirties* (T: CC 1972), a rich document collection, and Victor Hoar's edited collection, *The Great Depression* (T: CC nd). Still valuable are A.E. Safarian, *The Canadian Economy in the Great Depression* (T: UTP 1959), and H.A. Innis and A.F.W. Plumptre, *The Canadian Economy and its Problems* (T: CIIA 1934). Another important account is Irving Brecher's examination of *Monetary and Fiscal Thought and Policy in Canada 1919-39* (T: UTP 1957), a book that is extremely hard to come by. Alvin Finkel's account of *Business and Social Reform in the Thirties* (T: Lorimer 1979) goes some distance to turning the usual accounts of business attitudes on their ear. Business supported proposals for social welfare and government intervention, Finkel argues, hoping that this might bolster capitalism, and while the case has it seductive points, it is ultimately not proven. One excellent doctoral thesis, soon to be published, deserves mention, James Struthers's 'No Fault of Their Own: Unemployment and the Canadian Welfare State, 1914-41' (University of Toronto 1979). This is the fullest account of the development of unemployment insurance, and should be read with his article, 'Prelude to Depression: The Federal Government and Unemployment 1918-29,' CHR, 1977, and with Udo Sautter, 'The Origins of the Employment Service of Canada 1900-20,' *Labour*, 1980, all helpful accounts on piecing together the way the Depression ultimately produced some protection for workers.

The Bennett government, unhappily in command for the first (and worst) five years of the slump, has yet to be treated thoroughly. There is no full biography of Bennett and almost nothing on his ministers and their policies. Historians, like other Canadians, clearly have tried to forget. Lord Beaverbrook's *Friends* (L: Heine-

mann 1959) and Ernest Watkins, *R.B. Bennett* (T: Kingswood
House 1963), tell us little about the Conservative leader, and the
best source on the New Deal remains J.R.H. Wilbur's documents
book, *The Bennett New Deal* (T: CC 1968). Wilbur's little book on
H.H. Stevens (T: UTP 1977) and his articles 'H.H. Stevens and R.B.
Bennett, 1930-34,' CHR, 1962, and 'R.B. Bennett and the Reconstruction Party,' CHR, 1964, constitute the major scholarly opus on
the Tory government and give a good treatment to Bennett's difficulties with his minister of trade and commerce. Students will also
find material of interest in Donald Forster and C. Read's article,
'The Politics of Opportunism: The New Deal Broadcasts,' CHR,
1979, and can learn how the Tories got nowhere in Saskatchewan
from Norman Ward's 'The Politics of Patronage: James Gardiner
and Federal Appointments in the West 1935-57,' CHR, 1977. The
one account of the Tories for this period is Marc La Terreur, *Les
tribulations des conservateurs au Québec* (Q: PUL 1973), and there is
some startling material on Bennett's links to fascist movements in
Quebec in Lita-Rose Betcherman, *The Swastika and the Maple Leaf*
(T: Fitzhenry & Whiteside 1975). Jonathan Wagner has studied
domestic Nazis in 'The *Deutscher Bund Canada* 1934-39,' CHR,
1977; 'Nazi Party Membership in Canada: A Profile,' SH, 1981; and
Brothers beyond the Sea: National Socialism in Canada (Waterloo:
Wilfrid Laurier UP 1982).

THE BUREAUCRACY

The 1930s saw the beginnings of a competent public service in Canada. O.D. Skelton came to Ottawa in the mid-twenties and began to
build up the Department of External Affairs and to work to persuade King and Bennett that expertise was necessary if the state was
to have any influence in Canada. Over time he helped bring Clifford
Clark to the Finance department and Graham Towers to the newly-
created Bank of Canada, and all three were soon recruiting with
much success. The mandarinate was in formation.
    There is as yet no published history of the growth and change of
the civil service since the Depression. R.M. Dawson's *The Civil Service of Canada* (L: OUP 1929) is the best account of the earlier

period, and can be supplemented usefully with J.E. Hodgetts, *The Canadian Public Service: A Physiology of Government 1867-1970* (T: UTP 1973) and Hodgetts *et al.*, *The Biography of an Institution: The Civil Service Commission of Canada 1908-1967* (M: MQUP 1972). Also helpful, although badly outdated, is Taylor Cole, *The Canadian Bureaucracy* (Durham: Duke UP 1949). There is still only one departmental history, *Canada's Salesmen to the World: The Department of Trade and Commerce 1892-1939* (M: MQUP 1977); one book-length study of *Policy, Politics and the Treasury Board in Canadian Government* (Don Mills: SRA 1970) by W.L. White and J.C. Strick; and an article, 'An Examination of the Role of the Comptroller of the Treasury,' by R.D. MacLean, *Canadian Public Administration*, 1964. There is also a chatty history of the office of auditor general, Sonja Sinclair's *Cordial But Not Cosy* (T: M&S 1979), and two useful supplements to John Porter's treatment of the bureaucracy in *The Vertical Mosaic* (T: UTP 1965) – Dennis Olsen's *The State Elite* (T: M&S 1980) and Colin Campbell and George Szablowski, *The Super-Bureaucrats* (T: MAC 1979). J.L. Granatstein's *The Ottawa Men: The Civil Service Mandarins 1935-57* (T: OUP 1982) studies the twenty or so key members of the public service in their period of greatest influence.

Granatstein is also the author of the one academic study of a civil servant, *A Man of Influence: Norman A. Robertson and Canadian Statecraft 1929-68* (O: Deneau 1981). Robertson was one of Skelton's External Affairs recruits and played a decisive role in policy over a forty-year period in that department, in the Privy Council Office, and in all economic and trade policy. Joseph Schull's study of Donald Gordon, *The Great Scot* (M: MQUP 1979), uses oral history sources in an attempt to trace Gordon's role in the Bank of Canada, the Wartime Prices and Trade Board, and at the CNR. Among memoirs there is James Manion's *A Canadian Errant* (T: Ryerson 1960), an account by a trade commissioner; Dana Wilgress's *Memoirs* (T: Ryerson 1967), a lifeless account by a senior trade and foreign policy figure; and Arnold Heeney's *The Things that are Caesar's* (T: UTP 1972), a useful if not very frank account by the man who created the Privy Council Office into the powerful operation it is today. Additional works by foreign service officers will be treated in the next chapter.

THE LIBERALS

While there is no detailed account of the Liberal party during the Depression years, there is one book that deserves particular mention: Reginald Whitaker's *The Government Party: Organizing and Financing the Liberal Party of Canada 1930-58* (T: UTP 1977). This is the best study of a Canadian party that we have, a well-researched and written account of the way the Liberals picked up the pieces of their defeat in 1930 and put together the mixture of personnel and policy that brought them back to power in 1935 and kept them there for twenty-two years. This is a study of organization and finance, as the title says, but it is also a rich account of leadership and policy and of the ways the federal bureaucracy gradually became an agency of the Liberal party. Equally striking to an historian, Whitaker is one political scientist who gets his hands dirty in the archives and who seems to eschew opinion surveys and the increasingly arcane methodology much favoured in his discipline. Together with David Smith's *Prairie Liberalism: The Liberal Party in Saskatchewan, 1905-71* (T: UTP 1975), these are books that every student of twentieth-century Canadian politics must know.

THE CCF

Like most of the third parties in recent Canadian history, the Cooperative Commonwealth Federation has received substantial attention from scholars. There are several overall surveys of the party of which the best is Walter Young's *The Anatomy of a Party: The National CCF 1932-61* (T: UTP 1969). Based on solid research, Young's work grapples with the problems faced by a social movement that must act as a political party, and he is effective in analysing the role of the party bureaucracy. The key member of that bureaucracy, David Lewis, also published a posthumous volume of autobiography, *The Good Fight: Political Memoirs 1909-1958* (T: MAC

1981). This is an excellent memoir for historians, primarily because Lewis was everywhere and saw everything and in this volume he sets it all out with frankness. The result is good history, if not a warm human story. Still useful for the CCF's story is Dean McHenry, *The Third Force in Canada* (T: OUP 1950), an early scholarly look at the party. S.M. Lipset's able study of the Saskatchewan CCF, *Agrarian Socialism*, originally published in 1950, has been updated and supplemented with a series of essays in a new edition (NY: Doubleday 1968).

There are still more books on the party. Desmond Morton's *Social Democracy in Canada* (T: Samuel Stevens 1977) is a good, workmanlike survey of the CCF and its successor party, the NDP, and is much more reliable than Ivan Avakumovic's *Socialism in Canada* (T: M&S 1978) and much less ideological than Norman Penner's *The Canadian Left: A Critical Analysis* (T: PH 1977). Gerald Caplan's *The Dilemma of Canadian Socialism* (T: M&S 1973) is an examination of the CCF/NDP failure in Ontario while Leo Zakuta's *A Protest Movement Becalmed* (T: UTP 1964) studies change in the CCF, largely on the basis of remembered conversations. Gad Horowitz's *Canadian Labour in Politics* (T: UTP 1968) surveys the unions' role in the development of the CCF. Horowitz brilliantly postulates the thesis of the red-Tory, a peculiar Canadian hybrid, and for this alone his book is worth reading. More useful on labour, however, is I.M. Abella's *Nationalism, Communism and Canadian Labour* (T: UTP 1973).

Students should also be aware of O.D. Skelton's *Socialism: A Critical Analysis* (Boston: Houghton Mifflin 1911), a prize-winning dissection of the doctrine by the Queen's professor who went on to become the creator of the Department of External Affairs. Michiel Horn's book, *The League for Social Reconstruction: Intellectual Origins of the Democratic Left in Canada 1930-1942* (T: UTP 1980), also examines the roles of intellectuals in politics, and Gregory Baum's *Catholics and Canadian Socialism* (T: Lorimer 1980) is a useful reminder that not all Catholics opposed the CCF in its early days.

There are several CCF biographies. Much the best is Kenneth McNaught's fine study of J.S. Woodsworth, *A Prophet in Politics* (T: UTP 1959). Woodsworth's daughter, Grace McInnis, wrote *J.S. Woodsworth: A Man to Remember* (T: MAC 1953). There is also the sympathetic but sadly flawed *Tommy Douglas* (T: M&S 1975) by Doris Shackleton. Douglas here is the *nonpareil*, fighting evil inside the party and out, but the research is sloppy and errors abound. Biographies of other figures include Diane Lloyd's *Woodrow: A Biography of W.S. Lloyd* (np: Woodrow Lloyd Memorial Foundation nd) and Dorothy Steeves's study of Ernest Winch, *The Compassionate Rebel* (V: J.J. Douglas 1960).

SOCIAL CREDIT

There is also a large body of literature on Social Credit, that other radical product of the Depression. The major works are to be found in the Social Credit in Alberta series, published by the University of Toronto Press in ten volumes that looked widely into the origins and developments of the West. From a political history point of view, the most valuable books are J.R. Mallory, *Social Credit and the Federal Power in Canada* (1954); J.A. Irving, *The Social Credit Movement in Alberta* (1959); and C.B. Macpherson, *Democracy in Alberta: Social Credit and the Party System* (1953). Irving gets to the roots of Social Credit's appeal, while Macpherson erects the theory of the quasi-party to explain the phenomenon of one-party dominance in democratic states.

Other articles and books of note are John Saywell's 'Reservation Revisited: Alberta 1937,' CJEPS, 1962, and articles by Harold Schultz, notably 'The Social Credit Backbenchers' Revolt 1937,' CHR, 1960; 'A Second Term, 1940,' *Alberta Historical Review*, 1962; and 'Aberhart, the Organization Man,' *Alberta Historical Review*, 1959. The one biography is by L.P.V. Johnson and Ola McNutt, Aberhart's daughter, *Aberhart of Alberta* (Edmonton: 1970). There is also N.B. James's humorous *The Autobiography of a Nobody* (T: Dent 1947) and John Finlay's *Social Credit: The English Origins* (M: MQUP 1972). A good collection of documents is Lewis Thomas's *William Aberhart and Social Credit in Alberta* (T: CC 1977). Other articles include Hugh Whalen's 'Social Credit Measures in Alberta,' CJEPS, and Mary Hallett's examination of Social Credit's abortive pro-conscription offshoot in the 1940 election, 'The Social Credit Party and the New Democracy Movement, 1939-40,' CHR, 1966.

THE SECOND WORLD WAR

The politics of the war years have not yet been thoroughly examined. There is no full history of the Liberal party and no detailed studies of Mackenzie King or his key ministers. *The Mackenzie King Record*, of course, is invaluable, as is Norman Ward, ed., *A Party Politician: The Memoirs of Chubby Power* (T: MAC 1966), a frank, funny look at King's invaluable air minister and organization expert. John Hawkins, in *The Life and Times of Angus L* (Windsor, NS: Lancelot Press 1969), examines the Navy minister in an embarrassingly bad fashion, but Robert Bothwell and William Kilbourn's *C.D. Howe: A Biography* (T: M&S 1979) is a first-rate look at the man who made the Canadian war effort hum. Dale Thomson's *Louis St. Laurent, Canadian* (T: MAC 1967) is the first biography of King's successor written by a former aide and McGill political scientist. Thomson seems to have had access to the St. Laurent Papers, but the book fails to reveal much about its subject or his times. There is interesting and useful material in John Swettenham's *McNaughton*, II: *1939-43*, and III: *1944-69* (T: Ryerson 1969), particularly on political-military relations, the conscription crisis of 1944, and on McNaughton's period as minister of national defence. Mackenzie King's Ontario antagonist, *Mitch Hepburn*, is amusingly examined by Neil McKenty (T: M&S 1967) and there is also some useful political and attitudinal information in Vincent Massey's memoir, *What's Past is Prologue* (T: MAC 1963). An official biography of Massey by Claude Bissell is in process at the moment. The first volume, *The Young Vincent Massey* (T: UTP 1981), is brilliantly written and, in telling Massey's story to 1935, goes some distance to humanizing a young stuffed shirt. The second volume will be eagerly awaited.

The one study of the wartime King government is J.L. Granatstein's *Canada's War: The Politics of the Mackenzie King Government, 1939-45* (T: UTP 1975), a long book that looks at politics, social welfare, and conscription. That last subject is also examined for the Second World War in Granatstein and Hitsman, *Broken Promises*, and Granatstein has looked at the Conservative party in the same period in *The Politics of Survival: The Conservative Party of Canada, 1939-45* (T: UTP 1967). There is excellent material on Liberal party finance and organization during the war in Whitaker, *The Government Party*, and a more detailed account of party finances in Granatstein's 'Liberal Party Finances, 1935-45' in M.S. Cross and R. Bothwell, eds., *Policy by Other Means: Essays in Honour of C.P. Stacey* (T: CI 1972), and in his investigation of the Tories in the same period in *Studies in Canadian Party Finance* (O: QP 1966). *The Report of the Committee of Election Expenses* (O: QP 1966) and K.Z. Paltiel, *Political Party Financing in Canada* (T: McGraw-Hill 1970), together provide good narrative accounts of where the money comes from and goes.

Additional material on war politics can be found in C.P. Stacey's *Arms, Men and Governments: The War Policies of Canada 1939-45* (O: Information Canada 1970); in Graham's *Arthur Meighen*, III: *No Surrender* (T: CI 1965); in Robert Rumilly's massive *Duplessis et son temps* (M: Fides 1973); and in Conrad Black's even longer *Duplessis* (T: M&S 1977). Rumilly's *Histoire de la province de Québec*, tomes XXXVIII-XLI (M: Fides 1968, 1969), although a one-sided account of events, often provides otherwise unavailable documentation of war politics as seen from within Quebec. André Laurendeau's *La crise de la conscription de 1942*, a useful and revealing account of one Quebec intellectual's rejection of the federal government's war policy, fortunately is now available in translation in its entirety in Philip Stratford, ed., *André Laurendeau: Witness for Quebec* (T: MAC 1973). Additional material on Laurendeau, a genuinely fascinating character, can be found in Ramsay Cook and Michael Behiels, eds., *The Essential Laurendeau* (T: CC 1976).

One wartime subject that has attracted considerable interest in recent years is that of racism. The treatment of the Canadian Japanese in particular still arouses consider anger. Early studies include C.H. Young *et al.*, eds., *The Japanese Canadians* (T: UTP 1938), and F.E. LaViolette's *The Canadian Japanese and World War II* (T: UTP 1948), which remain the basic books on the subject and may still be the best. More recent accounts are Ken Adachi's *The Enemy that Never Was* (T: M&S 1976); Ann Sunahara, *The Politics of Racism* (T: Lorimer 1981); Peter Ward's *White Canada Forever* (M: MQUP 1978); and Barry Broadfoot's *Years of Sorrow, Years of Shame* (T: Doubleday 1977). The first three are based on extensive research;

Broadfoot's, much the least reliable, is based solely on edited conversations. One memoir by a wartime internee merits particular attention. T.U. Nakano's *Within the Barbed Wire Fence* (T: UTP 1980) is a fine piece of literature as well as a valuable account of the attitudes of those interned Japanese Canadians who hoped for a Japanese victory. The only account that does not totally condemn the government for its every action is to be found in Granatstein's *A Man of Influence*. Norman Robertson played a major role in creating the internment policy and as he was neither a racist nor a man without morality, the situation as he viewed it merits some consideration.

POLITICS TO 1957

The scholarly literature still remains relatively thin for the period after 1945. *Canada since 1945: Power, Politics, and Provincialism* by Robert Bothwell, Ian Drummond, and John English (T: UTP 1981) is lively, opinionated, anti-nationalist, and great fun to read, much more so than Donald Creighton's *Canada 1939-57: The Forked Road* (T: M&S 1976). This is the starting-point for work on the more recent period. Whitaker's *The Government Party* is similarly indispensable. Other very useful works include vols. III and IV of *The Mackenzie King Record* (T: UTP 1970); Thomson's *Louis St. Laurent*; and J.W. Pickersgill's *My Years with St. Laurent* (T: UTP 1975). The memoirs of Lester Pearson, *Mike*, vols. I and II (T: UTP 1972, 1973), tell Pearson's story down to the time he became leader of the opposition. Vol. I in particular is gracefully written and witty. The same cannot be said for John Diefenbaker's *One Canada: The Memoirs of the Rt. Hon. John G. Diefenbaker* (T: MAC 1975-7), the first volume of which tells Diefenbaker's story down to the election of 1957. There is some nostalgia and charm, but too much venom for all but the committed to enjoy. One of the Chief's targets, Dalton Camp, wrote a very fine memoir, *Gentlemen, Players and Politicians* (T: M&S 1970), a well-written study of a man's political education. The journalist Peter Stursberg has used oral history techniques to create a two-volume set on each of Diefenbaker and Pearson. *Lester Pearson and the American Dilemma* and *Lester Pearson and the Dream of Unity* (T: Doubleday 1978, 1980) and *Diefenbaker: Leadership Gained 1956-62* and *Diefenbaker: Leadership Lost 1962-67* (T: UTP 1975, 1976) have useful anecdotal material but can be trusted no more than one trusts any oral history source. Perhaps the surest guide to the period of Liberal ascendancy after the war is Bothwell and Kilbourn's *C.D. Howe*, a clear, concise, and well-researched account of the 'Minister of Everything' and his aims and attitudes. There is nothing on most of Howe's colleagues, many of whom – Abbott, Claxton, Martin – deserve to be studied. Walter Gordon's career, most important after 1963, of course, has drawn the attention of Denis Smith in his *Gentle Patriot* (Edmonton: Hurtig 1973), a fine study of an able man whose economic nationalism has often failed to endear him to the powerful or to many scholars. Gordon's own autobiography, *A Political Memoir* (T: M&S 1977), is useful on his early friendship with Pearson and his role in the Royal Commission on Canada's Economic Prospects, the Gordon Commission. David Lewis's autobiography, *The Good Fight*, provides a heavily detailed CCF account of the period, and Joey Smallwood's *I Chose Canada* (T: MAC 1973) gives an idiosyncratic view of events as seen from St John's. The view is clear, however, the comments sharp, and the book well worth study.

Journalists' memoirs for the period include Bruce Hutchison's *The Far Side of the Street* (T: MAC 1976); Grattan O'Leary's *Recollections of People, Press and Politics* (T: MAC 1977); Stuart Keate's *Paper Boy* (T: CI 1980); and John and Graham Fraser, eds., *Blair Fraser Reports: Selections 1944-68* (T: MAC 1969). Students of history will be amused at the astonishing number of factual slips to be found in the first two of these volumes. There is a need for a detailed look at that key group of journalists – Hutchison, Fraser, Grant Dexter, George Ferguson, and Kenneth Wilson – who were so close to the Liberal government during its postwar ascendancy as to form something approximating a federal department.

DIEFENBAKER, PEARSON, TRUDEAU

The Bothwell, English, Drummond book is indispensable for the period after 1957, and the autobiographies of Pearson, Diefenbaker, and Gordon must be consulted as well as the books examining these men.

Other studies on the politicians of the last quarter century include a substantial array of journalistic accounts, notably Peter Newman's *Renegade in Power* (T: M&S 1963), the first all-stops-pulled-out assault on a politician by a journalist to that point. Pearson failed to arouse similar passions, and John R. Beal's *The Pearson Phenomenon* (T: Longmans 1964) is adulatory. But Trudeau was more like Diefenbaker, and he has been roundly denounced by Walter Stewart in *Shrug: Trudeau in Power* (T: New Press 1972); sharply criticized by Antony Westell in *Paradox: Trudeau as Prime Minister* (T: PH 1972) and by Richard Gwyn, *The Northern Magus* (T: M&S 1980); and praised by George Radwanski, *Trudeau* (T: MAC 1978). Readers can pick their positions, but Gwyn's is much the best of the books. Robert Bothwell's *Pearson: His Life and World* (T: MHR 1978) is an attractive picture book with a sound text, while Bruce Thordarson's *Lester Pearson: Diplomat and Politician* (T: OUP 1974) is another brief life. Other political studies include Judy LaMarsh's feisty *A Bird in a Gilded Cage* (T: M&S 1969), which is very harsh on Pearson; Geoffrey Stevens's able examination of *Stanfield* (T: M&S 1973); and Jack Horner's *My Own Brand* (Edmonton: Hurtig 1980). The Stanfield biography is very favourable to the Tory leader who had the uncomfortable job of trying to hold the post-Diefenbaker party together, and Horner's memoir indicates just what a difficult job that must have been. It was difficult too for Joe Clark, the nine-month prime minister of 1979-80, the subject of a potboiler by David Humphreys, *Joe Clark: A Portrait* (O: Deneau & Greenberg 1980).

Biographical studies aside, the pickings are still thin. The best guide to national (and provincial) politics remains the *Canadian Annual Review*, published each year since 1960 by the University of Toronto Press. The CAR should be the first stopping-point for researchers of the period. Valuable political studies include John Meisel's books, *The Canadian General Election of 1957* (T: UTP 1962), *Papers on the 1962 Election* (T: UTP 1964), and *Working Papers on Canadian Politics* (M: MQUP 1975). J.M. Beck usefully collected statistical data on all elections to 1968 in *Pendulum of Power* (T: PH 1968), and there is a valuable collection of academic essays on the 1974 election in H.R. Penniman, ed., *Canada at the Polls: The General Election of 1974* (Washington: American Enterprise Institute 1975). The Liberals after 1958 have been examined by Joseph Wearing, a political scientist, in *The L-Shaped Party* (T: MHR 1981), a well-researched examination of the way the Grits have lost their support in the West. That subject is also dissected, and very neatly too, in David E. Smith's *The Regional Decline of a National Party: Liberals on the Prairies* (T: UTP 1981). The old-style party bosses of the Jimmy Gardiner ilk have disappeared, but their replacements with flow charts and ad-man's slogans have been ineffective. Two additional academic books can be mentioned. George Perlin's *The Tory Syndrome: Leadership Politics in the Progressive Conservative Party* (M: MQUP 1979) presents substantial data on the Conservative conventions of 1967 and 1976; Peter Regenstreif's *The Diefenbaker Interlude* (T: Longmans 1965) was one of the first books to be heavily based on polling data.

The Diefenbaker years have also been the subject of a number of insiders' accounts, often by journalists or by party officials. Robert Coates's *The Night of the Knives* (Fredericton: Brunswick Press 1969); Thomas Van Dusen's *The Chief* (T: McGraw-Hill 1968); and James Johnston's *The Party's Over* (T: Longman 1971) are by loyalists. Patrick Nicholson's *Vision and Indecision* (T: Longmans 1968) is a memoir by a journalist close to the Chief, one who revealed the 'secret memorandum' that was the occasion for one of Dief's most devastating House of Commons speeches. A usually forgotten study, *Eglinton* (T: Peter Martin 1965), Brian Land's analysis of the Toronto-Eglinton by-election of 1962, stands as one indicator of the way Ontario opinion was beginning to turn against the Tories by 1962. J.A. Laponce's study of opinion and attitudes in Vancouver-Burrard between 1963 and 1965, *People Versus Politics* (T: UTP 1969), is another.

The Pearson years have not attracted quite as much journalistic notice. There is Richard Gwyn's able analysis of *The Shape of Scandal* (T: CI 1965), a study of the messes that Pearson's ministers and aides got the government into, and there is Newman's *The Distemper of our Times* (T: M&S 1968), with its focus on the struggle between Pearson and Diefenbaker. On the early Trudeau years

there is Donald Peacock's *Journey to Power* (T: Ryerson 1968),
which looks at the 1968 election campaign, and Martin Sullivan's
Mandate '68 (T: Doubleday 1968) on the same subject. The Clark-
Trudeau struggles have been brilliantly analyzed by the acerbic Dal-
ton Camp in his *Points of Departure* (Ottawa: Deneau & Greenberg
1979); by Warner Troyer in *200 Days: Joe Clark in Power* (T: Personal Library 1980); and by Jeffrey Simpson in *Discipline of Power:
The Conservative Interlude and the Liberal Restoration* (T: Personal
Library 1980). The Troyer book is notable only for the Dalton
Camp introduction that begins it, but Simpson's book, based on a
substantial amount of documentary evidence, makes the case that
Clark failed because he simply was not tough enough for the prime
ministership. This book is the best place to begin a study of the
politics of the late 1970s and early 1980s.

FEDERALISM AND THE CONSTITUTION

There is a substantial literature on federalism, a preoccupation of
Canadian governments since the early 1960s, and the beginnings
of Quebec's dissatisfaction with the *status quo*. Among books that
should be consulted are J.S. Dupré et al., *Federalism and Policy Development* (T: UTP 1973); D.J. Savoie, *Federal-Provincial Collaboration*
(M: MQUP 1981); and Anthony Careless, *Initiative and Response*. All
three are policy oriented and examine specific cases. So too are Malcolm Taylor, *Health Insurance and Canadian Public Policy* (M: MQUP
1978) and *The Administration of Health Insurance in Canada* (T: OUP
1956), and Christopher Leman, *The Collapse of Reform: Political
Institutions, Policy and the Poor in Canada and the United States* (Cambridge: MIT 1980). R.M. Burns's very helpful book, *The Acceptable
Mean: The Tax Rental Agreements 1941-62* (T: Canadian Tax Foundation 1980), clarifies the fiscal arrangements between Ottawa and
the provinces, while Armstrong's *The Politics of Federalism* looks at
Ontario's traditional attitudes to Ottawa, a striking contrast to those
Queen's Park favoured during the drawn-out constitutional battle of
1980-1. Other titles of substantial value are Frank Scott's *Essays on
the Constitution* (T: UTP 1977), collected essays of the country's
leading constitutional scholar; Richard Simeon's *Federal-Provincial*

Diplomacy: The Making of Recent Policy in Canada (T: UTP 1972); and Claude Morin's *Quebec Versus Ottawa* (T: UTP 1976), an analysis by a Quebec civil servant and later PQ minister. Undoubtedly, Quebec was at the centre of the constitutional question for most of the period after 1960 and the Quiet Revolution. A vast array of books was produced on the Quebec question. One of the best was written by a career civil servant, Edward Corbett, *Quebec Confronts Canada* (Baltimore: Johns Hopkins UP 1967). Others include Edward McWhinney, *Quebec and the Constitution 1960-78* (T: UTP 1979); Richard Simeon, ed., *Must Canada Fail?* (M: MQUP 1977); André Bernard, *What Does Quebec Want?* (T: Lorimer 1978); Douglas Fullerton, *The Dangerous Delusion* (T: M&S 1978); R.M. Burns, ed., *One Country or Two?* (M: MQUP 1971); Gilles Lalande, *In Defence of Federalism* (T: M&S 1978); R.B. Byers and R.W. Reford, eds., *Canada Challenged* (T: CIIA 1979); and Douglas Auld *et al.*, *Canadian Confederation at the Cross-Roads* (V: Fraser Institute 1978). Long as it is, that list by no means exhausts the total. One more title should be added: *Western Separatism: The Myths, Realities and Dangers* (Edmonton: Hurtig 1981), edited by G. Stevenson and L. Pratt. The constitutional debate, at least, has employed countless political scientists, historians, and others.

J.L. GRANATSTEIN

Foreign and defence policy

'The scholarly literature on foreign and defence policy in Canada is still not large.' The chapter on foreign and defence policy in the two previous editions of this book began with those words. They are still true, but much less so than a few years ago, thanks to more generous access to the records of the Department of External Affairs, to government departments generally, and to the records left by political, diplomatic, and military personnel. There is now more material than one could have hoped for a decade ago, and the quality of the work is also good.

BIBLIOGRAPHIES

There is no detailed and critical bibliography on Canadian foreign and defence policy. The best basic sources are undoubtedly Claude Thibault's massive *Bibliographia Canadiana* (T: Longman 1973) and Grace Heggie's *Canadian Political Parties 1867-1968: A Historical Bibliography* (T: MAC 1977). The Heggie volume is better organized, and almost everything will be found in these two compendia. Smaller, but more directly useful for military historians, is O.A. Cooke, ed., *The Canadian Military Experience 1867-1967: A Bibliography* (O: Minister of Supply and Services 1979). For the period after 1945 there are two series of bibliographies. Donald Page's *A Bibliography of Works on Canadian Foreign Relations 1945-70* (T: CIIA 1973) has been succeeded by his *A Bibliography of Works on Canadian Foreign Relations 1971-75* (T: CIIA nd [1978?]). Both volumes are detailed, careful listings. The Canadian Institute of International Affairs also published *A Reading Guide to Canada in World Affairs 1945-71* (T: 1972), edited by L. Motiuk and M. Grant. Motiuk, a prolific bibliographer, also has produced the *Canadian Forces College Reading Guide for the Study of War, National Defence and Strategy* (T: mimeo 1967), and the *Strategic Studies Reading Guide* (O: National Defence 1970) to which a number of supplements, bound or on microfiche, have been prepared. The organization is cumbersome, but the range is extensive. A useful handbook on manuscript sources for the Second World War housed at the Public Archives of Canada, *Sources for the Study of the Second World War* (O: Public Archives 1979), is available free by writing the PAC.

OFFICIAL SOURCES

The basic source remains the House of Commons *Debates*. Well-indexed, the *Debates* provide a running historical commentary on the development of foreign and defence policy. More directly useful are the minutes of the Standing Committee on External Affairs and National Defence of the House of Commons, a body set up in the mid-1960s. The government-documents bibliographers in good libraries should be able to point researchers to earlier sources of foreign policy in Parliamentary committee proceedings, as well as to more recent materials. The Senate, desperately trying to find a role, has studied some foreign policy questions in recent years.

Other sources that should be sought out are the *Annual Reports* of External Affairs and National Defence and the various aid agencies. No earth-shaking material here, but basic data on personnel, budgets, and occasionally on policy are simply presented. The Department of External Affairs has also from time to time published small collections of documents on specific issues. There are, to cite a few, collections on the *Italo-Ethiopian Crisis* (1936), the *Outbreak of War* (1939), *Korea* (1950, 1951), and *The Suez Crisis* (1956, 1957). For twenty years after the Second World War, External Affairs also published annual volumes on *Canada and the United Nations*. The early volumes are chock-full of documents and speeches, but the more recent ones, perhaps reflecting the decline of the UN and the growing disinterest in Ottawa, are turgid. The department's *Report on the United Nations Conference on International Organization* (O: 1945) is a good collection of documentation on the San Francisco Conference of 1945 that established the world organization.

Easily the most valuable books published by External Affairs are the huge *Documents on Canadian External Relations*. Begun in 1967, the series has thus far produced ten volumes covering the years from the department's founding in 1909 through to 1946 (with a gap from 1944 to 1945). The quality of the volumes varies, with the first six much the least satisfactory. The source of the document was not cited in these volumes and the introductions were sometimes less than sound. But vol. XII, for example, that for 1946, corrects most of the flaws, offers a good range of documents, and also goes to enormous trouble to lay out the location and posting of virtually every member of External Affairs. An additional volume published by External Affairs must also be cited. P.A. Bridle, ed., *Documents on Relations between Canada and Newfoundland 1936-49* (1974), is the first of two volumes and a very good collection indeed. Researchers should also note that material relating to Canada is often found in the similar American series, *Foreign Relations of the United States*, and less often in *Documents on British Foreign Policy* and in *Documents on German Foreign Policy*.

There are a number of more ephemeral official publications. *External Affairs* began after the Second World War as a repository for press releases and speeches, although occasionally historical material slipped through the censors. The magazine has since died, a victim of budget cuts. After the Trudeau government came to office, External Affairs began to publish a glossy magazine, *International Perspectives*, a much better journal with articles by department personnel and outside experts. The journal has since fallen victim to the budget-cutting axe, as well, and is trying to survive on its own. Another useful source is the department's collection of *Statements and Speeches*, a long-running series, refreshed by countless annual infusions. Good libraries should have near-complete collections back to the late 1940s.

National Defence is much more reticent than its sister department. The *Canadian Defence Quarterly* was its journal in the interwar years, succeeded after the war by the *Canadian Army Journal*, the *Crowsnest*, and the *Roundel*. After unification, the three were consolidated into the glossy *Sentinel*. The department's White Papers, most notably those in 1964 and 1971, are important policy documents. Current information is most readily available in the yearly departmental reports, entitled *Defence 78*, *Defence 79*, etc.

PERIODICALS

Aside from *International Perspectives*, most of the periodical publishing in Canadian foreign policy is in the benevolent hands of the Canadian Institute of International Affairs. *International Journal*, its flagship publication, has been the best publication in the field since its establishment at the end of the Second World War. Its series, *Behind the Headlines*, presents a number of short essays on specific topics each year and has been doing so since 1940. *Etudes internationales*, published by the Quebec branch of the institute, has been in existence since 1969, and *Choix*, another publication of the branch, offers occasional longer pieces. The CIIA also publishes *Canada in World Affairs*, a long-running series of books that look at Canadian foreign and defence relations in two-year chunks (and that, regrettably, has been allowed to lag well behind events), and the Wellesley Papers, a series largely on strategic questions. The institute also sponsors the publication of a wide range of books. Its contribution to the field has been enormous.

The *Canadian Defence Quarterly*, founded by John Gellner, has been in operation for more than a decade now, attempting to create a forum for intelligent comment on defence issues. Many of the writers are serving officers. The result has been spotty, but there is a substantial amount of important material on armaments and doctrine to be discovered in CDQ's pages. Another journal, *International History Review*, published by the University of Toronto Press on behalf of the editors at Simon Fraser University, has recently made all of diplomatic history its province. Most issues contain an article on Canadian subjects.

GENERAL HISTORIES

George Glazebrook's *A History of Canadian External Relations* (T: OUP 1942; expanded 1950; 2 vol. ed., M&S 1962) has been superseded by Charles Stacey's *Canada and the Age of Conflict*. Vol. I covers the period from Confederation to 1921 (T: MAC 1977) and vol. II carries the story through to 1948 (T: UTP 1981). Stacey writes a fine, lively prose, the range of his research is wide, and his opinions are usually judicious and occasionally very tart. In the second volume a good deal of personal reminiscence intrudes (often pleasantly), and readers of Stacey's critical examination of Mackenzie King, *A Very Double Life* (T: MAC 1976), will likely be amused by the rather favourable treatment of King's policies. The two volumes constitute a splendid achievement, an invaluable examination of Canada's road from colony to linch-pin to a nation 'present at the creation' of the post-war world.

Other general studies that readers should note include R.A. MacKay and E.B. Rogers, *Canada looks Abroad* (T: OUP 1938), a good pre-war examination of Canadian policy; Stacey's *The Military Problems of Canada* (T: Ryerson 1940); and G.F.G. Stanley's *Canada's Soldiers* (T: MAC 1974), a popular history of Canada's wars and warriors. More recent and more opinionated than Stanley, Desmond Morton's *Canada and War* (T: Butterworth 1981) surveys defence policy from Confederation to the 1980s. J.B. Brebner's *North Atlantic Triangle: The Interplay of Canada, the United States and Great Britain* (T: Ryerson 1945) is still a suggestive interpretation. Brebner's was but one volume in the great series, The Relations of Canada and the United States, edited by J.T. Shotwell for the Carnegie Endowment for International Peace.

THE FIRST YEARS, 1867-1914

In this period when Canada could be said not to have had a foreign policy of her own, there is still much room for research. The result is that most books are either exceedingly narrow in focus or else so all inclusive as to be less than important for the student of external affairs.

The first place to begin is with the standard biographies of prime ministers, referred to in the National Politics section. Creighton's *Macdonald*, Thomson's *Alexander Mackenzie*, Skelton's *Laurier*, and Brown's *Borden*, are all good books that have substantial material about Canada's relations with Britain and the United States in them. Skelton's *Laurier* is particularly fascinating for what it tells us about its author, O.D. Skelton, the under-secretary of state for external affairs from 1925 to 1941 and the creator of the modern Department of External Affairs. Joseph Schull's *Laurier: The First Canadian* (T: MAC 1966) has not superseded Skelton's biography. Also worth note are Sir Charles Tupper, *Recollections of Sixty Years in Canada* (T: Cassell 1914); the two-volume *Life and Letters of Sir Charles Tupper* (T: Cassell 1916); and the subsequent *Supplement to the Life and Letters* (T: Ryerson 1926). In addition to a long political career that culminated briefly in the premiership, Tupper was high commissioner in London for a long period.

Other biographies of importance are J.M.S. Careless's fine *Brown of the Globe* (T: MAC 1959, 1963), particularly for its discussion of the abortive negotiations with the Americans on reciprocity questions during the Mackenzie administration, and O.D. Skelton's *Life and Times of Sir Alexander Galt* (T: OUP 1920), which carefully explores the financial links between British and Canadian capitalists and entrepreneurs. Sir John Willison's study of *Sir George Parkin* (L: MAC 1929) and W.L. Grant and Frederick Hamilton, *George Monro Grant* (T: Morang 1905), are studies of Canadian imperialists of the turn of the century. Goldwin Smith's *Canada and the Canadian Question* (reprint, T: UTP 1972) looks at the continentalist option of the same period, and D.J. Hall's *Clifford Sifton, I: The Young Napoleon, 1861-1900* (V: UBCP 1981) is a careful study, among other things, of Sifton's role in immigration, the International Joint Commission, and in maintaining order in the Klondike. Another biography, Robert Stewart's *Sam Steele: Lion of the Frontier* (T: Doubleday 1979), examines the career of a NWMP and army officer.

Any consideration of imperialism and nationalism at this time must take into account the excellent study by Carl Berger *The Sense of Power* (T: UTP 1970). Intellectual history, social history, and foreign policy – if one can describe the battle for the Canadian soul in this way – are brought into juxtaposition here. Berger has also collected documents together in his *Imperialism and Nationalism 1884-1914: A Conflict in Canadian Thought* (T: CC 1969). The student should read Norman Penlington's *Canada and Imperialism 1896-1899* (T: UTP 1965), a book that anticipated some of Berger's arguments.

In this era governors general still had some importance, influence, and power, and many hesitated not at all before using it. John Buchan, later a governor general himself as Lord Tweedsmuir, wrote the life of *Lord Minto* (L: Nelson 1925), and there are two interesting volumes in the publications of the Champlain Society. One is the *Dufferin-Carnarvon Correspondence 1874-1878*, edited by C.W. de Kiewiet and F.H. Underhill; the second is John Saywell's *The Canadian Journal of Lady Aberdeen, 1893-1898*, a marvellous, gossipy account by the wife of the governor general.

For general histories of the period, all of which devote space to Canada's relations with Britain and the United States, the first place to turn is to the generally excellent volumes of the Centenary series, published by McClelland and Stewart. W.L. Morton's *The Critical Years ... 1857-73* (1964); Peter Waite's *Canada 1874-96: Arduous Destiny* (1971); and R.C. Brown and Ramsay Cook's *Canada 1896-1921: A Nation Transformed* (1974) cover the first half-century of Confederation in considerable detail. The first two volumes have extensive bibliographies; all have detailed footnotes.

For the period around Confederation, the reader should refer first to Brian Jenkins's scholarly and definitive *Britain and the War for the Union*, (2 vols. M: MQUP 1974, 1980) and his *Fenians and Anglo-American Relations During Reconstruction* (Ithaca: Cornell UP 1969); to Robin Winks's *Canada and the United States: The Civil War Years* (Baltimore, Johns Hopkins UP 1960); and to David Farr, *The Colonial Office and Canada* (T: UTP 1955). An extraordinary scholar, J. Mackay Hitsman, completed *Safeguarding Canada 1763-1871* (T: UTP 1968) although he was desperately ill. The last two chapters cover this period and very well indeed, as does Charles Stacey's excellent *Canada and the British Army 1846-71* (revised ed., T: UTP 1963). Several of Stacey's voluminous articles cover the period, too, including 'Fenianism and the Rise of National Feeling in Canada at the Time of Confederation,' CHR, 1931; 'The Fenian Troubles and Canadian Military Development, 1865-71,' CHR, 1935; and 'Britain's Withdrawal from North America, 1864-71,' CHR, 1955. As with all Stacey's works, these are marked by splendid prose style and thorough research. For strong views, no one should miss Donald Creighton. His polemic, *Canada's First Century* (T: MAC 1970), covers this period and all others. His altering views on the United States and its influence on Confederation can be compared and contrasted with some of his earlier articles, notably 'Canada in the English-Speaking World,' CHR, 1945, and 'The United States and Canadian Confederation,' CHR, 1958.

American intentions to Canada were not always benevolent in practice. Basic studies include L.B. Shippee, *Canadian-American Relations 1849-74* (New Haven: Yale UP 1939); C.C. Tansill, *Canadian-American Relations 1875-1911* (New Haven: Yale UP 1943); and L.E. Ellis, *Reciprocity 1911* (New Haven: Yale UP 1939), all three being Carnegie series volumes and all three by American scholars. More useful, if more recent, are A.C. Gluek, *Minnesota and the Manifest Destiny of the American Northwest* (T: UTP 1965), and the suggestive book by D.F. Warner, *The Idea of Continental Union* (Lexington: University of Kentucky Press 1960). R.C. Brown's *Canada's National Policy 1883-1900: A Study in Canadian-American Relations* (Princeton, Princeton UP 1964) is very detailed and valuable because, unlike most of the books hitherto cited, it attempts to relate external questions and domestic politics.

Several studies put Canada into place in an Anglo-American context. C.S. Campbell, *Anglo-American Understanding 1898-1903* (Baltimore: Johns Hopkins UP 1957); A.E. Campbell, *Great Britain and the United States 1895-1903* (L: Longmans 1960); and Kenneth Bourne, *Britain and the Balance of Power in North America 1815-1908* (Berkeley: University of California Press 1967) all have much Canadian material, as does the long-forgotten work by A. Gordon Dewey, *The Dominions and Diplomacy: The Canadian Contribution* (L: Longmans 1929). For the complex Alaska Boundary dispute, reference can be made to John Munro, *The Alaska Boundary Dispute* (T: CC 1970), and to Norman Penlington, *The Alaska Boundary*

Dispute: A Critical Appraisal (T: MHR 1972). The Munro volume is a documents collection, but there are substantial differences in interpretation on the merits of the Canadian and American cases and on the British role between him and Penlington. Another useful documents collection is Paul Stevens, *The 1911 General Election: A Study in Canadian Politics* (T: CC 1970). Stevens assembles ample material to show the way commercial interests resisted any shift in the established trade patterns. In this same vein, students should read Robert Cuff's article, 'The Toronto Eighteen and the Election of 1911,' OH, 1965.

There are other interesting articles scattered throughout the periodicals. Donald Creighton's 'The Victorians and the Empire,' CHR, 1938, is still of value as is A.C. Cooke, 'Empire Unity and Colonial Nationalism 1884-1911,' CHAR, 1955. James Eayrs's examination of 'The Round Table Movement in Canada 1909-20,' CHR, 1957, should be supplemented by Carroll Quigley, 'The Round Table Groups in Canada 1908-38,' CHR, 1962, and most particularly by John Kendle's *The Round Table Movement and Imperial Union* (T: UTP 1975), the best and fullest treatment. See also A.C. Gluek's articles, 'The Invisible Revision of the Rush-Bagot Agreement, 1898-1914,' CHR, 1979, and 'Canada's Splendid Bargain: The North Pacific Fur Seal Convention of 1911,' CHR, 1982. Several articles are collected in Carl Berger, ed., *Imperial Relations in the Age of Laurier* (Canadian Historical Readings no 6; T: UTP 1969), along with a useful introduction and additional bibliographical listings.

For military subjects the Stacey and Hitsman books referred to above should be noted, as well as Richard Preston, *Canada and 'Imperial Defense'* (Durham: Duke UP 1967), and his *Canada's RMC* (T: UTP 1969), a well-done history of the Royal Military College, Kingston. An interesting curiosa is W.H. Russell's *Canada: Its Defences Condition and Resources* (L: 1865). On the Rebellion of 1885 the best source unquestionably is Desmond Morton's well-illustrated popular history, *The Last War Drum* (T: Hakkert 1972), which can be supplemented with his and R.H. Roy's *Telegrams of the North-West Campaign 1885* (T: CS 1972). Canada also despatched a party of voyageurs to the Nile expedition of 1884-5. On this see Charles Stacey, *Records of the Nile Voyageurs 1884-5* (T: CS 1959), and his article on the same subject, CHR, 1952.

There is no modern military history of the Boer War and the Canadian role in it, but Desmond Morton has published a biography of his ancestor, Gen. W.D. Otter, *The Canadian General* (T: Hakkert 1974), which is the best account of this subject available. Morton's 'Colonel Otter and the First Canadian Contingent in South Africa 1899-1900,' in M.S. Cross and R. Bothwell, eds., *Policy by other Means: Essays in Honour of C.P. Stacey* (T: CI 1972), is derived from his book. The able and prolific Morton's earlier book, *Ministers and Generals* (T: UTP 1970), is the best study of military-political relations for this period. Three contemporary Boer War accounts are still readily available: T.G. Marquis, *Canada's Sons on Kopje and Veldt*; S.M. Brown, *With the Royal Canadians*; and Sandford Evans, *The Canadian Contingents*, all full of tales of derring-do and romantic Victorianism. Very useful and very suggestive is Carman Miller's 'A Preliminary Analysis of the Socio-economic Composition of Canada's South African War Contingents,' SH, 1975, a detailed breakdown of the kinds and classes of men who joined up in the last little war.

One classic is George Taylor Denison's *Soldiering in Canada* (T: 1900), an account of Canadian military history from 1812 along with a memoir by the wild-eyed nationalist/imperialist militia officer. Other contemporary items that are interesting and now almost humorous are J.H. Burnham, *Canadians in the Imperial Naval and Military Service Abroad* (T: 1891), brief biographies of Canadian officers from lieutenant to general serving the Queen-Empress; Maj.-Gen. C.W. Robinson, *Canada and Canadian Defence* (L: 1910), an account of the ways Canada could defend against (or attack) the United States; and Christopher West, *Canada and Sea Power* (T: 1913), essentially a religio-militaristic tract calling on Canadians to think carefully before automatically offering to support the imperial fleet.

For French-Canadian attitudes to militarism, imperialism, and nationalism, Robert Rumilly's long biography of *Henri Bourassa* (M: Chantecler 1953) and Bourassa's own writings should be referred to. A useful Bourassa collection, translated into English, is Joseph Levitt, *Henri Bourassa on Imperialism and Bi-culturalism* (T: CC 1970). Desmond Morton's two articles, 'French Canada and the Canadian Militia 1868-1914,' (SH, 1969), and 'French Canada and

War, 1898-1917: The Military Background to the Conscription Crisis of 1917,' in J.L. Granatstein and R.D. Cuff, eds., *War and Society in North America* (T: Nelson 1971), are the best available analyses of the reasons Quebec was uneasy about military life, and there is additional material on this subject in his books cited above. Quebec scholarship on the subject has not been well done, as can be seen from an examination of C.M. Boissonault, *Histoire politico-militaire des Canadiens-francais* (Trois-Rivières: Editions du Bien Public 1967). An exception to this harsh comment is Jean-Yves Gravel, *L'Armée au Québec (1868-1900)* (M: BE 1974), a worthy attempt at writing the social history of French Canada's relations with military life after Confederation.

THE GREAT WAR

The basic biographies for the war include Skelton on Laurier, and Brown on Borden, referred to above, and two popular picture books with good, sound texts: Richard Clippingdale's *Laurier: His Life and World* (T:MHR 1979) and John English, *Borden: His Life and World* (T: MHR 1977). Henry Borden, ed., *Robert Laird Borden: His Memoirs* (T: MAC 1938), is a stripped-down memoir, completed after Borden's death and largely based on his diaries. Much better for the war years is Roger Graham, *Arthur Meighen*, I: *The Door of Opportunity* (T: CI 1960). Partisan as it is, Graham's account of war politics is, with Brown's *Borden*, still about the best we have.

Other biographies deserve mention. The commander of the Canadian Corps was Sir Arthur Currie, a civilian in arms and a better general for that. Currie made a number of difficulties for himself (see R.C. Brown and D.P. Morton, 'The Embarassing Apotheosis of a "Great Canadian": Sir Arthur Currie's Personal Crisis in 1917,' CHR, 1979), but he was badly treated by the politicians. A sympathetic account is H.M. Urquhart, *Arthur Currie: A Biography* (T: Dent 1950), and a good academic study is A.M.J. Hyatt, 'The Military Career of Sir Arthur Currie' (PHD thesis, Duke University 1965). General A.G.L. McNaughton was just beginning his long military career in the Great War, and his war service is well recounted in John Swettenham's *McNaughton*, I: *1887-1939* (T: Ryerson 1968). Another later general's story has been told by R.H. Roy in *For Most Conspicuous Bravery: A Biography of Major-General George R. Pearkes, V.C.* ... (V: UBCP 1977) and Morton's work on Otter is helpful on the war. There is still no satisfactory biography of Sam Hughes, the wartime minister of militia and defence. The gap has not been filled by C.F. Winter, *Lt. Gen. Sir Sam Hughes, Canada's War Minister* (T: MAC 1931), and even less so by Alan Capon, *His Faults lie Gently* (Lindsay, Ont.: Floyd Hall 1969). Both are uncritical pieces of devotion, as is the Hon. Leslie Frost's little pamphlet, *The Record on Sam Hughes set Straight* (np; nd). Much, much better is Frost's *Fighting Men* (T: CI 1967), a fine study of the effects of the war on Orillia, Ontario, and the men it sent to the front. There is one 'collective' biography of Canadian general officers, A.M.J. Hyatt's 'Canadian Generals of the First World War and the Popular View of Military Leadership,' SH, 1979. And there is one first-rate examination of a businessman, J.M. Bliss's *A Canadian Millionaire* (T: MAC 1978), a fine portrait of Sir Joseph Flavelle including his role in running the Imperial Munitions Board.

The official history of the army in the war is Col. G.W.L. Nicholson's *The Canadian Expeditionary Force 1914-19* (O: QP 1962), a thoroughly balanced and careful account, well illustrated and with splendid maps. There had been an earlier attempt at producing an official history, but only one volume of text and one of documents emerged. The text, Col. A.F. Duguid, *Official History of the Canadian Forces in the Great War 1914-1919* (O: KP 1939), is very dated, but the documents volume is a splendid piece of social history in its own right. The first volume of the official air force history, *Canadian Airmen and the First World War* (T: UTP 1980), by S.F. Wise and the staff of the Directorate of History at National Defence Headquarters, Ottawa, is a very well-done and detailed account of the thousands of Canadians who served in the Royal Flying Corps in a number of different theatres. Because there were few Canadian units, the story becomes difficult to follow, but that is a comment on Borden's policy and not on the book. Three additional volumes are projected for the RCAF history. *The Naval Service of Canada* (O: KP 1952) by G.N. Tucker is a good conventional history of the senior service. The first volume covers the period to 1939, and four chapters on the Great War sketch out the story. Also useful is Tucker's account of the great Naval bill controversy in the Laurier-Borden period.

For basic chronologies of the war and for extensive, useful quotations from newspapers and contemporary sources, every reader should be aware of J. Castell Hopkins's *Canadian Annual Review* for the war years, as well as his *Canada at War 1914-18* (T: 1919) and *The Province of Ontario in the War* (T: 1919).

A number of other books deserve mention. The best popular account of the war from a Canadian perspective is the late John Swettenham's *To Seize the Victory* (T: Ryerson 1965), which is also an able defence of Currie. Leslie Frost's book has already been noted; two other Tory politicians wrote on the war. George Drew's *Canada's Fighting Airmen* (T: 1930) is largely hero worship, but Col. Herbert Bruce's *Politics and the C.A.M.C.* (T: 1919) is a resounding assault on patronage, politicians, and Bruce's innumerable enemies who interfered with his efforts in the Canadian Army Medical Corps. Three collections are particularly interesting. Barbara Wilson's *Ontario and the First World War 1914-1918* (T: UTP 1977) gathers together documents from a vast array of sources and presents them neatly. Grace Morris Craig, *But This is Our War* (T: UTP 1981) traces the impact of the war on one family as the brothers and boy friends go overseas to fight and die. The result is deeply moving. The same can only partly be said for William Mathieson, *My Grandfather's War* (T: MAC 1981), a book that is flawed by poor arrangement and too many slips.

A few articles on military matters should be noted. Desmond Morton's prolific writings include 'The Cadet Movement in the Moment of Canadian Militarism 1909-14,' JCS, 1978; 'The Limits of Loyalty: French Canadian Officers and the First World War,' in Edgar Denton, ed., *Limits of Loyalty* (Waterloo: Wilfrid Laurier University Press 1980); 'The Supreme Penalty: Canadian Deaths by Firing Squad in the First World War,' QQ, 1972; 'Kicking and Complaining: Demobilization Riots in the Canadian Expeditionary Force, 1918-19,' CHR, 1980; and the best (if still unconvincing) examination of 'Polling the Soldier Vote: The Overseas Campaign in the Canadian General Election of 1917,' JCS, 1975.

Conscription is one subject that still stirs arguments. The best study of Quebec and conscription is Elizabeth Armstrong, *The Crisis of Quebec 1914-1918* (NY: Columbia UP 1938), a judicious, balanced account written before most of the archival sources opened up but one that has survived more than forty years. J.L. Granatstein and J.M. Hitsman, in *Broken Promises: A History of Conscription in Canada* (T: OUP 1977), use those archival sources to present the fullest modern account. A different view of the subject than the harshly critical one in *Broken Promises* can be found in A.M. Willms, 'Conscription 1917: A Brief for the Defence,' CHR, 1956. This tough-minded article argues that conscription was militarily necessary and by no means politically popular at the time Borden decided upon it. Willms's article is collected with several other good ones in Carl Berger, ed., *Conscription 1917* (Canadian Historical Readings no 8; T: UTP nd). A good account of conscientious objectors in the Great War – and the next one – is M. James Penton's *Jehovah's Witnesses in Canada* (T: MAC 1976). Two articles by R.M. Bray help put the English-Canadian mood during the war into focus. 'Fighting as an Ally: The English-Canadian Patriotic Response to the Great War,' CHR, 1980, and 'A Conflict of Nationalisms: The Win-the-War and National Unity Convention 1917,' JCS, 1980-1, are based on extensive manuscript and newspaper research, and can be read in conjunction with Brian Cameron, 'The Bonne Entente Movement, 1916-17: From Cooperation to Conscription,' JCS, 1978.

During the war Canada made substantial strides toward autonomy. Under Borden's lead and in response to the pressures of the war, great changes took place. Borden's account of these is in his *Canadian Constitutional Studies* (T: 1922), but the best accessible analysis is now in Craig Brown's biography of Sir Robert. A still useful collection of documents is R.M. Dawson, *The Development of Dominion Status* (L: OUP 1937) and other valuable studies include Kendle's *The Round Table Movement and Imperial Union*, the fullest examination of the group that exhilarated or frightened many Canadians. Kendle is also author of the standard study of *The Colonial and Imperial Conferences 1887-1911* (L: Longmans 1967), essential background to the Imperial War Conference of 1917. More material on autonomy has been gathered in Margaret Prang's *N.W. Rowell: Ontario Nationalist* (T: UTP 1975), a very long study of one of Borden's key Union government ministers. Another aspect of Canadian autonomy is studied by Robert Bothwell in 'Canadian Representation at Washington: A Study in Colonial Responsibility,' CHR, 1972, a careful examination of Ottawa's route to representation in the US. Additional articles include L.F. Fitzhardinge, 'Hughes, Borden and Dominion Representation at the Paris Peace Conference,' CHR, 1968; R.M. Dawson, 'Canada and Imperial War Cabinets,' in Chester Martin, ed., *Canada in Peace and War* (T: OUP 1941); M. Prang, 'N.W. Rowell and Canada's External Policy, 1917-21,' CHR, 1960; and J.W. Dafoe, 'Canada at the Peace Conference of 1919,' CHR, 1943. The sole monograph on Canada and the peace-making, George Glazebrook's brief *Canada at the Paris Peace Conference* (T: OUP 1942), can now be supplemented by the *Documents on Canadian External Relations*, vol. II (O: QP 1969), edited by R.A. MacKay. The best single examination of the difficult Anglo-Canadian relationship during the war and post-war period is now undoubtedly Philip Wigley, *Canada and the Transition to Commonwealth: British-Canadian Relations* 1917-26 (Cambridge: CUP 1977), a book that uses the substantial British manuscript sources to flesh out and reinterpret the traditional Canadian tale.

BETWEEN THE WARS

There are a number of good biographies dealing with the main figures of Canadian foreign and defence policy between the wars. The policy for the most part was that of Mackenzie King, the extraordinary man who dominated Canada, Canadian politics, and the Commonwealth from 1921 to 1948. The official King biography has three volumes. *William Lyon Mackenzie King*, vol. I (T: UTP 1958), covers the period 1874 to 1923; vols. II-III by H. Blair Neatby take the story to 1939. The Dawson volume is probably more sympathetic to King than Neatby's two, but both authors are calm and judicious and they establish a Mackenzie King who is somewhat different from the legend. Two other recent studies, Charles Stacey's *A Very Double Life* (T: MAC 1976) and Joy Esberey, *Knight of the*

Holy Spirit (T: UTP 1981), offer further looks at King, quite different in their emphasis, and both have something to say about foreign policy. There are a number of good essays on King's foreign policy in John English and John Stubbs, eds., *Mackenzie King: Widening the Debate* (T: MAC 1978).

Other important biographical studies include Kenneth Mc-Naught's fine study of J.S. Woodworth, the pacifist leader of the CCF, *A Prophet in Politics* (T: UTP 1959), and Roger Graham's able study of *Arthur Meighen*, II: *And Fortune Fled* (T: CI 1963). None of the biographies of Bennett shed much light on foreign policy (or anything else). There are bits and pieces of useful information in the biographies and memoirs of cabinet ministers. Chubby Power's *A Party Politician: The Memoirs of Chubby Power*, ed. Norman Ward (T: MAC 1966) is good reading and sheds significant light on Quebec attitudes to conscription and militarism in the interwar period. There should be some useful material in Marcel Hamelin, *Les mémoires du Senateur Raoul Dandurand* (Q: PUL 1967), for the senator was an important Canadian representative at the League during the 1920s. Regrettably, nothing of value found its way into print. The same thing can be said of E.M. Macdonald's *Recollections Political and Personal* (T: Ryerson 1938) which is quite unrevealing.

There is more in the books by and about civil servants and diplomats. Lester Pearson's *Mike: The Memoirs of the Right Honorable Lester B. Pearson*, I: *1897-1948* (T: UTP 1972) offers an engaging if not entirely frank look at Pearson's diplomatic career and attitudes to world events during the 1930s. There is some material in Charles Ritchie's engaging diary, *The Siren Years* (T: MAC 1974), on his pre-war postings and colleagues, and Arnold Heeney's discreet memoirs, *The Things that are Caesar's* (T: UTP 1972), gives us an insight into Mackenzie King's mind in the last months of peace – and through the war. Vincent Massey's memoirs, *What's Past is Prologue* (T: MAC 1963), can now be supplemented by the first volume of Claude Bissell's biography, *The Young Vincent Massey* (T: UTP 1981). Bissell's book is splendidly written, but in the light it sheds on Massey's work (or absence thereof) as a diplomat it is only marginally more revealing than the memoirs. *Public Servant: The Memoirs of Sir Joseph Pope*, ed. Maurice Pope (T: OUP 1960) indicates the slight influence that the under-secretary of state for external affairs from 1909, the department's formation, to 1925 exerted on policy. Dr O.D. Skelton, Pope's successor, had vast influence, but has not been favoured with a biography. The best treatment of Skelton thus far is G.N. Hillmer, 'The Anglo-Canadian Neurosis: The Case of O.D. Skelton,' in P. Lyon, ed., *Britain and Canada* (L: 1976). J.L. Granatstein's *A Man of Influence: Norman A. Robertson and Canadian Statecraft, 1929-68* (O: Deneau 1981) closely studies one of Skelton's key officers in the 1930s and looks at trade policy, in particular. Granatstein's *The Ottawa Men: The Civil Service Mandarins 1935-57* (T: OUP 1982) puts the External Affairs bureaucrats into perspective and contains studies of Pearson, Hume Wrong, Escott Reid, Loring Christie, and Robertson, with much on their 1930s' views. Dana Wilgress, another of those studied in *The Ottawa Men*, did *Memoirs* (T: Ryerson 1967), but these are unrevealing on Trade and Commerce. There are interesting anecdotes in Guy Sylvestre, ed., *A Canadian Errant* (T: Ryerson 1960), the memoirs of James P. Manion of Trade and Commerce. The first volume of Hugh L. Keenleyside's authobiography, *Strike the Golden Day* (T: M&S 1981), carries the story of his life and service in External Affairs to 1939, although there are sections, as on Pearson, that go into the 1970s. Robert Speaight, *Vanier: Soldier, Diplomat, & Governor General* (T: Collins 1970), offers some useful information on Vanier's diplomatic career in the 1930s, while General Maurice Pope, *Soldiers and Politicians* (T: UTP 1962), gives a view of life in the army and at National Defence Headquarters in the same period. Unquestionably, however, John Swettenham's *McNaughton*, vol. I, is the best biographical study of a military figure. The finest book on a newspaper man remains Ramsay Cook's *John W. Dafoe and the Free Press* (T: UTP 1963), which tells us a good deal about Dafoe's views on foreign policy and nationalism in the Great War and interwar years.

The very best source on defence policy in the interwar years in undoubtedly James Eayrs, *In Defence of Canada*, I: *From the Great War to the Great Depression* and II: *Appeasement and Rearmament* (T: UTP 1964, 1965). Eayrs has used some of the private papers and government records, and he has produced a brilliant, opinionated look at policy, policy-making, and policy-makers that is indispensable for researchers into the period. The confusion and mismanagement stand out in sharp detail, and Mackenzie King is generally the villain against whom occasionally far-sighted generals struggle. Some of the military, however, such as Col. J. Sutherland Brown, and revealed in a dream world of their own, planning strikes against the United States by mobile columns. By comparison, other studies of the period are lack-lustre. Aloysius Balawyder's *Canadian-Soviet Relations between the World Wars* (T: UTP 1972) and his *The Maple Leaf and the White Eagle: Canadian-Polish Relations, 1918-78* (Boulder: East European Monographs 1980) are rather too finely focused to be useful for any except the specialist. Equally, Michael Fry's *Illusions of Security: North Atlantic Diplomacy 1918-22* (T: UTP 1972) and Richard Kottman, *Reciprocity and the North Atlantic Triangle 1932-38* (Ithaca: Cornell UP 1968), are difficult books to push through, although like Balawyder they are based on extensive use of primary sources. One interesting book covering a little-known subject is Victor Hoar's *The Mackenzie-Papineau Battalion* (T: CC 1969), an account of the Canadians who went to Spain in the late 1930s to fight Franco's fascism.

Several other studies are quite valuable. Ian Drummond, *Imperial Economic Policy 1917-1939* (T: UTP 1974), is a superbly researched examination of a very complex subject. Richard Veatch, *Canada and the League of Nations* (T: UTP 1975), is a somewhat flawed look at an important subject, the first scholarly book on the League. As such it replaces S. Mack Eastman's *Canada at Geneva* (T: Ryerson 1946). These two volumes should be supplemented by the 30-year old study by Gwendolyn Carter, *The British Commonwealth and International Security* (T: Ryerson 1947), a thorough-going look at Commonwealth League attitudes and policy with good sections on Canada, and by R. Ovendale, *'Appeasement' and the English-Speaking World* (Cardiff: 1975). R.F. Holland's *Britain and the Commonwealth Alliance, 1918-39* (L: MAC 1981) demonstrates that British historians, like British politicians, fail to understand Canada and Canadians. An indispensable source for the entire period – and one that is generally flattering to Mackenzie King – is Nicholas Mansergh's

Survey of British Commonwealth Affairs: Problems of External Policy (L: OUP 1952). In the same *Survey* series the volumes by Sir Keith Hancock, *Problems of Nationality 1918-36* (L: OUP 1937) and *Problems of Economic Policy 1918-39, Part 1* (L: OUP 1942), are somewhat less satisfactory but are still gold mines of information – and footnotes.

In article literature, the 1920s are still very much the forgotten decade. The classic article by J.B. Brebner, 'Canada, the Anglo-Japanese Alliance and the Washington Conference,' *Political Science Quarterly*, 1935, was an early analysis of Arthur Meighen's triumph in helping to persuade the British not to renew their links with Japan. This should now be supplemented by Graham's work, by Fry's, and by J.S. Galbraith, 'The Imperial Conference of 1921 and the Washington Conference,' CHR, 1948. Ramsay Cook's two articles, 'J.W. Dafoe at the Imperial Conference of 1923,' CHR, 1960, and 'A Canadian Account of the 1926 Imperial Conference,' *Journal of Commonwealth Political Studies*, 1965, are useful primary sources with inside information on Canadian policy and planning. Finally, Donald Page's 'The Development of a Western Canadian Peace Movement' in Susan Trofimenkoff, ed., *The Twenties in Western Canada* (O: National Museum 1972), and his 'The Institute's Popular Arm: The League of Nations' Society in Canada,' *International Journal*, 1977-8, are useful attempts at analyzing the organization of public opinion on foreign policy in the interwar years. Norman Hillmer's 'A British High Commissioner for Canada 1927-28' *Journal of Imperial and Commonwealth History*, 1973, and 'Anglo-Canadian Relations 1927-34,' in *The Dominions between the Wars* (L: Institute of Commonwealth Studies 1972, use British and Canadian documents to explore the pressures in Ottawa and London that led to British diplomatic representation in Ottawa.

The 1930s have received somewhat more attention from scholars. Kenneth McNaught's 'Canadian Foreign Policy and the Whig Interpretation: 1936-1939,' CHAR, 1957, was the first attempt to suggest that Mackenzie King wanted to go to war in the late 1930s and manoeuvred so as to make it possible. Blair Neatby's fine article, 'Mackenzie King and National Unity,' in H.L. Dyck and H.P. Krosby, *Empire and Nations: Essays in Honour of Frederic P. Soward* (T: UTP

1969), worked something of the same ground and clearly demonstrated that King saw his task as keeping the country together – and getting it into the war 'at Britain's side.' Neatby's argument is carried further by J.L. Granatstein and R. Bothwell in ' "A Self-Evident National Duty": Canadian Foreign Policy 1935-9,' *Journal of Imperial and Commonwealth History*, 1975. For the (in)famous 'Riddell' incident at the League of Nations during the Italo-Ethiopian War the most recent source is Bothwell and John English, ' "Dirty Work at the Crossroads": New Perspectives on the Riddell Incident,' CHAR, 1972. These last two articles make extensive use of British, American, and Canadian primary sources, almost the first that do so. Unique in Canadian intellectual history is Lawrence Stokes's essay, 'Canada and an Academic Refugee from Nazi Germany: The Case of Gerhard Hertzberg,' CHR, 1976. Stokes studies one refugee's efforts to become accepted in Canada – and eventually to win a Nobel Prize. Refugees are also the focus of the fine article by Irving Abella and Harold Troper, ' "The line must be drawn somewhere": Canada and Jewish Refugees, 1939-9,' CHR, 1979, of their book on the same topic, *None is too Many* (T: Lester and Orpen Dennys 1982), and of Gerald E. Dirks, *Canada's Refugee Policy: Indifference or Opportunism?* (M: MQUP 1977). Questions of conscience are also examined in a little-known article, David Rothwell's 'United Church Pacifism – October 1939,' *The Bulletin* [of the United Church Archives Committee] 1973. A good documents collection on the period is R. Bothwell and G.N. Hillmer, *'The In-Between Time': Canadian External Policy in the 1930s* (T: CC 1975).

In the 1930s there was for the first time a substantial body of contemporary opinion and argument on foreign policy. A few references are all that can be ventured here. One such is *Canada, the Empire and the League* (T: Nelson 1938), a collection of speeches made at the 1938 Couchiching Conference. Most of the views were quite conventional. Less so is the section on foreign policy in Frank Scott's *Canada Today* (T: OUP 1938), still probably the finest analysis of depression-ridden Canada. Scott's articles were regularly featured in the *Canadian Forum* during the 1930s, along with those of Frank Underhill, G.M.A. Grube, and other left-wing intellectuals. They made the *Forum* into one of the best sources for anti-British and pacifist articles; surprisingly, perhaps, other such articles can be found in *Dalhousie Review* and *Queen's Quarterly* as well.

A few books on the Pacific area need mention. William Strange's *Canada the Pacific and War* (T: Nelson 1937) tried to explore Canada's interests in the Pacific and her possible military involvement there. More historically oriented is Charles Woodsworth's *Canada and the Orient* (T: MAC 1941), a detailed, academic survey of relations with the East dating back to the mid-nineteenth century. The extensive literature on the evacuation of Japanese Canadians from the Pacific Coast is covered in the first chapter.

This is also the place to refer again to the Canadian Institute of International Affairs. The CIIA has published a wide range of books and journals on foreign policy over the last forty years – three of the four titles cited in the last paragraph, for example, were sponsored by the Institute. In 1941 the CIIA launched its series *Canada in World Affairs* with the publication of F.H. Soward *et al., Canada in World Affairs: The Pre-War Years* (OUP). Thereafter, volumes have been issued to cover two-year periods, and the series as a whole, now numbering a dozen volumes, is the best generally available source on Canadian policy since the 1930s. The CIIA's pamphlet series, *Behind the Headlines*, is also very valuable, and since 1940 at least six titles have been issued each year. After the war, *International Journal*, the first scholarly journal of foreign policy in Canada, was started. The debt scholars owe the CIIA is immense. For a historical study on the 'Antecedents and Origins of the Canadian Institute of International Affairs,' the article by Edward Greathed in Dyck and Krosby, eds., *Empire and Nations*, is available.

THE SECOND WORLD WAR

The basic and best source for the Second World War is J.W. Pickersgill and D. Forster's *The Mackenzie King Record* (T: UTP 1960-70). Skilfully edited from the massive King diaries, the *Record* is an absolutely unique document giving the prime minister's views on people and events. Here, there is Mackenzie King's view on conscription, on the political tactics of elections, on foreign policy and social welfare. The *Record* is in four volumes, with vol. I covering the period from 1939 to 1944, vol. II that from 1944 to 1945, and vols. III-IV taking the story to 1948 and through the beginnings of the Cold War. This is the place to begin for all wartime topics, although now that the whole King diary is available on microfiche (T: UTP 1980), students may prefer to go to the original.

Other biographies of value include Pearson's *Mike*, vol. I; Graham's *Arthur Meighen*, III: *No Surrender* (T: CI 1965); Chubby Power's *A Party Politician*; the Massey memoirs; and David Lewis's *The Good Fight: Political Memoirs, 1909-58* (T: MAC 1981). John Swettenham's *McNaughton*, vols. II and III, is extremely useful on conscription in the Second World War, but less so on command questions. The biography of *Louis St. Laurent: Canadian* (T: MAC 1967) by Dale Thomson is lightly referenced and adds little for the war period; there are a few pages on St Laurent in the war years in J.W. Pickersgill's *My Years with Louis St. Laurent* (T: UTP 1975). Speaight's *Vanier* has some useful material on diplomatic life during the war, while Granatstein's *A Man of Influence* and his *The Ottawa Men* provide studies of some of the key bureaucratic players involved in foreign policy and international monetary and financial questions. The despatches and memos of a very able American diplomat, J. Pierrepont Moffat, the minister to Canada from 1940 to 1943, are collected in Nancy Hooker, ed., *The Moffat Papers 1919-43* (Cambridge: Harvard UP 1956). One soldier's autobiography is General E.L.M. Burns's *General Mud* (T: CI 1970); one sailor's is Jeffry V. Brock's *The Dark Broad Seas*, I: *With Many Voices* (T: M&S 1981), a first-class account of the war at sea; one airman's is Murray Peden's *A Thousand Shall Fall* (Stittsville, Ont.: Canada's Wings 1979, 1981). Peden's book is the best account of RCAF training and of the air war against Germany, a splendidly-written and deeply-moving account that deserves a very wide readership.

There are several official histories of the war. The RCN has two: Tucker's *The Naval Service of Canada*, vol. II, which treats service on shore, and Joseph Schull's more popular account, *The Far Distant Ships* (O: KP 1950). A good navy history remains to be written. The official RCAF history has yet to reach the war years. The official army history is in three volumes: C.P. Stacey's *Six Years of War* (O: QP 1955); G.W.L. Nicholson's *The Canadians in Italy* (O: QP 1957); and Stacey's *The Victory Campaign* (O: QP 1960). All are models of official history.

The best official book on the war is Stacey's *Arms, Men and Governments: The War Policies of Canada, 1939-45* (O: Information Canada 1970). This remains Stacey's finest work, a well-written and detailed analysis of Canadian policy in alliance warfare, a study of the homefront and conscription, of supply and development. The view of Mackenzie King is occasionally critical, and readers should refer to the second volume of Stacey's more recent work, *Canada and the Age of Conflict*, for more temperate – and sounder? – judgments.

One other official volume, not at all satisfactory, is J. de N. Kennedy, *History of the Department of Munitions and Supply* (O: KP 1950). Kennedy is only a guide to the many organizations within the department, not an analysis. Fortunately, Robert Bothwell and William Kilbourn's *C.D. Howe* (T: M&S 1979) provides a fine overview of Howe's work in mobilizing Canada's war production. One of the many American official histories deserves mention. S.W. Dziuban, *Military Relations between the United States and Canada* (Washington: Office of the Chief of Military History 1959), supplements the Canadian accounts.

As might be expected, conscription has been treated at length, particularly in the Swettenham and Stacey books. R. MacGregor Dawson, one of the official King biographers, was the posthumous author of *The Conscription Crisis of 1944* (T: UTP 1961), an incomplete account based on the King Papers. James Eayrs's study, *The Art of the Possible* (T: UTP 1961), is now outdated. There are long chapters on conscription in J.L. Granatstein's *Canada's War: The Politics of the Mackenzie King Government, 1939-45* (T: OUP 1975), in his *The Politics of Survival: The Conservative Party of Canada, 1939-45* (T: UTP 1967), and in Granatstein and Hitsman, *Broken Promises*. The last title is the most up-to-date and makes full use of the widest range of primary sources. R.H. Roy's biography of Gen. George Pearkes should also be consulted.

For Quebec and the war, the best single study remains André Laurendeau's evocative *La crise de la conscription* (M: Editions du Jour 1962), a fine account of the anti-conscription campaign waged by La Ligue de la défense du Canada. This work is translated in its entirety in Philip Stratford, *André Laurendeau: Witness for Quebec* (T: MAC 1973). Robert Rumilly's *Histoire de la province de Québec*, tomes XXXVIII-XLI (M: Fides 1968-9), and his massive *Maurice Duplessis et son temps* (M: Fides 1973) offer different perspectives, largely based on Duplessis's Papers. So too does Conrad Black's *Duplessis* (T: M&S 1977), a quite good book, but one that is weakest on the war period. J.-Y. Gravel has collected a number of articles on *Le Québec et la guerre* (M: BE 1974) and is also the author of a piece that argues that Quebec's disinterest in the war sprang from the discrimination against Francophones in the military (in the special Canadian issue of the *Revue de la Deuxième Guerre Mondiale* (oct. 1976)).

For foreign-policy subjects, J.W. Holmes's *The Shaping of Peace: Canada and the Search for World Order 1943-1957*, 2 vols. (T: UTP 1979, 1982); Stacey's *Canada and the Age of Conflict*; and Granatstein's *Canada's War* are useful. A number of essays on Canadian-American relations are collected in Robert Cuff and J.L. Granatstein, *Ties that Bind: Canadian-American Relations in Wartime* (2nd ed., T: Samuel Stevens 1977), including the most complete study of the Hyde Park Agreement of 1941. R.W. James's *Wartime Economic Cooperation* (T: Ryerson 1949) is more than thirty years old, but still contains a vast amount of valuable information, all filtered through the eyes of a participant. Similarly, A.F.W. Plumptre, *Three Decades of Decision: Canada and the World Monetary System, 1944-75* (T: M&S 1977), offers a bureaucrat's view of international monetary events and features a full-throated attack on Cuff and Granatstein. Among the many other articles on wartime foreign policy are John Hilliker's 'No Bread at the Peace Table: Canada and the European Settlement 1943-47,' CHR, 1980; Don Munton and Don Page, 'Planning in the East Block: The Post-Hostilities Problems Committees in Canada 1943-45,' *International Journal* 1977; Kim Nossal, 'Business as Usual: Canadian Relations with China in the 1940s,' CHAR, 1978; and Paul Couture, 'The Vichy-Free French Propaganda War in Quebec 1940-42,' CHAR, 1978. One study of Canadian war propaganda is W.R. Young, 'Academics and Social Scientists vs. the Press: The Policies of the Bureau of Public Information and the Wartime Information Board, 1939-45,' CHAR, 1978.

Two books about Canadians with extensive service in China are Munroe Scott, *McClure: The China Years* (T: Canec 1977), and Stephen Endicott, *James G. Endicott: Rebel out of China* (T: UTP

1980). Both suffer from serious problems as history, but that takes nothing away from the fascination of the stories of the different paths trodden by Canadian missionaries in the east.

Special note must be paid to the work of Ruth Pierson on women's roles during the war. Her articles, 'The Double Bind of the Double Standard: Venereal Disease Control and the CWAC in World War II,' CHR, 1981, 'Jill Canuck: CWAC of all Trades, but no Piston-Packing Momma,' CHAR, 1978, and 'Women's Emancipation and the Recruitment of Women into the Canadian Labour Force in World War II,' CHAR, 1976, are, despite the coy titles, first-class examples of research.

Among the recent books on the manifold aspects of the war only a few stand out. David Kaufman and Michiel Horn, *A Liberation Album* (T: MHR 1980), examines the impact of Canadian liberation of the Netherlands. Eric Koch's *Deemed Suspect* (T: Methuen 1980) lightly studies the internment in Canada of German Jews deported from England, while John Melady's *Escape from Canada!* (T: MAC 1981) looks at the German POWs incarcerated in Canada. Roy MacLaren's *Canadians behind Enemy Lines 1939-45* (V: UBCP 1981) gathers together all the available information on Canadians who served with Britain's SOE and other agencies in Nazi Europe or Japanese Asia. W.A.B. Douglas and B. Greenhous, *Out of the Shadows* (T: OUP 1977), is an unsentimental survey of the whole Canadian effort at home and at the fronts, and there are fine essays by John English, Robert Bothwell, and C.P. Stacey in Sidney Aster, ed., *The Second World War as a National Experience* (mimeo, O: Canadian Committee for the History of the Second World War 1981).

THE POST-WAR YEARS

The literature on the years since 1945 is very substantial, although most is ephemera and surprisingly little researched scholarship has yet been produced. As access to records becomes possible, however, this is bound to change. At present the best guides to events are the yearly volumes (from 1960) of *The Canadian Annual Review* (T: UTP 1961-).

As might be expected, the biographies are rather sketchy, with journalistic studies abounding. There are exceptions, however. *The*

Mackenzie King Record, vols. III and IV, is essential for the period to 1948, and the Pearson memoirs, *Mike*, vols. I-III (T: UTP 1972-5), cover the years to 1968 with a substantial coverage of foreign policy. John Diefenbaker's memoirs, *One Canada*, vols. I-III (T: MAC 1975-7), offer one view of events from 1957 to 1963 (and beyond), and there is also Walter Gordon's tart view of the Canadian-American relationship in his *A Political Memoir* (T: M&S 1977) and in Denis Smith's able study of Gordon, *Gentle Patriot* (Edmonton: Hurtig 1973). The Wilgress, Heeney, and Massey memoirs add their mite to the story, but there is more meat in Douglas LePan's *Bright Glass of Memory* (T: MHR 1979), particularly for its assessments of General McNaughton, Keynes, and Canadian international monetary policy, and the origins of the Colombo Plan. Charles Ritchie's *Diplomatic Passport: More Undiplomatic Diaries 1946-62* (T: MAC 1981) provide an amusing look at an untypical diplomat's life, and there are some useful tidbits in J.A. Roberts's memoir, *The Canadian Summer* (T: University of Toronto Bookroom 1981), an account by a soldier, civil servant, and diplomat. Arnold Smith's *Stitches in Time: The Commonwealth in World Politics* (T: General 1981) is a beautifully written, frank account of his years as the first secretary general of the Commonwealth. From 1965 to 1975 Smith wrestled with the British and a series of intractable problems, attempting – with substantial success – to keep the Commonwealth together. The Norman Robertson biography, *A Man of Influence*, offers one fully researched account of Canadian foreign policy to 1968, and Chester Ronning's *A memoir of China in Revolution* (NY: Pantheon 1974) tells the story of one old China hand in the Department of External Affairs, including some useful material on the Vietnam war.

Escott Reid merits a paragraph to himself. A very able officer in External Affairs for more than two decades, Reid produced two fine books. *Time of Fear and Hope* (T: M&S 1977) is one of the best accounts of the origins of the North Atlantic Treaty, a full, frank, and nicely researched story, marred only by some organizational weaknesses. His *Envoy to Nehru* (Delhi, T: OUP 1981) is a splendid account of his 1950s service in India, and Reid now has near completion a book of his letters from San Francisco and London in 1945 and 1946, the years when he played an important role in the making of the United Nations.

A few additional biographical studies might be mentioned. Peter Stursberg has put together four volumes of oral history, two each on Diefenbaker and Pearson. *Diefenbaker: Leadership Gained 1956-62* and *Diefenbaker: Leadership Lost 1962-67* (T: UTP 1975, 1976), and *Lester Pearson and the Dream of Unity* and *Lester Pearson and the American Dilemma* (T: Doubleday 1977, 1980) all contain some interesting material on foreign and defence policy. But, as with every book of oral history, the material is only as sound as the memory of the speaker and the integrity of the compiler. Stursberg's integrity is not in question; the memories are. No student should use such material without great care. Additional biographical material is mentioned in the first chapter.

There are two official histories of the Korean War, one each for the army and the navy. H.F. Wood's *Strange Battleground* (O: QP 1966) is a well-done account, but the book by T. Thorgrimsson and E.C. Russell, *Canadian Naval Operations in Korean Waters 1950-55* (O: QP 1965), is somewhat less satisfactory. *The Report of the Royal Commission on Bilingualism and Biculturalism*, vol. 3 A (O: QP 1969), has a long study on linguistic problems in the armed forces and there is also Gilles Lalande's helpful *The Department of External Affairs and Biculturalism* (O: QP 1969), another Bi-Bi study.

The best studies of post-war defence and foreign policy are in James Eayrs's *In Defence of Canada*. Vol. III: *Peacemaking and Deterrence* (T: UTP 1972) deals with Canadian policy to the UN, the Commonwealth, and the United States, and includes brilliant and acid personality sketches of the major Canadian personalities. Vol. IV: *Growing Up Allied* (T: UTP 1980) treats Canada and NATO, and two additional volumes are forthcoming to cover Korea, the Middle East, and Vietnam. Unquestionably Eayrs's work will stand as one of the major accomplishments of Canadian scholarship, all the more so because the prose is so good. *The Commonwealth and Suez* (T: OUP 1964) is a fine collection of documents on the 1956 crisis, and his volume in the *Canada and World Affairs* series for 1955-7 is one of the best accounts of Canadian policy.

Another splendid academic study is Denis Stairs's *The Diplomacy of Constraint: Canada, the Korean War and the United States* (T: UTP 1974), a detailed analysis of policy during the Korean War and of

Canada's difficulties in dealing with the United States. Those difficulties are also the subject of Robert Cuff and J.L. Granatstein, *American Dollars/Canadian Prosperity: Canadian-American Economic Relations 1945-50* (T: Samuel Stevens 1978). Included are examinations of the abortive free-trade talks of 1947-8, the relationship of Canada to the Marshall Plan, and the initial stages of joint defence-production planning. One fine thesis is J.T. Jockel's 'The United States and Canadian Efforts at Continental Air Defence 1945-57' (Johns Hopkins University 1978).

A useful survey of the entire period from 1945 is *Canada since 1945: Power, Politics, and Provincialism* (T: UTP 1981) by Robert Bothwell, John English, and Ian Drummond. Other studies include Hector Massey, ed., *The Canadian Military: A Profile* (T: CC 1972); J.C.M. Oglesby, *Gringos from the Far North: Essays in Canadian-Latin American Relations, 1867-1967* (T: MAC 1976); Alistair Taylor *et al.*, *Peacekeeping: International Challenge and Canadian Response* (T: CIIA 1968); and John McLin's very useful examination of *Canada's Changing Defence Policy 1957-63* (Baltimore: Johns Hopkins UP 1967).

Jocelyn Ghent's University of Illinois doctoral thesis (1976) on 'Canadian-American Relations and the Nuclear Weapons Controversy, 1958-63' is a valuable analysis of the events covered by McLin, her judgments being based on substantial archival and interview research. Two articles by Ghent are readily accessible: 'Canada, the United States and the Cuban Missile Crisis,' *Pacific Historical Review*, 1979, and 'Did he Fall or Was he Pushed? The Kennedy Administration and the Collapse of the Diefenbaker Government,' *International History Review*, 1979. Peyton Lyon's 1961-3 volume in the *Canada in World Affairs* series is indispensable for this subject as is Granatstein's *A Man of Influence*. Another aspect of Canadian-American relations is fully covered in Neil Swainson, *Conflict over the Columbia: The Canadian Background to an Historic Treaty* (M: MQUP 1979).

There are several important essay collections, John Holmes's excellent and voluminous essays are collected in *The Better Part of Valour* and *Canada: A Middle-Aged Power* (T: M&S 1970, 1975), and a series of lectures, *Life with Uncle: The Canadian-American Rela-*

tionship (T: UTP 1981), offers a wise look at Canada's major relationship – and problem. Three special issues of *International Journal* are particularly valuable. The winter 1973-4 issue was devoted to essays on L.B. Pearson, the summer 1967 number offered retrospective looks at Canadian foreign policy, and the summer 1976 issue was on 'The U.S. and Us.' Also helpful is King Gordon, ed., *Canada's Role as a Middle Power* (T: CIIA 1966); Stephen Clarkson, ed., *An Independent Foreign Policy for Canada?* (T: M&S 1968); Norman Hillmer and Garth Stevenson, eds., *Foremost Nation: Canadian Foreign Policy and a Changing World* (T: M&S 1977); P.V. Lyon and Tareq Ismael, eds., *Canada and the Third World* (T: MAC 1976); Barbara Johnson and M.W. Zacher, eds., *Canadian Foreign Policy and the Law of the Sea* (V: UBCP 1977); H.E. English, ed., *Canada-United States Relations* (NY: Praeger 1976); Andrew Axline, *et al.*, eds., *Continental Community? Independence and Integration in North America* (T: M&S 1974); and K.A.J. Hay, ed., *Canadian Perspectives on Economic Relations with Japan* (M: Institute for Research on Public Policy 1980).

Occasional essays in these collections take a revisionist perspective. But there can be little doubt that revisionism in Canada lags behind that in the United States (and a good thing, too, some will say). One effort at a revisionist perspective, Cuff and Granatstein's *Ties That Bind*, was not warmly received. See, for example, Don Page and Don Munton, 'Canadian Images of the Cold War,' *International Journal*, 1977. The material on Canada in the Pentagon Papers and Charles Taylor's *Snow Job: Canada, the United States and Vietnam (1954-1973)* (T: Anansi 1974), however, suggests that revisionism is far from finished or unnecessary.

Finally, five studies of Trudeau-style foreign and defence policy deserve noting. Bruce Thordarson's *Trudeau and Foreign Policy* (T: UTP 1972) is a fine analysis of policy-making during the heralded review that Trudeau launched soon after taking office. Peter Dobell's *Canada's Search for New Roles* (L: OUP 1972) is generally wise, while Colin Gray's *Canadian Defence Priorities* (T: CI 1972) is tough-minded and realistic. So too are Brian Cuthbertson, *Canadian Military Independence in the Age of the Superpowers* (T: Fitzhenry & Whiteside 1977), and Gerald Porter, *In Retreat: The Canadian Forces in the Trudeau Years* (O: Deneau & Greenberg nd).

This listing, admittedly, barely skims the surface of the literature since 1945. Researchers are advised to make full use of the bibliographies with which this chapter began; they should also remember that simply because there is a vast amount of literature does not mean that subjects are closed. Few subjects in Canadian defence and foreign policy have been exhausted, and there are still stereotypes to be destroyed and ikons to be shattered.

MICHAEL BLISS

Economic and business history

Many historians are dissatisfied with the state of our knowledge of post-Confederation economic and business history. In the 1930s and early 1940s much of the best writing about Canada was in the field of economic history, by such economists as W.A. Mackintosh and H.A. Innis and historians like Donald Creighton and A.R.M. Lower. After the Second World War, however, the study of economics in Canada became less historically-oriented and more influenced by theoretical and statistical analysis. Many economists neglected traditional economic history; many of those still interested in economic history produced quantitative studies that are difficult for the layman to understand. On their part, Canadian historians tended to concentrate on political subjects, perhaps partly discouraged by the complexity and sophistication of the new economics. Business history, long recognized in other countries as a field of study in its own right, languished in Canada until the 1970s from lack of interest by historians and businessmen. Consequently, a survey of what needs to be done in Canadian economic and business history – there is no history of Canadian manufacturing, no satisfactory survey of post-Confederation economic history, no readable work on a wide range of industries and companies, etc., etc. – might be as long as or longer than an article on the existing literature.

But professional complaints about the inadequacies of the field will not impress the beginning student of Canadian history, who in this as in every other field finds that historians have already written more than anyone can (or should) read. The older generation of economic historians produced a massive amount of valuable writing, most of which has stood up remarkably well over time. A few outstanding economists and historians continued to develop themes in economic and business history through the 1950s and 1960s. It seems that many younger Canadian historians are once again becoming interested in economic and business topics and, as well, the quantitative approach of the new economic historians is beginning to pay off in important studies challenging key aspects of the older interpretations. Despite the gaps in the literature, then, the existing work is already far too extensive to be more than touched upon in a short essay. The titles mentioned in the following sections are only a small fraction of the existing literature. The bias in selection is towards introductory and standard works and, taking account of the problem most history students have with advanced economics, slightly away from some of the more technical studies.

SURVEYS AND INTERPRETATIONS

For many years the standard textbook has been W.T. Easterbrook and Hugh G.J. Aitken, *Canadian Economic History* (T: MAC 1956). Heavily reflecting the traditional 'staples approach' to Canadian economic history (in which the exploitation of a succession of staple products is seen as providing the basic framework of Canadian economic development), it is strongest in its treatment of primary industries and transportation, weakest on manufacturing, business-government relations, and the period after approximately 1930. Two newer textbooks, intended to replace Easterbrook and Aitken, fail to do so satisfactorily. *Canada: An Economic History* (T: MAC 1980) by William L. Marr and Donald G. Paterson is almost unusable because of the way its thematic organization destroys a reader's sense of the Canadian economy developing through time. History students will also find the book marred by economists' jargon and charts; but readers who persist will find much useful material, including a handy bibliography. Richard Pomfret's *The Economic Development of Canada* (T: Methuen 1981) requires little persistance because it is so short (202 pages). At best a useful introduction to some of the recent debates on some of the main themes of Canadian economic development, the book can be used as a text only at students' peril.

A number of older texts and studies can be usefully consulted. M.Q. Innis, *Economic History of Canada* (2nd ed., T: Ryerson 1954), and A.W. Currie, *Canadian Economic Development* (T: Nelson 1942), resemble Easterbrook and Aitken in their strengths and weaknesses. The formative years of post-Confederation economic history are analyzed very accessibly in Book I of the *Report of the Royal Commission on Dominion-Provincial Relations* (O: KP 1940), which is available in a 1963 Carleton Library paperback edition edited by Donald V. Smiley and entitled *The Rowell/Sirois Report, Book I*. Alternatively, W.A. Mackintosh, *The Economic Background of Dominion-Provincial Relations* (O: KP 1939; reprinted T: M&S 1964), was the special study for the Rowell-Sirois Commission upon which much of the economic history in Book I was based. Both volumes give special attention to the regional impact of national economic policies as well as to their effects upon dominion-provincial relations.

O.J. Firestone's *Canada's Economic Development, 1867-1953* (L: Bowes & Bowes 1958) is not so much a survey of Canadian economic development as a pioneering reconstruction of statistical series. Much of Firestone's data has been incorporated in the more comprehensive, indeed indispensable, *Historical Statistics of Canada* (T: MAC 1965), edited by M.C. Urquhart and K.A.H. Buckley. It can usefully be supplemented by Warren E. Kalbach and Wayne W. McVey, *The Demographic Bases of Canadian Society* (T: McGraw-Hill 1971).

A standard general anthology of articles covering many themes of Canadian economic history is W.T. Easterbrook and M.H. Watkins, eds., *Approaches to Canadian Economic History* (T: M&S 1967). One of the more important interpretive articles published in recent years and an excellent introduction to the work of the new economic historians is Kenneth H. Norrie, 'The National Policy and the Rate of Prairie Settlement: A Review,' JCS, 1970. It can be supplemented by Peter J. George and Ernest H. Oksanen, 'Recent Developments in the Quantification of Canadian Economic History,' SH, 1969. The death of the older economic history and the shortcomings of new scholarship, particularly neo-Marxist, is the theme of R.F. Neill's valuable article, 'The Passing of Canadian Economic History,' JCS, 1977.

Two anthologies, David S. Macmillan, ed., *Canadian Business History: Selected Studies, 1497-1971* (T: M&S 1971), and Glenn Porter and Robert Cuff, eds., *Enterprise and National Development: Essays in Canadian Business and Economic History* (T: Hakkert 1972), illustrate the strengths and weaknesses (much too often the weaknesses in the Macmillan volume) of Canadian business history. All of these titles contain good bibliographies or bibliographical articles as guides for further reading. Although most of the articles and theoretical assumptions in H.A. Innis, *Essays in Canadian Economic History* (T: UTP 1956), are dated, it is still an indispensable collection of the shorter writings of Canada's greatest economic historian. Innis's work can also be approached through Robin Neill's *A New Theory of Value: The Canadian Economics of H.A. Innis* (T: UTP 1977), and the articles in the special Innis issue of the *Journal of Canadian Studies*, winter 1977.

Tom Naylor's two-volume work, *The History of Canadian Business, 1867-1914* (T: Lorimer 1976), is eclectically radical and factually unreliable. Some reviewers have found it brilliant; others, including this author, judge it useless. Naylor has about the same low opinion of Michael Bliss's *A Living Profit: Studies in the Social History of Canadian Business, 1883-1911* (T: M&S 1974), which has been considered a pioneering study of business attitudes on such issues as competition and trade unions.

PERIODS AND REGIONS

Canadian economic history since 1945 is now very accessible thanks to the excellent chapters on economic matters in *Canada since 1945: Power, Politics, and Provincialism* (T: UTP 1981) by Robert Bothwell, Ian Drummond, and John English. Because of the weaknesses of all the textbooks, this work is indispensable for bringing the history of the Canadian economy up-to-date. A still useful guide to the main themes of government management of the economy from the mid-1940s through the early 1960s is the collection of essays, *Canadian Economic Policy since the War*, published in 1965 by the Canadian Trade Committee of the Private Planning Association of Canada. The one survey of an important special theme is A.F.W. Plumptre, *Three Decades of Decision: Canada and the World Monetary System, 1944-75* (T: M&S 1977). No one should attempt detailed study of Canadian economic developments since 1960 without referring to the articles in the annual series, the *Canadian Annual Review*, published by the University of Toronto Press. There are few surveys or syntheses of the economic history of other specific time periods of post-Confederation history. An important exception to the vacuum in chronological studies is A.E. Safarian, *The Canadian Economy in the Great Depression* (T: UTP 1959; T: M&S 1970), a fairly technical study but essential to the understanding of that decade. More technical but also important is Edward Marcus, *Canada and the International Business Cycle, 1927-1939* (NY: Bookman Associates 1954).

Not surprisingly, the province of Quebec has been the region most singled out for special attention, particularly by French-Canadian economic historians. The best short introduction to Quebec's post-Confederation economic history is still the essay by A. Faucher and M. Lamontagne, 'History of Industrial Development,' most readily available in Marcel Rioux and Yves Martin, eds., *French-Canadian Society*, vol. I (T: M&S 1964). Jean Hamelin and Yves Roby, *Histoire économique du Québec, 1851-1896* (M: Fides 1971), is an important synthesis for the second half of the nineteenth century; and the collection of articles edited by Robert Comeau, *Economie Québécoise* (M: PUQ 1969), contains several pertaining to twentieth-century economic development and French-Canadian economic thought. A good general introduction to the problem of French-Canadian economic 'backwardness' is René Durocher and Paul-André Linteau, eds., *Le 'retard' du Québec et l'infériorité économique des Canadiens-français* (TR: BE 1971). There is an excellent chapter on French Canada and the new industrialism in Robert Craig Brown and Ramsay Cook, *Canada 1896-1921: A Nation Transformed* (T: M&S 1974). William F. Ryan, *The Clergy and Economic Growth in Quebec (1896-1914)* (Q: PUL 1966), has been the single most important study suggesting a reconsideration of the belief that the church deliberately retarded industrial development. Vigorous counter-arguments to the view that Quebec stagnated under Duplessis are advanced in Conrad Black's massive *Duplessis* (T: M&S 1977). Regionalism and regional economic development have attracted considerable interest recently, undoubtedly because of the perception of growing decentralization of the country in the 1970s. Perhaps the best introduction to recent work on the theme are the articles in David Jay Bercuson and Philip A. Buckner, eds., *Eastern and Western Perspectives: Papers from the Joint Atlantic Canada/Western Canadian Studies Conference* (T: UTP 1981). An older collection of articles edited by Bercuson, *Canada and the Burden of Unity* (T: MAC 1977), is also useful.

By far the best recent studies of the economic history of a region have been carried out by historians of Atlantic Canada, whose work is most commonly found in the indispensable journal *Acadiensis*. An uneven sample is also contained in Lewis R. Fisher and Eric W. Sager, eds., *The Enterprising Canadians: Entrepreneurs and Economic Development in Eastern Canada, 1820-1914* (St. John's: Memorial University 1979). The most influential of the new Maritime economic historians has been the late David Alexander, whose untimely death was a major loss to Canadian scholarship. His most significant work, *The Decay of Trade: An Economic History of the Newfoundland Saltfish Trade, 1935-65* (St. John's: Memorial University 1977), covers far more than its title might suggest. The UTP is scheduled to publish a collection of Alexander's articles, the most important of which is 'Economic Growth in the Atlantic Region, 1880 to 1940,' *Acadiensis*, 1978. On a more limited topic, one of the best and most useful of the new regional studies is Ernest R. Forbes, *The Maritime Rights Movement, 1919-1927: A Study in Canadian Regionalism* (M: MQUP 1979). The only general economic history of a Canadian region remains S.A. Saunders, *The Economic History of the Maritimes* (O: KP 1939).

The North and mid-north are treated extremely well in Morris Zaslow, *The Opening of the Canadian North, 1870-1914* (T: M&S 1971), which is also generally useful for Canadian resource policy as a whole during that period. For more recent history consult K.J.

Rea, *The Political Economy of the Canadian North* (T: UTP 1968). In *Prairie Capitalism: Power and Influence in the New West* (T: M&S 1979), John Richards and Larry Pratt provide not only an excellent study of western economic development since 1945 but perhaps the best single historical introduction to the key issues of post-war Canadian resources policy.

THE STAPLE INDUSTRIES

Although of diminishing importance by the time of Confederation, Canada's first two great staple industries were still significant to the economy. Their post-Confederation history is outlined in the later chapters of H.A. Innis's two classic studies, *The Fur Trade in Canada: An Introduction to Canadian Economic History* (New Haven: Yale UP 1930; rev. ed., T: UTP 1956) and *The Cod Fisheries: The History of an International Economy* (New Haven: Yale UP 1940; T: UTP 1978). Even though the substantive issues are largely outside post-Confederation history, no student should miss the recent controversy about Innis's treatment of the fur trade raised by W.J. Eccles, 'A Belated Review of Harold Adam Innis, *The Fur Trade in Canada*,' CHR, 1979, and continued in the exchange between Hugh M. Grant and Eccles in the September 1981 CHR.

The replacement of the square timber trade by that in lumber as the chief forest industry is treated in detail in A.R.M. Lower, *The North American Assault on the Canadian Forest: A History of the Lumber Trade between Canada and the United States* (T: Ryerson 1938). The best study of the later development of pulp and paper as the dominant forest industry is J.A. Guthrie, *The Newsprint Paper Industry* (Cambridge: Harvard UP 1941). G.W. Taylor's *Timber: History of the Forest Industry in B.C.* (V: J.J. Douglas 1975) contains much new material on the modern industry in that province. A useful study of a dominant pulp and paper company in Quebec is Jorge Niosi, 'La Laurentide (1887-1928): pionnière du papier journal au Canada,' RHAF, 1975. Donald MacKay's *The Lumberjacks* (T: MHR 1978) stands alone in Canadian historiography as a model dissection of how an industry actually worked. One of the few studies stressing the development of conservation is *Renewing Nature's Wealth* (T: Department of Lands and Forests 1967) by Richard S. Lambert and

Paul Pross, a history of the Department of Lands and Forests in Ontario.

There is no complete history of Canadian mining. H.A. Innis, *Settlement and the Mining Frontier* (T: MAC 1936), is still the best introduction to the development of mineral resources. It can be supplemented by E.S. Moore, *American Influence on Canadian Mining* (T: UTP 1941), and two popular histories: D.M. LeBourdais, *Metals and Men* (T: M&S 1957), and Arnold Hoffman, *Free Gold: The Story of Canadian Mining* (NY: Rinehart 1946). O.W. Main's *The Canadian Nickel Industry* (T: UTP 1955) is a particularly good study of problems of monopoly and marketing in that industry. The later development of uranium is discussed in W.D.G. Hunter, 'The Development of the Canadian Uranium Industry: An Experiment in Public Enterprise,' CJEPS, 1962. For the modern potash industry in Saskatchewan see Richards and Pratt, *Prairie Capitalism*.

Studies of post-Confederation agricultural history should begin with John McCallum, *Unequal Beginnings: Agriculture and Economic Development in Quebec and Ontario until 1870* (T: UTP 1980), which puts most themes of central Canadian agricultural history in the perspective of a powerful (if rather shakily documented) restatement of the staple thesis. Attention then shifts to Western Canada, where the standard study of federal land policy remains *'Dominion Lands' Policy* by Chester Martin (T: MAC 1938), reprinted in the Carleton Library series in 1973 with an introduction by L.H. Thomas. Two of the better studies of the settlement of the Prairies are A.S. Morton, *A History of Prairie Settlement* (T: MAC 1938), and with special emphasis on ethnic groups, Robert England, *The Colonization of Western Canada* (L: P.S. King 1936). Canada's finest agricultural historian was Vernon C. Fowke. His *National Policy and the Wheat Economy* (T: UTP 1957) is one of the great works in Canadian economic history, a sweeping study of agricultural development in the context of national development policies. Fowke's earlier work, *Canadian Agricultural Policy: The Historical Pattern* (T: UTP 1946), is also essential, particularly for the role of government in the stimulation of agricultural research. The leading historian of the development of the wheat economy was D.A. MacGibbon in his two volumes, *The Canadian Grain Trade* (T: MAC 1932) and *The Canadian Grain Trade, 1931-1951* (T: UTP 1952). Everything anyone ever wanted to know about the operations of the Canada Wheat Board can be found in C.F. Wilson, *A Century of Canadian Grain* (Saskatoon: Western Producer Prairie Books 1978). Much can be learned about the economic and social patterns of western agriculture from G.E. Britnell's *The Wheat Economy* (T: UTP 1939). An excellent explanation of the transition from classical agrarian protest to the modern farm lobby for ever more marketing boards is an article by Ian Macpherson, 'An Authoritative Voice: The Reorientation of the Canadian Farmers' Movement, 1935 to 1945,' CHAR, 1979. Macpherson is also the author of a good history of the co-operative movement, *Each for All* (T: MAC 1979).

Canadian historians are gradually beginning to correct their neglect of the history of energy resources. The one fine historical study of the utilization of an energy resource is John H. Dales's model economic history, *Hydroelectricity and Industrial Development: Quebec, 1898-1940* (Cambridge: Harvard UP 1957). Merrill Denison's *The People's Power: The History of Ontario Hydro* (T: M&S 1960) is the most recent of several works on Ontario Hydro. A pioneering and very useful study of coal resources in the context of national energy policy is A.A. den Otter, 'Railways and Alberta's Coal Problem, 1880-1960,' in Anthony Rasporich, ed., *Western Canada Past and Present* (Calgary: M&S West, 1975). David Breen supplies an even more important pioneering study of energy policy in 'Anglo-American Rivalry and the Evolution of Canadian Petroleum Policy to 1930,' CHR, 1981. The study of 'national' energy policy can then be continued through H.V. Nelles's unorthodox, well-documented article, 'Canadian Energy Policy, 1945-80: A Federalist Perspective,' in R.K. Carty and W. Peter Ward, eds., *Entering the Eighties: Canada in Crisis* (T: OUP 1980), and Richards and Pratt's *Prairie Capitalism*.

The early history of the petroleum industry itself is sketched in Victor Ross, *Petroleum in Canada* (T: Southam Press 1917), and a popular history, Eric J. Hanson's *Dynamic Decade* (T: M&S 1958), which describes the first great oil boom in Alberta. There is one very good history of a Canadian oil company, Philip Smith's *The Treasure-Seekers: The Men who built Home Oil* (T: MAC 1978). William Kilbourn's *Pipeline* (T: CI 1970) is a good account of the building, financing, and parliamentary debate about Canada's first national natural gas pipeline. Most of the publications relating to Canadian energy policy before 1981 (including, in part, the Nelles article) have been out-paced by events, particularly the launching of the National Energy Policy in 1980 and the accords reached between Ottawa and the producing provinces in 1981.

TRANSPORTATION

The standard introduction is still G.P. de T. Glazebrook, *History of Transportation in Canada* (T: Ryerson 1938; reissued in two volumes, T: M&S 1964). Its concentration on railways accurately reflects the overwhelmingly central role these have played in Canadian transportation history. Some of the reasons for this emerge from the remarkable writings of T.C. Keefer, recently republished as *Philosophy of Railroads and Other Essays* (T: UTP 1972), with a particularly fine introduction by H.V. Nelles. Canadians' continuing fascination with railways has been shown by the extraordinary popularity of Pierre Berton's two-volume history of the building of the Canadian Pacific Railway, *The National Dream* and *The Last Spike* (T: M&S 1970, 1971). These are immensely colourful narrative histories containing a good deal of material on aspects of the CPR little noticed in the more scholarly histories, such as surveying and land speculation, and have been reasonably well received by professional historians. A more general history of the CPR, taking the story well into the twentieth century, is W. Kaye Lamb, *History of the Canadian Pacific Railway* (NY: MAC 1977). It is still profitable to consult H.A. Innis, *A History of the Canadian Pacific Railway* (1923; T: UTP 1971), particularly the reissue which contains a foreword by Peter J. George raising important questions about profitability and the subsidies given to the corporation. It is also both useful and entertaining to consult an important critical review of Berton's first volume by H.V. Nelles in the November-December 1970 issue of the *Canadian Forum* and the resulting exchange between Nelles and Berton in the February 1971 issue.

The Canadian National Railway system has been well served by G.R. Stevens, whose two-volume *Canadian National Railways* (T: CI 1960, 1962) is a complete history of all of the railways that had become the CNR by 1921, including the Grand Trunk, Canadian Northern, Grand Trunk Pacific, and National Transcontinental.

Stevens condensed these volumes and added new material on the CNR in the 1920s and 1930s in his *History of the Canadian National* (NY: MAC 1973). With the publication of T.D. Regehr's *The Canadian Northern Railway: Pioneer Road of the Northern Prairies 1895-1915* (T: MAC 1976) we now have both a definitive study of a magnificent failure as well as a model of first-class scholarship in business history. It supersedes Regehr's earlier article, 'The Canadian Northern Railway: The West's Own Product,' CHR, 1970. Of the many other studies of major or minor railways in Canada three worth consulting are Albert Tucker, *Steam into Wilderness: Ontario Northland Railway 1902-1962* (T: Fitzhenry & Whiteside 1978); A.W. Currie, *The Grand Trunk Railway of Canada* (T: UTP 1957); and Howard Fleming, *Canada's Arctic Outlet: A History of the Hudson Bay Railway* (Berkeley and Los Angeles: University of California Press 1957). A valuable study of railway systems in a continental perspective is William J. Wilgus, *The Railway Interrelations of the United States and Canada* (T: Ryerson 1937). There are a number of biographies, varying greatly in quality, of railway leaders. The best of these both deal with CPR presidents: Heater Gilbert, *Awakening Continent: The Life of Lord Mount Stephen*, I: *1824-1891* (Aberdeen: University of Aberdeen Press 1965), and Walter Vaughan, *The Life and Work of Sir William Van Horne* (L: OUP 1926). Railway leaders are among the chief targets of Gustavus Myers's muckraking *A History of Canadian Wealth* (1914; T: James Lewis and Samuel 1972). Much can be learned about the tangled thickets of railroading and politics from Brian J. Young, *Promoters and Politicians: The North-Shore Railways in the History of Quebec, 1854-1885* (T: UTP 1978).

Other forms of transportation in the post-Confederation years have been generally neglected by economic historians. John F. Due, *The Intercity Electric Railway Industry in Canada* (T: UTP 1966), contains a mass of factual data on the golden age of electric street railways. The best introductions to the history of aviation in Canada are Frank H. Ellis, *Canada's Flying Heritage* (2nd ed., T: UTP 1961), and C.A. Ashley, *The First Twenty-Five Years: A Study of Trans-Canada Air Lines* (T: MAC 1963). William Willoughby's *The St. Lawrence Seaway: A Study in Politics and Diplomacy* (Madison: University of Wisconsin Press 1961) is a study of the most recent attempt to recreate the empire of the St Lawrence.

Another of the many products of the flourishing historiography of Atlantic Canada has been new work on ships and shipbuilding. See the review article 'Wooden Ships and Iron Men Revisited' by David Sutherland in *Acadiensis* (autumn 1978); the publications arising from the Atlantic Canada Shipping Project, particularly Keith Matthews and Gerald Panting, eds., *Ships and Shipbuilding in the North Atlantic Region* (St John's: Memorial University 1978); and the important article, 'Patterns of Investment in the Shipping Industries of Atlantic Canada, 1820-1900,' by Eric Sager and Lewis Fischer, *Acadiensis*, 1979.

FINANCE

Canadian financial institutions and policy have, on the whole, been well studied by economists and historians. R. Craig McIvor's *Canadian Monetary, Banking and Fiscal Development* (T: MAC 1958) is a comprehensive introduction to almost all aspects of Canadian financial history. Indispensable reference volumes on the history of taxation in Canada are J. Harvey Perry's *Taxes, Tariffs and Subsidies: A History of Canadian Fiscal Development*, 2 vols. (T: UTP 1955). They are updated in A. Milton Moore, J. Harvey Perry, and Donald I. Beach, *The Financing of Canadian Federation: The First Hundred Years* (T: Canadian Tax Foundation 1966), and R.M. Burns, *The Acceptable Mean: The Tax Rental Agreements, 1941-1962* (T: Canadian Tax Foundation 1980). For the earlier period of dominion-provincial financial relations, J.A. Maxwell, *Federal Subsidies to the Provincial Governments in Canada* (Cambridge: Harvard UP 1937), is the best guide. The often hilarious history of Parliament's attempts to control government spending is recounted in Norman Ward, *The Public Purse: A Study in Canadian Democracy* (T: UTP 1962). Irving Brecher, *Monetary and Fiscal Thought and Policy in Canada, 1919-1939* (T: UTP 1957), is a helpful study of the problems of monetary policy in those transitional years. The relevant chapters in the Bothwell, English, Drummond book, *Canada since 1945* are a particularly good guide to post-war fiscal and monetary policy.

The best introduction to the history of banking in Canada is a documentary collection edited by E.P. Neufeld, *Money and Banking in Canada: Historical Documents and Commentary* (T: M&S 1954).

Neufeld's own book, *The Financial System of Canada: Its Growth and Development* (T: MAC 1972), is a masterly study of the growth of all forms of financial intermediaries, like Perry an indispensable reference work. Few of the company-sponsored histories of banks and insurance companies are noteworthy. The best of these is Victor Ross and A. St L. Trigge, *A History of the Canadian Bank of Commerce*, 3 vols. (T: OUP 1920-34). The appearance of Ronald Rudin's good article, 'A Bank Merger unlike the Others: The Establishment of the Banque Canadienne Nationale,' CHR, 1980, suggests what fertile fields there are to be tilled in the history of Canadian banking. A useful introduction to the phenomenon of Quebec's *caisses populaires* is Yves Roby's *Alphonse Desjardins et les caisses populaires* (M: Fides 1964).

THE TARIFF AND SECONDARY INDUSTRY

The history of Canadian manufacturing is inseparable from that of the government policy which was designed to stimulate and protect the manufacturing sector of the economy. The National Policy of tariff protection became the single most controversial economic policy adopted by a Canadian government. In recent years historical judgment on the protective tariff has been harsh, strongly influenced by John H. Dales's *Protective Tariff in Canadian Development* (T: UTP 1966). Because of the heavy reliance on economic theory in that work the beginning student might consult Dales's article, 'Protection, Immigration and Canadian Nationalism,' in Peter Russell, ed., *Nationalism in Canada* (T: McGraw-Hill 1966). In the same volume Craig Brown's 'The Nationalism of the National Policy' is a good explanation of the assumptions held by the politicians who established the National Policy. For the political situation that led to the National Policy, however, consult Benjamin Forster, 'The Coming of the National Policy: Business, Government and the Tariff, 1876-1879,' JCS, 1979. That issue of the *Journal of Canadian Studies*, commemorating the centenary of the National Policy, contains a number of useful articles, some of them very sweeping in their interpretations. O.J. McDiarmid, *Commercial Policy in the Canadian Economy* (Cambridge: Harvard UP 1946), is a good, detached survey of commercial policy to 1939. An older, very hostile, but still useful history of protection in Canada is Edward Porritt, *Sixty Years of Protection in Canada* (Winnipeg: Grain Growers Guide 1913).

A good starting-point for the history of Canadian-American tariff negotiations is D.C. Masters, *Reciprocity, 1846-1911* (O: CHA Booklet no 12 1961). The movement for commercial union, along with other economic problems in Canadian-American relations, is dealt with in R. Craig Brown, *Canada's National Policy, 1883-1900* (Princeton: Princeton UP 1964). L.E. Ellis, *Reciprocity 1911: A Study in Canadian-American Relations* (New Haven: Yale UP 1939), is still the best account of that critical election. The sometimes neglected history of Canadian tariff policy in the 1930s is most easily approached through Richard N. Kottman, *Reciprocity and the North Atlantic Triangle, 1932-1938* (Ithaca: Cornell UP 1968), and in the 1940s through Robert Cuff and J.L. Granatstein, *American Dollars/Canadian Prosperity: Canadian-American Economic Relations 1945-50* (T: Samuel Stevens 1978) and Granatstein's *A Man of Influence: Norman A. Robertson and Canadian Statecraft, 1929-68* (O: Deneau 1981). Douglas H. Arnett, *British Preferences in Canadian Commercial Policy* (T: Ryerson 1948), is also useful.

There is still no single work on the history of manufacturing industries. The best study of the regional growth and national integration of manufacturing in the late nineteenth and early twentieth centuries is an unpublished doctoral thesis by T.W. Acheson, 'The Social Origins of Canadian Industrialism: A Study in the Structure of Entrepreneurship' (University of Toronto 1971). The chapter of the thesis published as 'The National Policy and the Industrialization of the Maritimes, 1880-1910,' *Acadiensis*, 1972, is a particularly valuable study of manufacturing in that region which has spawned various offspring articles, particularly L.D. McCann's excellent study of 'The Mercantile-Industrial Transition in the Metal Towns of Pictou County, 1857-1931,' *Acadiensis*, 1981.

There is a fine chapter on the rise of manufacturing in Jacob Spelt's *Urban Development of South-Central Ontario* (1955; T: M&S 1972). For Quebec the works cited above should be consulted. An important statistical overview is Gordon W. Bertram, 'Historical Statistics on Growth and Structure in Manufacturing in Canada.

1870-1957,' Canadian Political Science Association, *Conference on Statistics, Papers, 1962-3* (T: UTP 1963).

The secondary literature on specific manufacturing industries is particularly sporadic. Works by Main and Guthrie on the nickel and newsprint paper industries have already been mentioned. William G. Phillips, *The Agricultural Implement Industry of Canada* (T: UTP 1956), is a solid economic study. Within that industry Merrill Denison has written a popular history of Massey-Ferguson, *Harvest Triumphant* (T: M&S 1948), and E.P. Neufeld has produced what seemed to be a model contemporary history of a model multinational corporation in *A Global Corporation: A History of the International Development of Massey-Ferguson Limited* (T: UTP 1969). The trouble with Neufeld's work, however, was that in celebrating success it made Massey's virtual collapse in the 1970s almost incomprehensible, or at least a complete surprise. Therefore it has to be supplemented by the useful survey of the whole history of the Massey enterprise, Peter Cook's *Massey at the Brink* (T: Collins 1981). William Kilbourn's history of the Steel Company of Canada, *The Elements Combined* (T: CI 1960), is one of the few other first-class histories of a manufacturing enterprise. For further information on the nineteenth- and early twentieth-century iron and steel industries W.J. Donald's older study, *The Canadian Iron and Steel Industry* (Boston and NY: Houghton Mifflin 1915), is still useful. A short history of the asbestos industry in Quebec can be found in Robert Armstrong, 'L'industrie de l'amiante au Québec, 1878-1929,' RHAF, 1979. Meat-packing, munitions, philanthropy, the Toronto financial community, and many other subjects relating to modern Canadian business are discussed in Michael Bliss's thick biography of a businessman who had his finger in most Canadian pies around the turn of the century, *A Canadian Millionaire: The Life and Business Times of Sir Joseph Flavelle, Bart., 1858-1939* (T: MAC 1978).

Attention is just beginning to turn to the marketing of goods and services in post-Confederation Canada. Douglas McCalla's *The Upper Canada Trade, 1834-1872* (T: UTP 1979), a study of the business of the Buchanan family, contains much detailed information on the commercial network in mid-century. A more systematic and very useful pioneering study is Gaetan Gervais, 'Le commerce de détail au Canada (1870-1880,' RHAF, 1980. Retailing was another of Flavelle's activities, so *A Canadian Millionaire* is useful for both department stores and the creation of an early chain-store system. C.L. Burton's *A Sense of Urgency* (T: CI 1952) is the best autobiography written by a Canadian businessman and contains much useful material on Simpson's (which Burton headed after 1929) and on the philanthropic activities of Toronto businessmen. Another good biography of a retailer, written by a professional historian, is Alan Wilson, *John Northway: A Blue-Serge Canadian* (T: Burns & McEachern 1965).

THE STATE AND ECONOMIC LIFE

The interaction of businessmen and governments in the development and regulation of Canadian economic activity, particularly during the transformation to an urban, industrialized society, is a subject of growing interest to business historians and to Canadian historians generally. For introductory surveys of the role of Canadian governments in economic life two articles by Hugh G.J. Aitken should be consulted: 'Defensive Expansion: The State and Economic Growth in Canada,' in Easterbrook and Watkins, eds., *Approaches to Canadian Economic History*, and 'Government and Business in Canada: An Interpretation,' *Business History Review*, 1964. The idea that government involvement in the Canadian economy has generally been beneficial has recently been challenged by Michael Bliss in '"Rich by Nature, Poor by Policy": The State and Economic Life in Canada,' in Carty and Ward, *Entering the Eighties: Canada in Crisis*. An influential popular restatement of that idea, however, has been Herschel Hardin, *A Nation Unaware: The Canadian Economic Culture* (V: J.J. Douglas 1974).

J.A. Corry, *The Growth of Government Activities since Confederation* (O: KP 1939), is a straightforward survey of the growth of government involvement in the economy, weak on the period before 1914 but containing much useful factual information. H.V. Nelles, *The Politics of Development: Forests, Mines, and Hydro-electric Power in Ontario, 1849-1941* (T: MAC 1974), is a superb analysis of the interaction of political and business groups in the shaping and development of resources policy in Ontario. Nelles's work challenges a number of traditional assumptions about the uses of state power in Canada, is a mine of information on the industries discussed, and should be a model and stimulant for similar studies of other provinces.

Aside from Nelles, historians are only beginning to produce case studies of the relations of businessmen, corporations, and governments. A good example of an attempt to generalize about business-government relations in the Laurier period, in conscious comparison with recent American historiography, is Christopher Armstrong and H.V. Nelles, 'Private Property in Peril: Ontario Businessmen and the Federal system, 1898-1911,' in Porter and Cuff, eds., *Enterprise and National Development*. Patricia Roy, who has written several fine articles on the British Columbia Electric Railway, discusses its lobbying tactics in 'The Fine Arts of Lobbying and Persuading: The Case of the B.C. Electric Railway,' in Macmillan, ed., *Canadian Business History*, and discusses state regulation of its activities in 'Regulating the British Columbia Electric Railway: The First Public Utilities Commission in British Columbia,' BCS, 1971. A number of themes of business-government relations in the 1920s are brought together very sensitively in Tom Traves's *The State and Enterprise: Canadian Manufacturers and the Federal Government 1917-1931* (T: UTP 1979). Also in the Porter and Cuff volume, Michael Bliss discusses the early years of Canadian competition policy in 'Another Anti-Trust Tradition: Canadian Anti-Combines Policy, 1889-1910.' For the general theme of competition and consolidation in the Canadian economy, however, students should consult Lloyd G. Reynolds, *The Control of Competition in Canada* (Cambridge: Harvard UP 1940), and, with emphasis on the more recent period, L.A. Skeoch, ed., *Restrictive Trade Practices in Canada* (T: M&S 1966).

Historians are also beginning to appreciate the immense importance of business-government relations in wartime. An article like Robert Cuff's 'Organizing for War: Canada and the United States during World War I,' CHAR, 1969, is very suggestive of the themes to be developed in future studies. At present, however, there is still limited material on the Canadian economy in the two world wars.

The chapter on the war economy in Brown and Cook, *A Nation Transformed*, is an excellent introduction to economic organization in the war of 1914-18. Special attention to the impact of the war on the western Canadian economy is given by John Herd Thompson in *The Harvests of War: The Prairie West, 1914-1918* (T: M&S 1978), and munitions-making is treated in Bliss, *A Canadian Millionaire* and in his article, 'War Business as Usual: Canadian Munitions Production, 1914-18,' in N.F. Dreisziger, ed., *Mobilization for Total War* (Waterloo: Wilfrid Laurier UP 1981).

The much more complex World War II economy can best be approached through an excellent general survey, J.L. Granatstein's *Canada's War: The Politics of the Mackenzie King Government, 1939-45* (T: OUP 1975), followed by Robert Bothwell and William Kilbourn's biography of the Canadian government's central economic manager, *C.D. Howe* (T: M&S 1979). Bothwell has a good summary of the war production record in ' "Who's Paying for Anything these days?": War Production in Canada 1939-45' in Dreisziger, ed., *Mobilization for Total War*.

The dominion government's interest in supporting commercial development is usefully traced in O. Mary Hill, *Canada's Salesman to the World: The Department of Trade and Commerce, 1892-1939* (M: MQUP 1977). The mixed and unhappy record of government attempts to stimulate industrial development in the 1960s is the subject of Philip Mathias's valuable little book (which would be more valuable if someone would revise and update it), *Forced Growth: Five Studies of Government Involvement in the Development of Canada* (T: James Lewis and Samuel 1971); two good journalists' books apropos of the same subject are H.A. Fredericks and Allan Chambers, *Bricklin* (Fredericton: 1977), and Garth Hopkins, *Clairtone: The Rise and Fall of a Business Empire* (T: M&S 1978). Roy E. George's *The Life and Times of Industrial Estates Limited* (Halifax: Institute of Public Affairs, Dalhousie University 1974) is a pioneering scholarly assessment of a development agency. Ottawa's groping in the 1970s towards something that might be called an 'industrial strategy' is analyzed in Richard D. French, *How Ottawa Decides: Planning and Industrial Policy-Making, 1968-1980* (T: Lorimer 1980).

FOREIGN OWNERSHIP

The emergence of a new Canadian economic nationalism in the 1960s sparked a continuing interest in the role of foreign capital, technology, and enterprise in Canadian economic development. Although much has been written about French and English involvement in the British North American economy before Confederation, the material on the post-Confederation years, particularly on American investment in Canada, is still limited and uneven in quality. Hugh G.J. Aitken's *American Capital and Canadian Resources* (Cambridge: Harvard UP 1961) remains the best survey of the situation as it had developed through the 1950s. It can usefully be supplemented by the essays in Aitken, ed., *The American Economic Impact on Canada* (Durham: Duke UP 1959). An older study which is still a standard source for the period before 1940 is Herbert Marshall, Frank A. Southard, Jr, and Kenneth W. Taylor, *Canadian-American Industry: A Study in International Investment* (1936; T: M&S 1976).

Among the more recent attempts to explore the growth of American influence in Canadian manufacturing are Stephen Scheinberg's provocative article, 'Invitation to Empire: Tariffs and American Economic Expansion,' in Cuff and Porter, eds., *Enterprise and National Development*, and Michael Bliss's comment on the ironies of the National Policy, 'Canadianizing American Business: The Roots of the Branch Plant,' in Ian Lumsden, ed., *Close the 49th Parallel, Etc.: The Americanization of Canada* (T: UTP 1970). Mira Wilkins set the American spillover into Canada in a much wider context in *The Emergence of Multinational Enterprise: American Business Abroad from the Colonial Era to 1914* (Cambridge: Harvard UP 1970) and *The Maturing of Multinational Enterprise: American Business Abroad from 1914 to 1970* (Cambridge: Harvard UP 1974). For American involvement in resource industries and the tensions between nationalism and continentalism in development policy, Nelles's *The Politics of Development* is invaluable. The most commented upon of the socialist/nationalist attempts at an historical explanation of the foreign ownership problem is R.T. Naylor's long essay, 'The Rise and Fall of the Third Commercial Empire of the St. Lawrence,' in Gary Teeple, ed., *Capitalism and the National Question in Canada* (T: UTP

1972). Naylor refines and somewhat alters his thesis in *The History of Canadian Business, 1867-1914*. L.R. MacDonald directly challenges Naylor's basic conceptualization in 'Merchants against Industry: An Idea and its Origins,' CHR, 1975.

As the debate on foreign ownership developed in the 1960s it produced an extraordinary volume of analysis and polemic, much of it directed against the free-trade, anti-nationalist views held by most Canadian economists in the 1950s and early 1960s and set out most clearly in several of the articles in Harry G. Johnson's *The Canadian Quandary* (T: McGraw-Hill 1963). One of the first and most articulate of the new nationalists was Abraham Rotstein, whose articles have been collected in *The Precarious Homestead: Essays on Economics, Technology and Nationalism* (T: New Press 1973). Denis Smith's biography of Walter Gordon, *Gentle Patriot* (Edmonton: Hurtig 1973), is an outstanding source of information on Gordon's attempts to convert the Liberal party to economic nationalism. Kari Levitt's *Silent Surrender: The Multinational Corporation in Canada* (T: MAC 1970) was the most widely-read attack on foreign ownership. The most prominent of the economists with grave doubts about the new economic nationalism was A.E. Safarian, whose position is set out most accessibly in 'Foreign Investment in Canada: Some Myths,' JCS, 1971. The whole foreign ownership debate and its effects on economic policy are given a judicious and appropriate evaluation in Bothwell, Drummond, and English's *Canada since 1945*. The only flaw in their treatment is their assumption that the debate is unlikely to be important in the 1980s.

GILBERT A. STELTER

Urban history

THE NATURE OF URBAN HISTORY

Urban history is often defined as a subdiscipline of social history, but urban history is clearly both less and more than social history. It is less in the sense that the urban dimension represents only a portion of a total society; it is more in that the history of towns and cities touches on many topics beyond the scope of social history. Precise definitions are not desirable or even possible because of the complexity of the subject matter, but to many of those who write urban history, it is not a single discipline or subdiscipline in any exclusive respect; rather, it is a field of knowledge in which many disciplines converge. In Canada, historians and geographers, but also planners, architects, economists, and political scientists have made major contributions to an understanding of the urban past.

During the past decade there has been a growing recognition of the importance of urban developments in Canada's past by historians and social scientists, even for periods of our history when the urban proportion of the population was relatively small. Towns and cities obviously were nodal points of leadership and change within the larger society. Some of the interest in the urban past stemmed directly from some of the traditional interpretations of Canadian history. For example, major historians such as Harold Innis, Donald Creighton, and Arthur Lower emphasized metropolitan relationships in their studies of the staples trades. This was first consciously applied to all of Canadian history in the pathbreaking article by J.M.S. Careless, 'Frontierism and Metropolitanism in Canadian History,' CHR, 1954. During the 1960s and early 1970s much of the stimulation for the study of urban history was due to the importation of American concepts and methodology, for urban history was originally highly developed in the United States. Particularly influential was Sam Bass Warner who explained how spatial expansion of cities through suburbanization led to a class and racial sorting out of society. Also important was Stephan Thernstrom's work on social mobility which heralded the beginning of a massive turn to systematic analysis of society. Unfortunately, Canadian scholars often treated Canadian cities as if they were mere extensions of the United States system without even asking if the border made a difference. By the late 1970s a reaction to this approach was apparent, for we had been ignoring what might have been indigenous to the Canadian scene. In particular, some scholars are now stressing that the urban dimension is only one aspect of a society – that is, towns and cities are subsystems within a larger political and social system and have to be examined from the perspective of that larger system.

These developments have been traced in a number of articles including Gilbert Stelter, 'The Historian's Approach to Canada's Urban Past,' SH, 1974, and John Weaver, 'Living in and Building up the Canadian City,' *Plan Canada*, 1975. A geographer's perspective is James Lemon, 'Study of the Urban Past: Approaches by Geographers,' CHAR, 1973. An excellent analysis of the development of urban history in Quebec is Annick Germain, 'Histoire urbaine et histoire de l'urbanisation au Québec,' UHR, 1979. At the international level, Bruce Stave has done a number of informal interviews with urban historians such as Warner, H.J. Dyos, and Richard Wade. Recently he has interviewed two Canadian historians, Alan Artibise, UHR, 1980, and Gilbert Stelter, *Journal of Urban History*, 1980.

BIBLIOGRAPHIES

A major reference work, Artibise and Stelter, *Canada's Urban Past: A Bibliography to 1980 and Guide to Canadian Urban Studies* (V: UBCP

1981), is now available which should make it possible for students to find quickly what literature exists on a multitude of topics. This volume contains more than 7000 entries for books, articles, and theses, and is an indication of the wealth of material which was often lost in obscure journals or hidden behind disciplinary boundaries. The Bibliography includes a lengthy listing of general works on growth and economic development, population, urban environments, and municipal government. For each province there is a separate section on general works, and divisions for the major cities – the oldest and largest of which are divided into historical time periods. There are extensive indexes – author, place, and subject – allowing the researcher to find comparable material for a variety of places. The first annual supplement to the bibliography, prepared by Elizabeth Bloomfield, appeared in the October 1981 issue of the *Urban History Review*. The Guide section of *Canada's Urban Past* provides a listing and critique of organizations involved in urban research and a detailed description of major sources of urban data in archives across the country.

Several specialized bibliographies are useful aids to finding one's way through particular aspects of urban history. For planning history, older periodical literature is carefully covered in Ian Cooper and David Hulchanski, *Canadian Town Planning, 1900-1930: An Historical Bibliography* (T: Centre for Urban and Community Studies, University of Toronto 1978). Volume I covers planning; volume II, housing; volume III, public health. The most extensive listing of planning material for one particular city is in A.J. Dakin and P. Manson-Smith, *Toronto Urban Planning: A Selected Bibliography* (Monticello, Ill.: CPL Exchange Bibliography no 670 1974). The remarkable usefulness of a specialized group of maps is described in Robert Hayward, 'Sources for Urban Historical Research: Insurance Plans and Land Use Atlases,' UHR, 1973, and his *Fire Insurance Plans in the National Map Collection* (O: PAC 1977). Despite its title, the most comprehensive guide to architectural history is Douglas Richardson, ed., *Architectural Conservation and the History of Architecture ...* (Kingston: Ontario Heritage Foundation 1976), which covers all regions of the country.

JOURNALS

The most important journal for urban history is the *Urban History Review*, published three times a year by the National Museum of Man. The UHR contains several significant articles in each issue, as well as information on current research, reviews, thesis abstracts, conferences, and notes on recent archival acquisitions. It occasionally publishes special issues. In the past these have included 'The Canadian City in the Nineteenth Century' (1975); 'Approaches to the History of Urban Reform' (1976); 'Immigrants and the City' (1978); 'Fire, Disease and Water in the Nineteenth Century City' (1979); 'Aspects of Urban Heritage' (1980). A word of advice may be necessary for those searching for this periodical in the library stacks. Because the Museum of Man is a government agency, many libraries insist on cataloguing it with government documents, not with other journals, where it belongs.

Several major journals should also be regularly consulted as guides to new work on Canadian communities. *The Canadian Historical Review* and the *Revue d'histoire de l'Amérique française* regularly list recent publications, many of which are directly related to urban development. Of the regional journals, the most useful in this regard is *Acadiensis*, which specializes in the history of the Atlantic provinces. *Prairie Forum* and *BC Studies* are essential for western topics. Other Canadian journals which specialize in urban studies often include material of interest to the urban historian. Among these are *Plan Canada*, the journal of the Canadian Institute of Planners; *Urban Focus*, a newsletter emphasizing urban government; *Trace*, a magazine about architecture; and the *Canadian Geographer*. Canadian material is also regularly included in major international urban history journals, especially the *Urban History Yearbook* and the *Planning History Bulletin* from Britain, and the *Journal of Urban History* and *Urbanism Past and Present* from the United States.

GENERAL STUDIES

There is no comprehensive general account of Canadian urban history as yet. The most detailed survey is found in portions of George

Nader's two-volume *Cities of Canada* (T: MAC 1976, 1977), which stresses population and economic growth. This is a useful reference work, but one looks in vain for any discussion of the role of individual entrepreneurs or organized groups such as Boards of Trade in explanations of growth, nor does one find mention of the place of interest groups or even municipal government in the physical evolution of cities. A useful, brief overview which deals with some of these deficiencies is J.M.S. Careless, *The Rise of Cities in Canada before 1914* (T: CHA Booklet no 32 1978). The closest thing to an urban history text at the moment is Gilbert Stelter and Alan Artibise, eds., *The Canadian City: Essays in Urban History* (T: M&S 1977), a collection of seventeen articles on a variety of themes such as economic development, physical form, government, and society. The introductions to each section provide a brief outline of major trends. A new edition of this volume will incorporate some of the best of the recent literature.

Although there is no book-length study, several articles trace the general patterns of urbanization in Canada. The policies of private and government agencies is stressed in Peter Goheen, 'Some Aspects of Canadian Urbanization from 1850 to 1921,' in Woodrow Borah, Jorge, Hardoy, and Gilbert Stelter, eds., *Urbanization in the Americas* (O: National Museum of Man 1980). The growth of an urban system is described by Richard Preston, 'The Evolution of Urban Canada: The Post-1867 Period,' in R.M. Irving, ed., *Readings in Canadian Geography* (T: HRW 1978). 'City forming' activities are outlined by Gilbert Stelter, 'The City-Building Process in Canada,' in Stelter and Artibise, eds., *Shaping the Urban Landscape: Aspects of the Canadian City-Building Process* (O: Carleton UP 1982).

THE URBAN BIOGRAPHY

The most popular form of urban history is the book-length study of a single city's evolution. We usually refer to this type of study as an urban biography because the community as a whole is treated as a personality with distinguishable characteristics. A positive feature of the best urban biographies is that the author tries to relate several of the complex facets of a city. This concern for the totality of the urban experience is usually not present in thematically-oriented studies. Of the older biographies, the most important were W.H. Atherton, *Montreal, 1534-1914*, 3 vols. (M: Clarke 1914); J.E. Middleton, *The Municipality of Toronto: A History*, 3 vols. (T: Dominion 1923); and T. Aikins, *The History of Halifax City* (1895; Belleville: Mika 1973). A succession of more popular biographies have since appeared which often give a useful overview of a city's development. Among the best are G. Glazebrook, *The Story of Toronto* (T: UTP 1971); Kathleen Jenkins, *Montreal: Island City of the St. Lawrence* (NY: Doubleday 1966); Thomas Raddall, *Halifax: Warden of the North* (L: Dent 1950); J.G. MacGregor, *Edmonton: A History* (Edmonton: Hurtig 1967); and A. Morley, *Vancouver: From Milltown to Metropolis* (V: Mitchell 1975).

The first of the modern biographies that was also first-rate urban history was Donald C. Masters, *The Rise of Toronto, 1850-1890* (1947; T: UTP 1974). Masters traced the establishment of Toronto's hegemony over Ontario and the competition with Montreal for domination of the national urban scene. This work successfully related social and cultural development to the city's stages of economic growth. A second good example is John Cooper, *Montreal: A Brief History* (M: MQUP 1967), which provides a neat review of the relationship between various aspects of urban life – transportation, municipal government, physical expansion, and social organizations. Other studies of individual cities, such as Jacob Spelt, *Toronto* (T: Collier-Macmillan 1973), and Walter Hardwick, *Vancouver* (T: Collier-Macmillan 1974), are not essentially historical in orientation but contain a good deal of information on economic growth and spatial expansion. Another approach to urban biography involves a collective effort in which several authors deal with different aspects of one community's development. The most effective venture of this kind, with several outstanding chapters, is Gerald Tulchinsky, ed., *To Preserve and Defend: Essays on Kingston in the Nineteenth Century* (M: MQUP 1976).

The model of modern biographies, against which others must now be judged, is Alan Artibise, *Winnipeg: A Social History of Urban Growth, 1874-1914* (M: MQUP 1975). This book not only provides a rounded and intelligent outline of the early city's development, but it is based on a well-documented thesis: the domination of the city's political, economic, and social life by a growth-conscious commercial elite. Artibise successfully shows how an obsessive commitment to the growth ethic led directly to the elite's lack of concern for social and economic problems and ultimately to a class and ethnically divided city. Artibise has also been influential in promoting some of the more desirable qualities of the urban biography at the national level. He is general editor of the History of Canadian City series, a joint publishing venture of the National Museum of Man and James Lorimer, which envisages the publication of as many as thirty commissioned volumes. Three have appeared to date: Artibise, *Winnipeg: An Illustrated History* (1977); Max Foran, *Calgary: An Illustrated History* (1978); Patricia Roy, *Vancouver: An Illustrated History* (1980); and volumes on Hamilton, Toronto, Halifax, and Montreal are to appear soon. These volumes are consciously designed to become more than a series of disconnected local histories, for each author follows a set of guidelines that includes an emphasis on comparable themes.

At this point the reader may well wonder what the difference is between urban biography and what is often referred to as local history. As a rule of thumb, local history is usually interested in the unique qualities of a particular community, while urban history falls somewhere between the specifics of the local and, on the other hand, the social scientific search for general or even universal patterns. Local histories are often carefully assembled and well-written accounts of a town's or city's history, although some give the impression of indiscriminate lists of data and events or have a booster tone in which the place is seen as a continuously unfolding success story, where all residents, regardless of class, supposedly share common goals. An example which illustrates both the strengths and weaknesses of local history is Paul O'Neill's two-volume *The Story of St. John's, Newfoundland* (Erin, Ont.: Porcépic 1975, 1976). O'Neill is obviously a careful researcher and a skilful storyteller, but the reader is overwhelmed by local minutiæ, and the topically organized chapters inhibit any conception of the town's development over time.

THEMATIC APPROACHES

Economic growth and metropolitan development
The economic development of Canadian cities has received considerable attention from historians and social scientists. They continue to ask the central questions: 'Why do cities grow or not grow? What are the crucial factors stimulating or inhibiting growth?' The answers seem to be confusing, for some emphasize the role of local initiative; others, broad impersonal forces over which no individuals or cities have any control. Some stress the generative nature of urban economic activities for regions and the country as a whole; others argue that urban vitality depends on the level of staples production at the regional and national levels.

To some extent this confusion evaporates if one realizes that scholars generalize from different scales of explanation. For example, at the first level – that of the local city – biographers tend to emphasize the significance of individuals, organized groups, or municipal governments in promoting economic growth. In his work on Winnipeg and other Prairie cities, Artibise has defined an 'urban ethos' which provided guidance in the community's formulation of its urban policy. His article, 'Boosterism and the Development of Prairie Cities, 1871-1913,' in a volume he edited, *Town and City: Aspects of Western Canadian Urban Development* (Regina: Canadian Plains Research Center 1981), isolates several characteristics of this ethos. Artibise has also described the 'booster' activities of Prairie elites as they attracted railways, industry, and immigrants, or, in a more negative sense, promoted premature city incorporations and boundary extensions and insisted on deficit financing for huge public-work projects in 'Continuity and Change: Elites and Prairie Urban Development, 1914-1950,' in Artibise and Stelter, eds., *The Usable Urban Past: Planning and Politics in the Modern Canadian City* (T: MAC 1979).

In a similar vein, scholars have described booster ideology and practices in a variety of other communities. Entrepreneurs and community leaders who believed that industry was the key for growth and prosperity have been examined in Paul-André Linteau's excellent monograph, *Maisonneuve: Comment les promoteurs fabriquent une ville* (M: BE 1981), and in Leo Johnson, *History of Guelph, 1827-1927* (Guelph: Guelph Historical Society 1977). The practice of bonusing – that is, of granting incentives to new industries by municipal governments – was widely adopted. Tom Naylor's colourful account of bonusing in *The History of Canadian Business*, vol. 2 (T: Lorimer 1976), should be supplemented by Elizabeth Bloomfield's critique, 'Municipal Bonusing of Industry: The Legislative Framework in Ontario to 1930,' UHR, 1981. Very often, a community's activities were led by Boards of Trade who managed to get public support for their programs. The leadership and their policies are effectively analyzed by Douglas McCalla, 'The Commercial Politics of the Toronto Board of Trade, 1850-1869,' CHR, 1969, and by David Sutherland, 'The Personnel and Policies of the Halifax Board of Trade, 1890-1914,' in L.R. Fischer and Eric Sager, eds., *The Enterprising Canadians: Entrepreneurs and Economic Development in Eastern Canada, 1820-1914* (St John's: Memorial University 1979).

Even tiny places engaged in aggressive promotional activities in an effort to improve or at least maintain their position in the urban hierarchy. Good examples of this are E.J. Noble, 'Entrepreneurship and Urban Growth: A Case Study of Orillia, Ontario, 1867-1898,' UHR, 1980, and articles in Artibise, ed., *Town and City*, especially Barry Potyondi, 'In Quest of Limited Urban Status,' and Paul Voisey, 'Boosting the Small Prairie Town, 1904-1931.' But many small communities were not in a position to determine their own future, regardless of the potential dynamism of their leadership. These included railroad towns like early Vancouver as described in Norbert MacDonald, 'The Canadian Pacific Railway and Vancouver's Development to 1900,' BCS, 1977. The power of large corporations was even more apparent in most resource industry towns. Hundreds of company and company-dominated towns have been created by mining and pulp and paper companies, and their economic viability continues only by corporate fiat. The nature of these towns is delineated by Stelter and Artibise, 'Canadian Resource Towns in Historical Perspective,' *Plan Canada*, 1978.

A second level of analysis in terms of economic development is the city or town in its regional context. J.M.S. Careless and Larry

McCann have effectively described this level in several articles on the west and in the Atlantic region. Careless has always emphasized the reciprocal relations between cities and their regional hinterlands; among the best of his many important articles on this theme is 'Aspects of Metropolitanism in Atlantic Canada,' in Mason Wade, ed., *Regionalism in the Canadian Community* (T: UTP 1969). McCann relates the emergence of a regional system directly to the expansion of a staple economy in his 'Urban Growth in a Staple Economy: The Emergence of Vancouver as a Regional Metropolis' in L.J. Evendon, ed., *Vancouver: Western Metropolis* (Victoria: Dept. of Geography, University of Victoria 1977) and in 'Staples and the New Industrialism in the Growth of Post-Confederation Halifax,' *Acadiensis*, 1979. The best study of the place of towns and cities in the development of southern Ontario is still Jacob Spelt, *Urban Development in South Central Ontario* (T: M&S 1972). Because Canada is so regionally oriented, the concept of a functional region based on an underlying structure of cities will probably become a significant approach in future urban historical research.

A third level of analysis, that of the national system, has had little work so far, except for the pioneering work of Careless on the concept of metropolitanism, and that of economic geographers such as James Simmons. One characteristic that both emphasize is the degree of openness of the Canadian urban system – that is, the extent to which it is influenced by external forces. To a large extent, the economic function of Canadian cities has always involved the export of raw materials from fur and fish in the earliest years to lumber and wheat in the nineteenth century to minerals in the twentieth. Fluctuations in the international demand for these products has had an immediate and direct effect on urban growth. Another characteristic that has been outlined by Careless and Simmons is the extent to which cities form a central component of what has become known as a national heartland-hinterland, or core-periphery system in Canada. Careless's ideas in this regard are most developed in his thoughtful 'Metropolis and Region: The Interplay Between City and Region in Canadian History Before 1914,' UHR, 1979. Those of Simmons are outlined in 'The Evolution of the Canadian Urban System,' in Artibise and Stelter, eds., *The Usable Urban Past*.

One of the future tasks of urban history is to sort out the processes of growth at various scales. Historians have traditionally emphasized the human agency – people able to use their opportunity – and this must be synthesized with the social scientists' emphasis on impersonal and mechanistic forces. A successful example of such a combination is a chapter entitled 'Growth Forces' in Leonard Gertler and Ronald Crowley, *Changing Canadian Cities* (T: M&S 1977).

Urban society

The standard work on the dimensions and characteristics of the country's urban population is still Leroy Stone's census monograph, *Urban Development in Canada* (O: Dominion Bureau of Statistics 1967). There has been surprisingly little comparable data produced for individual cities from the published census. Exceptions are the volumes in The History of Canadian Cities series which each contain a very useful collection of data about nativity, ethnicity, religion, and occupation. Students of Quebec cities are also well served in this respect through the statistics included in the chapters on urban development in a valuable provincial history: Paul-André Linteau, René Durocher, and Jean-Claude Robert, *Histoire du Québec contemporain* (M: BE 1979).

The urban immigrant is finally receiving some attention. Leaders in this area are Robert Harney and Harold Troper who have edited special issues of *Canadian Ethnic Studies* (1977) and the *Urban History Review* (1978) entitled 'Immigrants in the City.' Particularly important in these issues are essays by Lillian Petroff on the evolution of the Macedonian community in Toronto, and Harney's work on the boarding-house. Harney and Troper have also produced *Immigrants: A Portrait of the Urban Experience, 1890-1930* (T: Van Nostrand 1975), an illustrated history of some aspects of immigration in Toronto. The extent to which non-English-speaking immigrants were spatially segregated into foreign ghettoes is well documented in Artibise, 'Divided City: The Immigrant in Winnipeg Society, 1874-1921,' in Stelter and Artibise, *The Canadian City*. How the urban experience changed Irish immigrants has been examined in important new work by Murray Nicolson in an analysis of Irish Catholics in Victorian Toronto. In 'The Irish Catholics and Social Action in Toronto, 1850-1900,' *Studies in History and Politics*, 1980, Nicolson shows how Irish Catholics consciously created a parallel structure of education, health, and welfare, and even of employment in order to resist assimilation into the predominantly Protestant milieu of the city.

The major study of the social structure of nineteenth-century Canadian urban society is Michael Katz, *The People of Hamilton, Canada West: Family and Class in a Mid-Nineteenth Century City* (Cambridge: Harvard UP 1975). In this careful reconstruction of social and family patterns during the decade of the 1850s, Katz discovered a tremendous degree of transiency and inequality. He suggests a three-class division of society – entrepreneurial, artisan, and labouring – and suggests that this social hierarchy was not governed by birth but by achievement. This pathbreaking work fairly bristles with intriguing questions, many of which are being taken up by those studying other places. In a consciously comparative study, Chad Gaffield and David Levine, 'Dependence and Adolescence on the Canadian Frontier: Orillia, Ontario in the Mid-Nineteenth Century,' *History of Education Quarterly*, 1979, found that the economic development of a small place also led to increased social inequality, but that there were significant differences in patterns of school attendance, employment, and age at marriage between smalltown and urban Ontario. Another comparative study, Sheva Medjuck, 'The Importance of Boarding for the Structure of the Household in the Nineteenth Century,' SH, 1980, emphasizes the close relationship between household structure and local economic conditions. Bettina Bradbury, 'The Family Economy and Work in an Industrializing City: Montreal in the 1870's,' CHAR, 1979, shows that the percentage of nuclear families in portions of Montreal was much lower than in Hamilton and other places, and points to the necessity for further comparative research on family structure.

The social landscape of cities, defined as how people and functions are sorted out, has become increasingly researched. The first systematic study was Peter Goheen, *Victorian Toronto 1850 to 1900: Pattern and Process of Growth* (Chicago: University of Chicago, Dept. of Geography Research Paper no 127 1970), which showed a dramatic societal change during a period of rapid industrialization. Goheen found that Toronto's society in the 1850s was characterized by a 'social jumble' in which rich and poor lived close together and most people lived near their work. By 1900 most of the affluent segregated themselves from the rest of society and many people travelled fairly long distances to work.

One of Goheen's concerns was the significant shift in the scale of the industrial units of production as many small workshops with a few employees were consolidated into larger factories, each with a considerable number of employees. Much of the recent literature on working-class history is directly relevant to this phenomenon. That industrialization's benefits were not evenly distributed in class terms is convincingly portrayed in Terry Copp's *The Anatomy of Poverty: The Condition of the Working Class in Montreal, 1897-1929* (T: M&S 1974) and in a parallel study, Michael Piva, *The Condition of the Working Class in Toronto, 1900-1921* (O: University of Ottawa Press 1979). The exploitation of women workers in particular is graphically outlined in two significant studies: D. Suzanne Cross, 'The Neglected Majority: The Changing Role of Women in Nineteenth-Century Montreal,' in Stelter and Artibise, eds., *The Canadian City*, and Marie Lavigne and Jennifer Stoddart, 'Women's Work in Montreal at the Beginning of the Century,' in Marylee Stephenson, ed., *Women in Canada* (T: General Publishing 1977). The best work to date on how industrialization affected the organization of the working class is Gregory Kealey, *Toronto Workers respond to Industrial Capitalism* (T: UTP 1980). Less useful is Bryan Palmer, *A Culture in Conflict: Skilled Workers and Industrial Capitalism in Hamilton, Ontario, 1860-1914* (M: MQUP 1979), for the urban environment is only a vague backdrop to the author's interest in labour relations.

The form of the city

One of the most active areas of urban history is that which deals with the evolution of the built environment. Most of the work in the history of city planning is concentrated on the reform movement of the early twentieth century when planning became professionalized and subject to the influences of the city beautiful and garden city movements. A fine anthology of contemporary speeches and papers is Paul Rutherford, ed., *Saving the Canadian City, 1880-1920* (T: UTP 1974). Recent research in this area is represented in the collection of articles, *The Usable Urban Past*, especially Thomas Gunton, 'The Ideas and Policies of the Canadian Planning Profession, 1909-1931,' and P.J. Smith, 'The Principle of Utility and the Origins of Planning Legislation in Alberta, 1912-1975.' An overview of the federal government's role in planning is provided by Artibise and Stelter, 'Conservation Planning and Urban Planning: The Canadian Commission of Conservation in Historical Perspective,' in Roger Kain, eds., *Planning for Conservation: An International Perspective* (L: Mansell 1981). Walter Van Nus has traced planners' evolution from a romance with grandiose city beautification schemes to the more prosaic emphasis on zoning restrictions in order to protect property values in two important articles: 'The Fate of City Beautiful Thought in Canada, 1893-1930,' in Stelter and Artibise, eds., *The Canadian City*, and 'Towards the City Efficient: The Theory and Practise of Zoning, 1919-1939,' in Artibise and Stelter, eds., *The Usable Urban Past*.

The relationship between planners' ideals and the hard practical realities of actual city-building is detailed in Elizabeth Bloomfield, 'Economy, Necessity, Political Reality: Town Planning Efforts in Kitchener-Waterloo, 1912-1925,' UHR, 1980. Thousands of private developers, large corporations, and city councils all had a hand in determining the final shape of the communities. The decentralized and unregulated character of mid-nineteenth century land development is stressed by Michael Doucet, 'Speculation and the Physical Expansion of Mid-Nineteenth Century Hamilton,' in Stelter and Artibise, eds., *Shaping the Urban Landscape*. Paul-André Linteau's work on Maisonneuve, cited earlier, shows how promoters reaped windfall profits on land they owned by controlling municipal councils. An excellent case study of a planned suburb in the early twentieth century is John Weaver, 'From Land Assembly to Social Maturity: The Suburban Life of Westdale (Hamilton), Ontario, 1911-1951,' SH, 1978. Building practises were closely related to land development. The best example of research in this area is Susan Buggey, 'Building Halifax, 1841-1871,' *Acadiensis*, 1980. The great demand for public and residential building in a growing Halifax led to substantial changes in the organization of builders as well as in their methods of construction and design. The financial aspects of residential construction are analysed in two older articles: K.A.H. Buckley, 'Urban Building and Real Estate Fluctuations in Canada,' CJEPS, 1952, and James Pickett, 'Residential Capital Formation in Canada, 1871-1921,' CJEPS, 1963, but housing remains a neglected subject. Unfortunately, the best survey, John Saywell, *Housing Canadians: Essays on the History of Residential Construction in Canada* (O: Economic Council of Canada, Discussion Paper no 24 1975), is not readily available to students.

Interest in urban architectural history has grown rapidly in recent years, inspired perhaps by the struggles in each city to preserve significant buildings. Two review articles survey and evaluate this work: Harold Kalman, 'Recent Literature on the History of Canadian Architecture,' *Journal of the Society of Architectural Historians*, 1972, and Deryck Holdsworth, 'Built Forms and Social Realities: A Review Essay of Recent Work on Canadian Heritage Structures,' UHR, 1980. The standard work on Canadian architecture is still Alan Gowans, *Building Canada: An Architectural History of Canadian Life* (T: OUP 1966). This provocative and individualistic interpretation has not received the credit it deserves for its insights into the relationship between society's ideals and its built forms. As for work on particular cities, the best work has been done in Quebec and especially on Montreal. The architectural urban biography that everyone will now attempt to emulate is Jean-Claude Marsan's *Montreal in Evolution* (M: MQUP 1981), first published in 1974 and recently translated. To a far greater extent than other architectural historians, Marsan has related the physical dimensions of a city to its society and economy. Also important for Montreal is the work of Phyllis Lambert, 'The Architectural Heritage of Montreal: A Sense of Community,' *Artscanada*, 1975-6, and 'Building in Montreal: A Break with Tradition,' *Canadian Collector*, 1978. For Quebec City, Luc Noppen, C. Paulette, and M. Tremblay, *Québec: Trois siècles d'architecture* (Q: Libre Expression 1979), provides a sensitive view of the evolution of our oldest city. The destruction of historic buildings has led to some excellent architectural history about what has been lost. Luc D'Iberville-Moreau, *Lost Montreal* (T: OUP 1975), and William

Dendy, *Lost Toronto* (T: OUP 1978), are both in this tradition. Dendy's work on individual buildings is far superior to that in Eric Arthur's *Toronto, No Mean City* (T: UTP 1974), but because the organization is based on these buildings rather than on a period, the reader gets very little appreciation of the development of the city over time.

The spatial expansion of modern Canadian cities was greatly accelerated by improvements in internal transportation which made possible growth beyond the compact, walking-distance city of the mid-nineteenth century. The horse-drawn and then the electrically driven streetcar encouraged decentralization and suburbanization. In some cases such as Vancouver, streetcar line extensions and inter-urban radial railroads preceded development, but in Winnipeg they were drawn to areas that had already been developed, as is shown in H.J. Selwood, 'Urban Development and the Streetcar: The Case of Winnipeg,' UHR, 1978, and in J.E. Rea, 'How Winnipeg was Nearly Won,' in A.R. McCormack and Ian MacPherson, eds., *Cities in the West* (O: National Museum of Man 1975). In Toronto the Mackenzie and Mann-controlled transit company also refused to build lines to suburban areas, preferring to ensure a good profit from heavy ridership possible in a compact, densely built-up city. This story and its implications is well told in Michael Doucet, 'Mass Transit and the Development of Toronto in the Early Twentieth Century,' in Stelter and Artibise, eds., *Shaping the Urban Landscape*, and Donald Davis, 'Mass Transit and Private Ownership: An Alternative Perspective on the Case of Toronto,' UHR, 1979. A lively account of the way the streetcar system became a popular political issue, Christopher Armstrong and H.V. Nelles, *The Revenge of the Methodist Bicycle Company: Sunday Streetcars and Municipal Reform in Toronto, 1880-1897* (T: Peter Martin 1977), should be supplemented by Sharon Meen, 'Holy Day or Holiday? The Giddy Trolley and the Canadian Sunday,' UHR, 1980. Much useful information on electric streetcar history is available in the work of the street railway buffs, for virtually every city has a respectable history in this regard. Among the best are F.F. Angus and R.J. Sandusky, *Loyalist City Streetcars: The Story of Street Railway Transit in Saint John, New Brunswick* (T: Railfare 1979); Richard Binns, *Montreal's*

Electric Streetcars: An Illustrated History of the Tramway Era, 1872-1959 (M: Railfare 1973); Colin Hatcher, *Stampede City Streetcars: The Story of Calgary's Municipal Railway* (M: Railfare 1975).

Urban government and politics
General studies of municipal government, such as D.J. Higgins, *Urban Canada: Its Government and Politics* (T: MAC 1977), usually include a brief chapter on historical background, but there is no full-length survey of Canadian urban government. Research activity is currently concentrated on the era of reform between 1880 and 1920, roughly parallelling the American Progressive movement, when Canadians experimented with American models of centralized decision-making and scientific management such as boards of control, city managers, and commission government. The reformers have received a sympathetic assessment in the work of Paul Rutherford, 'Tomorrow's Metropolis: The Urban Reform Movement in Canada, 1880-1920,' in Stelter and Artibise, eds., *The Canadian City*. But most commentators disagree, arguing that the reformer's rhetoric hid their desire to make cities less democratic by expanding bureaucracies and increasing regulatory powers at the expense of the newcomers and the poor. Examples of this interpretation are John Weaver, *Shaping the Canadian City: Essays on Urban Politics and Policy, 1890-1920* (T: Institute of Public Administration 1977); James Anderson, 'The Municipal Government Reform Movement in Western Canada, 1880-1920,' in Artibise and Stelter, eds., *The Usable Urban Past*; and Melvin Baker, 'The Politics of Municipal Reform in St. John's, Newfoundland, 1888-1892,' UHR, 1976. The importance of moral issues such as alcohol or Sunday observance is developed by Desmond Morton, *Mayor Howland: The Citizen's Candidate* (T: Samuel Stevens 1973).

One of the traditions stemming from this period of reform was the notion of non-partisanship in municipal government. J.K. Masson and James Anderson, eds., *Emerging Party Politics in Urban Canada* (T: M&S 1972), explores several aspects of this tradition. But the tradition, supposedly in direct contrast to the American experience, may have been more apparent than real. In a stimulating overview of urban government, John Taylor, 'Mayors à La Mancha: An

Aspect of Depression Leadership in Canadian Cities,' UHR, 1981, argues that 'conventional' city politics, although technically non-partisan, were in fact loosely identified with Liberal and Conservative urban elites. Their colours quickly became apparent when they were challenged by representatives of broader-based groups including the Socialists and the Charismatics, such as Camillian Houde, who had personal followings. The existence of two unacknowledged parties has been strongest in Winnipeg, perhaps, where the 'citizen' and 'labour' groups and their policies have been clearly identified by J.E. Rea in several publications including 'The Politics of Conscience: Winnipeg after the Strike,' CHAR, 1971.

The activity of city governments in coping with the problems of growth by providing a variety of services has not been extensively studied as yet. One area that has received some attention is the municipal ownership of utilities. It seems clear from the work of Artibise on Winnipeg and Johnson on Guelph that local pressure for public ownership came from local businessmen who stood to benefit from more efficient water, power, and transportation systems. Where municipal ownership was delayed, as was the case with the Toronto waterworks, arguments were based on practical, not ideological grounds as shown by Elwood Jones and Douglas McCalla, 'Toronto Waterworks, 1840-1877: Continuity and Change in Nineteenth Century Toronto Politics,' CHR, 1979. Another area of growing research interest in municipal government services is the public health movement. A useful survey of the literature and of available sources for future research is Paul A. Bator, 'Public Health Reform in Canada and Urban History: A Critical Survey,' UHR, 1980. Several articles can be found in the special issue of the *Journal of Canadian Studies*, spring 1979, on Dependency and Social Welfare.

IRVING ABELLA

Labour and working-class history

Canadian labour history has finally arrived! When the first edition of
this book was published in 1974 just over two pages were devoted to
works on Canadian unions. Three years later, in the second edition,
the situation had somewhat improved. Appended at the end of the
chapter on business history, room was found for four pages on
'labour and industrial relations, trade unions and working-class life.'
Now, in the present edition, recognizing what has occurred over the
past decade, the editors have given labour history its due place as
one of the major areas of study in this country. And indeed, there
has been an almost exponential growth in the number of studies
and – more significantly – students, in the field of working-class history since the early 1970s.

What explains the fact that for the first hundred years of our existence Canadian scholars assiduously avoided the topic? Perhaps it
was because not until the 1960s and 70s was there a large number of
academics with working-class backgrounds. Before then, before the
days of Canada Council fellowships and the vast expansion of the
university system, most historians came from the middle and upper
classes of society, since only they could afford the time and money
required to undertake research. Or perhaps it has more to do with
the students of the 1960s coming of age. Most of the authors mentioned in this chapter were at school in the 1960s and early 1970s
and were decidedly influenced by the activist aura of the period. As

well, the work of British and American social and labour historians had a profound effect on many young Canadians looking for new avenues of research into the Canadian past.

It cannot be denied, however, that until recently for most Canadian historians the Canadian worker never existed. Somehow, a country came into being, railways laid across a continent, canals dug, ships built, coal mined, lumber cut, fish caught and canned, and goods manufactured – without workers. They were scarcely mentioned in most Canadian history books, and only came to our attention when they were doing nasty things, such as opposing conscription, closing down railways, plants, and mines, or rioting in the streets. Now, all that has changed. Indeed, one new popular history refers to the working-class as the 'real builders' of this nation.

GENERAL HISTORIES

Yet despite this phenomenal growth in the literature there is still no entirely satisfactory one-volume history of the Canadian labour movement. Perhaps as good a place as any to begin a study of the Canadian working class, therefore, is with two short introductory booklets published by the Canadian Historical Association: Eugene Forsey, *The Canadian Labour Movement 1812-1902* (O: CHA Booklet no 27 1974), and Irving Abella, *The Canadian Labour Movement 1902-1960* (O: CHA Booklet no 28 1975). The former is a detailed account of the growth of unionism in the nineteenth century; the latter, though it stresses trade union developments, is more anecdotal and deals with social and political matters as well. Of the popular surveys, by far the best is Desmond Morton with Terry Copp, *Working People: An Illustrated History of Canadian People* (O: Deneau & Greenberg 1980). This is a well-written book full of splendid photographs. Its major fault is that the authors seemingly could not decide whether they wanted a narrative or pictorial history of the Canadian worker. Thus neither the text nor the photos are entirely satisfactory. Nonetheless, theirs is a sympathetic account of the growth and development of our union movement and should provide students with an easy and stimulating introduction to Canadian labour history. The same cannot be said for Charles Lipton, *The Trade Union Movement in Canada* (3rd ed., T: NC Press 1967). Though it contains much useful material, it is a highly tendentious and partisan book, and a difficult one to read. Where Morton and Copp provide an unabashedly social-democratic view of Canadian labour history, Lipton's is a curious combination of eccentric Marxism and an unyielding nationalism. Also of interest is Harold Logan's classic *Trade Unions in Canada* (T: MAC 1948). For years this was the standard account of the history of trade unionism in Canada. It has now, of course, suffered the fate of most pioneering works – it has become badly dated, and many of its facts and analyses have been successfully challenged. Two other books, written by veteran trade-unionists, Morden Lazarus, *Years of Hard Labour* (Don Mills: Ontario Federation of Labour 1974), and Jack Williams, *The Story of Unions in Canada* (T: Dent 1975), provide highly-readable 'official' histories. Finally, undoubtedly the best overview of Canadian labour in the twentieth century was never meant to be a book. Rather, Stuart Jamieson's *Times of Trouble: Labour Unrest and Industrial Conflict in Canada, 1900-1966* (O: Privy Council Office 1968) was intended as a study of strikes for the federal government's Task Force on Labour Relations. Notwithstanding its narrow focus on industrial disputes, it provides an excellent framework for a study of trade union history in this century.

Since there are no completely satisfactory histories of the Canadian labour movement, it goes without saying that there is certainly no adequate history of the Canadian working class. We know very little about the life and conditions of work of Canadian workers over the past two hundred years. Two useful anthologies which bring together much fascinating material on these conditions are Michael Cross, ed., *The Canadian Workingman in the Nineteenth Century* (T: OUP 1974), and Irving Abella and David Millar, eds., *The Canadian Worker in the Twentieth Century* (T: OUP 1978). Both are documentary histories containing largely eye-witness accounts describing the day-to-day activities of workers at home, at play, and at work. Taken together with Greg Kealey's excellent *Canada Investigates Industrialism* (T: UTP 1973), which is a condensed version of the massive Royal Commission on Capital and Labour – without question the best social history source on nineteenth-century Canada, these provide a suggestive and enlightening introduction to the life of the Canadian worker.

Even though real working-class history in this country is only about a decade old, this has not prevented the creation of two schools of interpretation – of two very different conceptions of what labour history is really all about. Even though proponents of both schools are roughly the same age, have similar educational backgrounds, and wrote at about the same time, one of the protagonists has described the cleavage as a 'generation' gap. Though this description confuses more than it elucidates, it would be fair, I think, to describe one group as 'culturalist' and the other as 'labourist.' The former is largely Marxist; the latter, though it has no coherent ideology, is largely social-democratic. To the 'culturalist' what is worth studying is not so much unions as the 'work process.' They are more concerned with the 'class experience' than they are with organization, more with 'culture' than politics. With some notable exceptions their work is largely in the nineteenth century and community-centred, and their concerns and methodology are heavily influenced by such leading British and American scholars as E.P. Thompson, Herbert Gutman, Eric Hobsbawm, and David Montgomery. Through the study of voluntary societies, leisure activities, workplace behaviour, and family life they are trying to recreate – if they ever existed – the class-consciousness and 'culture' of Canadian working men and women.

The so-called 'labourist' school is much more heterogeneous. They are less ideological and concerned more with unions than with individual workers. Their studies often concern entire regions and even the whole country rather than select communities. For the most part their histories are largely institutional and political. Little attention is paid in these studies to either 'class conflict' or 'culture.' There are some who argue – correctly, I think – that too much has been made of the differences between the two schools, that actually in many ways their works are not very dissimilar. And in fact, despite what they say, historians of both schools deal with workers, unions, politics, and working conditions in much the same way, though obviously their emphases are different.

PRE-CONFEDERATION

There is no better book to begin a study of Canadian labour history than with Clare Pentland's long-time underground study *Labour and Capital in Canada* (T: Lorimer 1981). Though in his lifetime he never wrote a book, through his articles, lectures, and ideas Pentland had a profound impact on the study of labour in this country. This posthumous work was Pentland's 1950 doctoral dissertation and was widely read by scholars in the field. Now that it is readily available it should be basic reading for students of Canadian labour history. It provides the framework for understanding how a labour movement came into being and – from a quasi-Marxist point of view – describes the evolution of industrial capitalism in Canada. Important as well, but a far different book, is Eugene Forsey's massive *History of Canadian Labour 1812-1902* (T: UTP 1982). It is a book very heavy on facts and figures, but very light on analysis. Though, as Forsey himself admits in his introduction, the study is dated, since he completed his research in the 1960s, it is nonetheless the single most important reference book for nineteenth-century Canadian labour history.

Because these are the only two monographs for this period, we are dependent on a series of articles for our knowledge of the Canadian working class in these years. Fortunately, these are of a uniformly high quality and, taken together, provide a fairly comprehensive account of the pre-Confederation worker. Right from the beginning Canadian workers realized they lived in an eight-month country which could not provide steady work on a year-round basis. For them winter was sheer purgatory. Many succumbed before its ferocity, its numbing coldness, its depressing boredom. Judith Fingard's gripping 'The Winter Tale: Contours of Pre-Industrial Poverty in British America 1815-1860,' CHAR, 1974, describes in graphic detail the impact of winter on Canadian workers and their families. Also of some note is her study of 'The Decline of the Sailor as a Ship-Labourer in Nineteenth Century Timber Ports,' *Labour*, 1977. Undoubtedly the most important group of workers in this period were those men digging the canals which would connect Montreal and Europe to the settlements in Upper Canada and beyond. Two important studies of this group are Clare Pentland, 'The Lachine Strike of 1843,' CHR, 1948, and Ruth Bleasdale, 'Class Conflict on the Canals of Upper Canada in the 1840s,' *Labour*, 1981. These workers were almost entirely Irish and their influence on the early labour movement was profound. Two articles by Michael Cross, 'The Shiners War: Social Violence in the Ottawa Valley in the 1830s' CHR, 1973, and 'Stony Monday 1849: The Rebellion Losses Bill in Bytown,' OH, 1971, also discuss the peculiarities and significance of these Irish. The attitude of the 'Great Rebel' towards workers is described in Fred Armstrong's 'Reformer as Capitalist: William Lyon Mackenzie and the Printers Strike of 1836,' OH, 1967. Of some limited interest as well is a two-part article by Stephen Langdon, 'The Emergence of the Canadian Working Class Movement 1845-75,' JCS, 1973, which makes the case for such a movement without much supporting data. Finally, a study of one of the first unions in Canada may be found in J.I. Cooper's turgid but informative 'The Quebec Ship Labourers Benevolent Society,' CHR, 1949.

POST-CONFEDERATION

It has become commonplace to state that the history of post-Confederation Canada's union movement begins with the *Globe* strike of 1872. Two good introductions to the strike are John Battye, 'The Nine Hour Pioneers: The Genesis of the Canadian Labour Movement,' *Labour*, 1979, and Sally F. Zerker, 'George Brown and the Printers Union,' JCS, 1975. For an entirely different point of view see Donald G. Creighton, 'George Brown, Sir John A. Macdonald and the Working Man,' CHR, 1943. Still the best overview of the role of labour in this decade is Bernard Ostry, 'Conservatives, Liberals and Labour in the 1870s,' CHR, 1960. One of the first large strikes in our history is ably dealt with in Desmond Morton, 'Taking on the Grand Trunk: The Locomotive Engineers Strike of 1876-6,' *Labour*, 1977.

The 1880s is the era of the Knights of Labor in Canada. Historians are just now beginning to learn how significant was the role of this strange band of unionists from south of the border who spread their labour gospel throughout most of the cities and towns of Canada.

The most thorough study of the Knights is Gregory Kealey and Bryan Palmer, *Dreaming of What Might Be: The Knights of Labor in Ontario* (NY: Cambridge UP 1982). This has now replaced Douglas Kennedy, *The Knights of Labor in Canada* (L: University of Western Ontario 1956), as the standard account. For the Knights in Quebec the most useful study is Fernand Harvey, 'Les Chevaliers du Travail, les Etats-Unis et la société québécoise 1882-1902,' in F. Harvey, ed., *Aspects historiques du mouvement ouvrier au Québec* (M: BE 1979). A thoughtful article on the Knights and journalists is Russell Hann, 'Brainworkers and the Knights of Labor: E.E. Sheppard, Phillips Thompson and the Toronto News 1883-1887,' in G. Kealey and P. Warren, eds., *Essays in Canadian Working Class History* (T: M&S 1970). Eugene Forsey, 'The Telegraphers Strike of 1883,' TRSC, 1971, details the role of the Knights in this first nation-wide work stoppage in Canadian history.

The outstanding labour figure of these years, Daniel O'Donoghue, a man called by some 'the father of Canadian labour,' is memorialized in a much-too-sympathetic biography by Doris French, *Faith, Sweat and Politics* (T: M&S 1972). O'Donoghue, it turns out, was not the friend of labour, French though he was. For a much better look at these years there is a fine article by Frank Watt, 'The National Policy, the Workingman and Proletarian Ideas in Victorian Canada,' CHR, 1959, which examines the issues affecting workers and discusses the lively labour press of this period. Also of some merit is Bernard Ostry, 'Conservatives, Liberals and Labour in the 1880s,' CJEPS, 1961.

It seems that the 1870s and 80s have become fertile grounds of research for social historians of the 1970s and 80s. In Kealey and Warren, eds., *Essays in Canadian Working Class History*, there are three solid articles on this period: Harvey Graff, 'Respected and Profitable Labour: Literacy, Jobs and the Working Class in the Nineteenth Century'; Michael Doucet, 'Working Class Housing in a Small Nineteenth Century Canadian City: Hamilton, Ontario 1852-1881'; and Gregory Kealey, 'The Orange Order in Toronto: Religious Riots and the Working Class.' In addition, an intriguing article by Bryan Palmer, 'Discordant Music: Charivaris and Whitecapping in Nineteenth Century North America,' *Labour*, 1978, attempts to argue – not entirely successfully – that these customs were part of a working-class culture which threatened the 'developing bourgeois hegemony.'

The labour literature of this period, however, is dominated by two books – Bryan Palmer, *A Culture in Conflict: Skilled Workers and Industrial Capitalism in Hamilton Ontario 1860-1914* (M: MQUP 1979), and Gregory S. Kealey, *Toronto Workers respond to Industrial Capitalism 1867-1892* (T: UTP 1980). The major concern of both authors is to describe how workers of a pre-industrial society responded to the onslaughts of industrial capitalism. Neither, but especially Palmer, are very much concerned with unions or politics; each devotes most of his book to a discussion of working-class culture and consciousness. Their critics have pointed out – perhaps correctly – that their conclusions are suggestive rather than definitive and that by ignoring the impact of ethnicity and religion they have not really discovered a 'unique' working-class culture. Nonetheless, both are seminal studies and are key to an understanding of working-class experiences in the late nineteenth century.

EARLY TWENTIETH CENTURY, 1900-19

Any study of the Canadian labour movement in the twentieth century should begin with a look at the ideas of the man who, for better or for worse, would dominate labour policy in this century. Mackenzie King saw himself as a friend of the workingman, as an arbiter of their needs and desires. He helped found the federal Department of Labour, was its first deputy minister, and as such devised much of the labour legislation of this period. For years the best description of the man and his labour policies was H.C. Ferns and B. Ostry, *The Age of Mackenzie King: The Rise of a Leader* (L: Heinemann 1955; reprinted T: Lorimer 1975). Though it is still a devastating account and well worth reading, a new book, Paul Craven, *An Impartial Umpire: Industrial Relations and the Canadian State 1900-1911* (T: UTP 1981) has taken its place as the standard study. This is a sprawling sketch, whose aim it is to provide a detailed analysis not only of King and his peculiar ideas, but of the labour relations of these years as well. For those interested in wading through King's thoughts firsthand – an experience not to everyone's tastes – his *Industry and Humanity: A Study in the Principles Underlying Industrial Reconstruc-*

tion (T: UTP 1973), which was first published in 1918, has now been reprinted. Perhaps a better idea would be to read the exchange between Reg Whittaker and Paul Craven (*Labour*, 1977, 1979) concerning King's intellectual background and his contributions to Canadian labour relations before the First World War.

This was also the period in which international unions guided by the head of the American Federation of Labor, Sam Gompers, launched a massive organizational campaign – using, by the way, Canadian funds and organizers – and took over control of Canada's labour centre, the Trades and Labor Congress. The story of this invasion and its implications is fully detailed in Robert Babcock, *Gompers in Canada: A Study of American Continentalism before the First World War* (T: UTP 1974). This is, clearly, the best study of American unions in Canada in this period, and though some critics take exception to Babcock's conclusion – that the AFL took over the TLC largely because of Gomper's 'imperialist' concepts – no one can quarrel with the breadth of his research. The saga of the significant Berlin (Kitchener, Ontario) Conference of 1902, when Gompers made his move, is well told in Babcock's 'Sam Gompers and the Berlin Decision of 1902' in R. Preston, ed., *The Influences of the United States on Canadian Development* (Durham: Duke UP 1972). The impact of this conference in Quebec is the subject of Jacques Rouillard's 'Le Québec et le congrès de Berlin, 1902,' *Labour*, 1976.

A useful introduction to the labour politics of this period is Martin Robin, *Radical Politics and Canadian Labour 1880-1930* (Kingston: Industrial Relations Centre, Queen's University 1968). Though heavy on detail – some of it wrong – and difficult to read, the book does provide a worthwhile account of the development of socialism and radicalism amongst Canadian workers. There is no better description of the life of the working class in this period than Terry Copp's startling *The Anatomy of Poverty: The Condition of the Working Class in Montreal 1897-1927* (T: M&S 1974). Copp paints a picture of urban poverty and distress which is so horrifying, so unbelievable, that one can only sit back and wonder how such adversity – Montreal had the highest infant mortality rate in the world, next to Calcutta – could exist in Canada's largest city in this century. For the nation's second-largest city, Michael Piva, *The Condition of the*

Working Class in Toronto, 1900-1921 (O: University of Ottawa Press 1979), presents a less devastating analysis, which nonetheless concludes that both living and working conditions were disgraceful. Perhaps because of this situation there was much labour unrest in the years before the First World War. As Desmond Morton concludes in his important article, 'Aid to the Civil Power: The Canadian Militia in Support of the Social Order 1867-1911,' CHR, 1970, governments were always prepared to support their industrial and business allies with anything at their disposal – including troops – to help weaken a nascent labour movement. The most detailed description of the attitude of businessmen towards unions is Michael Bliss, *A Living Profit: Studies in the Social History of Canadian Business 1883-1911* (T: M&S 1974).

An interesting approach to the causes of strikes in this period is Craig Heron and Bryan Palmer, 'Through the Prism of the Strike: Industrial Conflict in Southern Ontario 1901-1914,' CHR, 1977. Its thesis is that most strikes in this period were fought over the issue of workshop control. Similar conclusions – that an artisanal culture was trying to come to terms with a voracious industrial capitalism – are drawn in articles on Toronto by Wayne Roberts, 'The Last Artisans: Toronto Printers 1897-1914,' in Kealey and Warren, eds., *Essays in Canadian Working Class History*, and 'Artisans, Aristocrats and Handymen: Politics and Unionism among Toronto Skilled Building Trades Workers 1897-1914,' *Labour*, 1976. For Hamilton workers see Craig Heron, 'The Crisis of the Craftsman: Hamilton's Metal Workers in the Early Twentieth Century,' *Labour*, 1980. Though immigrants obviously played a key role in the labour events of these years, few historians have studied their impact. A singular exception is Robert Harney, whose work on Italian immigration is of great significance. Most helpful for students of labour is his 'Montreal's King of Italian Labour: A Case Study of Padronism,' *Labour*, 1979. In addition, a very good article on immigrant workers is Jean Morrison, 'Ethnicity and Violence: The Lakehead Freight Handlers Before World War I,' in Kealey and Warren, eds., *Essays in Canadian Working Class History*.

The course of labour history in this country changes with the onset of the First World War. A very good overview of these changes can be found in R.C. Brown and G.R. Cook, *Canada 1892-1921: A*

Nation Transformed (T: M&S 1974). The life of a worker – in this case a miner – is ably portrayed in Doug Baldwin, 'A Study in Social Control: The Life of the Silver Miner in Northern Ontario,' *Labour*, 1977. A complement to this article is Bryan Hogan, *Cobalt: Year of the Strike 1919* (Cobalt: Highway Book Shop 1978). Relations with the federal government were badly strained in these years as is made clear by David Bercuson, 'Organized Labour and the Imperial Munitions Board,' *Industrial Relations*, 1973, and Myer Semiatycki, 'Munitions and Labour Militancy: The 1916 Hamilton Machinists' Strike,' *Labour*, 1978. The attitude of labour towards conscription is nicely documented in Martin Robin, 'Registration, Conscription and Independent Labour Politics 1916-1917,' CHR, 1966. The most crucial developments affecting the labour movement, however, were not taking place in eastern or central Canada where most of the country's workers were, but rather in the west, where radicalism was strongest.

WESTERN CANADA, 1900-21

Why western Canadian workers were so much more radical than their eastern counterparts has been the subject of much historical debate. Scholars have devoted much time and energy to examining the nature of this radicalism and explaining its growth. Most active has been David Bercuson. His *Confrontation at Winnipeg: Labour, Industrial Relations and the General Strike* (M: MQUP 1974) provides the most thorough account of this most traumatic event in our labour past. Almost as useful – with the advantage of being shorter – is *The Winnipeg Strike 1919* (T: Longman 1974) which he wrote with K.W. McNaught, or his article, 'Winnipeg 1919,' in Irving Abella, ed., *On Strike: Six Key Labour Struggles in Canada* (T: Lorimer 1974). Bercuson has also written a colourful – and definitive – study of the *One Big Union, Fools and Wise Men: The Rise and Fall of the One Big Union* (T: MHR 1978). In addition, his provocative 'Labour Radicalism and the Western Frontier 1897-1919,' CHR, 1977, deals in an intriguing way with the question of the origins of western radicalism. A much more comprehensive examination of western radicalism may be found in A. Ross McCormack's excellent study,

Reformers, Rebels and Revolutionaries: The Western Canadian Radical Movement (T: UTP 1978).

Both Bercuson and McCormack emphasize the role of immigrants in the creation of a militant labour movement on the Prairies and in British Columbia. So far, the only book to be devoted to these newcomers is Donald Avery, *Dangerous Foreigners: European Immigrant Workers and Labour Radicalism in Canada 1896-1932* (T: M&S 1979). His concerns, however, veer more towards government policy and domestic nativism than to the immigrants themselves. Thus, though the book provides a wealth of information, it does not tell us all that much about the 'dangerous foreigners.' It does tell us more, however, than Jack Scott's study of the Industrial Workers of the World in British Columbia, *Plunderbund and Proletariat* (V: New Star 1975), which is simply a pastiche of quotes taken from elsewhere. An infinitely better history of the IWW can be found in McCormack's book. Useful as well for events in British Columbia in these years is Stanley Scott, 'A Profusion of Issues: Immigrant Labour, the World War and the Cominco Strike of 1917,' *Labour*, 1977. For a cursory but helpful overview of that province's trade union movement see Paul Phillips, *No Power Greater: A Century of Labour in British Columbia* (V: British Columbia Federation of Labour 1967). Carlos Schwantes, *Radical Heritage: Labor, Socialism and Reform in Washington and British Columbia* (V: Douglas and McIntyre 1979), is an insightful comparison of Pacific Northwest labour developments on both sides of the border. Perhaps the most poignant description of frontier working conditions – because it was written by an eye-witness – is Edmund Bradwin, *The Bunkhouse Men* (reprinted T: UTP 1972). Similarly, the most moving and graphic description of the Winnipeg strike comes from the participants themselves in Norman Penner, ed., *Winnipeg 1919: The Strikers own History of the Winnipeg General Strike* (T: Lorimer 1973).

Though superseded by other scholarly work, Donald Masters, *The Winnipeg General Strike* (T: UTP 1950), is still worth reading, as is the chapter on the strike in K.W. McNaught, *A Prophet in Politics: A Biography of J.S. Woodsworth* (T: UTP 1959). Two useful pre-strike analyses of the growth of militance in the west are Clare Pentland,

'The Western Canadian Labour Movement 1897-1919,' *Canadian Journal of Social and Political Thought*, 1976, and Paul Phillips, 'The National Policy and the Development of the Western Canadian Labour Movement,' in A. Rasporich and H.C. Klassen, eds., *Western Perspectives 2* (T: HRW 1973). A very good analysis as well is Gerald Friesen, 'Years in Revolt: Regionalism, Socialism and the Western Canadian Labour Movement,' *Labour*, 1976. Less good is Larry Peterson, 'The One Big Union in International Perspective: Revolutionary Industrial Unionism 1900-1925,' *Labour*, 1981. Finally, Warren Caragata, *Alberta Labour: A Heritage Untold* (T: Lorimer 1979, presents a brief survey of that province's colourful labour past.

SINCE 1920

It seems that following the Winnipeg strike not only was the steam knocked out of the labour movement, but out of labour historians as well. Few of them have made any effort to research the years following this cataclysmic event. There is, for example, not one study of the Canadian labour movement from the collapse of the OBU in 1921 to the rise of the CIO in 1936. Perhaps because this was also a period of unparalleled labour weakness, few historians have chosen to write about it. Like everyone else, historians prefer writing about times of activity rather than quiescence, of successes rather than defeats, of growth rather than stagnation. With only one exception, this was a period of unmitigated failure for Canada's trade union movement. The exception was in Nova Scotia – or more accurately, Cape Breton Island – in which fully 50 per cent of the strikes in this period occurred. A very sympathetic study of the Cape Breton labour situation may be found in Paul MacEwan, *Miners and Steelworkers: Labour in Cape Breton* (T: Samuel Stevens, Hakkert 1976). Though too much of the book concentrates on politics and too little on the conditions of life and work in the region, it is, still, an excellent introduction to the labour history of that area. Also useful are David Frank, 'Class Conflict in the Coal Industry: Cape Breton, 1922,' in Kealey and Warrian, eds., *Essays in Working Class History*, and Don McGillivary, 'Military Aid to the Civil Power: The

Cape Breton Experience in the 1920s,' *Acadiensis*, 1974. For a change of pace, Dawn Fraser, *Echoes from Labor's War: Industrial Cape Breton in the 1920s* (T: New Hogtown Press 1976), tells the same story – with more vigour – in verse form.

A major reason for labour's impotence in this decade was the increasingly sophisticated anti-union techniques adopted by industrialists across the country. Why break unions and strikers with scabs or troops when it could more easily – and more efficiently – be done by company unions? The experience of one plant is graphically documented in Bruce Scott, 'A Place in the Sun: The Industrial Council at Massey-Harris 1914-1929,' *Labour*, 1976. The difficulties of organizing in this era are also depicted in James A. Prendergast, 'The Attempts at Unionization in the Automobile Industry in Canada, 1928,' OH, 1978. A good description of the plight of the white-collar salaried employee in the 1920s is Anthony Thomson, 'The Large and Generous View: The Debate on Labour Affiliation in the Canadian Civil Service 1918-1928,' *Labour*, 1977.

Yet the 1920s also saw the introduction into Canada of a movement which would have a profound effect on trade-unionism in this country. The two best surveys of the Communist party are William Rodney, *Soldiers of the International: A History of the Communist Party of Canada, 1919-1929* (T: UTP 1968), and Norman Penner's fine study, *The Canadian Left: A Critical Analysis* (T: PH 1977). Of less use, since it scarcely deals with the party's activities in the labour movement, is Ivan Avakomovic, *The Communist Party of Canada: A History* (T: M&S 1975). Intriguing, but dubious as history, are the memoirs of two party activists, *Your's in the Struggle: Reminiscences of Tim Buck*, edited by William Beeching and Phylis Clarke (T: NC Press 1977), and Tom McEwen, *The Forge Glows Red: From Blacksmith to Revolutionary* (T: Progress Books 1974). Both are highly partisan but interesting accounts of the role of the Communists in Canada. Also of some value are the reminiscences of an ethnic union organizer and party stalwart, in Irving Abella, ed., 'Portrait of a Jewish Professional Revolutionary: The Recollections of Joshua Gershman,' *Labour*, 1977.

The high point of Communist success – at least within the labour movement – coincided with the onset of the Depression. The Workers Unity League was founded by the party in 1929 and before it was disbanded in 1935 it had organized – and radicalized – thousands of Canadian workers, had led vast protest marches and campaigns, and had been responsible for the vast majority of strikes in these years. Two of these, 'Estevan 1931' by Stanley Hanson and 'Aid to the Civil Power: The Stratford Strike of 1933' by Desmond Morton may be found in Irving Abella, ed., *On Strike*. As well, John Herd Thompson and Allen Seager, 'Workers, Growers and Monopolists: The "Labour Problem" in the Alberta Beet Sugar Industry During the 1930s,' *Labour*, 1978, examine the organization of a unique type of labour organization in Canada – a union of agricultural workers. Fascinating, first-hand accounts of the party's activity amongst workers can also be gleaned from Ronald Liversege, *Recollections of the On-to-Ottawa Trek* (T: M&S 1973), and Myrtle Bergen's highly-coloured tale of woodworkers in British Columbia, *Tough Timber: The Loggers of British Columbia: Their History* (T: Progress Books 1966). Party activities are also highlighted in Sydney Hutcheson's often-touching memoir, *Depression Stories* (V: New Star 1976), and Patricia Shultz's brief booklet, *The East York Workers Association: A Response to the Great Depression* (T: New Hogtown Press 1975).

Undoubtedly, the most important event for Canadian unionism since the Winnipeg General Strike was the arrival of the Congress of Industrial Organization – the CIO. This marked the birth of industrial unionism in Canada. The only book which discusses the activities of the CIO as well as the role of the Communist party and its social democratic rival, the CCF, within the labour movement is Irving Abella, *Nationalism, Communism and Canadian Labour: The CIO, the Communist Party and the Canadian Congress of Labour, 1935-1956* (T: UTP 1973). It contains much information on the creation and growth of such potent industrial unions as the Automobile Workers, Steel Workers, Wood Workers, Electrical Workers, and Mine, Mill, and Smelter Workers. Also of some interest is Abella's article on the strike which gave the CIO its first foothold in Canada, 'Oshawa, 1937,' in Abella, ed., *On Strike*. An earlier CIO strike is well described in Duart Snow, 'The Holmes Foundry Strike of March 1937,' OH, 1977. Later CIO developments in southern Ontario are ably presented in a series of articles in Terry Copp, ed., *Industrial Unionism in Kitchener, 1937-1947* (Elora: Commock Press 1976). In a thoughtful article, 'Minto, New Brunswick: A Study in Class Relations Between the Wars,' *Labour*, 1980, Allen Seager describes the impact of the CIO in the coal towns of New Brunswick.

The CIO invasion brought to a head the struggle for power within a rapidly expanding labour movement between the CCF and the Communist party. A significant study of this conflict is Gad Horowitz, *Canadian Labour in Politics* (T: UTP 1968). Horowitz supports the CCF position and has little use for the Communists. A slightly different point of view may be gleaned from Irving Abella, 'American Unions, Communism and the Canadian Labour Movement: Some Myths and Realities,' in R.A. Preston, ed., *The Influences of the United States on Canadian Development*. Also useful – but extremely derivative – is Arnold Bennett, 'Red-Baiting – Trade Union Style: Cold War Factionalism in the Canadian Trade Union Movement,' *Our Generation*, 1979. This concentration on the internal battles within the house of labour in these years has diverted the attention of historians away from what was a more important struggle – the attempt by the union movement to force out of a hostile government legislation which would bring industry to the bargaining table. Eventually labour succeeded and a new industrial relations pattern came into being. Aside from one badly dated survey, Harold Logan, *State Intervention and Assistance in Collective Bargaining: The Canadian Experience, 1943-1956* (T: UTP 1956), there is only one article, Laurel Sefton MacDowell, 'The Formation of the Canadian Industrial Relations System during World War Two,' *Labour*, 1975, which deals with this watershed in our labour history. The first test of this new system during the Ford strike immediately following the war is the subject of a commendable article by David Moulton, 'Ford, Windsor 1945,' in Abella, ed., *On Strike*.

A helpful introduction to the new, strengthened labour movement which emerged from the Second World War is R.U. Miller and Fraser Isbester, eds., *Canadian Labour in Transition* (T: PH 1971). The attempts of the representatives of organized labour to lobby government officials is described in David Kwavnick, *Organized Labour and Pressure Politics: The Canadian Labour Congress 1956-*

1968 (M: MQUP 1972). Much better reading, though more suspect as history, are the eye-witness stories told by union leaders of their involvement in the important labour events of this period in Gloria Montero, *We Stood Together: First Hand Accounts of Dramatic Events in Canada's Labour Past* (T: Lorimer 1979). A similar book, equally superficial, though easy to read, is Walter Stewart, *'Strike!'* (T: M&S 1974). Neither of these books should be taken very seriously. Two opposing points of view on the performance – and indeed the viability – of international unions in Canada are John Crispo, *International Unionism: A Study in Canadian American Relations* (T: McGraw-Hill 1967), and Robert Laxer's acerbic attack on American unions, *Canada's Unions* (T: Lorimer 1976). Even more polemical is Rick Salutin's hagiography of a labour nationalist, *Kent Rowley: A Canadian Hero* (T: Lorimer 1979).

The most recent phenomenon of Canadian unionism – the remarkable growth of white-collar and public sector unions – has, as yet, received almost no attention from historians. There are some relevant articles in H.D. Jain, ed., *Canadian Labour and Industrial Relations: Public and Private Sector* (T: MHR 1975). Bruce McLean, *'A Union Amongst Government Employees': A History of the British Columbia Government Employees Union, 1919-1979* (Burnaby: BC Government Employers Union 1979), is an official account of the growth of one such union. Another is Jackie Ainsworth, ed., *An Account to Settle: The Story of the United Bank Workers* (SORWVC) (V: Press Gang Publishers 1979). The autobiography of the notorious leader of Canada's postal workers in the 1970s, Joe Davidson and John Deverall, *Joe Davidson* (T: Lorimer 1978), tells the inside story of his union's growing militance throughout this decade.

UNION AND REGIONAL LABOUR HISTORIES

Despite the impressive publishing record of labour historians since 1970, most have shied away from institutional history. There are few accounts of individual unions or labour congresses. The most thorough history of a local union is Sally F. Zerker, *The Rise and Fall of the Toronto Typographical Union: A Case Study of Foreign Domination* (T: UTP 1982). Since the union has an almost complete set of records from its creation in the nineteenth century, Zerker's book tells us a great deal about early unionism in this country. A far less scholarly book is John Stanton's lamentable *Life and Death of a Union: The History of the Canadian Seamen's Union 1936-1959* (T: Steel Rail Press 1978). A different perspective on this union is John Allan (Pat) Sullivan's bitterly anti-Communist diatribe, *Red Sails on the Great Lakes* (T: MAC 1955). More scholarly – and far more useful – is Terry Copp's brief history, *The IUE in Canada* (Kitchener: Cumnock Press 1979), which tells the fascinating story of the International Union of Electrical Workers relatively unsuccessful attempts to destroy the left-wing United Electrical Workers union. Two anecdotal accounts of left-wing British Columbia unions are G.A. North, *A Ripple, a Wave*, ed. Harold Griffin (V: Fishermen Publishing Society 1974), which is the story of the efforts to build a union in the Pacific fishing industry, and *Man Along the Shore: The Story of the Waterfront as told by Longshoremen Themselves 1860s-1975*, ed. H. Deppies and Ben Swankey (V: International Longshoremen's and Warehousemen's Union Local 500 Pensioners 1975). For the Nova Scotia fishing industry a very good study is Silver Donald Cameron, *The Education of Everett Richardson: The Nova Scotia Fishermen's Strike 1970-1* (T: M&S 1977).

Except for the West and Quebec, regional studies of Canadian trade unionism are almost non-existent. For Newfoundland there is R.A. Hattenhauer's 'A Brief Labour History of Newfoundland,' in the *Report for the Royal Commission on Labour Legislation in Newfoundland and Labrador* (O: QP 1970), which is difficult to obtain. There are very few labour histories of the Maritime provinces – outside, of course, of Cape Breton Island – and, most surprisingly, of the country's industrial heartland, Ontario, though for the latter, at least, the Ontario Historical Studies Commission is sponsoring a two-volume history.

QUEBEC

Though in many instances the history of unionism in Quebec parallels that of the rest of Canada, there are enough fundamental differences to warrant a special section in this chapter. For students of

Quebec labour, the most important sources are the bulletins and research reports of the Regroupement de Chercheurs en Histoire de Travailleurs Québécois [RCHTQ], entitled *Histoire des travailleurs québécois: Bulletin RCHTQ*, and its 'Collection histoire des travailleurs québécois,' a multi-volume series on the history of the Quebec working class. The most accessible general history of Quebec, Fernand Harvey, éd., *Le mouvement ouvrier au Québec* (M: BE 1980), is a collection of interpretative essays with a very good critical bibliography. An older history is Richard Desrosiers and Denis Héroux, *Les travailleurs québécois et le syndicalisme* (M: PUQ 1971). A briefer, more popular – and more partisan – history is *Histoire du mouvement ouvrier au Québec (1825-1976)* (M: Confédération des Syndicats Nationaux 1979). For the nineteenth century the most important books are Jean Hamelin et Noel Belanger, éds., *Les travailleurs québécois: 1851-1896* (M: PUQ 1973), and Harvey, éd., *Aspects historiques du mouvement ouvrier au Québec*. Dealing with an even earlier period is J.-P. Hardy et P.-T. Ruddell, *Les apparantis artisans à Québec 1660-1815* (M: PUQ 1977).

For Quebec labour in the twentieth century the premier scholar is Jacques Rouillard. His three books, *Les travailleurs du coton au Québec 1900-1915* (M: PUQ 1974), *Les syndicats nationaux au Québec de 1900 à 1930* (Q: PUL 1979), and *Histoire de la CSN 1921-1981* (M: BE 1981), cover the story of the province's labour movement in this century. Each of these studies surveys a different aspect of the union movement; the first examines the egregious working conditions of textile workers; the second traces the growth of national unionism in the province; the third is a comprehensive history of one of Quebec's premier organizations, the Confederation of National Trade Unions [CNTU]. Naturally there are gaps in Rouillard's books and there are a number of books which provide additional information. Two interesting examinations of the Communist party are Marcel Fournier, *Communisme et anti-communisme au Québec 1920-1950* (M: Edition coopérative Albert Saint Martin 1979), and R. Comeau and B. Dionne, *Les communistes au Québec 1936-1956: Sur le parti Communiste du Canada* (M: PUQ 1981). Perhaps of more use – because it has been translated into English – is Evelyn Dumas, *Bitter Thirties in Quebec* (M: Black Rose Books 1975). Complementary to this study of strikes and working conditions during the Depression is J.P. LeFebvre, éd., *En grève! L'histoire de la CSN et des luttes menées par ses militants de 1937 à 1963* (M: Editions du Jour 1963).

Undoubtedly the most significant strike of all – at least from the point of view of the labour movement – was the famous asbestos strike of 1949. Several years later a group of academics, journalists, and union leaders – most of whom were participants in the strike, and most of whom would later go on to achieve prominence throughout Canada – put together a crucially important book of essays. Now translated into English this study, edited by a young law professor, Pierre-Elliot Trudeau, entitled *The Asbestos Strike* (T: Lorimer 1974), became a milestone in the social and political history of the province. A much briefer version of the strike is Fraser Isbester's 'Asbestos 1949,' in Abella, ed., *On Strike*.

Few Canadian labour leaders have had either the time or the talent to write their memoirs. A singular exception has been Alfred Charpentier, one of Quebec's most venerable unionists. His *Cinquante ans d'action ouvrier: les memoires de l'Alfred Charpentier* (Q: PUL 1971) is an engaging book and one of few first-hand accounts extant of a French-Canadian worker's experiences in the sub-arctic slums of Montreal in the late nineteenth century. Indefatigable, even at an advanced age he wrote 'La conscience syndicale lors des grèves du textile en 1937 et de l'amiante en 1949,' *Labour*, 1978, which was a rejoinder to the conclusions arrived at by L.A. Tremblay in his *Le syndicalisme québécois: Idéologie de la CSN et de la FTQ 1940-1970* (M: PUM 1972).

WOMEN

Over the past decade, concomitant with the rise of the feminist movement, increasing numbers of scholars have begun devoting their attention to the long-benighted area of the role of women in the labour movement. One of the first – and still amongst the best – studies was Janice Acton *et al.*, ed., *Women at Work: Ontario 1850-1930* (T: Women's Educational Press 1974), a fascinating anthology of articles on the condition of women's work in this period. A more recent collection, Linda Kealey, *A Not Unreasonable Claim: Women and Reform in Canada, 1880s-1920s* (T: Women's Educational Press 1979), also contains several relevant articles. Wayne Roberts, who has articles in both these readers and has extensively researched the working class in Toronto in the Laurier period, has also written a concise history of women workers in Toronto in these years, *Honest Womanhood* (T: New Hogtown Press 1976). Although his conclusions concerning the class consciousness of women workers may not be supported by the evidence, the evidence alone is illuminating. A thoughtful discussion of a strike in this period is Joan Sangster, 'The 1907 Bell Telephone Strike: Organizing Women Workers,' *Labour*, 1978.

Though neither is exclusively about labour, both Gwen Matheson, ed., *Women in the Canadian Mosaic* (T: Peter Martin 1976), and Susan Mann Trofimenkoff and Alison Prentice, eds., *The Neglected Majority* (T: M&S 1977), contain important essays on working women. Two other anthologies which are also of some use are *Women Unite!* (T: Women's Educational Press 1972) and Marylee Stephenson, ed., *Women in Canada* (T: General Publishing 1973). A fine collection of articles on Quebec women – including several which deal with the working women of the province – is Marie Levigne and Yolande Pinard, éds., *Les femmes dans la société québécoise* (M: BE 1977). More comprehensive is Francine Berry, *Le travail de la femme au Québec: L'évolution de 1940 à 1970* (M: RHCTQ 1977). A more specific study is Gail Cuthbert Brandt, ' "Weaving it Together": Life Cycle and the Industrial Experience of Female Cotton Workers in Quebec, 1910-1950,' *Labour*, 1981.

For the period after the First World War, Veronica Strong-Boag has published two fine articles, 'The Girl of the New Day: Canadian Working Class Women in the 1920s,' *Labour*, 1976, and 'Wages for Housework: Mother's Allowances and the Beginning of Social Security in Canada,' *JCS*, 1979. For Quebec women workers in this period see Marie Levigne and Jennifer Stoddart, 'Les travailleuses montréalaises entre les deux guerres,' *Labour*, 1977. But probably the most telling description is Rolf Knight's history of his immigrant mother's experiences in Canada, *A Very Ordinary Life* (V: New Star 1974). There has been little written on working-class women during the Second World War, but there is some material on the years since the war. Both the Department of Labour and Statistics Canada have published overviews, the most useful of which are *Women at Work in Canada* (Department of Labour 1974) and *The Female Worker in Canada* (Dominion Bureau of Statistics 1968). Also of some use is Julie White, *Women and Unions* (Canadian Advisory Council on the Status of Women 1980), and Pat and Hugh Armstrong, *The Double Ghetto* (T: M&S 1978).

A very important source for the study of women's history in Canada is a journal entitled *Atlantis*. Since it first began publication in the mid-1970s it has published some very good articles on working women. The best of these are Susan Trofimenkoff, '"One Hundred and Two Muffled Voices": Canada's Industrial Women in the 1880s' (1977), and Alison Prentice, 'Writing Women into History: The History of Women's Work in Canada' (1978).

GOVERNMENT DOCUMENTS AND BIBLIOGRAPHIES

For those interested in further research on the Canadian labour movement, without any question the best sources can be found in the government document section of any good library. In 1900 one of the first decisions of the newly appointed deputy minister of labour was to publish a monthly report on labour activities throughout the country. This was perhaps Mackenzie King's greatest legacy to historians of the Canadian working class. The *Labour Gazette*, appearing every month for nearly eighty years, is an unequalled mine of information on our trade-union movement. Sadly, in order to save a small amount of money, in 1978 the federal government senselessly ordered its termination. Fortunately, it did not liquidate another of King's creations, and an excellent source as well, the Department of Labour's *Annual Report on Labour Organization*. Another treasure-chest of information are the various Royal Commissions set up by both federal and provincial governments to investigate aspects of working-class life and conditions in this country. Their reports, and often the evidence on which these reports are based, can be found in most research libraries. They provide an almost inexhaustible source for the student of Canadian labour and social history. The most important of these commissions are the 1889 study on the Relations of Labour and Capital, the 1896 study on the sweating system, the 1903 investigation of railway workers, the 1904 exposé of Italian immigration, the 1907 enquiry on the Bell telephone strike, the 1913 examination of technical education, the significant 1919 survey of industrial unrest, and the 1930s commissions on price spreads, relief camps, and textile plants. There are many more, especially for the period following the Second World War.

An excellent introduction to most of this research material is Russell Hann *et al.*, eds., *Primary Sources in Canadian Working Class History 1860-1930* (Kitchener: Dumont Press 1973). Also useful to researchers is the 'Working Class Record' with articles by Abella, Hann, and Kealey in a special edition of *Archivaria* in 1977. The most comprehensive bibliography of Canadian labour is G.D. Vaisey, ed., *The Labour Companion* (H: Committee on Canadian Labour History 1980). As well, there is a regular updating of books and articles in *Labour*. Indeed, there is no better way to keep abreast of the latest developments and research in the area of Canadian labour and working-class history than by regularly reading this journal – the only one in the country devoted entirely to labour history.

CARL BERGER

Social and intellectual history

The literature on Canadian social and intellectual history varies enormously in range and quality and is quite eclectic in method. This listing is highly selective and isolates the more recent work which has clustered around the theme of the impact of industrial and urban change and upon groups and classes which found only an incidental place in traditional historical writing.

SURVEYS AND REGIONAL STUDIES

There are no comparative surveys of social developments since Confederation, certainly nothing to match R.C. Harris and J. Warkentin, *Canada at Confederation* (T: OUP 1974), which provides a superb picture of the regional societies at mid-century. In an introductory, documentary survey, *The Social Development of Canada* (T: UTP 1942), S.D. Clark focused on the problems of social dislocation that occurred in frontier areas throughout the country's past. His *Church and Sect in Canada* (T: UTP 1948) illustrates how staple exploitation in new areas led to dissatisfaction with formal and traditional religious organizations and services and ultimately to religious movements of protest. This analysis extends from the mid-eighteenth century to 1900 and the discussions of the Methodist church and the urban scene in the late nineteenth century are extremely valuable. *Canadians in the Making* (T: Longmans 1958) by Arthur Lower is a personal and opinionated disquisition on the bad effects of Calvinism, colonialism, and unselective immigration. Two collections of essays that mirror a concern with social class and class consciousness and protest are *Studies in Canadian Social History*, ed. Michiel Horn and Ronald Sabourin (T: M&S 1974), and *Prophecy and Protest: Social Movements in Twentieth-Century Canada*, ed. Samuel D. Clark, J. Paul Grayson, and Linda M. Grayson (T: Gage 1975). John Porter, *The Vertical Mosaic: An Analysis of Social Class and Power in Canada* (T: UTP 1965), is an examination of class structure and elite groups in the mid-twentieth century. This work is seminal for the range of questions it suggests about the past as well as for the richness of its historical illustrative material. Robert Craig Brown and Ramsay Cook, *Canada, 1896-1921: A Nation Transformed* (T: M&S 1974), interprets these crucial decades in terms of the repercusions of profound and extensive economic and social change.

Some of the best literature that explicitly relates political economy, social structure, and political culture concentrates on the regions or provinces. James Hiller and Peter Neary, eds., *Newfoundland in the Nineteenth and Twentieth Centuries* (T: UTP 1980), should be read in conjunction with S.J.R. Noel, *Politics in Newfoundland* (T: UTP 1971), which is an appraisal of a unique political culture and not merely a political history. Patrick O'Flaherty, *The Rock Observed: Studies in the Literature of Newfoundland* (T: UTP 1979), is a lively and incisive examination of literature, history, and culture. Although Ernest R. Forbes, *The Maritime Rights Movement, 1919-1927: A Study in Canadian Regionalism* (M: MQUP 1979), deals with one phase of that region's political protest against injustice, the analysis is set within a broad social and economic perspective. Jean Daigle, ed., *Les Acadiens des Maritimes: Etudes Thématique* (Moncton: Centre d'études acadiennes 1980), includes essays on education, religion, and material culture.

The major developments and issues involved in the evolution of French Canada from a rural to a predominantly industrial and urban society are set out in two excellent collections of articles, Marcel Rioux and Yves Martin, eds., *French-Canadian Society* (T: M&S 1964), and Jean C. Falardeau, éd., *Essais sur le Québec contemporain/Essays on Contemporary Quebec* (Q: PUL 1953). An important and revisionist work, William F. Ryan, *The Clergy and Economic Growth in Quebec (1896-1914)* (Q: PUL 1966), challenges the view that the church impeded economic growth by analysing the encouragement that the clergy gave to various industrial enterprises in an effort to retain French Canadians within the province. The general conclusion is that there were no ascertainable theological barriers to economic growth but rather that the failure of French Canadians to control their own economic development arose from accidental circumstances. This is but one aspect of a complex debate over the question of the 'economic inferiority' of French Canada, a debate which involves not only questions of economics but also of culture and social values generally. A collection of articles representing a variety of approaches to this problem is René Durocher and Paul-André Linteau, éds., *Le 'Retard' du Québec et l'infériorité économique des Canadiens français* (TR: BE 1971). Michel Brunet, 'Trois dominantes de la pensée canadienne-française: l'agriculturisme, l'anti-étatisme et le messianisme,' in his *Présence anglaise et les Canadiens* (M: Beauchemin 1958) is a classic dissection of the elements of the traditional French-Canadian outlook which are held to have impeded that society's ability to control its own economic life. Jean Hulliger, *L'enseignement social des évêques canadiens de 1891-1950* (M: Fides 1950), is a useful but not profound analysis of the social pronouncements of the clergy based on their public statements. Much has been written about the exodus of French Canadians to the United States and A. Faucher, 'L'émigration des Canadiens français au XIXe siècle: Position du problème et perspectives,' *Recherches sociographiques*, 1964, is a good introduction to this literature and the problems of the topic.

Paul-André Linteau, René Durocher, and Jean-Claude Robert, *Histoire du Québec contemporain de la Confédération à la crise (1867-1939)* (Q: BE 1979; trans. T: Lorimer 1982), is generally successful in providing a comprehensive analysis of French-Canadian society that is firmly based on economic and class factors. Both Denis Monière, *Le développement des idéologies au Québec: des origines à nos jours* (M: Editions Québec/Amérique 1977; trans. T: UTP 1981), and Gilles Bourque and Nicole Laurin-Frenette, 'Classes sociales et idéologies nationalistes au Québec (1760-1970),' *Socialisme québécois*,

1970, are more notable for their points of view than for the freshness of their material. There is a good listing of additional literature in René Durocher and Paul-André Linteau, *Histoire du Québec: bibliographie sélective (1867-1970)* (TR: BE 1970).

For Ontario, G.P. de T. Glazebrook, *Life in Ontario: A Social History* (T: UTP 1968), is rather conventional and descriptive; Donald Swainson, ed., *Oliver Mowat's Ontario* (T: MAC 1972), includes, in addition to studies in politics, a delightful evocation of an 'un-Victorian' society by Peter Waite, and important essays on the prohibition movement in the nineties, social change in rural Ontario, and the flight from competition among businessmen. The conclusions of a recent effort to analyse the social realities of mid-nineteenth-century Hamilton, Ontario, through the statistical analysis of patterns of class and social structure are presented in publications by Michael Katz: 'Social Structure in Hamilton, Ontario,' in Stephen Thernstrom and Richard Sennett, eds., *Nineteenth-Century Cities: Essays in the New Urban History* (New Haven: Yale UP 1969); 'The People of a Canadian City: 1851-2,' CHR, 1972; and *The People of Hamilton, Canada West: Family and Class in a Mid-Nineteenth-Century City* (Cambridge, Harvard UP 1975). A similar approach to a rural district, which illustrates how the shortage of land in a mature agricultural community affected the family, life experiences, and social mobility, is David Gagan, *Hopeful Travellers: Families, Land, and Social Change in Mid-Victorian Peel County, Canada West* (T: UTP 1981). Olga Bishop, comp., *Bibliography of Ontario History, 1867-1976*, 2 vols. (T: UTP 1980), is an exhaustive inventory of all aspects of the province, including social developments.

Few regions have as rich and extensive a literature of social history as western Canada, as may be seen in Alan F. Artibise, comp., *Western Canada since 1870: A Select Bibliography* (V: UBCP 1978). Histories of provinces – such as W.L. Morton, *Manitoba: A History* (T: UTP 1957), or John Archer, *Saskatchewan: A History* (Saskatoon: Western Producer Prairie Books 1980), necessarily pay a good deal of attention to the moulding of distinctive agricultural societies. Doug Owram, *Promise of Eden: The Canadian Expansionist Movement and the Idea of the West, 1856-1900* (T: UTP 1980), examines how perceptions of the Prairies changed from that of an inhospitable wilderness to that of a garden, and how eastern Canadian expansionists who actually settled in the west became in effect exponents of a regional outlook. R.C. MacLeod, *The Northwest Mounted Police and Law Enforcement, 1873-1905* (T: UTP 1976), analyses the institutional and social character of the force and the interplay between the police and society. Thomas Flanagan, *Louis 'David' Riel: Prophet of the New World* (T: UTP 1979), attempts to make sense of the Métis leader's religious ideas in terms of messianic movements that sprang up elsewhere among similar downtrodden groups. John H. Thompson's *The Harvests of War: The Prairie West, 1914-1918* (T: M&S 1978) explores the impact of war on industry and agriculture, ethnic relations, politics, and reform. The theme of the literary imagination coming to terms with a new and unknown landscape and society is traced out in Dick Harrison, *Unnamed Country: The Struggle for a Canadian Prairie Fiction* (Edmonton: University of Alberta Press 1977).

Two fine collections of articles on the Pacific coast are J. Friesen and H.K. Ralston, eds., *Historical Essays on British Columbia*, which contains a select bibliography (T: M&S 1976), and W. Peter Ward and Robert A.J. McDonald, eds., *British Columbia: Historical Readings* (V: Douglas and McIntyre 1981), which highlights labour history and industrial conflict, urban growth, economic and business history, and race relations.

An able analysis of frontier expansion is presented in Morris Zaslow, *The Opening of the Canadian North, 1870-1914* (T: M&S 1971), which contains a particularly illuminating assessment of the goldrush society of the Yukon and a comparison of settlement in northern Ontario and Quebec.

A listing of new literature in social, intellectual, and cultural history is to be found in each issue of the *Canadian Historical Review*, and the main journals devoted to regional or provincial history – *Acadiensis*, *Revue d'histoire de l'Amérique française*, *Ontario History*, and *BC Studies* – not only report on recent publications but sometimes contain bibliographies of works on special themes in social history. *Histoire sociale/Social History*, though not exclusively Canadian in focus, also publishes occasional bibliographies, such as the listing by André Larose of current work on population and demographic studies (May 1979).

URBAN STUDIES

The best introduction to recent urban studies is Gilbert A. Stelter and Alan F.J. Artibise, eds., *The Canadian City: Essays in Urban History* (T: M&S 1977), which contains studies of metropolitan growth and urban society, and also a reflective survey of approaches to the field and a selective bibliography. Artibise and Stelter have also prepared a detailed bibliography (V: UBCP 1981), together with an excellent introductory essay. The programmatic statement of the metropolitan approach which called attention to the need to trace the relationship between urban communities and their hinterlands is J.M.S. Careless, 'Frontierism, Metropolitanism, and Canadian History,' in C. Berger, ed., *Approaches to Canadian History* (T: UTP 1967). Jacob Spelt, *Urban Development of South-Central Ontario* (1955; T: M&S 1973), analyses the political, geographic, and economic factors behind Toronto's dominance over the region; a more limited but still useful survey is D.C. Masters, *The Rise of Toronto, 1850-1890* (T: UTP 1947). Though a rather difficult book, *Victorian Toronto, 1850 to 1900: Pattern and Process of Growth* (Chicago: University of Chicago Press 1970) by Peter Goheen is especially notable for its explanation of class segregation within the city. A balanced and informative but all too brief account of the relations of classes and ethnic groups within another metropolis is given in J.I. Cooper, *Montreal* (M: MQUP 1969). A.F.J. Artibise, *Winnipeg: A Social History of Urban Growth, 1874-1914* (M: MQUP 1975), provides an excellent survey of the processes of growth, class and ethnic segregation, and urban politics of that prairie centre.

Three selections of essays provide a disconnected but still illuminating picture of urban centres on the prairies: Anthony W. Rasporich and Henry Klassen, eds., *Frontier Calgary: Town, City, and Region, 1875-1914* (Calgary: M&S West 1975); A.R. McCormack and Ian Macpherson eds., *Cities in the West* (O: National Museum of Man, Mercury Series 1975), contains both general papers on the urban frontier as well as research on such subjects as municipal politics, sport, and businessmen and reform; and Alan F. Artibise, ed., *Town and City: Aspects of Western Canadian Urban Development* (Regina: Canadian Plains Research Center 1981). The National Museum of Man is sponsoring the publication of a series of illustrated histories of Canadian centres: three volumes have appeared – Alan Artibise, *Winnipeg* (T: Lorimer 1977); Max Foran, *Calgary* (T: Lorimer 1978); and Patricia Roy, *Vancouver* (T: Lorimer 1980). General overviews of the urban reform movements are to be found in Paul Rutherford, 'Tomorrow's Metropolis: the Urban Reform Movement in Canada, 1880-1920,' CHAR, 1971; John C. Weaver, *Shaping the Canadian City: Essays on Urban Politics and Policy, 1890-1920* (Monographs on Canadian Urban Government, Institute of Public Administration of Canada 1977); and C. Armstrong and H.V. Nelles, *The Revenge of the Methodist Bicycle Company: Sunday Streetcars and Municipal Reform in Toronto, 1888-1897* (T: Peter Martin 1977). The chief journal in Canadian urban studies is the *Urban History Review/Revue d'histoire urbaine*.

LABOUR AND BUSINESS

Labour history or, more exactly, the history of the working class, has become one of the most vital and exciting aspects of Canadian historical writing. Since a separate section is devoted to it in this volume, only those works of the most general interest are mentioned here. Gregory S. Kealey and Peter Warrian, eds., *Essays in Canadian Working Class History* (T: M&S 1976), presents not only a program of the 'new' labour history but substantial illustrations of how valuable the approach can be in reinterpreting familiar subjects like the Orange Order and developing new ones like the artisan traditions of the Toronto printers. Two studies of work, wages, and standards of living of the urban working class are Michael Piva, *The Condition of the Working Class in Toronto, 1900-1921* (O: University of Ottawa Press 1979), and Terry Copp, *The Anatomy of Poverty: The Condition of the Working Class in Montreal, 1897-1929* (T: M&S 1974), the second of which attributes the low income of labour to structural rather than cultural peculiarities of the port city. Gregory

S. Kealey, *Toronto Workers Respond to Industrial Capitalism, 1867-1892* (T: UTP 1980), demonstrates in great detail how factory production undermined the relatively independent status of skilled workers, and how the working class adapted to the new society through unions and participation in politics. A more controversial study, Bryan Palmer, *A Culture in Conflict: Skilled Workers and Industrial Capitalism in Hamilton, Ontario, 1860-1914* (M: MQUP 1979), argues that these workers attained not only a high degree of class consciousness but an independent culture as expressed in their associational activities, traditions, reform ideology, and unions. *Reformers, Rebels, and Revolutionaries: The Western Canadian Radical Movement, 1899-1919* (T: UTP 1977) by A. Ross McCormack is a fine, discriminating analysis that does full justice to reform and revolutionary ideologies. A succinct and incisive analysis of the status of unskilled Central and Eastern European immigrant workers and their radical ethnic and political associations is offered in Donald Avery, *'Dangerous Foreigners': European Immigrant Workers and Labour Radicalism in Canada, 1896-1932* (T: M&S 1979). An institutional study that is especially good on the church and the working class is Jacques Rouillard, *Les synicats nationaux au Québec de 1900 à 1930* (Q: PUL 1979).

F.W. Watt, 'The National Policy, the Workingman, and Proletarian Ideas in Victorian Canada,' CHR, 1959, analyses the attitudes of the more radical fringe of labour spokesmen in Ontario toward capitalism in the late nineteenth century, and Ramsay Cook, 'Henry George and the Poverty of Canadian Progress,' CHAR, 1976, deals with one influential strand in early labour thought. The writings of one radical have been collected in *The Politics of Labour* by T. Phillips Thompson (1887; T: UTP 1975).

Additional literature is listed in G. Douglas Vaisey, comp., *The Labour Companion: A Bibliography of Canadian Labour History based on Materials printed from 1950 to 1975* (Halifax: Committee on Canadian Labour History 1980). The best recent work is to be found in the journal *Labour/Le Travailleur*.

In contrast to labour studies, the social – as distinct from the economic – history of business is thin and undernourished. Glen Porter and Robert D. Cuff, eds., *Enterprise and National Develop-*

ment: Essays in Canadian Business and Economic History (T: Hakkert 1973), contains a good analysis by T.W. Acheson of 'Changing Social Origins of the Canadian Industrial Elite,' and Michael Bliss, *A Living Profit: Studies in the Social History of Canadian Business, 1883-1911* (T: M&S 1974), is especially informative on the formation of self-protective associations and on the ways in which business spokesmen perceived success, competition, the tariff, and labour. The latter's *A Canadian Millionaire: The Life and Times of Sir Joseph Flavelle, Bart. 1859-1939* (T: MAC 1978) is a splendid full-scale biography dealing with business practices and touching upon an astonishing range of subjects including Methodism, philanthropy, and domestic architecture.

WOMEN'S HISTORY

The dominant themes in this field are the changing economic and social status of women and the movement for political and social equality. *Women at Work: Ontario 1850-1930*, ed. Janice Acton *et al.* (T: Women's Educational Press 1974), offers a series of essays on females in the workforce. Catherine L. Cleverdon, *The Woman Suffrage Movement in Canada* (1950; T: UTP 1974), is a complete account of the struggle for the franchise. *The Proper Sphere: Woman's Place in Canadian Society*, ed. Ramsay Cook and Wendy Mitchison (T: OUP 1976), a selection of documents, presents a full picture of legal rights, education, work, organizations, and prescriptive morality. Three collections of studies that deal with both work and reform are Susan Mann Trofimenkoff and Alison Prentice, eds., *The Neglected Majority: Essays in Canadian Women's History* (T: M&S 1977), which ranges from the feminization of the teaching profession and the evolution of national organizations to the recruitment of women into the labour force in World War II; Marie Lavigne and Yolande Pinard, *Les femmes dans la société québécoise* (M: BE 1977), which includes studies of the participation of women in the labour force in Montreal and the struggle for the provincial suffrage; Linda Kealey, ed., *A Not Unreasonable Claim: Women and Reform in Canada, 1880s-1920s* (T: Women's Educational Press 1979), contains, in addition to an informative introduction placing the feminist movement into historical context, essays dealing with the revolt against dependency, female medical doctors, and the Women's Christian Temperance Union. Georgina Binnie-Clark, *Wheat and Woman* (1914; T: UTP 1979), is an autobiographical account of an observant and determined homesteader. The experiences of a female medical student are conveyed in V. Strong-Boag, ed., *A Woman with a Purpose: The Diaries of Elizabeth Smith, 1872-1884* (T: UTP 1980). More directly related to the politics of reform is Nellie McClung's *In Times Like These* (1915; T: UTP 1972), an illuminating statement by an early feminist on the ideology of social regeneration; Ramsay Cook, 'Francis Marion Beynon and the Crisis of Christian Reformism,' *The West and the Nation*, ed. C. Berger and R. Cook (T: M&S 1976), is a penetrating critique of this strain of utopianism in feminist and social gospel thought. V. Strong-Boag, *The Parliament of Women: The National Council of Women of Canada, 1893-1929* (O: Museum of Man 1976), traces the remarkably diverse concerns of this organization through the high-tide of optimism to the deflation of reform in the twenties. Another reminder of how little things changed after a whole generation of effort is her 'The Girl of the New Day: Canadian Working Women in the 1920s,' *Labour/Le Travailleur*, 1979.

The fullest guide to the literature in this field is Beth Light and V. Strong-Boag, comps., *True Daughters of the North: Canadian Women's History – An Annotated Bibliography* (T: OISE 1980). *Atlantis: A Woman's Studies Journal/Journal d'études sur la femme* contains a number of articles on women's history.

ETHNICITY AND IMMIGRATION

The literature on immigration and particularly the history of specific ethnic groups other than French or British is extensive, as may be seen even in such a limited listing as Andrew Gregorovich, *Canadian Ethnic Groups Bibliography* (T: Ontario Department of the Provincial Secretary 1972), or in the occasional bibliographies published in *Canadian Ethnic Studies/Etudes ethniques au Canada*. A few of the more adequate studies of individual groups and their place in the social and political milieu are George Woodcock and Ivan Avakumovic, *The Doukhobors* (T: OUP 1968); Robin Winks, *The Blacks in Canada* (New Haven: Yale UP 1971); J.G. MacGregor, *Vilni Zemli* (Free Lands): the *Ukrainian Settlement of Alberta* (T: M&S 1969); John Norris, *Strangers Entertained: A History of the Ethnic Groups of British Columbia* (V: BC Centennial Committee 1971); Frank H. Epp, *Mennonites in Canada, 1786-1920: The History of a Separate People* (T: MAC 1974); and Howard Palmer, *Land of the Second Chance: A History of Ethnic Groups in Southern Alberta* (Lethbridge: Lethbridge Herald 1972). Stephen A. Speisman, *The Jews of Toronto* (T: M&S 1980), a fine study, is especially sensitive to tensions within that community. Robert F. Harney and J.V. Scarpaci, eds., *Little Italies in North America* (T: Multicultural History Society of Ontario 1981), includes studies of the Italian communities in Montreal, Toronto, and the Lakehead. And Frances Swyripa, *Ukrainian Canadians: A Survey of their Portrayal in English-Language Works* (Edmonton: Institute of Ukrainian Studies 1978), is far more than a bibliographical inventory.

More limited works that are still useful both for detail and their points of view are Wilhelm Kristjanson, *The Icelandic People in Manitoba* (Winnipeg: Wallingford Press 1965); Victor Peters, *All Things Common: The Hutterian Way of Life* (Minneapolis: University of Minnesota Press 1965); B.G. Sack, *History of the Jews in Canada* (M: Harvest House 1965); Mykhailo Marunchak, *The Ukrainian Canadians: A History* (Winnipeg: Ukrainian Free Academy of Sciences 1970); Wiktor Turek, *The Poles in Manitoba* (T: Polish Research Institute of Canada 1967); John Gellner and John Smerk, *The Czechs and Slovaks in Canada* (T: UTP 1968). In addition, the first six volumes of Generations: A History of Canada's Peoples have been published by McClelland and Stewart for the Multiculturalism Program of the Department of the Secretary of State. These are Grace Anderson and David Higgs, *A Future to Inherit: Portuguese Communities in Canada* (1976); Henry Radecki with Benedykt Heydenkorn, *A Member of a Distinguished Family: The Polish Group in Canada* (1976); W.S. Reid, ed., *The Scottish Tradition in Canada* (1976); G. Loken, *From Fjord to Frontier: A History of the Norwegians in Canada* (1980); P.D. Chimbos, *The Canadian Odyssey: The Greek Experience in Canada* (1980); and Baha Abu-Laban, *An Olive Branch on the Family Tree*, on the Arabs in Canada (1980).

Though all these books touch upon Canada's immigration policy, three articles focus upon it more directly: David Hall, 'Clifford Sifton: Immigration and Settlement Policy, 1896-1905,' in H. Palmer, ed., in *Settlement of the Prairie West* (Calgary: University of Calgary 1977); Donald Avery, 'Canadian Immigration Policy and the Foreign Navy, 1896-1914,' CHAR, 1972, which argues that while policy at the turn of the century aimed mainly at recruiting farmer settlers, it increasingly also sought to import an industrial proletariat; and Irving Abella and Harold Troper, '"The line must be drawn somewhere": Canada and Jewish Refugees, 1933-39,' CHR, 1979, a scathing indictment of prejudice and indifference. Gerald Dirks, *Canada's Refugee Policy: Indifference or Opportunism?* (M: MQUP 1978), deals with the period since 1930.

Attitudes towards Oriental immigrants and exclusionist policies have been examined in three exceptionally good monographs. W. Peter Ward, *White Canada Forever: Popular Attitudes and Public Policy toward Orientals in British Columbia* (M: MQUP 1978), traces the evolving stereotype from the mid-nineteenth century to the decision to evacuate the Japanese-Canadians from the West coast during the Second World War. Hugh Johnston, *The Voyage of the Komagata Maru: The Sikh Challenge to Canada's Colour Bar* (Delhi: OUP 1979), examines not only Canada's rejection of these people but the repercussions of their return to India. And Ken Adachi, *The Enemy that Never Was: A History of the Japanese Canadians* (T: M&S 1976), is noteworthy both for its portrayal of generational differences within that community and its wealth of detail on the evacuation.

One of the most pathetic groups of Canada's immigrants were the some eighty thousand children sent out by British philanthropic organizations between 1880 and 1930. The background, institutional setting, and dispersal in Canada has been analyzed in J.G. Parr, *Labouring Children: British Immigrant Apprentices to Canada, 1869-1924* (M: MQUP 1980); and the experience of individuals has been evoked in Kenneth Bagnell, *The Little Immigrants* (T: MAC 1980).

Three thoughtful and provocative articles dealing with the general question of the degree to which ethnic groups were compelled to assimilate to a single pattern are J.E. Rea, 'The Roots of Prairie Society,' in D. Gagan, ed., *Prairie Perspectives* (T: HRW 1970); Allan Smith, 'Metaphor and Nationality in North America,' CHR, 1970; and Howard Palmer, 'Mosaic versus Melting Pot? Immigration and Ethnicity in Canada and the United States,' *International Journal*, 1976.

David E. Smith, *Prairie Liberalism: The Liberal Party in Saskatchewan, 1905-71* (T: UTP 1975), examines a concrete case of the integration of immigrant voters into a provincial political machine and the defeat of that party by an outburst of nativism and prejudice in the election of 1929. There is no better source for understanding the emotional and human dimensions of the experience of a young boy from an immigrant background accommodating himself to the dominant Anglo-Saxon culture than John Marlyn's novel, *Under the Ribs of Death* (T: M&S 1957).

POLITICAL AND SOCIAL THOUGHT

Much of the best literature on Canadian politics has been in the form of political biographies, and these must necessarily provide the basis for any assessment of Canadian political thought and traditions. George P. de T. Glazebrook, *A History of Canadian Political Thought* (T: UTP 1966), is not a systematic examination of political ideas but a series of extended reflections on Canadian political problems. There are, however, a relatively large number of essays, written for the most part by political biographers, which attempt to summarize in a general fashion the major convictions and beliefs of their subjects. J.M.S. Careless, the biographer of the Liberal George Brown, for example, has examined the impact of British Manchester liberalism and its modifications in the colonial environment in 'Mid-Victorianism in Central Canadian Newspapers, 1850-67,' CHR, 1950, and 'The Toronto *Globe* and Agrarian Radicalism, 1850-67,' CHR, 1948, and gave a short assessment of his subject in 'George Brown' in *Our Living Tradition*, Second and Third Series, ed. Robert L. McDougall (T: UTP 1959). F.H. Underhill analysed Canadian liberalism in the generation after Confederation in a number of essays, among them 'Political Ideas of the Upper Canadian Reformers, 1867-1878,' in his *In Search of Canadian Liberalism* (T: MAC 1960), and 'Edward Blake and Liberal Nationalism,' in *Essays in Canadian History* (T: UTP 1939), ed. R. Flenley. J.D. Livermore, 'The Personal Agonies of Edward Blake,' CHR, 1975, is a brilliant examination of his psychology and mental agonies. D.G. Creighton, 'Sir John A. Macdonald,' in *Our Living Tradition: Seven Canadians* (T: UTP 1957), ed. C.T. Bissell, is a forceful defence of the Conservative leader's conviction that Canadian survival could only be ensured by a centralized federation and the alliance with Britain. Though J.K. Johnson, 'John A. Macdonald,' in *The Pre-Confederation Premiers: Ontario Government Leaders, 1841-1867,* ed. J.M.S. Careless (T: UTP 1980), deals with the early years, the observations made about Macdonald's political style and his business involvements and contacts are most suggestive for understanding his entire career.

The ideology of imperialism has been analysed in C. Berger, *The Sense of Power: Studies in the Ideas of Canadian Imperialism, 1867-1914* (T: UTP 1970), which suggests how English-Canadian nationalism fused a loyalty to Canada with a deep commitment to the British empire, and in Robert Page, 'Canada and the Imperial Idea in the Boer War Years,' JCS, 1970. The life and ideas of the leading critic of imperialism in Canada and an advocate of continental unity are lucidly analysed in Elizabeth Wallace, *Goldwin Smith: Victorian Liberal* (T: UTP 1957). The best source of Smith's thought is his *Canada and the Canadian Question* (1891; T: UTP 1972). J.R. Miller, *Equal Rights: The Jesuits' Estates Act Controversy* (M: MQUP 1979), adds much to our understanding of the French-English cultural conflicts of the late eighties by thoroughly examining the sense of crisis over the future of Confederation and explaining the social concerns of the advocate of 'equal rights.' A.I. Silver, *The French-Canadian Idea of Confederation, 1864-1900* (T: UTP 1982), is an important analysis of the way in which French-Canadian opinion changed from an almost exclusive concern with the future of the culture in Quebec to an intense concern with the minority throughout a bicultural country.

A rather uneven collection, *The Political Ideas of the Prime Ministers of Canada* (Ottawa: University of Ottawa Press 1968), ed. Marcel Hamelin, contains short assessments of Sir Robert Borden by R.C. Brown, Arthur Meighen by Roger Graham, and W.L.M. King by Blair Neatby. Perhaps the most revealing source for Mackenzie King's convictions about the nature of society, politics, and unseen forces is his *Industry and Humanity* (1919; T: UTP 1973). Reginald Whitaker, 'The Liberal Corporatist Ideas of Mackenzie King,' *Labour*, 1977, is a superb interpretation of King's enduring views on class relations and the question of resolving industrial conflict. Paul Craven, *'An Impartial Empire': Industrial Relations and the Canadian State, 1900-1911* (T: UTP 1980), not only examines King's intellectual development but shows how his views moulded Canada's policy on labour and capital. John English, *The Decline of Politics: The Conservatives and the Party System, 1901-20* (T: UTP 1977), is an exemplary social and intellectual study of the transformation of politics. The role of one ideological obstacle to a recognition of the problems of an industrial society is assessed in Allan Smith, 'The Myth of the Self-Made Man in English Canada, 1850-1914,' CHR, 1978. J.H.R. Wilbur, 'R.B. Bennett as a Reformer,' CHR, 1969, deals with the question of the seriousness of that conservative Prime Minister's belated commitment to reform. In a provocative essay at the beginning of his *Canadian Labour in Politics* (T: UTP 1968), Gad Horowitz advanced the notion that Canadian political culture possessed a 'tory touch' which explained not only why socialism appeared stronger in Canada than in the United States, but also why conservatives like Bennett sometimes resorted, without any serious inhibitions, to the use of state power to ensure national ends.

The essays collected in *Idéologies au Canada français, 1850-1900*, dir. Fernand Dumont, Jean-Paul Montminy et Jean Hamelin (Q: PUL 1971), and *Idéologies au Canada français, 1900-1929*, dir. Fernand Dumont, Jean Hamelin, Fernand Harvey, et Jean-Paul Montminy (Q: PUL 1974), provide good introductions to the preoccupations of the intellectuals, the press, and the clergy. The social thought of the French-Canadian nationalist movement which centred on Henri Bourassa in the two decades after 1900 has been analysed in Joseph Levitt, *Henri Bourassa and the Golden Calf: The Social Program of the Nationalists of Quebec, 1900-1914* (O: University of Ottawa Press 1969), which finds that Bourassa's attempt to come to terms with economic changes was moulded by his moralism and above all by his fear that any enhancement of the power of the secular state would decrease that of the church to which he gave his primary allegiance. The other two main subjects of the nationalist program are generously represented in *Henri Bourassa on Imperialism and Bi-culturalism 1900-1918* (T: CC 1970), ed. Joseph Levitt. Ramsay Cook, ed., *French-Canadian Nationalism* (T: MAC 1969), is a very useful anthology of nationalist advocacy and analysis ranging from the mid-nineteenth century to the Quiet Revolution of the 1960s. An indispensible older work by a foreign observer, André Siegfried, *The Race Question in Canada* (1970; T: M&S 1966), offers a penetrating analysis of the different outlooks of the two peoples and is effective in isolating the religious bases of these outlooks.

The standard account of the nationalist movement in the interwar period is Michael Oliver, 'The Social and Political Ideas of French Canadian Nationalists, 1920-1945' (PHD thesis, McGill University 1956). Susan M. Trofimenkoff, ed., *Abbé Groulx: Variations on a Nationalist Theme* (T: CC 1973), is an introduction to the thought of the major figure, and her *Action Française: French Canadian Nationalism in the Twenties* (T: UTP 1975) offers a lucid account of the organization which he founded. His autobiography, *Mes mémoires*, 4 vols. (M: Fides 1970-4), and J.-P. Gaboury, *Le nationalisme de Lionel Groulx* (O: University of Ottawa Press 1970), are helpful for an understanding of the historical mythology underpinning his outlook.

SOCIAL REFORM AND PROTEST

Canadian development in the period after 1880 generated a considerable volume of social criticism and a middle-class, moralistic, reform movement which reached its climax during World War I. This general progressive impulse included urban reform, temperance, and female suffrage but its common denominator was a revival of social concern among the Protestant denominations. Historians of religious institutions have not generally paid much attention to the influence of religious conviction in the broad social sense but a survey, *The Christian Church in Canada* (T: Ryerson 1956), by

H.H. Walsh, does describe the problems faced by the churches and the major religious developments in a lucid, summary fashion. John Moir, *Enduring Witness: A History of the Presbyterian Church in Canada* (T: Presbyterian Church in Canada 1974), deals very effectively with one denomination's contributions to social service and missions and contains a lucid account of the church union movement. The crucial work for understanding the 'social gospel' is Richard Allen's *The Social Passion: Religion and Social Reform in Canada, 1914-28* (T: UTP 1971), in which the desire to create the kingdom of God on earth is seen as the master impulse behind the reform movements, and an attempt is made not to analyse its ideology abstractly but to trace its impact in concrete action relating to the labour churches, church union, prohibition, social work, the Winnipeg General Strike, and the Progressive party. One major figure in the movement, J.S. Woodsworth, is the subject of a sympathetic biography, *A Prophet in Politics* (T: UTP 1959), by Kenneth McNaught, and two of his works have been recently reprinted; *Strangers within our Gates* (1909; T: UTP 1972) deals with the challenge of massive immigration, and *My Neighbor* (1911; T: UTP 1972) with conditions in the growing cities, and the need for urban reform.

Gerald Hallowell's *Prohibition in Ontario, 1919-1923* (T: Ontario Historical Society 1972) is a detailed appraisal of the success of prohibition, the difficulties in enforcing it, and its eventual repudiation. Graeme Decarie, 'Something Old, Something New ...: Aspects of Prohibitionism in Ontario in the 1890s,' in *Oliver Mowat's Ontario*, ed. D. Swainson (T: MAC 1972), is a sardonic analysis of the motives behind the campaign for the abolition of the use of liquor. The abuse of alcohol and the prohibition movement in another region has been colorfully examined in James Gray, *Booze: The Impact of Whiskey on the Prairie West* (T: MAC 1972), and its connection with another 'social evil' is developed in his equally sensationalist study of prostitution, *Red Lights on the Prairies* (T: MAC 1971). E. Forbes, 'Prohibition and the Social Gospel in Nova Scotia,' *Acadiensis*, 1971, is a very fine study of the abandonment of the prohibition experiment in favour of government control. Clifford Rose, *Four Years with Demon Rum*, ed. E.R. Forbes and A.A. MacKenzie (Fredericton: Acadiensis Press 1980), offers a mordant and ironical comment on the prohibition experiment in Nova Scotia by a one-time inspector.

The social roots and ideas of farmer protest during the first three decades of the century have been treated in such essentially political studies as W.L. Morton, *The Progressive Party in Canada* (T: UTP 1950), and Paul Sharp, *The Agrarian Revolt in Western Canada* (Minneapolis: University of Minnesota Press 1948). C.B. Macpherson, *Democracy in Alberta* (T: UTP 1953), contains an excellent analysis of the political philosophy of the United Farmers of Alberta based on the writings of Henry Wise Wood and William Irvine as well as a convincing explanation of how their ideas of government based on economic groups was a rationalization of the peculiar features of the prairie economy. W.L. Morton, 'Social and Political Philosophy of Henry Wise Wood,' *Agricultural History*, 1948, is a useful assessment. W.R. Young, 'Conscription, Rural Depopulation, and the Farmers of Ontario, 1917-19,' CHR, 1972, is a good study of the social background of the surge of farmer protest in the province at the end of the First World War. W.C. Good's autobiography, *Farmer Citizen* (T: Ryerson 1958), is an honest and illuminating statement of the farmers' case seen in retrospect. Ian Macpherson, *Each for All: A History of the Co-operative Movement in English Canada, 1900-1945* (T: MAC 1979), does full justice to the variety of interest groups involved, including the Prairie wheat growers and Maritime fishermen.

Considerable attention has been devoted to the Depression and especially its impact on Prairie society and political radicalism. James Gray, *The Winter Years: The Depression on the Prairies* (T: MAC 1966), is a memoir of that period illuminating life in Winnipeg, the relief system, and make-work projects, and, to a lesser extent, revealing conditions of life in rural areas. A more systematic economic study of the effects of the Depression on income and expenditure, provincial and municipal institutions, standards of living, and rehabilitation in Saskatchewan is George Britnell, *The Wheat Economy* (T: UTP 1939). A fine article which describes the relief system is Blair Neatby, 'The Saskatchewan Relief Commission, 1931-1934,' in D. Swainson, ed., *Historical Essays on the Prairie Provinces* (T: M&S 1970). A documentary collection edited by Michiel Horn,

The Dirty Thirties: Canadians in the Great Depression (T: CC 1972), illustrates governmental policy at all levels. *Recollections of the On-to-Ottawa Trek by Ronald Liversedge with Documents Related to the Vancouver Strike and the On-to-Ottawa Trek* (T: M&S 1973), ed. Victor Hoar, contains a radical's description of conditions in the camps for the single unemployed and the Regina riot. Lita-Rose Betcherman, *The Swastika and the Maple Leaf: Fascist Movements in Canada in the Thirties* (T: Fitzhenry & Whiteside 1975), concentrates on anti-semitic groups – some insignificant; others, like Adrien Arcand's National Social Christian party, of more than passing curiosity.

The political protest movements of the 1930s – particularly the Cooperative Commonwealth Federation and the Social Credit Movement – have been studied in numerous works, two of which, S.M. Lipset's *Agrarian Socialism: The Cooperative Commonwealth Federation in Saskatchewan: A Study in Political Sociology* (NY: Anchor 1968) and John A. Irving, *The Social Credit Movement in Alberta* (T: UTP 1959), are fine examples of social-intellectual history. David R. Elliott, 'Antithetical Elements in William Aberhart's Theology and Political Ideology,' CHR, 1978, and 'William Aberhart: Right or Left,' in *The Dirty Thirties in Prairie Canada*, ed. R.D. Francis and H. Ganzevoort (V: Tantalus 1980), are convincing explanations of the Social Credit leader's curious combination of fundamentalist religion and progressivism. Michiel Horn, *The League for Social Reconstruction: Intellectual Origins of the Democratic Left in Canada, 1930-1942* (T: UTP 1980), is a comprehensive assessment of the reformist intellectuals and their role in the national CCF. Norman Penner, *The Canadian Left: A Critical Analysis*, is best on the ideology of the Communist party in the interwar years; Ivan Avakamovic, *The Communist Party of Canada: A History* (T: M&S 1975), is a full-scale institutional study.

The pattern of Prairie protest has generated several thoughtful inquiries both on the nature of populism and on the problem of explaining the apparent divergent political traditions of Alberta and Saskatchewan. Three especially penetrating articles are V. Conway, 'The Prairie Populist Response to the National Policy,' JCS, 1979; P. Sinclair, 'Class Structure and Populist Protest,' *Society and Politics in*

Alberta, ed. Carlo Caldarola (T: Methuen 1979); and N. Wiseman, 'The Pattern of Prairie Politics,' QQ, 1981. Roger Gibbins, *Prairie Politics & Society: Regionalism in Decline* (T: Butterworth 1980), is an effective analysis of developments since World War II.

SOCIAL WELFARE

The essential outlines of the evolution of the welfare state are given in Richard B. Splane, *Social Welfare in Ontario, 1791-1893* (T: UTP 1965), and Denis Guest, *The Emergence of Social Security in Canada* (V: UBCP 1980). An informative biography of the first superintendent of neglected and dependent children in Ontario is Andrew Jones and Leonard Rutman, *In the Children's Aid: J.J. Kelso and Child Welfare in Ontario* (T: UTP 1980). A fine survey of broad scope, Neil Sutherland, *Children in English-Canadian Society* (T: UTP 1976), deals not only with 'progressive' education but also with the public health movement and the treatment of juvenile delinquents. A special issue of the *Journal of Canadian Studies* (spring 1979) on dependency and social welfare contains articles on health reform, mothers' allowances, and the emergence of the professional social worker, and James Struthers, 'Prelude to Depression: The Federal Government and Unemployment, 1918-29,' CHR, 1977, examines the brief life of a forward-looking initiative in social policy. Malcolm Taylor, *Health Insurance and Canadian Public Policy* (M: MQUP 1978), reconstructs the contexts of seven political decisions that cumulatively laid the basis for the country's health insurance system. The influence of the Second World War upon social welfare legislation is one of the themes in J.L. Granatstein, *Canada's War: The Politics of the Mackenzie King Government, 1939-1945* (T: OUP 1975).

PUBLIC EDUCATION

A critical survey of the development of public school systems and educational thought and practice which attempts – sometimes successfully – to relate the history of education to the social context is J. Donald Wilson, Robert M. Stamp, and Louis-Philippe Audet, eds., *Canadian Education: A History* (T: PH 1970). Louis-Philippe

Audet, *Histoire de l'enseignement du Québec*, 2 vols. (T: HRW 1971), is an able summary. Two revisionist works that interpret the evolution of the public educational system as a conservative instrument of class control are Alison Prentice, *The School Promoters: Education and Social Class in Mid-Nineteenth Century Upper Canada* (T: M&S 1977), which concentrates upon changing attitudes to children and the threats to social order from the 1840s to the 1870s, and Michael B. Katz and Paul H. Mattingly eds., *Education and Social Change: Themes from Ontario's Past* (NY: New York UP 1975). Harvey J. Graff, *The Literacy Myth: Literacy and Social Structure in the Nineteenth Century City* (NY: Academic Press 1980), is a rather contentious attempt to show, on the basis of some evidence drawn from Kingston, Hamilton, and London, that there was little connection between literacy and economic success and social mobility. Neil McDonald and Alf Chaiton, eds., *Egerton Ryerson and his Times* (T: MAC 1978), offer diversity of perspectives on a figure whose influence on public education extended to all of English Canada.

UNIVERSITIES

Older histories of universities, like W.S. Wallace, *A History of the University of Toronto, 1827-1926* (T: UTP 1927), tend to concentrate upon administrations and make little systematic effort to relate the institutions to their social settings; nor are they informative about the intellectual developments within them. Three recent official histories which go part way to remedying these defects and convey a feeling for the unique traditions of centres of higher learning are Hilda Neatby, *Queen's University*, I: *1841-1917, And Not to Yield* (M: MQUP 1978); Stanley B. Frost, *McGill University: For the Advancement of Learning*, I: *1801-1895* (M: MQUP 1980); and Charles M. Johnston, *McMaster University*, I: *The Toronto Years*; II: *The Early Years in Hamilton, 1930-1957* (T: UTP 1976, 1981). Robin S. Harris, *A History of Higher Education in Canada, 1663-1960* (T: UTP 1976), devotes most attention to the development of the curriculum and research. Harris and A. Tremblay have compiled an indispensible guide, *A Bibliography of Higher Education in Canada* (T: UTP 1960; supplements 1971, 1981).

S.E.D. Shortt, *The Search for an Ideal: Six Canadian Intellectuals and their Convictions in an Age of Transition 1890-1930* (T: UTP 1976), analyses the thought of six university figures, not only on national and social issues but also on culture and, above all, religion. An important study of far-reaching implications, A.B. McKillop, *A Disciplined Intelligence: Critical Inquiry and Canadian Thought in the Victorian Era* (M: MQUP 1979), is most informative on the philosophy taught in universities. An interesting counterpoint is Yvan Lamonde, *La philosophie et son enseignement au Québec (1665-1920)* (Q: HMH 1980).

The major forces which have shaped historical writing on Canada are examined in Carl Berger, *The Writing of Canadian History: Aspects of English Canadian Historical Literature and Thought* (T: OUP 1976), and Serge Gagnon, *Le Québec et ses historiens de 1840 à 1920: La Nouvelle France de Garneau à Groulx* (Q: PUL 1978).

Canadian economic history has been dominated by the staples thesis of H.A. Innis whose life has been sympathetically recorded by D.G. Creighton in *H.A. Innis: Portrait of a Scholar* (T: UTP 1957), and whose work has been assessed by Robin Neill in *A New Theory of Value: The Canadian Economics of H.A. Innis* (T: UTP 1972) and in a special issue of the *Journal of Canadian Studies*, winter 1977.

SCIENCE AND MEDICINE

A Curious Field-Book: Science & Society in Canadian History, ed. Trevor H. Levere and Richard A. Jarrell (T: OUP 1974), a collection of documents, and *Pioneers of Canadian Science*, ed. G.F.G. Stanley (T: UTP, Royal Society of Canada 1966), are good introductions with useful bibliographies. Morris Zaslow, *Reading the Rocks: The Story of the Geological Survey of Canada, 1842-1972* (T: MAC 1975), is an outstanding, comprehensive study of the government scientific agency. Charles F. O'Brien, *Sir William Dawson: A Life of Science and Religion* (Philadelphia: American Philosophical Society 1971), provides a rigorous analysis of the writings of a tenacious opponent of Darwin's evolution theory. Janet Foster, *Working for Wildlife: The Beginnings of Preservation in Canada* (T: UTP 1978), explores the origins and early successes of the conservation movement. S.E.D.

Shortt, ed., *Medicine in Canadian Society: Historical Perspectives* (M: MQUP 1981), is an excellent collection of articles that deals with such subjects as epidemics, birth control, pre-Freudian attitudes to sex, lunatic asylums, and the medical profession. It also includes a very useful bibliography to the literature on this topic.

THE MEDIA

A succinct survey that ranges from the rise of the press to the multi-media is Paul Rutherford, *The Making of the Canadian Media* (T: MHR 1978). His book, *A Victorian Authority: The Daily Press in Late Nineteenth-Century Canada* (T: UTP 1982), examines the popular press. M. Prang, 'The Origins of Public Broadcasting in Canada,' CHR, 1965, looks at the activities of the Canadian Radio League and other interests that advocated a national system. Two volumes by Frank Peers, *The Politics of Canadian Broadcasting, 1920-1951* and *The Public Eye: Television and the Politics of Canadian Broadcasting, 1952-1968* (T: UTP 1969, 1979), are detailed studies of policy decisions made by governments. Peter Morris, *Embattled Shadows: A History of the Canadian Cinema, 1895-1939* (M: MQUP 1978), tells the story of movie making up to the creation of the National Film Board. A partial picture of developments since then may be pieced together from Forsyth Hardy, *John Grierson: A Documentary Biography* (T: OUP 1979), and a special issue of the *Journal of Canadian Studies* on the film in English Canada, spring 1981.

SOCIETY AND CULTURE

The relationship between social and intellectual history, and imaginative literature and painting, is an extremely complex one and though there are numerous descriptive histories of literature and the arts there have been few systematic attempts to relate them in a general cultural history. The two standard guides to literature are Carl F. Klinck, ed., *Literary History of Canada* (T: UTP 1976), and Pierre de Grandpré, dir., *Histoire de la littérature française du Québec*, 4 vols. (M: Beauchemin 1967-70). Russell Harper, *Painting in Canada* (T: UTP 1966; 2nd ed., 1979), is a good introduction to both the main developments and additional writing in the field. Douglas Cole, 'The History of Canadian Art,' *Acadiensis*, 1980, discusses the chief works on painting since 1867.

General attempts to relate the themes that writers of fiction have dealt with to the culture of the country have been more notable for their boldness than for their general acceptance. Margaret Atwood, *Survival: A Thematic Guide to Canadian Literature* (T: Anansi 1972), stresses the defeatist preoccupation with mere existence in some Canadian fiction and poetry; a more convincing as well as more limited study, Ronald Sutherland, *Second Image: Comparative Studies in Quebec/Canadian Literature* (T: New Press 1971), suggests, for example, the pattern of puritanism in both literatures. Outstanding examples of occasional essays collected by two interpreters of Canadian culture are Jean-Charles Falardeau, *Notre société et son roman* (M: Beauchemin 1962), and Northrop Frye, *The Bush Garden: Essays on the Canadian Imagination* (T: Anansi 1971).

PATRICIA E. ROY

British Columbia

British Columbia's post-colonial historiography is, in many instances, a case of poverty in the midst of plenty. Entering the vast extent of British Columbia's historical literature is relatively easy, charting a course through it is more difficult, and finding first-rate material on a particular subject is more a matter of good luck than careful planning. British Columbians have always been interested in their history and the province has seldom lacked popular historians whose perspectives have tended to be parochial and whose scholarship has been uneven. There is an intellectual tradition in the province but it is more notable for its genteel qualities than for its academic discipline. Until the last decade or so rarely have more than one or two professional historians at any one time been actively engaged in the research and writing of British Columbia history. Today, at the campuses of the three provincial universities and at some of the regional colleges, courses in British Columbia history are a regular offering. Most of the teachers of such courses are themselves actively engaged in research and some supervise graduate students. Nevertheless, the writing of the history of British Columbia in the post-colonial era is still very much in a pioneering stage.

From the student's point of view, the most accessible, comprehensive, and up-to-date route into British Columbia historical writing is through *Western Canada since 1870*, edited by Alan Artibise (V: UBCP 1978). This volume, which includes books, articles, and some theses, should be supplemented with Frances Woodward's bibliography of recent British Columbia books, articles, and government documents that regularly appears in the quarterly, *BC Studies*. Woodward has also compiled *Theses on British Columbia History and Related Subjects* (V: UBC Library 1971; supplement 1974) and has occasionally published lists of recent theses in BCS. Two older guides to government documents prepared by Marjorie C. Holmes are still useful. They are *Publications of the Government of British Columbia, 1871-1947* (Victoria: KP 1947) and *Royal Commissions and Commissions of Inquiry Under the 'Public Inquiries Act' in British Columbia, 1872-1942: A Checklist* (Victoria: KP 1945). A superb retrospective bibliography of printed material is the *Dictionary Card Catalog of the Provincial Archives of British Columbia* (Boston: G.K. Hall 1971). This unique catalogue includes subject, author, and title cards for periodical articles and chapters in books as well as for books and pamphlets. Two volumes of *A Bibliography of British Columbia*, one edited by Barbara J. Lowther, *Laying the Foundations, 1849-1899* (Victoria: University of Victoria 1968), the other edited by M.H. Edwards and J.C.R. Lort, *Years of Growth, 1900-1950* (Victoria: University of Victoria 1975), are of greater use to bibliophiles than to students writing term papers but do provide useful information about authors of books and pamphlets. An extensive guide to published and unpublished material on resource industries and regional studies is Duncan Ket, comp., *British Columbia: A Bibliography of Industry, Labour, Resources and Regions for the Social Sciences* (V: UBCP 1978). Students should note that all of the bibliographies listed above aim to be inclusive rather than selective within their proclaimed parameters; inclusion in a bibliography is not necessarily an *imprimatur* of scholarly quality.

INTERPRETATIONS

The best overview of British Columbia historiography, Allan Smith's trenchant essay, 'The Writing of British Columbia History,' BCS, 1980,* places the historical work on British Columbia over the last hundred years in a broad conceptual framework. As well, his bibliographic footnotes offer a guide to some of the more important works in provincial historiography. Smith's essay, which also serves as the introduction to a collection of essays on British Columbia history, *British Columbia: Historical Readings*, edited by W.P. Ward and R.A.J. McDonald (V: Douglas & McIntyre 1981), may be usefully supplemented by Jean Friesen's introduction to an older collection of representative articles, *Historical Readings on British Columbia* (T: M&S 1976), which Friesen edited with H.K. Ralston. The Friesen and Ralston collection itself was chosen and arranged to reflect the editors' interpretation of the evolution of British Columbia historiography. [For convenience's sake articles that are reprinted in Ward and McDonald are noted *; those in Friesen and Ralston, #.]

As yet, many of the attempts to explain British Columbia have been undertaken by social scientists other than historians who are often more interested in the contemporary scene than in the historical background they sketch. Good examples are R.M. Burns's perceptive essays on British Columbia's relations with the rest of Canada, 'British Columbia and the Canadian Federation' in R.M. Burns, ed., *One Country or Two?* (M: MQUP 1971), and 'British Columbia: Perceptions of a Split Personality' in Richard Simeon, ed., *Must Canada Fail?* (M: MQUP 1977). E.R. Black, another political scientist, in 'British Columbia: The Politics of Exploitation,' in R.A. Shearer, ed., *Exploiting Our Economic Potential* (T: HRW 1968), sees a preoccupation with material things as a major characteristic of provincial politics.

The cleavages within British Columbia society have also commanded attention. In 'The Social Basis of Party Politics,' QQ, 1966, Martin Robin, a political scientist, argued that 'class cleavage' has been the most important conflict in British Columbia history. Since then he has modified his views. In a 1978 essay, 'British Columbia: The Company Province,' in his edited collection, *Canadian Provincial Politics* (2nd ed., T: PH 1978), Robin suggests 'it is difficult to say which cleavage, class or regional, is more critical in determining the structure of British Columbia politics.' In 'Class and Race in the Social Structure of British Columbia, 1870-1939,' BCS, 1980,* W. Peter Ward, an historian, has directly challenged the applicability of the class conflict model to British Columbia and asserted that 'the major cleavages in British Columbia's social structure ... were those based upon race.' That view, in turn, has been attacked in 'Race and Class in British Columbia: A Comment' by the sociologist, Rennie Warburton, BCS, 1981. Both Ward and Warburton make thoughful observations that invite further investigation. Should their debate be followed by well-informed discussion, British Columbia historiography can only benefit.

GENERAL STUDIES

Although it was published in 1958 (a 1971 edition included only a few minor revisions), Margaret A. Ormsby's *British Columbia: A History* (T: MAC) has stood the test of time remarkably well. It is more than just a basic reference text. Essentially political in framework, it includes material on the economy and social life and offers, almost *en passant*, many stimulating insights into the nature of British Columbia society. As an interpretive work it should be read in conjunction with Ormsby's museful 1966 presidential address to the Canadian Historical Association, CHAR, 1966, and John Norris's examination of Ormsby's writings, 'Margaret Ormsby,' BCS, 1976-7. The earlier 'standard' work, volume 2 of F.W. Howay, *British Columbia* (Winnipeg: S.J. Clarke 1914), is still a handy reference for lists of MLAs and some statistics. Howay's *The Making of a Province* (T: Ryerson 1928) is such a drastic condensation of the earlier work that its usefulness is limited. The only other book-length survey of modern British Columbia history, Martin Robin's two-volume work, *The Company Province – The Rush for Spoils, 1871-1933* and *Pillars of Profit, 1934-1972* (T: M&S 1972, 1973), is almost exclusively political history. While the volumes develop some of the provocative ideas expressed in Robin's articles, they are marred by sloppy scholarship and should be used with care. Some of the vigour of the debate engendered by the publication of *The Rush for Spoils* is illustrated by the exchange between a reviewer, Norman Ruff, and Robin (BCS, 1973). The debate, alas, was more over accuracy of detail than matters of substance. A detailed comment on some of the ideas of 'The Company Province' may be found in ' "The Company Province" and its Centennials: A Review of Recent British Columbia Historiography' by Patricia E. Roy, *Acadiensis*, 1974.

THE CONFEDERATION ERA

As yet, there is no thorough or systematic study of British Columbia in the Confederation era. Although the essays in it are uneven in quality, W. George Shelton, ed., *British Columbia & Confederation* (Victoria: University of Victoria 1967), is a good overall introduction to the period and its footnotes provide leads to older articles on aspects of Confederation by such historians as F.W. Howay, W.E. Ireland, and W.N. Sage. Confederation era politics are discussed in a brief and lively fashion in chapter 17 of P.B. Waite, *The Life and Times of Confederation* (T: UTP 1962). These older works should be augmented by recent works relating to some of the participants in the Confederation movement. *The Reminiscences of Doctor John Sebastian Helmcken*, ed. Dorothy Blakey Smith (V: UBCP 1975), a model of careful and detailed annotation, includes the recollections of an important convert to Confederation and his diary of the negotiations in 1870. The views of a more reluctant supporter of Confederation are sketched by Gordon R. Elliott in 'Henry P. Pellew Crease: Confederation or No Confederation,' BCS, 1971-2. Some of the thoughts of British officials in the colony of British Columbia are outlined in two 1974 articles in BCS, 'Frederick Seymour: The Forgotten Governor' by Margaret A. Ormsby and 'The Hankin Appointment' by Robert L. Smith, and in an MA thesis by Kent M. Haworth, 'Governor Musgrave, Confederation, and Responsible Government' (University of Victoria 1975). Leading British Columbia political figures speak for themselves in the Confederation Debates of 1870 reprinted as an appendix in volume V of the *Journals of the Colonial Legislatures of the Colonies of Vancouver Island and British Columbia, 1851-1871*, ed. James E. Hendrickson (Victoria: Provincial Archives of British Columbia 1980).

THE FIRST THREE DECADES OF CONFEDERATION

From an historical point of view, provincial politics before 1903 are a virtual *terra incognita*. In *The Company Province* Martin Robin dismisses the period in one chapter. His work in no way replaces the relevant chapters of Ormsby's *British Columbia* as really the only helpful source on the period. Two old articles are of limited use. W.N. Sage, 'Federal Parties and Provincial Groups in British Columbia, 1871-1903,' *British Columbia Historical Quarterly*, 1948, tries to find some order in the confusion of the political groups that existed before 1903 while Edith Dobie, 'Some Aspects of Party History in British Columbia, 1871-1903,' *Pacific Historical Review*, 1932, is largely an account of federal political campaigns in Victoria. Of the fourteen premiers who held office between 1871 and 1903, only John Robson (1889-92) has been the subject of a modern MA thesis, Ivan Antak, 'John Robson: British Columbian' (University of Victoria 1972). Some indication of the confused state of British Columbia politics at the turn of the century may be gained from an examination of two essays on the Laurier government's dismissal of Lieutenant-Governor T.R. McInnes: J.T. Saywell, 'The McInnes Incident in British Columbia,' *British Columbia Historical Quarterly*, 1950, and G.F.G. Stanley, 'A "Constitutional Crisis" in British Columbia,' CJEPS, 1955.

British Columbia's troubled relations with Ottawa in this period have been slightly better treated by historians. Initially, delays in the construction of the railway were the main source of conflict. Margaret A. Ormsby's article, 'Prime Minister Mackenzie, the Liberal Party and the Bargain with British Columbia,' CHR, 1945, offers a more detailed account of this incident than her general history. Ottawa views of the controversy are set forth in Dale Thomson, *Alexander Mckenzie: Clear Grit* (T: MAC 1960), and C.W. de Kiewiet and F.H. Underhill, eds., *The Dufferin-Carnarvon Correspondence, 1874-1878* (T: CS 1955).

The completion of the Canadian Pacific Railway brought only temporary peace to British Columbia's dealings with the federal government. The financial grievances which lay at the heart of the Better Terms movement, a political ploy long favoured by provincial premiers, are clearly sketched in J.A. Maxwell, *Federal Subsidies to the Provincial Governments in Canada* (Cambridge: Harvard UP 1937). The province's long-standing claims are buttressed with plentiful statistics in *British Columbia in the Canadian Confederation* (Victoria: KP 1938), the province's submission to the Royal Commission on Dominion-Provincial Relations.

The theme of the Canadianization of British Columbia was explored in two essays published in the 1940s. Margaret Ormsby's 'Canada and the New British Columbia,' CHAR, 1948,# argues that integrating forces such as religious ties and political practices existed before the completion of the Canadian Pacific Railway while W.N. Sage in 'British Columbia becomes Canadian, 1871-1901,' QQ, 1945,# describes the CPR as the 'greatest single Canadianizing force in British Columbia.' Recently, R.A.J. McDonald, in 'Victoria, Vancouver, and the Economic Development of British Columbia, 1886-1914'* in A.F.J. Artibise, ed., *Town and City: Aspects of Western Canadian Cities* (Regina: Canadian Plains Research Center 1980), has persuasively argued that initially the railway had 'surprisingly little impact on existing economic patterns along the B.C. Coast.'

By the turn of the century, however, the CPR had directly or indirectly changed the relationship between the older city and capital, Victoria, and the new CPR terminus, Vancouver. Victoria's decline is documented in Stanley Ruzicka, 'The Decline of Victoria as a Metropolitan Centre, 1885-1901' (MA thesis, University of Victoria 1973). A useful case study of how a Victoria entrepreneur coped with change is G.W.S. Brooks, 'Edgar Crow Baker: An Entrepreneur in Early British Columbia,' BCS, 1976. The role of business elites, especially railroad and real estate interests, in establishing Vancouver is the subject of R.A.J. McDonald, 'City-Building in the Canadian West: A Case Study of Economic Growth in Early Vancouver, 1886-1893,' BCS, 1979. A study specifically directed to the effects of the CPR on Vancouver is Norbert MacDonald, 'The Canadian Pacific Railway and Vancouver's Development to 1900,' BCS, 1977.* MacDonald has also examined the competition among Victoria, Vancouver, and Seattle for the control of the Klondike trade in 'Seattle, Vancouver and the Klondike,' CHR, 1968.

THE ECONOMY

What every British Columbia historian would like is a comprehensive economic history of the province. The best effort towards such a study so far is chapter 2 of R.A.J. McDonald, 'Business Leaders in

Early Vancouver, 1886-1914,' (PHD thesis, UBC 1977). This chapter synthesizes a wide range of sources but, of course, is largely confined to the years 1885-1914. Some of the material is included in McDonald's articles cited above. Two old but still useful sources are the essays on fishing, forestry, farming, and mining in volume 22 of *Canada and its Provinces*, ed. Adam Shortt and Arthur Doughty (T: Publishers' Association of Canada 1914), and F.W. Howay, W.N. Sage, and H.F. Angus, *British Columbia and the United States* (T: Ryerson 1942; reprinted NY: Russell & Russell 1970). The latter work, which was written for the Carnegie series on the Relations of Canada and the United States, is 'concerned with the fortunes of various attempts to exploit the rich natural resources of the region and with international disputes incidental to these attempts.' Many of its observations invite further inquiry.

Writing in 1972, A.D. Scott observed the absence of local economic studies. Work by Scott and other members of the Economics Department at the University of British Columbia has overcome some of that problem. Although relating primarily to the contemporary scene, some of the essays in a special edition of *BC Studies* edited by Scott (1972) and in R.A. Shearer, ed., *Exploiting our Economic Potential* (T: HRW 1968), occasionally include historical background sketches. From a historian's point of view, one of the most important articles to emanate from the UBC Department of Economics is D.G. Paterson, 'European Financial Capital and British Columbia: An Essay on the Role of the Regional Entrepreneur,' BCS, 1974.* Paterson demonstrates that regional entrepreneurs, using imported capital, 'did fulfill a vital function' in the provincial economy before World War I. A case study of a significant exception may be found in Patricia E. Roy, 'Direct Management from Abroad: The Formative Years of the British Columbia Electric Railway,' *Business History Review*, 1973.

British Columbia's major industries are based on the exploitation of natural resources. A good outline of how the provincial government distributed land, timber, and minerals before 1914 is Robert E. Cail, *Land, Man and the Law: The Disposal of Crown Lands in British Columbia, 1871-1913* (V: UBCP 1974). Historians have given individual industries very limited attention. In 'Agricultural Development in British Columbia,' *Agricultural History*, 1945, Margaret Ormsby briefly traces the history of agriculture. An earlier article of hers appeared with several other papers on agriculture in BC in *Scientific Agriculture*, 1939. Little work on agricultural history has been done since apart from G.E.G. Thomas, 'The British Columbia Ranching Frontiers, 1858-1896' (MA thesis, UBC 1976), an examination of the economic and social aspects of the cattle industry, and Morag MacLachlan, 'The Success of the Fraser Valley Milk Producers' Association,' BCS, 1974-5, an analysis of an important agricultural co-operative. A different approach to the study of agriculture is the work of David C. Jones on agricultural education. Two examples of his work are 'The *Zeitgeist* of Western Settlement: Education and the Myth of the Land' in J. Donald Wilson and David C. Jones, eds., *Schooling and Society in 20th Century British Columbia* (Calgary: Detselig 1980), and '"We cannot allow it to be run by those who do not understand education" – Agricultural Schooling in the Twenties,' BCS, 1978.

According to its title, *The British Columbia Fisheries* by W.A. Carrothers (T: UTP 1941), should be a comprehensive study but it is in fact largely a study of the salmon fisheries and is most useful for its extensive statistical tables. Anyone wishing detailed factual information on the salmon industry may find it in the encyclopedic *Salmon: Our Heritage* (V: BC Packers 1969) by Cicely Lyons, who spent almost forty years as a secretary to senior officers of BC Packers Ltd. In contrast is a scholarly work by Keith Ralston modestly titled 'The 1900 Strike of the Fraser River Sockeye Salmon Fishermen' (MA thesis, UBC 1965). Ralston's thesis is an extensive study of the salmon industry in the late nineteenth and early twentieth centuries. He has also published an important article on British Columbia's trade relations with California and London, 'Patterns of Trade and Investment on the Pacific Coast, 1867-1892: The Case of the British Columbia Salmon Canning Industry,' BCS, 1968-9. Two articles by J.M.S. Careless, 'The Lowe Brothers, 1852-1870: A Study in Business Relations on the North Pacific Coast,' BCS, 1969, and 'The Business Community in the Early Development of Victoria, British Columbia,' in D.S. Macmillan, ed., *Canadian Business History* (T: M&S 1972), deal only incidentally with the fisheries but they should be read in association with the Ralston article to develop the picture of late nineteenth-century trading relationships.

Two old works still serve as the best studies of the interior mining industry. They are the relevant chapters in Howay, Sage, and Angus, *British Columbia and the United States*, and in H.A. Innis and A.R.M. Lower, *Settlement on the Forest and Mining Frontier* (T: MAC 1938). A very detailed account of changing investment patterns is J.S. Church, 'Mining Companies in the West Kootenay and Boundary Region of British Columbia, 1890-1900,' MA thesis, UBC 1961. There is no good overview of the coastal coal-mining industry. The only recent work, Daniel T. Gallacher, 'Men, Money, Machines: Studies Comparing Colliery Operations and Factors of Production in British Columbia's Coal Industry to 1891,' PHD thesis, UBC 1979 narrowly focuses on management and production.

Despite its importance in the provincial economy, historians have almost ignored the lumber industry. Apart from W.A. Carrothers's good survey in A.R.M. Lower, ed., *The North American Assault on the Canadian Forest* (T: Ryerson 1938), most works on forestry are more concerned with individuals than with the industry as a whole. This is as true of *Timber: A History of the Forest Industry in B.C.* (V: J.J. Douglas 1975) by G.W. Taylor, a retired newspaperman, as it is of the oral history, *First Growth: The Story of British Columbia Forest Products Limited*, co-ordinated by Sue Baptie (V: BC Forest Products 1975), or of Myrtle Bergren's *Tough Timber* (T: Progress Books 1967; reprinted V: Elgin 1979), an account of how Bergren's husband and other Communist sympathizers organized the International Woodworkers of America on Vancouver Island during the 1930s. The later conflicts between the 'reds' and the 'whites' in the IWA are examined from somewhat different perspectives in Irving Abella, *Nationalism, Communism, and Canadian Labour: The CIO, the Communist Party, and the Canadian Congress of Labour, 1935-56* (T: UTP 1972), chapter 7, and in Jerry Lembcke, 'The International Woodworkers of America in British Columbia, 1942-1956,' Labour, 1980.

LABOUR

The most comprehensive study of labour, Paul Phillips's pioneering work *No Power Greater: A Century of Labour in British Columbia* (V:

BC Federation of Labour 1967), was written as the BC Federation's 1967 centennial project. It is an excellent starting-point but it is not a definitive study as it concentrates on formal institutions and was unable to take advantage of major collections of labour records which have since become available in archives, notably those of the University of British Columbia, Special Collections. In *Radical Heritage: Labor, Socialism and Reform in Washington and British Columbia, 1895-1917* (V: Douglas & McIntyre 1979) Carlos A. Schwantes tells a familiar story to readers of British Columbia labour history but, by putting it in a comparative perspective, raises new questions. Although Stuart Jamieson's primary object was to examine industrial relations 'crises' throughout Canada in the first two-thirds of this century, his *Times of Trouble: Labour Unrest and Industrial Conflict in Canada, 1900-66* (O: Task Force on Labour Relations 1968) inevitably contains a great deal of material on British Columbia and incorporates much of his 1962 CJEPS article on the 1950s, 'Regional Factors in Industrial Conflict: The Case of British Columbia.'*#

British Columbia events are a major part of several studies of radical labour, including Martin Robin, *Radical Politics and Canadian Labour, 1880-1930* (Kingston: Queen's University, Industrial Relations Centre 1968). More recently, both Ross McCormack and David Bercuson have published more sophisticated studies on major aspects of radical labour. McCormack, in *Reformers, Rebels and Revolutionaries: The Western Canadian Radical Movement, 1899-1919* (T: UTP 1977), skilfully dissects the various strands of the radical labour movement and shows that the revolutionary strand was most likely to flourish in British Columbia. An extended version of McCormack's account of 'The Industrial Workers of the World in Western Canada, 1905-1914' appeared in CHAR, 1975, while an earlier version of one chapter appeared as 'The Emergence of the Socialist Movement in British Columbia,' BCS, 1974. Bercuson's study, *Fools and Wise Men: The Rise and Fall of the One Big Union* (T: MHR 1978), a much broader work than its title immediately suggests, includes a brief introduction to labour and working conditions, especially in the interior mining industry, and to conflicts within organized labour in Vancouver during World War I. Bercuson has also written a provocative and wide-ranging article, 'Labour

Radicalism and the Western Industrial Frontier, 1897-1919,' CHR, 1977.*

The troubles of the Vancouver Island coal fields are discussed in most general works on labour relations as well as in more specific studies. The 1903 strike, which had extended repercussions because of its alleged link with a strike of CPR employees and the influence of the Royal Commission established to investigate it, is examined in A.D. Orr, 'The Western Federation of Miners and the Royal Commission on Industrial Disputes in 1903 with Special Reference to the Vancouver Island Coal Miners Strike' (MA thesis, UBC 1968). On the 'great strike' of 1912-14, the most recent and sophisticated work is 'The Vancouver Island Coal Miners, 1912-1914: A Study of an Organizational Strike,' BCS, 1980, in which John Norris draws on such basic secondary sources as A.J. Wargo, 'The Great Coal Strike: The Vancouver Island Coal Miners' Strike, 1912-1914' (BA essay, UBC 1962), and employs new evidence, the letters of his father who served with the militia in Nanaimo, to examine the union's organizational problems and their relationship to the subsequent riot.

Two case studies deal with specific labour disputes during World War I. In 'A Profusion of Issues: Immigrant Labour, the World War, and the Cominco Strike of 1917,' Labour, 1977, Stanley Scott outlines the issues, including the eight-hour day, which caused a five-week long strike at the Trail smelter. In 'The British Columbia Electric Railway and its Street Railway Employees: Paternalism in Labour Relations,' BCS, 1972-3, Patricia Roy shows how apparently harmonious relations between a utility company and its employees broke down during the war and resulted in four strikes between 1917 and 1919. Labour history, even in British Columbia, does not always deal with disputes. In a pioneering study, 'Union Maids: Organized Women Workers in Vancouver, 1900-1915,' BCS, 1979, Star Rosenthal has rescued, almost from oblivion, the efforts of women workers such as telephone operators and waitresses to organize themselves. Covering some of the same ground but written primarily as an argument against the discrimination practised by male labour leaders is Marie Campbell, 'Sexism in British Columbia Trade Unions, 1900-1920,' in Barbara Latham and Cathy Kess, eds., In Her Own Right: Selected Essays in Women's History in B.C.

(Victoria: Camosun College 1980). Susan Wade's essay in the same volume, 'Helena Gutteridge: Votes for Women and Trade Unions,' sketches the ideas of a woman prominent in the trade-union movement.

British Columbia also has a small library of Marxist histories of the labour movement that are popular and polemical rather than scholarly and systematic. William Bennett, *Builders of British Columbia* (V: Broadway Printers 1937), is an early example. Later works include Harold Griffin, *British Columbia: The People's Early Story* (T: Tribune 1958), and Jack Scott, *Plunderbund and Proletariat: A History of the I.W.W. in British Columbia* (V: New Star 1975).

POLITICS

Richard McBride, who is credited with introducing party lines to provincial politics in 1903, is the subject of two MA theses, P.R. Hunt, 'The Political Career of Sir Richard McBride' (UBC 1953), and B.R.D. Smith, 'Sir Richard McBride: A Study in the Conservative Party of British Columbia, 1903-1916' (Queen's University 1959). Both, especially the Smith thesis, set a high standard in their time but neither should be regarded as the final word on Sir Richard. Surprisingly, McBride, who left a large collection of papers, has not attracted the attention of many historians but in 'Progress, Prosperity and Politics: The Railway Policies of Richard McBride,' BCS, 1980, Patricia Roy explores an important aspect of McBride's administration and illustrates how he attempted to cope with a province that is composed of many regions. The same theme of competing regions emerges in a splendid article by the historical geographer, R. Cole Harris, 'Locating the University of British Columbia,' BCS, 1976-7. This essay brilliantly captures the mood *circa* 1910 of 'a new place where energy went to development rather than to social thought and where the idea of the modern world encountered a novel setting that British Columbians themselves did not yet understand.' In ' "Pretty Sleek and Fat": The Genesis of Forest Policy in British Columbia' (MA thesis, UBC 1979), Robert H. Marris argues that British Columbia largely borrowed from experiences elsewhere in evolving a forest policy the primary purpose of which was to raise revenue. The difficulties of the provincial Liberals in the McBride era are examined in Melva J. Dwyer, 'Laurier and the British Columbia Liberal Party, 1896-1911: A Study in Federal-Provincial Party Relations' (MA thesis, UBC 1961).

Apart from a short MA thesis by Victor Dailyde, 'The Administration of W.J. Bowser, Premier of British Columbia, 1915-1916' (University of Victoria 1976), little has been written of McBride's immediate successor. The Liberal administration which followed Bowser has fared no better historiographically. James Morton, *Honest John Oliver* (T: Dent 1933), is a friend's posthumous tribute to the premier, 1918-27. Nevertheless, several Liberal reforms, including the enfranchisement of women, are considered in two essays in Latham and Kess, eds., *In Her Own Right*: Diane Crossley, 'The B.C. Liberal Party and Women's Reforms,' and Michael Cramer, 'Public and Political: Documents of the Women's Suffrage Campaign in British Columbia, 1871-1917: The View from Victoria.' The best study of the suffrage question is, however, Linda Hale, 'The British Columbia Woman Suffrage Movement, 1890-1917' (MA thesis, UBC 1977).

The major third parties to emerge in the tens and twenties have been the subject of separate articles. Margaret Ormsby's essay, 'The United Farmers of British Columbia: An Abortive Third Party Movement,' *British Columbia Historical Quarterly*, 1953, also includes a short survey of wartime and post-war agricultural problems. The curious story of how part of the United Farmers' movement was absorbed into the Provincial party, a group formed in Vancouver by dissident Conservative businessmen, is also outlined in Ian Parker, 'The Provincial Party,' BCS, 1970-1. Edith Dobie's survey, 'Party History in British Columbia, 1903-1933,' *Pacific Northwest Quarterly*, 1936,* deals mainly with the Simon Fraser Tolmie government, 1928-33. The best introduction to that sad administration is Ian D. Parker, 'Simon Fraser Tolmie: The Last Conservative Premier of British Columbia,' BCS, 1971.* An important aspect of that government, the role of businessmen in it, is examined in Robert E. Groves, 'Business Government: Party Politics and the British Columbia Business Community, 1928-1933' (MA thesis, UBC 1976). With the collapse of the Conservatives, the Liberals under T.D. Pattullo came to power in 1933. Pattullo's premiership, particularly his relationship with Mackenzie King and his social reform plans, have been carefully examined by Margaret Ormsby in 'T. Dufferin Pattullo and the Little New Deal,' CHR, 1962.* Pattullo's interest in the north is described in Daniel J. Grant, 'T.D. Pattullo's Northern Empire: The Alaskan Highway and the Proposed Annexation of the Yukon Territory, 1933-1941' (MA thesis, University of Victoria 1980), while his work as a party organizer is the subject of J. Neil Sutherland, 'T.D. Pattullo as a Party Leader' (MA thesis, UBC 1960). Some of the educational reforms proposed by G.M. Weir, a professional educator and Pattullo's minister of education, are discussed in Jean Mann, 'G.M. Weir and H.B. King: Progressive Education or Education for the Progressive State' in Wilson and Jones, eds., *Schooling and Society*.

The Coalition era (1941-52) awaits its historian although Donald K. Alper's doctoral dissertation, 'From Rule to Ruin: The Conservative Party of British Columbia, 1928-1954' (UBC 1976), includes a survey of the Coalition administration. Alper's article, 'The Effects of Coalition Government on Party Structure: The Case of the Conservative Party in B.C.,' BCS, 1977, is of greater interest to political scientists than to historians. It is still too early to expect a study of the twenty years of W.A.C. Bennett's Social Credit administration though one important and complicated event, the negotiation of the Columbia River treaty, has been analysed in scholarly detail in Neil A. Swainson, *Conflict Over the Columbia: The Canadian Background to an Historic Treaty* (M: MQUP 1979). Paddy Sherman's *Bennett* (T: M&S 1966) represents a shrewd reporter's observations of the early years of the Bennett government. Martin Robin's *Pillars of Profit* includes a good deal of material on the Bennett era but must be used with caution. A very sympathetic and sketchy work is *The Wonderful World of W.A.C. Bennett* (T: M&S 1971) by Ronald Worley, Bennett's one time executive assistant.

While neither of the two major national parties has fared very well at the hands of British Columbia electors or historians, socialists have enjoyed relative political, and historiographical success. The close relationship between labour and socialism helps explain the comparatively extensive literature on left-wing politics. In addition to some of the titles listed under Labour, readers interested in the Marxian-Socialist tradition should consult Ross A. Johnson, 'No Compromise – No Political Trading: The Marxian Socialist Tradition in British Columbia' (PHD thesis, UBC 1975). The CCF/NDP has its own corpus of literature including even Daisy Webster, *Growth of the NDP in B.C., 1900-1970* (V: NDP 1970), a biographical dictionary of eighty-one BC socialists elected to the Legislature or Parliament. One of the few published biographies of a British Columbia politician is *The Compassionate Rebel: Ernest E. Winch and his Times* by Dorothy G. Steeves (V: Boag Foundation 1960; reprinted V: J.J. Douglas 1977). This sympathetic study of one of the founders of the CCF in BC is especially useful for its account of the times in which socialist ideas flourished. Although primarily concerned with the national CCF, Walter Young's *Anatomy of a Party: The National CCF, 1932-1961* (T: UTP 1969) includes British Columbia material. In an article, 'Ideology, Personality and the Origin of the CCF in British Columbia,' BCS, 1976-7),* Young has shown the importance of personality as well as ideology in dividing the party. The notes accompanying the article are a useful guide to much of the thesis literature on the CCF.

SOCIETY

The 'new' social history has not yet come to British Columbia; nevertheless, an extensive but uneven literature does provide glimpses of various aspects of British Columbia society. The history of education provides a good example. *Schooling and Society*, Wilson and Jones, eds., is like a breath of fresh air as its contributors get away from the more traditional histories of education such as F.H. Johnson, *A History of Public Education in British Columbia* (V: UBCP 1964), which is essentially an outline of the history of the administration of education as is H.T. Logan's *Tuum Est: A History of the University of British Columbia* (V: UBC 1958). Yet, without such institutional histories, the tasks of the contributors to *Schooling and Society* – all recent graduate students in the Faculty of Education at the University of British Columbia – would have been more difficult. This new generation of scholars do set educational development in a broad context of provincial society and they are aware of the literature of the 'new' social history but they do not really apply it to the British Columbia situation. Their problem, like that of all British Columbia historians, is the scarcity of solid secondary material from which one can safely undertake more adventuresome and sophisticated journeys into the past.

The provincial government only began providing limited financial support for schools outside the non-sectarian public school system in 1977 but other schools did exist. Although private schools, apart from those operated by the Roman Catholic church, faded in the late nineteenth century as the public school system evolved, Jean Barman in 'Marching to Different Drummers: Public Education and Private Schools in British Columbia, 1900-1950,' *British Columbia Historical News*, 1980, demonstrates that private schools reappeared after the turn of the century in response to the desires of British immigrants to provide their sons with a British style of education. 'Growing up British in British Columbia: The Vernon Preparatory School, 1914-1946,' Barman's contribution to Wilson and Jones, eds., *Schooling and Society*, is a case study of one such school. While Barman deals only with boys, the only extensive study of the Roman Catholic schools, Edith E. Down, *A Century of Service, 1858-1958: A History of the Sisters of Saint Ann and their Contribution to Education in British Columbia, the Yukon and Alaska* (Victoria: 1966) is almost exclusively concerned with the education of girls. Although there are no historical studies of them apart from some 'in house' volumes, private schools for girls existed as did Catholic schools for boys. The difficulties of the public schools in teaching children of such minority groups as native Indians, Asians, and Doukhobors are reviewed in Mary Ashworth, *The Forces Which Shaped Them* (V: New Star 1979).

Of the various denominations, the Anglicans and Roman Catholics were most active in missionary work. Of the Anglicans, the best known and most thoroughly studied missionary is *William Duncan of Metlakatla: A Victorian Missionary in British Columbia* (Ottawa: National Museums of Canada 1974), whose career has been well analysed by Jean Usher. Duncan's Methodist neighbour is the subject of Clarence R. Bolt, 'Thomas Crosby and the Tsimshian of Port

Simpson, 1874-1897' (MA thesis, Simon Fraser University 1981).
The general history of the Anglican church in British Columbia to
the mid-1920s is sketched in Frank A. Peake, *The Anglican Church
in British Columbia* (V: Mitchell 1959), an institutional history written to commemorate the centennial of the establishment of the Dio-
cese of British Columbia. To celebrate the centennial of their arrival
in British Columbia, a Roman Catholic order of men, the Oblates of
Mary Immaculate, commissioned an anecdotal history of their
work: Kay Cronin, *Cross in the Wilderness* (V: Mitchell 1960). One
Oblate mission, that of the Cariboo, is the subject of a more scholarly study, Margaret Whitehead, *The Cariboo Mission: A History of
the Oblates* (Victoria: Sono Nis 1981).

As the paucity of work on missionaries suggests, religion has not
been a popular topic for historical inquiry, yet religious beliefs – or
possibly the lack of them – have undoubtedly had a role in shaping
British Columbia society. Aspects of the Social Gospel are con-
sidered in a brief reminiscence, H.T. Allen, 'A View from the
Manse: The Social Gospel and Social Crisis in British Columbia,
1929-1945,' in Richard Allen, ed., *The Social Gospel in Canada*
(Ottawa: National Museum 1975). Two MA theses also deal with the
Social Gospel. Sheila P. Mosher, 'The Social Gospel in British
Columbia: Social Reform as a Dimension of Religion, 1900-1929'
(University of Victoria 1974), is a general overview; Marilyn J. Harrison, 'The Social Influence of the United Church of Canada in British Columbia, 1930-1948' (UBC 1975), is a more detailed account of
a later period. The reform for which the Protestant churches were
best known in the early twentieth century, prohibition, was not
exclusively a religious crusade in BC. See A.M. Hiebert, 'Prohibition
in British Columbia' (MA thesis, Simon Fraser University 1969).

Although some denominations established medical facilites such
as hospitals and welfare institutions such as orphanages, private initiative and local government traditionally played a significant role in
offering health and welfare services. Several medical doctors have
written anecdotal accounts of their profession. These include R.G.
Large, *Drums and Scalpel: From Native Healers to Physicians on the
North Pacific Coast* (V: Mitchell 1968); Robert E. McKechnie II,
Strong Medicine: History of Healing on the Northwest Coast (V: J.J.

Douglas 1972); and T.F. Rose, *From Shaman to Modern Medicine: A Century of Healing Arts in British Columbia* (V: Mitchell 1972). Recently, professional historians have begun a systematic study of the medical profession. In articles heavily larded with statistical tables and graphs, John Norris, 'The Country Doctor in British Columbia, 1887-1975: An Historical Profile,' BCS, 1981, and Margaret Andrews, 'Medical Attendance in Vancouver, 1886-1920,' BCS, 1978-9, have found considerable mobility among practitioners. Andrews has also written a fine commentary on the effect of an epidemic on public health policy in 'Epidemic and Public Health: Influence in Vancouver, 1918-1919,' BCS, 1977.

A very brief foray into proposals to pay medical costs through insurance is 'A Report on Health Insurance: 1919' by D.L. Matters, BCS, 1974. A broader study of early programs for various kinds of social welfare is her article 'Public Welfare Vancouver Style, 1910-1920,' JCS, 1979. Matters is also the author of a unique study of juvenile delinquents, 'A Chance to Make Good: Juvenile Males and the Law in Vancouver, B.C., 1910-1945' (MA thesis, UBC 1978), and of 'The Boys' Industrial School: Education for Juvenile Offenders' in Wilson and Jones, eds., *Schooling and Society*. On matters relating to children, Neil Sutherland's path-breaking study, *Children in English-Canadian Society: Framing the Twentieth-Century Consensus* (T: UTP 1976), should be consulted since many of its examples are drawn from British Columbia sources. Some of the problems of the distressed, and especially efforts to improve the legal position of women and children, are vividly described in *My Mother the Judge: A Biography of Judge Helen Gregory MacGill* by Elsie Gregory MacGill (T: Ryerson 1955; reprinted T: Peter Martin 1981). Women on the other side of the law are the subject of another essay in the same volume. In 'The "Social Evil": Prostitution in Vancouver, 1900-1920,' Deborah Nilsen argues that prostitution cannot be understood without an examination 'of the economic circumstances of female workers.'

In an article that challenges much of the methodology used by other Canadian historians to determine the real wages of the working classes, Eleanor Bartlett in 'Real Wages and the Standard of Living in Vancouver, 1901-1929,' BCS, 1981, concludes that 'Vancouver working men may have benefitted less from rapid economic expansion, accompanied by inflation in the final years of the century and during the war, than from the more modest growth of the 1920s.' The question of unemployment runs through Bartlett's essay. For a fuller account of how the city coped with unemployment see Patricia E. Roy, 'Vancouver: The "Mecca of the Unemployed," 1907-1929,' in Artibise, ed., *Town and City*.

Almost all of the studies of health and welfare concentrate on Vancouver, the province's largest city. Although several general anecdotal histories exist, the only scholarly overview is Patricia E. Roy, *Vancouver: An Illustrated History* (T: Lorimer 1980). In addition to the previously mentioned works by R.A.J. McDonald and Norbert MacDonald, two splendidly researched articles by Norbert MacDonald, 'A Critical Growth Cycle for Vancouver, 1900-1914,' BCS, 1973, and 'Population, Growth and Change in Seattle and Vancouver, 1880-1960,' *Pacific Historical Review*, 1970,# provide extensive detail. The latter article is an example of that all too rare genre, the comparative study.

Every British Columbia town and city seems to have at least one history of itself, often the legacy of one or other of the three centennials the province celebrated between 1958 and 1971. Frequently they are the works of devoted local residents or hired professional publicists and are of local interest only. Occasionally, some of the better ones can be used to flesh out the background of a particular theme or to add detail about particular industries. For example, Elsie G. Turnbull, *Trail between the Wars* (Victoria: 1980), tells the story of the Cominco Strike of 1917 from the company's point of view. Unfortunately, it suffers from a phobia that so often affects local historians – a fear of footnotes.

From the late 1920s through the 1950s regional topics were a popular subject for the only graduate history students in the province – those enrolled as MA candidates at the University of British Columbia. While many of their authors later went on to distinguished careers, most of the theses they left behind now seem old-fashioned. Nevertheless, they do include useful information and, in many cases, are the only historical studies of the region. Among the examples of such works are W.W. Bilsland, 'The History of Revelstoke and the Big Bend' (1955); Mollie Cottingham, 'A History of the West Kootenay District in British Columbia' (1947); J.E. Gibbard, 'Early History of the Fraser Valley, 1808-1885' (1937); M.H. Matheson, 'Some Effects of Coal Mining upon the Development of the Nanaimo Area' (1950); M.A. Ormsby, 'A Study of the Okanagan Valley of British Columbia' (1931); Sylvia Thrupp, 'A History of the Cranbrook District in East Kootenay' (1929); and G.B. White, 'A History of the Eastern Fraser Valley Since 1885' (1937).

In the late 1960s and early 1970s there was a brief flurry of interest at all three provincial universities in examining the impact of the Depression of the 1930s on particular regions or communities. Two studies concerned chiefly with municipal financial problems are Bettina Bradbury, 'The Road to Receivership: Unemployment and Relief in Burnaby, North Vancouver City and District and West Vancouver, 1929-1933' (MA thesis, Simon Fraser University 1975), and Daniel T. Gallacher, 'City in Depression: The Impact of the Years 1929-1939 on Greater Victoria, B.C.' (MA thesis, University of Victoria 1969). Two MA theses which examine the broader social and economic impact of the Depression on their respective regions are William A. Sloan, 'The Crowsnest Pass during the Depression: A Socio-Economic History of Southeastern British Columbia, 1918-1939' (University of Victoria 1968), and A.J. Wright, 'The Winter Years in Cowichan: A Study of the Depression in a Vancouver Island Community' (UBC 1967).

The controversy among the various levels of government over the responsibility of providing for single unemployed men is the subject of a splendid BA Honours essay: Marion E. Lane, 'Unemployment during the Depression: The Problem of the Single Unemployed Transient in British Columbia, 1930-1938' (UBC 1966). The most dramatic protest of the unemployed, the On-to-Ottawa Trek, is recounted in Ronald Liversedge, *Recollections of the On-to-Ottawa Trek*, ed. Victor Hoar (T: M&S 1973). Although really a study in labour history, Richard McCandless, 'Vancouver's "Red Menace" of 1935: The Waterfront Situation,' BCS, 1974, should be read along with the studies of the unemployed to show why Vancouver authorities were so fearful of disorder.

A few recent published works suggest both the great variation of regions in the province and the potential wealth of material available for future research. In chapter 2 of *The Opening of the Canadian*

North, 1870-1914 (T: M&S 1971), Morris Zaslow succinctly surveys the often forgotten northern half of the province. Two volumes in the University of British Columbia Press series, Recollections of the Pioneers of British Columbia, offer insights on two isolated parts of the province and especially on the experiences of pioneer women. *A Pioneer Gentlewoman in British Columbia*, the memoirs of Susan Allison, with an introduction and notes by Margaret A. Ormsby (V: UBCP 1976), is the interesting story of a courageous woman who, in addition to raising fourteen children in the isolated Similkameen Valley in the late nineteenth century, wrote a paper on the Similkameen Indians that was published by the British Association for the Advancement of Science. The published diaries of an Anglican lay missionary to white settlers, *God's Galloping Girl: The Peace River Diaries of Monica Storrs, 1929-1931*, ed. W.L. Morton (V: UBCP 1979), demonstrates that as late as the 1930s much of British Columbia was very much pioneer country.

While regional studies seem out of fashion, ethnic studies are currently much in vogue. The only general study of ethnic groups is *Strangers Entertained: A History of the Ethnic Groups of British Columbia*, which John Norris edited for the British Columbia Centennial '71 Committee (V: 1971). The contributions, mainly by members of the ethnic groups themselves, are very uneven in quality but Norris's introductory analysis merits careful perusal.

Until recently, the study of native Indians was largely the preserve of anthropologists. Some idea of the extent of their work can be gained by an examination of 'A Select Bibliography of Anthropology in British Columbia,' BCS, 1973. Moreover, the best basic introduction to the field is still Wilson Duff's *The Indian History of British Columbia*, I: *The Impact of the White Man* (Victoria: Provincial Museum 1964). Tragically, volume 2 never appeared. Undoubtedly the finest work by a historian on the place of native Indians in BC society is Robin Fisher, *Contact and Conflict: Indian-European Relations in British Columbia, 1774-1890* (V: UBCP 1977). Unfortunately, all but the last chapter is primarily on the pre-Confederation era as is much of Fisher's earlier article, 'Joseph Trutch and Indian Land Policy,' BCS, 1971-2. However, Fisher has also written a study of one episode of post-Confederation problems with Indian lands, 'An

Exercise in Futility: The Joint Commission on Indian Land in British Columbia, 1875-1880,' CHAR, 1975. The general basis of Indian lands policy is set out in Cail, *Land, Man and the Law*. A fresh approach to the study of Indians is Rolf Knight, *Indians at Work: An Informal History of Native Indian Labour in British Columbia, 1858-1930* (V: New Star 1978). This very informal history demonstrates that Indians were engaged in wage labour in almost all of British Columbia's primary industries from their beginnings. An aspect of Indian organization is examined in E. Palmer Patterson, 'Andrew Paull and the Early History of British Columbia Indian Organization,' in Ian Getty and Donald B. Smith, eds., *One Century Later: Western Canadian Reserve Indians since Treaty 7* (V: UBCP 1978). One of the best ways to appreciate Indian culture and society is to read works by Indians themselves such as George Clutesi, *Potlatch* (Sidney: Gray 1969), and James Sewid, *Guests Never Leave Hungry: The Autobiography of James Sewid*, ed. James P. Spradley (New Haven: Yale UP 1969).

The British immigrants who played an important role in British Columbia's history are seldom studied as an ethnic group though Jean Barman's work on private schools suggests that they can be as in her essay, 'The World that British Settlers Made: Class, Ethnicity and Private Education in the Okanagan Valley,' in Ward and McDonald, *British Columbia: Historical Readings*, a revised and extended version of her earlier essay in Wilson and Jones, eds., *Schooling and Society*. A fascinating case study of one group of British immigrants whose fate illustrates the false hopes raised by real estate promoters is Nelson Riis, 'The Walhachin Myth: A Study in Settlement Abandonment,' BCS, 1973. Most British immigrants did readily assimilate into BC society. So too did the Scandinavians, including the Finns. Some of their individual settlements have been examined. For example, Lester R. Peterson, *The Cape Scott Story* (V: Mitchell 1974), is an account of the Danes who attempted an agricultural settlement at the north end of Vancouver Island at the turn of the century. Irene Howard, *Vancouver's Svenskar: A History of the Swedish Community in Vancouver* (V: Vancouver Historical Society 1970), is an eclectic collection of material about Swedes in the province. British Columbia has also provided a home for various utopian settlements.

Several of them are discussed in A.W. Rasporich, 'Utopian Ideals and Community Settlements in Western Canada, 1880-1914,' in H.C. Klassen, ed., *The Canadian West* (Calgary: Comprint 1977). The best documented utopian community is Sointula, a socialist colony founded by Finns in 1901. Its history has been examined in John I. Kolehmainen, 'Harmony Island: A Finnish Utopian Venture in British Columbia,' *British Columbia Historical Quarterly*, 1941, while the ideas of its founder are explored in J. Donald Wilson, 'Matti Kurikka: Finnish-Canadian Intellectual,' BCS, 1973-4.

During and immediately after World War I, the German settlers who had previously moved easily about in British Columbia society before the war experienced considerable hostility. The problem of the enemy alien is the subject of Tracy Reynolds, 'A Case Study in Attitudes towards Enemy Aliens in British Columbia, 1914-1919' (MA thesis, UBC 1973). An account of the Victoria riot protesting the sinking of the *Lusitania* is Charles Humphries's lively essay, 'War and Patriotism: The *Lusitania* Riot,' *British Columbia Historical News*, 1971. Humphries has also indicated the strength of anti-German, anti-Roman Catholic, and anti-French-Canadian sentiment in 'The Banning of a Book in British Columbia,' BCS, 1968-9, an account of how W.L. Grant's *History of Canada* was withdrawn from the schools of the province.

The most controversial ethnic groups have generated an extensive body of literature. A guide, now somewhat dated, to the writings on the Doukhobors is Maria Horvath, comp., *A Doukhobor Bibliography* (V: UBC Library, 1968-70). The best introduction to the Doukhobors is George Woodcock and Ivan Avakumovic, *The Doukhobors* (T: OUP 1968; reprinted T: M&S 1977). A very brief introduction to the subject and to one important aspect of controversy is F.H. Johnson, 'The Doukhobors of British Columbia: The History of a Sectarian Problem in Education,' QQ, 1963.

The list of books and articles on Asians is a long one. A critical guide to studies of the place of Chinese and Japanese in British Columbia is '"White Canada Forever": Two Generations of Studies,' *Canadian Ethnic Studies*, 1979, by Patricia E. Roy. This essay includes an extended review of W. Peter Ward, *White Canada Forever: Popular Attitudes and Public Policies towards Orientals in Brit-*

ish Columbia (M: MQUP 1978), the most comprehensive study of the British Columbia response to Asians, Chinese, Japanese, and East Indians. Ward's argument that psychological tensions were more important than socio-economic ones in explaining anti-Orientalism in BC has been challenged by Roy in 'British Columbia's Fear of Asians, 1900-1950,' SH, 1980,* which suggests that Asians provided sufficient economic, social and military competition to warrant deep fears among white British Columbians anxious to maintain their dominant position. The climax of these fears was, of course, the wartime removal of the Japanese from the coast of British Columbia. The reasons for that decision, its consequences for the Japanese community, and the formation of federal government policy vis-à-vis the Japanese from 1941 to 1950 when the government refused to pay further claims for Japanese property losses are carefully documented in Ann Gomer Sunahara, *The Politics of Racism: The Uprooting of Japanese Canadians during the Second World War* (T: Lorimer 1981).

A comprehensive guide to literature on East Indians in British Columbia is an integral part of Norm Buchignani, 'A Review of the Historical and Sociological Literature on East Indians in Canada,' *Canadian Ethnic Studies*, 1977. An article and book published since that review merit attention. In 'The British Columbia Franchise and Canadian Relations with India in Wartime, 1939-1945,' BCS, 1980, J.F. Hilliker shows how British Columbia's prejudices embarrassed Mackenzie King's attempts to become involved in shaping Commonwealth policy towards India. A generation earlier, in 1914, the decision of the Canadian government to respect British Columbia's wishes and deny entry to most of the 376 Indian would-be immigrants on board the chartered vessel, the *Komagata Maru*, set off repercussions in India which have been skilfully analysed by Hugh Johnston in *The Voyage of the Komogata Maru: The Sikh Challenge to Canada's Colour Bar* (Delhi: OUP 1979).

British Columbia, despite the efforts of its residents to restrict certain immigrants, is an ethnically diverse society. It has always been, of course, diverse geographically. British Columbia is also a very young society where hitherto the past has been more frequently the subject for adventures in nostalgia than for scholarly investigation. The beginnings of historiographical debate is a promising sign but there are still many gaps in British Columbia historiography and much of what has been written needs re-examination with a critical, questioning eye. Nevertheless, the totality of the existing literature demonstrates that British Columbia is indeed a province worthy of serious historical inquiry.

HARTWELL BOWSFIELD

The Prairie provinces

There is no general history covering the Prairie provinces in the
post-Confederation period. The one attempt to treat the West as a
unit, A.S. Morton's classic study, *A History of the Canadian West to
1870-71* (1939; T: UTP 1973), ends with the entry of the region into
Confederation. Similarly, Douglas Hill's *The Opening of the Canadian West* (L: Heinemann 1967), a lively, readable account, covers
the story of the West only to the formation of the provinces of Saskatchewan and Alberta in 1905.

Each of the western provinces has at present a periodical devoted
to its area of interest, and which covers both the pre- and post-Confederation periods. The oldest of these periodicals is the *Transactions
of the Historical and Scientific Society of Manitoba*, first issued in
1882. Publication, however, was not continuous, and the first series
ended in 1906; a second was published between 1926 and 1930. A
third series began in 1944-5 and continued until 1979 when it was
superseded by *Manitoba History*. The Saskatchewan Archives Board
has issued *Saskatchewan History* since 1944, while the *Alberta Historical Review*, published by the Alberta Historical Society, first
appeared in 1953. *Prairie Forum*, first published in 1976 by the
Canadian Plains Research Center, University of Regina, contains
articles on a wide variety of topics from agriculture and architecture
to ecology, native culture, and urbanization, and a regular listing of
theses on Prairie subjects.

Bruce Peel's revised *A Bibliography of the Prairie Provinces to 1953* (2nd ed., T: UTP 1973) contains some items written in the post-1953 period. The volume includes an author and title index and short biographical notes on the authors. Alan F.J. Artibise, *Western Canada since 1870: A Select Bibliography and Guide* (V: UBCP 1978), covering the Prairie provinces and British Columbia, lists books, pamphlets, periodical articles, and theses. The Select Subject Index is, however, inadequate. The *Canadian Plains Bulletin*, issued by the Canadian Plains Research Center, contains a bibliographical section on new publications.

INTERPRETATION

Throughout much of his writing, W.L. Morton, the West's foremost historian, has assigned to the Canadian Prairies a decisive role in the Confederation movement and in the interpretation of Canadian history. A summary account of Canadian and American interest in the West and how the Prairies and British Columbia were brought into Confederation is his *The West and Confederation 1857-1871* (O: CHA Booklet no 9 1965). In his article 'Clio in Canada: The Interpretation of Canadian History,' *University of Toronto Quarterly*, 1946, Morton stated that the West could not accept the Laurentian interpretation which was based on the economic subordination of the West. He asserted that the key factors or 'decisive' sections in Canadian history were French survival, the domination of Ontario, and the subordination of the West. The Maritimes and British Columbia did not rank so high because they had always possessed destinies alternative to that of incorporation in Canada. Without them there might have been a Canada, Morton claimed, but there could have been no Canada without the decisive sections. The theme of the subordination of the West is further expanded in his article 'The Bias of Prairie Politics,' TRSC, 1955, where the process of resistance to central Canada is divided into three periods: the struggle for political equality; the agrarian protest movement; and the attempt to build a political utopia through Social Credit and the CCF.

A number of Canadian historians have considered the applicability of Frederick Jackson Turner's frontier thesis to Canada. A survey of some of their writings is found in Morris Zaslow, 'The Frontier Hypothesis in Recent Historiography,' CHR, 1948; in Michael Cross, ed., *The Frontier Thesis and the Canadas: The Debate on the Impact of the Canadian Environment* (T: CC 1970); and in Maurice Careless's historiographical article 'Frontierism, Metropolitanism, and Canadian History,' CHR 1965. A more general but related treatment of the role of the frontier in shaping social and institutional life is found in S.D. Clark, *The Developing Canadian Community* (2nd ed., T: UTP 1968), and Russell Ward, 'Frontierism and National Stereotypes,' CHAR, 1964. Turner advanced the proposition that the frontier promoted the formation of a composite nationality, developed the powers of the national government, and fostered democracy and individualism. A systematic study of the application of this proposition to the Canadian West has to date not been undertaken.

COLLECTIONS

Since 1969 the University of Calgary has sponsored annually the Western Canadian Studies Conference. The papers presented at this conference have been published under a variety of titles: David Gagan, ed., *Prairie Perspectives* (T: HRW 1970); A.W. Rasporich and Henry C. Klassen, eds., *Prairie Perspectives 2* (T: HRW 1973); S.M. Trofimenkoff, ed., *The Twenties in Western Canada* (O: National Museum 1972); David Bercuson, ed., *Western Perspectives 1* (T: HRW 1974); A.W. Rasporitch, ed., *Western Canada Past and Present* (Calgary: University of Calgary and M&S West 1975); Howard Palmer, ed., *The Settlement of the West* (Calgary: University of Calgary 1977); Henry C. Klassen, ed., *The Canadian West* (Calgary: University of Calgary 1977); R.D. Francis and H. Ganzevoort, eds., *The Dirty Thirties in Canada* (V: Tantalus 1980); Howard Palmer and Donald Smith, eds., *The New Provinces: Alberta and Saskatchewan, 1905-1980* (V: Tantalus 1980). David Bercuson and Philip A. Buckner, eds., *Eastern and Western Perspectives* (T: UTP 1981) is a collection of papers presented at the Joint Atlantic Canada/Western Canadian Studies Conference in 1978.

The stated purpose of the conference is to present the research of established and younger scholars, and, as J.E. Rea says in *Western*

Perspectives 1, to provide a corrective to the emphasis on the history of the West as an agrarian experience and to explore the urban, labour, and immigrant 'fact' in western development. The papers published cover a wide variety of subjects: the urban and labour scene, native peoples, religion, education, the physical landscape, the West in fiction. A similar interdisciplinary approach is taken in the publications of the Canadian Plains Research Center, notably the collections of papers edited by Richard Allen: *A Region of the Mind: Interpreting the Western Plains* (1973) and *Religion and Society in the Prairie West* (1974). A valuable overview article included in the *Region of the Mind* is T.G. Regehr, 'Historiography of the Canadian Plains after 1870.' *The West and the Nation* (T: M&S 1976), a collection of papers edited by Carl Berger and Ramsay Cook, contains an article by Berger analysing the writings of W.L. Morton which should be required reading for any student of the history of the West.

The theme of western alienation is covered in John J. Barr and Owen Anderson, eds., *The Unfinished Revolt: Some Views on Western Independence* (T: M&S 1971), a collection of articles by Albertans. The tone expressed is strident and angry, raising the question of western economic independence and separation. *Proceedings of One Prairie Province: A Question for Canada*, ed. David K. Elton (Lethbridge: University of Lethbridge and Lethbridge Herald 1970), is a selection of papers presented at a 1970 conference in Lethbridge considering the feasibility and implications of a merger of the three prairie provinces. Donald Swainson, ed., *Historical Essays on the Prairie Provinces* (T: M&S 1970), brings together excerpts from some nineteenth-century historians of the West and diverse articles from western historical journals. In Larry Pratt and Garth Stevenson, eds., *Western Separatism: The Myths, Realities & Dangers* (Edmonton: Hurtig 1981), will be found an analysis of the current separatist movement in the West. Of this collection the article by Kenneth Norrie and Michael Percy, 'The Economics of a Separate West,' is probably the most helpful in challenging the economic arguments of the pro-separatists. Roger Gibbins in *Prairie Politics & Society: Regionalism in Decline* (T: Butterworth 1980) argues that the 'radicalism and regionalized political behaviour' of the Prairies has 'largely disintegrated.' Social and technological change, he says, have eroded the earlier distinctiveness of Prairie society and fostered 'a more homogeneous national culture.'

MANITOBA

No history of a province can compare with the achievement of W.L. Morton's *Manitoba: A History* (T: UTP 1957, 1967). Morton's work is both a narrative and an analysis of the political, economic, social, and cultural life of a distinct provincial society, yet it is never parochial. 'With this volume,' said a reviewer in 1957, 'provincial history has come of age, both as a subject of study itself and as a field where a most striking contribution can be made to Canada as a whole.' James A. Jackson's *The Centennial History of Manitoba* (T: M&S 1970) is a sound, readable volume, while Murray Donnelly's *The Government of Manitoba* (T: UTP 1963), is a carefully researched study of the province's political institutions.

Documents relating to Manitoba's entry into Confederation in 1870 have been collected in W.L. Morton, ed., *Manitoba: The Birth of a Province* (Altona: Manitoba Record Society 1965). Included in the volume are excerpts from the House of Commons debate on the Manitoba bill; the Journal of the Rev. N.J. Ritchot, one of the delegates appointed to negotiate the terms of Manitoba's entry into Confederation; and three of the four 'Lists of Rights' drawn up in the Red River Settlement. American interest in the Canadian West at the time of the first Riel rebellion may be followed in Alvin C. Gluek, *Minnesota and the Manifest Destiny of the Canadian Northwest* (T: UTP 1965), and in Hartwell Bowsfield, ed., *James Wickes Taylor Correspondence 1859-1870* (Altona: Manitoba Record Society 1968). Taylor was the special agent of the American State Department appointed to report on Red River affairs; he became American consul at Winnipeg in 1870.

The Manitoba Act of 1870 guaranteed a system of denominational schools and French as a legal language in the province. To what extent this was the recognition of a bicultural compact made at the time of Confederation in 1867 has been a matter of dispute. Donald Creighton, in 'John A. Macdonald, Confederation, and the Canadian West,' in R.C. Brown, ed., *Minorities, Schools and Politics* (T: UTP 1969), argues that the bicultural nature of the Manitoba Act resulted from Riel's 'dictatorship' and the need for a quick resolution of the difficulties at Red River. This interpretation, as well as Creighton's view regarding the establishment of denominational schools and the recognition of French in the Northwest Territories, is challenged in a harsh rebuttal by Ralph Heintzman, 'The Spirit of Confederation: Professor Creighton, Biculturalism and the Use of History,' CHR, 1971. Heintzman suggests that the bicultural institutions established in the West were not, as Creighton characterized them, the result of accident and improvisation. The decisions, he asserts, were made with deliberate intent and with the implications clearly in mind.

ALBERTA AND SASKATCHEWAN

The scholarly treatment of the territorial period of Alberta and Saskatchewan history is Lewis H. Thomas, *The Struggle for Responsible Government in the North West Territories, 1870-1897* (T: UTP 1956), and C.C. Lingard, *Territorial Government in Canada: The Autonomy Question in the Old North West Territories* (T: UTP 1946). This period and the struggle for provincial status are covered in summary form in Lewis H. Thomas, *The North-West Territories 1870-1905* (O: CHA Booklet no 26 1970). Documentary source material will be found in volume 2 of E.H. Oliver, *The Canadian North West: Its Early Development and Legislative Records* (O: KP 1915). *The Prairie West to 1905: A Canadian Source Book* (T: UTP 1975), with an introduction by Lewis G. Thomas, covers such post-1867 topics as government and politics, law and order, the ranching frontier, and the development of transportation and communication. Douglas Owram, ed., *The Formation of Alberta: A Documentary History* (Calgary: Historical Society of Alberta 1979), with an introduction by Lewis G. Thomas and Lewis H. Thomas, provides a collection of documents covering the territorial period of Alberta to the gaining of provincial status in 1905.

The best history of Saskatchewan is that by John H. Archer, *Saskatchewan: A History* (Saskatoon: Western Producer Prairie Books 1980), containing an extensive and useful bibliographical essay. The best analysis of the political scene in Saskatchewan is Norman Ward and Douglas Spafford, eds., *Politics in Saskatchewan* (T: Longmans

1968), a collection that deserves imitators for every province in Canada. To counter-balance the traditional picture of Saskatchewan as a province of 'radical' politics, Evelyn Eager, 'The Conservatism of the Saskatchewan Electorate,' argues that voters have 'withheld support from any movement which has not trimmed its radical edges and included practical benefits among its proposals.' The most recent volume on the political life of the province is David Smith's examination of the Liberal party in *Prairie Liberalism: The Liberal Party in Saskatchewan 1905-71* (T: UTP 1975). Evelyn Eager in *Saskatchewan Government, Politics and Pragmatism* (Saskatoon: Western Producer Prairie Books 1980) looks at the province's political institutions.

There has been no scholarly history of the province of Alberta. James G. MacGregor's *A History of Alberta* (Edmonton: Hurtig 1972) is a popular account with only a limited attempt to see provincial developments within the national context. In *The Liberal Party in Alberta: A History of Politics in the Province of Alberta 1905-1921* (T: UTP 1959) Lewis G. Thomas refers to Alberta as a province with a reputation for 'political eccentricity.' For fifty years (1921-71) Alberta was ruled by the United Farmers of Alberta and Social Credit. Thomas examines the Liberal dominance of the years 1905-21 as a characteristic of Alberta politics and relates this both to a non-party tradition and to the failure of oppostion parties to provide an acceptable alternative to the government in power. An excellent study of the Alberta political scene is Carlo Caldarola, ed., *Society and Politics in Alberta* (T: Methuen 1979), which examines party politics, political culture, voting patterns, and class, status, and power in the province. Alberta politics, the editor points out, is largely a product of 'western alienation,' and the province's 'resource autonomy' with its 'accompanying prosperity.' A splendid study of *Prairie Capitalism: Power and Influence in the New West* (T: M&S 1979) has been written by John Richards and Larry Pratt, with much use of primary sources.

LOUIS RIEL

The life of Louis Riel and the rebellions of 1869-70 and 1885 have received profuse attention. The scholarly biography is George Stanley, *Louis Riel* (T: Ryerson 1963). It is, and is likely to remain for some time, the definitive work. Joseph Kinsey Howard, in *Strange Empire: A Narrative of the Northwest* (NY: William Morrow 1952), presents Riel as a symbol of the North American frontier, doomed, as were the Métis and Indian people, by the advance of white society. Other biographies of Riel include W.M. Davidson, *Louis Riel, 1844-1885* (Calgary: Albertan Publishing Co 1955); E.B. Osler, *The Man Who Had to Hang: Louis Riel* (T: Longmans Green 1961); and Hartwell Bowsfield, *Louis Riel: The Rebel and the Hero* (T: OUP 1971). Thomas Flanagan in *Louis 'David' Riel: 'Prophet of the New World'* (T: UTP 1979) emphasizes Riel's religious ideas and beliefs, and argues here, as elsewhere (JCS, 1974), that the thesis that Riel was insane cannot be maintained.

George Stanley, in *The Birth of Western Canada: A History of the Riel Rebellions* (L: Longmans Green 1936), treats the rebellions in terms of cultural conflict, the clash between a primitive and a civilized society. The value of this pioneering study is enhanced by Stanley's analysis of the years between the two rebellions and the development of Indian, Métis, and white grievances against the federal government. The 1880s are seen within the context of cultural conflict and the beginnings of a western agrarian protest movement. The theme of cultural conflict is found also in Stanley's booklet *Louis Riel: Patriot or Rebel?* (O: CHA Booklet no 2 1954).

W.L. Morton has rejected Stanley's cultural conflict interpretation as related to the 1869-70 rebellion, arguing that the Red River Settlement by 1869 was not a primitive but rather a civilized society. He interprets Riel's resistance to the Canadian government in 1869 as an extension of the traditional racial and religious tension of eastern Canada to the West. Morton's discerning analysis of the situation at Red River in 1869-70 is found in his introduction to *Alexander Begg's Red River Journal and Other Papers Relative to the Red River Resistance of 1869-1870* (T: CS 1960).

Among contemporary accounts of the two rebellions are Alexander Begg, *The Creation of Manitoba: or a History of the Red River Troubles* (T: 1871); Charles A. Boulton, *Reminiscences of the North West Rebellions* (T: 1886); and C.P. Mulvaney, *The History of the North West Rebellion of 1885* (T: 1885). A recent account of the

1885 rebellion by Desmond Morton, *The Last War Drum: The North West Campaign of 1885* (T: Hakkert 1972), deals with the campaign itself in detail. R.E. Lamb's *Thunder in the North* (NY: Pageant Press 1957), while lacking analysis, presents an abundant selection of contemporary reactions to Riel – excerpts from the newspapers and the political debate. A collection of contemporary accounts, documents, and recent interpretations has been brought together in Hartwell Bowsfield, *Louis Riel: Rebel of the Western Frontier or Victim of Politics and Prejudice?* (T: CC 1969). The report of the House of Commons committee investigating the rebellion of 1869-70 and the promise of an amnesty to Riel is in *Journals of the House of Commons*, vol. 8, appendix 6, 1874. The trial of Riel is found in *Canada Sessional Papers*, 1886, vol. 19, no 43, and reprinted in Desmond Morton, ed., *The Queen versus Louis Riel* (T: UTP 1974). *The Diaries of Louis Riel* (Edmonton: Hurtig 1979) contains an introduction by Thomas Flanagan.

There are two histories of the Métis people: Marcel Giraud, a French historian and sociologist, *Le Métis canadien* (Paris: Université de Paris, Institut d'Ethnologie 1945), and A.H. de Trémaudan, *Histoire de la nation métisse dans l'ouest canadien* (M: Editions Albert Lévesque 1936). George Woodcock in *Gabriel Dumont: The Métis Chief and His Lost World* (Edmonton: Hurtig 1975) asks why Canadians chose to celebrate the martyr Riel and not the hero Dumont. The choice, he says, reflects the complexities of the Canadian inner feeling. Riel symbolizes Canadian alienation and defeat as a people. Canadians see themselves as a besieged minority. His biography of Dumont is an effective piece of writing outlining the social, political, and economic decline of the Métis people.

THE NATIONAL POLICY

The combination of railway, settlement, and tariff programs called the National Policy which was intended to develop a viable transcontinental economy but which provoked western protest is the subject of V.C. Fowke's *The National Policy and the Wheat Economy* (T: UTP

1957). Fowke's brilliant study traces also the grain marketing problems of the West and the development of the wheat pool system. In 'The National Policy – Old and New,' CJEPS, 1952, he provides a good summary of the role of the National Policy in integrating the West in the Canadian economy. Similar studies are W.A. Mackintosh's 1939 work for the Rowell-Sirois Commission on Dominion-Provincial Relations, *The Economic Background of Dominion-Provincial Relations* (reprinted T: M&S 1964), and R.C. Brown, 'The Nationalism of the National Policy,' in Peter Russell, ed., *Nationalism in Canada* (T: McGraw-Hill 1966). The same volume contains John Dales's 'Protection, Immigration and Canadian Nationalism,' which effectively questions some of the traditional interpretations of the value of the National Policy.

A comparison between the National Policies of Canada and the United States is found in Melville H. Watkins, 'The "American System" and Canada's National Policy,' *Bulletin of the Canadian Association for American Studies*, 1967. A similar but more probing comparison is V.C. Fowke, 'National Policy and Western Development in North America,' *Journal of Economic History*, 1956.

The best theoretical approach to the controversy between protectionism and free trade in Canadian economic development is J.H. Dales, 'Some Historical and Theoretical Comment on Canada's National Policies,' QQ, 1964, and his suggestive *The Protective Tariff in Canada's Development* (T: UTP 1966). Western attitudes toward the National Policy can be found in Edward Porritt, *The Revolt in Canada against the New Feudalism: Tariff History from the Revision of 1907 to the Uprising in the West in 1910* (L: Cassell 1911). Criticism of national economic policies, not entirely dissimilar to Porritt's, remains part of the current western attitude towards Confederation. A number of the readings referred to above reflect these attitudes. Kenneth Norrie, 'The National Policy and Prairie Economic Discrimination, 1870-1930,' in Donald H. Akenson, ed., *Canadian Papers in Rural History* (Gananoque: Langdale Press 1978), analyses statistically the costs of production to the Prairie farmer (price of land, price of machinery, railway rates, etc.) and questions whether those farmers had legitimate economic grievances.

IMMIGRATION, SETTLEMENT, AND RAILWAYS

Towards the end of the nineteenth century and as part of the National Policy, the Canadian government embarked upon an aggressive immigration program directed toward the settlement of the prairies. The result was a phenomenal growth in population, western development, and an increase in the number of immigrants from southern and eastern Europe. An excellent general account of this period is R.C. Brown and Ramsay Cook, *Canada 1896-1921: A Nation Transformed* (T: M&S 1974).

D.C. Corbett, *Canada's Immigration Policy: A Critique* (T: UTP 1957), while emphasizing Canadian immigration policies in the post-1945 period when immigration was urban, not agriculturally oriented, has background on the earlier periods. Corbett's specific interest is in the economic effects of immigration. Another general history, Norman Macdonald, *Canada: Immigration and Colonization, 1841-1903* (T: MAC 1966), has extended coverage of immigration to the West and provides information on specific ethnic groups. An older but still valuable study, with helpful statistical tables, is W.G. Smith, *A Study in Canadian Immigration* (T: Ryerson 1920). Smith deals with specific immigrant groups, and notes the problem of assimilation which had been first brought to the attention of the Canadian public in 1909 by J.S. Woodsworth in *Strangers within our Gates: or, Coming Canadians* (1909; T: UTP 1972). The attempted assimilation of European groups in Saskatchewan is covered by Robert England, *The Central European Immigrant in Canada* (T: MAC 1929). England's *The Colonization of Western Canada: A Study of Contemporary Land Settlement (1869-1934)* (L: P.S. King 1936) is the story of the adaptation of individuals and group communities to the environment from 1870 to the depression years of the 1930s. Howard Palmer, ed., *Immigration and the Rise of Multiculturalism* (T: CC 1975), is a collection of documents covering the period 1896-1971.

The movement of hundreds of thousands of Americans, one of the largest immigrant groups, into the Prairie provinces is covered by Karel Bicha, *The American Farmer and the Canadian West 1896-*

1914 (Lawrence, Kansas: Coronado Press 1972), and by Harold Troper, *Only Farmers Need Apply* (T: Griffin House 1972).

A number of the volumes of the Macmillan Canadian Frontiers of Settlement series are of fundamental importance to the study of immigration and settlement. Especially valuable are W.A. Mackintosh, *Prairie Settlement, the Geographical Setting* (1934), which covers the land, climate, railways, and the spread of settlement; C.A. Dawson, *Group Settlement, Ethnic Communities in Western Canada* (1936), which deals with specific groups (Doukhobors, Mennonites, Mormons, German Catholics, French Canadians), referring to them as 'cultural islands' inhibiting the process of assimilation; and C.A. Dawson and E.R. Yonge, *Pioneering in the Prairie Provinces: The Social Side of the Settlement Process* (1940), which covers the western economy, agricultural practices, and the establishment of educational and religious institutions. Originally published with A.S. Morton, *A History of Prairie Settlement* (T: MAC 1938), as one volume in the series, Chester Martin's *Dominion Lands' Policy* analyses federal regulations and the administration of public lands. An abridged edition of Martin's work was published (T: M&S) in 1973.

The periodical *Canadian Ethnic Studies* (University of Calgary, 1969-) has extensive bibliographical data on ethnic groups in Canada. Other bibliographical sources are Andrew Gregorovich, ed., *Canadian Ethnic Groups Bibliography* (T: Ontario Department of the Provincial Secretary and Citizenship 1972), and a series of bibliographies covering both published and unpublished sources issued by the federal Department of Citizenship and Immigration and its successor department, Manpower and Immigration.

The policy of railway land grants and the administration of lands granted to the Canadian Pacific Railway is traced in J.B. Hedges, *The Federal Railway Land Subsidy Policy of Canada* (Cambridge: Harvard UP 1934), and in his *Building the Canadian West: The Land and Colonization Policies of the Canadian Pacific Railway* (NY: MAC 1939).

The romance and high drama of the building of the transcontinental railway abounds in Pierre Berton's two volumes, *The National Dream: The Great Railway 1871-1881* and *The Last Spike: The Great Railway 1881-1885* (T: M&S 1970, 1971). The serious student of the Canadian Pacific Railway should not miss, in addition, the more prosaic but fundamental study by Harold Innis, *A History of the Canadian Pacific Railway* (1923; T: UTP 1970), or L.B. Irwin, *Pacific Railways and Nationalism in the Canadian-American Northwest 1845-1873* (1939; NY: Greenwood Press 1968). A recent attempt at debunking the 'national dream' school of Berton and criticizing the relationship between the CPR and the federal government is Robert Chodos, *The CPR: A Century of Corporate Welfare* (T: James Lewis and Samuel 1973).

Myth-making has also been the rule in much that has been written about the Royal Canadian Mounted Police. The centenary of the organization of the force in 1973 saw reprints of a number of earlier titles. J.P. Turner's *The North-West Mounted Police 1873-1893*, 2 vols. (O: Department of Justice 1950) is basically a chronology. Ronald Atkin, *Maintain the Right: The Early History of the North West Mounted Police, 1873-1900* (L: MAC 1973), covers familiar ground well, and provides many human touches. Nora and William Kelly, *The Royal Canadian Mounted Police: A Century of History 1873-1973* (Edmonton: Hurtig 1973), is too defensive toward the force and so uncritical that Lorne and Caroline Brown's *An Unauthorized History of the RCMP* (T: James Lewis and Samuel 1973), in which the Mounties are seen as strike-breakers and persecutors of radicals and immigrants, is almost welcome. The only balanced and analytical study to date is R.G. Macleod, *The North West Mounted Police and Law Enforcement 1873-1905* (T: UTP 1976), which places the police within the framework of politics and political ideology. The official reports of the commissioner of the RNWMP for the years 1874-87 have been reprinted in facsimile editions under the three titles *Opening up the West*, *Settlers and Rebels*, and *Law and Order* (T: Coles 1973).

MANITOBA SCHOOL QUESTION

In 1890 the Manitoba legislature withdrew financial support from denominational schools thought to have been guaranteed under the Manitoba Act of 1870. An introduction to the complex religious and racial problem which resulted and which bedevilled Canadian political life throughout the 1890s is Lovell Clark, ed., *The Manitoba*

School Question: Majority Rule or Minority Rights? (T: CC 1968). This compilation provides a sampling of contemporary opinion as well as both legal and historical interpretations. Clark's personal approach is that the controversy was not inherent in the local situation but resulted from the actions of a 'demagogue and bigot,' D'Alton McCarthy from Ontario, who succeeded in arousing the prejudices of Anglo-Saxon, Protestant Manitoba. In his history of Manitoba W.L. Morton suggests that Manitoba could have settled the school question 'quietly' had outside forces and events not intervened. Why Manitoba responded so readily to McCarthy and why Manitoba, usually spoken of as an extension of Ontario society, refused to accept the separate school system established in Ontario are questions which still need exploration.

John S. Ewart's *The Manitoba School Question* (T: CC 1894) is a compilation of the legislation and legal proceedings related to the controversy by a lawyer who had argued cases on behalf of the Roman Catholic minority in Manitoba. Ewart's participation is analysed in W.T. Shaw, 'The Role of John S. Ewart in the Manitoba School Question' (MA thesis, University of Manitoba 1959).

The attack on the denominational school system in Manitoba in the 1870s and the disappearance of the issue in the 1880s is dealt with by R.E. Clague, 'The Political Aspects of the Manitoba School Question, 1890-1896' (MA thesis, University of Manitoba 1939). The convulsive effect of the question on national political parties and its place in the 1896 federal election is examined in most of the studies on Wilfrid Laurier, and readers should consult H. Blair Neatby, *Laurier and a Liberal Quebec* (T: M&S 1973). See also John Saywell, ed., *The Canadian Journal of Lady Aberdeen, 1893-1898* (T: CS 1960); Ellen Cooke, 'The Federal Election of 1896 in Manitoba' (MA thesis, University of Manitoba 1943); and Lovell Clark, 'The Conservative Party in the 1890's,' CHAR, 1961. The most comprehensive study is Paul Crunican, *Priests and Politicians: Manitoba Schools and the Election of 1896* (T: UTP 1974). The only full-length study of the schools question in the Northwest Territories is Manoly Lupul, *The Roman Catholic Church and the North-West School Question: A Study in Church-State Relations in Western Canada, 1875-1905* (T: UTP 1974).

WINNIPEG GENERAL STRIKE, 1919

D.C. Masters, *The Winnipeg General Strike* (T: UTP 1950), remains
the standard and perhaps the most objective account of the origins
of the great strike of 1919. Masters concludes that despite 'wild
talk' by some radicals, the strike was exactly what it purported to
be – an effort to secure collective bargaining, not a seditious conspiracy or a Bolshevik plot. A contemporary interpretation of the
strike as a conspiracy is in the *Canadian Annual Review*, 1919. In
this interpretation the strike was a deliberate attempt by labour to
capture the government of Winnipeg and eventually 'overthrow
the existing system of National government and replace it by one
of workmen only.' The strike as part of Canadian labour history is
covered in H.A. Logan, *Trade Unions in Canada* (T: MAC 1948),
and by Eugene Forsey, 'History of the Labour Movement in Canada,' *Canada Year Book 1957-58*. The strike in terms of class
conflict is dealt with by Kenneth McNaught in his biography of J.S.
Woodsworth, *A Prophet in Politics* (T: UTP 1959); by Martin Robin
in *Radical Politics and Canadian Labour, 1880-1930* (Kingston:
Queen's University 1968); and by H.C. Pentland, 'Fifty Years
After,' *Canadian Dimension* 1969. The workers' account of the
events is in Norman Penner, ed., *Winnipeg 1919: The Strikers' Own
History of the Winnipeg General Strike* (T: James Lewis and Samuel
1973). David Bercuson, *Confrontation at Winnipeg* (M: MQUP 1974),
focuses on the industrial background of the strike, examining
labour-management relations in Winnipeg from the turn of the
century to 1919. Kenneth McNaught and David Bercuson, *The
Winnipeg General Strike 1919* (T: Longman 1974), provide a short,
general survey and a helpful chapter on 'pivotal' interpretations.
Two Royal Commission reports on the strike were made, one by
the federal government (Mathers Report), the other by the government of Manitoba (Robson Report). David Bercuson, *Fools and
Wise Men* (T: MHR 1978), analyses the rise and fall of the One Big
Union which was in the process of formation at the time of the
1919 strike. A. Ross McCormack, *Reformers, Rebels, and Revolutionaries* (T: UTP 1977), covers the development of western Canadian radical movements for the period 1899-1919.

THIRD PARTIES

The West has been the birthplace for a succession of new political movements. Regional politics and third parties are covered in Hugh Thorburn, ed., *Party Politics in Canada* (T: PH 1972); John C. Courtney, *Voting in Canada* (T: PH 1967); Paul Fox, *Politics in Canada* (T: McGraw-Hill 1966); and F.C. Engelmann and Mildred Schwartz, *Political Parties and the Canadian Social Structure* (T: PH 1967). Desmond Morton's *NDP: The Dream of Power* (T: Hakkert 1974) treats the NDP governments in the West as well as the national party. Martin Robin's *Canadian Provincial Politics: The Party Systems of the Ten Provinces* has a chapter on each of the Prairie provinces and British Columbia. In *Democracy and Discontent* (1969; 2nd ed., T: MHR 1978) Walter D. Young looks at the Progressive, Social Credit, and CCF parties.

The basic study of Canada's first 'third' party is W.L. Morton, *The Progressive Party in Canada* (T: UTP 1950), which was issued as the first of a ten-volume series designed to cover the background and development of Social Credit in Alberta. The Progressives' electoral triumph of 1921 is represented as the culmination of western agrarian discontent. Morton's study includes coverage of the western provincial political scene, the conflicting rivalries within the Progressive party, and its decline in the 1920s. Paul Sharp, in *The Agrarian Revolt in Western Canada* (Minneapolis: University of Minnesota Press 1948), makes a comparison between the American and Canadian agrarian protest movements, while Louis Aubrey Wood, *A History of Farmers' Movememnts in Canada* (T: UTP 1975), presents an historical survey of the agrarian movement covering the establishment of the Grange in Ontario in 1872, the Patrons of Industry, the grain growers' associations on the Prairies, the struggle against the tariff 1896-1911, and the Progressive party.

The populist background of the American-born Alberta agrarian leader Henry Wise Wood and his theory of occupational representation and group government is analysed in W.L. Morton, 'The Social Philosophy of Henry Wise Wood, the Canadian Agrarian Leader,' *Agricultural History*, 1948. The attempt to put Wood's theory into practice by Alberta Progressives in the 1920s and the problem faced by third parties in the parliamentary system is covered by W.L. Morton in 'The Western Progressive Movement and Cabinet Domination,' CJEPS, 1946. The origins of the Progressive movement and the conflict between Wood's followers and those of the Manitoban Thomas Crerar, who preferred traditional party practices and sought to avoid 'class' politics, is looked at in his 'The Western Progressive Movement, 1919-1921,' CHAR, 1950. W.K. Rolph's biography, *Henry Wise Wood of Alberta* (T: UTP 1950), includes the story of Wood's leadership of the United Farmers of Alberta and his organization of wheat pools. There is no biography of Crerar as yet.

Indispensable to the study of Social Credit in Alberta are John A. Irving, *The Social Credit Movement in Alberta* (T: UTP 1959), and C.B. Macpherson, *Democracy in Alberta* (T: UTP 1953, 1962). Irving's narrative approach covers the years from 1932, when William Aberhart embraced the monetary theories of Major C.H. Douglas to the Social Credit electoral victory of 1935. Since the success of the movement was so largely dependent on the personality of one man, Irving devotes considerable attention to Aberhart's career as a school teacher, fundamentalist, and radio evangelist. He investigates the background of a number of secondary leaders and, based on interviews, provides a psychologist's picture of the response of followers to Aberhart and his teachings. To Irving, the rise of Social Credit can be attributed to the failure of the United Farmers of Alberta government to cope with the Depression of the 1930s and to Aberhart's personal appeal and organizational abilities. An article-length study of the rise of Social Credit is his 'The Evolution of the Social Credit Movement,' CJEPS, 1948. John J. Barr, *The Dynasty: The Rise and Fall of Social Credit in Alberta* (T: M&S 1974), carries the story of the party to the electoral victory of Peter Lougheed and the Conservatives in 1971.

In Macpherson's book the reader will find an extended analysis of Social Credit monetary theory and a theoretical approach to the reasons Alberta turned from the traditional two-party system, first to the United Farmers of Alberta in 1921 and then to Social Credit in 1935. Macpherson dismissed the UFA and Social Credit as third parties and characterized Alberta as having a 'quasi-party' system in which the dominance of one party was the result of a homogeneous electorate. The electorate acted as it did because Alberta was a petit-bourgeois, quasi-colonial society in rebellion against the political and economic power of central Canada. In 'The Political Theory of Social Credit,' CJEPS, 1949, Macpherson considers the relationship of Social Credit theory to parliamentary democracy and class politics. Although concentrating on the Social Credit movement in Quebec, Maurice Pinard, in *The Rise of a Third Party: A Study in Crisis Politics* (Englewood Cliffs: PH 1971), puts forward a general hypothesis regarding the rise of third parties which is relevant to the Alberta situation. He rejects Macpherson's quasi-party thesis and argues that Alberta has always been an area of one-party dominance.

Denis Smith, 'Prairie Revolt, Federalism and the Party System,' printed in Thorburn's *Party Politics*, also challenges Macpherson's theory. Macpherson's suggestion that the alternate party system never took firm root in western Canada must be modified, he says, since the dominance of one party as reflected in the number of seats in a provincial legislature is not reflected in the popular vote: 'No prairie party has received more than fifty-eight percent of the popular vote in a provincial election since 1917,' In the same article Smith also challenges Frank Underhill's thesis in *Canadian Political Parties* (O: CHA 1957) that third parties at the provincial level constitute the real centre of political opposition to the federal government. In 'Liberals and Conservatives on the Prairies, 1917-1968' in David Gagan, ed., *Prairie Perspectives*, he contends that the two traditional national parties have always maintained 'a substantial presence' in western Canada.

J.R. Mallory's study, *Social Credit and the Federal Power in Canada* (T: UTP 1954), covers the Alberta scene from 1935-45 but goes beyond the details of the disallowance of Alberta's Social Credit legislation. He includes an historical survey of the federal disallowance power from 1867 to 1936 and places the struggle between Alberta and the federal government within the context of a revival of federal control over the provinces. The disallowance of the 1937 Social Credit legislation is dealt with by Mallory in 'Alberta Social Credit Legislation of 1937,' CJEPS, 1948.

W.E. Mann, *Sect, Cult, and Church in Alberta* (T: UTP 1955), looks at the religious background of the Alberta community. The relationship between the evangelical religious movement and Social Credit is examined by S.D. Clark in 'The Religious Sect in Canadian Politics,' *American Journal of Sociology*, 1945, and in his *The Developing Canadian Community*. Lewis H. Thomas, ed., *William Aberhart and Social Credit in Alberta* (T: CC 1977), is a helpful collection of documents on the man and the movement. David Elliott in 'Antithetical Elements in William Aberhart's Theology and Political Ideology,' CHR, 1978, provides a careful analysis of Aberhart's religious fundamentalism.

A number of 'radicals' or 'left-wing' leaders in the 1920s and 1930s, for example, E.A. Partridge, in *A War on Poverty* (Winnipeg: c1925), argued that farmers and workers, both victims of the capitalist, free-enterprise system, should join in establishing a co-operative society. The role of such leaders in moving the farm organizations in Saskatchewan toward the co-operative and socialist goal is examined by Duff Spafford, 'The Left Wing 1921-1931,' in Ward and Spafford, eds., *Politics in Saskatchewan*. S.M. Lipset, in *Agrarian Socialism: The Cooperative Commonwealth Federation in Saskatchewan; A Study in Political Sociology* (Berkeley: University of California Press 1950), identified the agrarian protest and co-operative movement as a socialist movement. He makes it clear, however, that as the CCF approached success in 1944 it was not a doctrinaire socialist party. A second edition of Lipset's work (NY: Doubleday 1968) contains several articles which examine the CCF movement after the electoral victory of 1944 in Saskatchewan. These cover an analysis of class voting behaviour, the doctors' strike of 1962, and the medicare program. In one of these articles, 'Agrarian Pragmatism and Radical Politics,' John W. Bennett and Cynthia Drueger challenge Lipset's interpretation of the leftward swing in the agrarian movement and claim that evidence of collective action should not be equated with socialism. They point out that the grass-roots support of the CCF in Saskatchewan was interested primarily in remedying specific economic grievances and that by 1944 the socialist ideology of the party had been much diluted. Dean E. McHenry, in *The Third Force in Canada: The Cooperative Commonwealth Federation, 1932-1948* (Berkeley: University of California Press 1950), notes the relationship between the British and Canadian socialist movement. The emphasis in his work is on party organization and structure. The meaning of the 'Third Force' in his title is his belief that the CCF was a middle way between the extremes of reaction and revolution.

In 'The League for Social Reconstruction and the Development of a Canadian Socialism, 1932-1936,' JCS, 1972, Michiel Horn argues that the Regina Manifesto of 1933 was in large part worked out by eastern intellectuals and that Canadian socialism, though British in origin, had its unique Canadian content. Useful on the background of the socialist movement in Canada to 1920 is Paul Fox, 'Early Socialism in Canada,' in J.H. Aitchison, ed., *The Political Process in Canada* (T: UTP 1963, 1971). Gad Horowitz, *Canadian Labour in Politics* (T: UTP 1968), offers a study of Louis Hartz's thesis of fragment cultures applied to Canada and of the role of socialism in Canada and its relationship to organized labour.

The CCF movement in Saskatchewan is covered also by Walter D. Young in his excellent history of the national party, *The Anatomy of a Party: The National CCF 1932-1961* (T: UTP 1969). The only scholarly biography of the 'father' of the CCF is McNaught's *A Prophet in Politics*, which covers Woodsworth's various careers as preacher, social worker, Winnipeg striker, pacifist, and socialist politician. A personal account of Woodsworth's life is that by his daughter, Grace McInnis, *J.S. Woodsworth: A Man to Remember* (T: MAC 1953). A collection of Woodsworth's writings has been put together in Edith Fowke, ed., *Towards Socialism: Selections from the Writings of J.S. Woodsworth* (T: Ontario Woodsworth Memorial Foundation 1948). A useful compilation reflecting the changes in the party's political philosophy is found in *The Decline and Fall of a Good Idea: CCF-NDP Manifestoes 1932 to 1969*, introd. Michael Cross (T: New Hogtown Press 1974).

DEPRESSION, 1930s

Undiversified economy plus a series of drought years made the Prairies tragically vulnerable to the Depression of the 1930s. Comprehensive examinations of the period are A.E. Safarian, *The Canadian Economy in the Great Depression* (T: UTP 1959); W.A. Mackintosh, *Economic Problems of the Prairie Provinces* (T: MAC 1935); and the

Report of the Royal Commission on Dominion-Provincial Relations (O: KP 1940). H. Blair Neatby, *The Politics of Chaos: Canada in the Thirties* (T: MAC 1972), and Ramsay Cook, ed., *Politics of Discontent* (T: UTP 1967), have articles on Woodsworth, Aberhart, and T. Dufferin Pattullo of British Columbia. Victor Hoar has edited a collection of articles and reminiscences, *The Great Depression* (T: CC 1969), as well as *The On-To-Ottawa Trek* (T: CC 1970), which deals with the relief camp strike in British Columbia and the Regina riot of 1935. *Recollections of the On-To-Ottawa Trek* (T: M&S 1973) is a personal account by a participant, Ronald Liversedge. James Gray, in *The Winter Years: The Depression on the Prairies* (T: MAC 1966), captures brilliantly the essence of the Depression years in human and social terms. *Ten Lost Years 1929-1939* (T: Doubleday 1973) is an oral history collection of personal memories of the 1930s compiled by Barry Broadfoot.

SUMMARY

Writing on the Canadian West is dominated by studies in political and economic history, by the east-west relationship, and western political dissent. Despite this emphasis it has been suggested that there is a need for more primary research in Prairie politics. David Smith makes this comment in 'Interpreting Prairie Politics,' JCS, 1972, a survey of the political literature on the Prairie provinces with extensive bibliographic references. There are, Smith argues, many gaps in the study of political culture and institutions. One of these gaps has been filled by his own study, *The Regional Decline of a National Party: Liberals on the Prairies* (T: UTP 1981), in which it is argued that the national party has failed to understand the 'rural fundamentalism' of the Prairies and its regional economic needs. The most obvious gap is in the field of biography. Few full-length studies on political and other figures have been undertaken; there is, for instance, no serious biography of William Aberhart. John Kendle's *John Bracken: A Political Biography* (T: UTP 1979); D.J. Hall's *Clifford Sifton, I: The Young Napoleon, 1861-1900* (V: UBCP 1981); Anthony Mardiros's *The Life of a Prairie Radical: William Irvine* (T: Lorimer 1979) represent recent examples of work in this field. One of the themes in writings on the Prairie provinces is that the West was invaded by an eastern culture. Studies of the cultural carriers – the newspaper editors, clergymen, teachers, professional class, agrarian and political leaders – are needed to represent both the process of Canadianization of the West as well as the regionalization of its people. This theme has received attention in Doug Owram's excellent study, *Promise of Eden: The Canadian Expansionist Movement and the Idea of the West, 1856-1900* (T: UTP 1980).

The political and economic 'domination' of the West by central Canada has been treated extensively within the context of the Laurentian and Metropolitan interpretations of Canada history. The Metropolitan thesis outlines how such centres as Montreal and Toronto attached an economic, political, and cultural hinterland to their respective metropolitan bases. In the hinterland a sub-metropolis, Winnipeg or Vancouver, attached sub-hinterlands. The analysis of this secondary process has begun but remains a fertile field for investigation. The suggestion by J. Maurice Careless in '"Limited Identities" in Canada,' CHR, 1969, that the true Canadian experience has been regional rather than national should prompt not only further studies of regionalism in Canada, but also an examination of the economic, political, and cultural relationships between urban and rural areas in the Canadian West. Inquiry might be made into the influence and role of urban newspapers or educational institutions.

The only study to date of a Prairie city, comparable to D.C. Masters's examination of the rise of Toronto, is Alan F.J. Artibise, *Winnipeg: A Social History of Urban Growth 1874-1914* (M: MQUP 1975). Reuben Bellan, *Winnipeg: First Century* (Winnipeg: Queenston House Publishing Co 1978), describes the origins and economic development of Winnipeg to the 1970s. Alan F.J. Artibise has edited a collection of documents on the same city under the title *Gateway City: Documents on the City of Winnipeg, 1873-1913* (Altona: Manitoba Record Society 1979). The role of the Hudson's Bay Company in the early development of Winnipeg and other Prairie communities is outlined in Hartwell Bowsfield, ed., *The Letters of Charles John Brydges, 1879-1882*, with an introduction by Alan Wilson (Winnipeg: Hudson's Bay Record Society 1977). A.R. McCormack and Ian Macpherson, eds., *Cities in the West* (O: National Museums of Canada 1975), a collection of papers presented at the Western Canada Urban History Conference in 1974, and Alan F.J. Artibise, ed., *Town and City: Aspects of Western Canadian Urban Development* (Regina: Canadian Plains Research Center 1981), provide a sample of the research underway in the field of urban history. The contribution such research might make is manifest in such articles as J.M.S. Careless, 'Aspects of Urban Life in the West, 1870-1914,' in *Prairie Perspectives 2*, and 'Development of the Winnipeg Business Community, 1870-1890,' TRSC, 1970, or Karl Lenz, 'Large Urban Places in the Prairie Provinces – Their Development and Location,' in R.L. Gentilcore, *Canada's Changing Geography* (T: PH 1967).

In his 'Clio in Canada,' W.L. Morton commented that Frederick Jackson Turner's sectional interpretation of American history was relevant to Canada and argued that western sectionalism 'in different terms' was as justified as Quebec nationalism or the British nationalism of Ontario. The centrality and emphasis in historical writing about the Prairies as an agricultural region has been overcome. The work of the Canadian Plains Research Center and of the Western Canadian Studies Conference symbolizes a new direction in which research is directed at broader aspects of Prairie life, its ecology and urban development, its native peoples and its literature.

PETER OLIVER

Ontario

There has still been surprisingly little effort by Canadian historians consciously to write the regional history of Ontario. As a result, while there has been much history written by Ontario historians and while there is much about Ontario in that work, there does not at the moment exist a historical literature devoted to Ontario in the sense that such may be said to exist for other Canadian regions. This is not intended to signify that there are not studies of the development of education, of political systems, of business interests, and other facets of Ontario life which are comparable to those done elsewhere but merely that in contrast to the spirit and method of work done, say about the west or Quebec, that which has taken Ontario for its subject has not always had Ontario as its theme. Put simply, there seems to have been a tacit, almost unthinking, assumption that no regional history of this province is required or even appropriate.

In explanation of this phenomenon, Morris Zaslow, a past president of the Ontario Historical Society, has commented that 'the regionalism of Ontario is often so closely identified with Canadian nationalism that many Ontarians fail to regard Ontario as a region at all and equate the larger Dominion with the purposes of Ontario.' Witness, for example, the role played by Ontario writers in the general development of Canadian historical scholarship. From the day of Wrong, Kennedy, and Skelton to that of Innis, Creighton, and

Careless, the major concern of Ontario scholars, on the face of it at least, was not the province but the nation. Let the westerners write about their wheat economy and the French Canadians their nationalism; any study of the work of Ontario historians will show that they took all Canada for their subject.

Yet while national politics, the federal government, and the Canadian economy provided them with subjects, such interests could not disguise the fact that many of the assumptions and values on which their analysis rested, or to which their interpretations pointed, attested to the Ontario origins of their authors. They were products of the same society that produced politicians determined that 'Ontario must lead the way' and churchmen bent on the 'Canadianization' of the west. Seldom do they seem to have recognized that the work they were doing might reflect a regional bias just as surely as did that whose subject matter was explicitly regional, but nonetheless theirs was a brand of national history with which those living elsewhere than in Ontario must have had some difficulty in identifying. The Manitoba historian, W.L. Morton, perceived this when he noted of the influential Laurentian interpretation propounded by Innis and Creighton that 'its implications cannot be but misleading both to those brought up in the metropolitan area and those brought up in the hinterlands. Teaching inspired by the historical experience of metropolitan Canada cannot but deceive, and deceive cruelly, children of the outlying sections.'

Eventually, the historian of ideas will draw upon the rich lode of national historical scholarship produced by Ontarians to explain many of that society's values and prejudices. This does not, however, provide adequate compensation for that which other Canadian regions already have in somewhat greater measure – that is, a respectable brand of regional history. That most historical scholarship produced here has been directed towards national themes has meant that in a very real way Ontario, so far as written history is concerned, must be classified as a have-not province. There has, in short, been no sustained effort to delineate and explain Ontario's regional characteristics. Furthermore, the bulk of the work that has been done has focused on Upper Canada and Canada West and generations of students in the schools might have noticed, but probably did not, that after 1867 Ontario, at the very moment of its creation as a province within Confederation, seemed to drop from sight in the textbooks and the classrooms.

In part this was because this province, wealthy, stable, sure of its role in Confederation, could perhaps be taken for granted. Many Ontario academics have studied the phenomenon of sectional unrest in the west and the fascinating nationalism of French Canada while ignoring the society in which they themselves lived and taught. As well, as industrialization and urbanization contributed to the destruction of the values of old Ontario, the region, we are told, became all but indistinguishable in its character from other North American industrial societies. This circumstance caused one scholar, A.R.M. Lower, to raise the question: 'Ontario – Does It Exist?' OH, 1968, and to respond with a resounding 'No.' The very size of the province, its own internal regional diversification, and, most of all, the eroding power of unchecked urbanization and industrialization, destroyed the region's sense of identity more completely than happened in any other Canadian region until Lower could conclude that no more are there Ontarians but only people who happen to live in Ontario. Yet such a conclusion will seem strange to those Canadians who live outside the province's borders, to Nova Scotians, to Albertans, to Québécois, who seldom hesitate to offer their own views of the province's peculiar characteristics, often views which are less than complimentary. And to Ontarians as well Lower's conclusion should seem premature if only because it was made in a period when historians, novelists, and poets had not yet directed their attention in any sustained way to understanding and defining Ontario's regional characteristics.

That situation now is changing but at present Ontario history is in a somewhat peculiar state of transition. The last decade has seen an enormous amount of work dealing with post-Confederation Ontario subjects. In part this is a result of the infusion of provincial funds through the Ontario Historical Studies Series and several volumes of the OHSS now are in print. Mostly, however, the greatly increased volume of historical scholarship may be attributed to the number of Canadian historians now at work in university history departments as well as to exciting new developments in such fields as social, labour, education, and intellectual history. The bibliographical guides described herein attest to the hundreds of articles, theses, and books being written about Ontario subjects and the present selection necessarily is idiosyncratic, reflecting to a degree the interests of the author. But in relatively few cases does this bulk of work take a consciously regional approach. In the late 1960s Maurice Careless, Ramsay Cook, and others argued that the Canadian reality can best be understood by first coming to terms with Canada's regions and undoubtedly regional approaches in the 1970s became more respectable than ever before.

Yet for Ontario at least, notwithstanding the work of the OHSS and the increasing number of courses in Ontario history offered in the universities, the regional approach has not prevailed. While it is true that more than ever before the Ontario regionalist may draw on a profusion of riches, in social and economic if not in political history, yet Ontario has yet to develop a distinguished school of historians whose approach first and foremost is regional and whose work allows us to say with assurance that we now understand what is unique and what is universal about this province's regional characteristics.

In Ontario regional history remains a significant but secondary approach. What seems to be happening is that the profusion of interest in labour, educational, and other studies is making available a body of material which will become grist for the regionalist's mill. Instead of starting an inquiry with questions about Ontario as a region, it seems likely that in the province the regionalist will be the synthesizer who takes the pieces of economic, social, cultural, and political history and pieces them together into some coherent whole. In written history, then, as in other respects, Ontario, it is clear, is not a region like the others.

BIBLIOGRAPHICAL WORKS

The most comprehensive bibliographical tool is Olga B. Bishop *et al.*, eds., *Bibliography of Ontario History, 1867-1976: Cultural, Economic, Political, Social*, 2 vols (T: UTP for Ontario Historical Studies Series 1980). Organized topically, it includes books, periodical articles, government reports, and Royal Commissions. Also invaluable are the Book Notes published annually in *Ontario History*. Since 1980 these have been published separately by the Ontario Historical Society in an 'Annual Bibliography of Ontario History.' Loraine Spencer and Susan Holland compiled *Northern Ontario: A Bibliography* (T: UTP 1968). In 1972 Laurentian University Press published *Community Development in Northeastern Ontario: A Selected Bibliography* compiled by Gilbert A. Stelter and John Rowan. As well, Professor Stelter's *Canadian Urban History: A Selected Bibliography* (Sudbury: Laurentian UP 1972) contains a useful section on Ontario. Benjamin Fortin and Jean-Pierre Gaboury have prepared a *Bibliographie analytique de l'Ontario français* (Cahiers du Centre de Recherche en Civilisation Canadienne-Française, l'Université d'Ottawa 1975). The Centre de Recherche has also published numerous other guides and bulletins respecting Franco-Ontarian materials. Andrew Gregorovich's *Canadian Ethnic Groups Bibliography: A Selected Bibliography of Ethno-Cultural Groups in Canada and the Province of Ontario* appeared in 1972 under the auspices of the Ontario Department of the Provincial Secretary and Citizenship. *Ontario Ethno-Cultural Newspapers, 1835-1972*, an annotated checklist, was compiled by Duncan McLaren (T: UTP 1973). In an important project, the Toronto Area Archivist's Group in co-operation with the Boston Mills Press has undertaken to prepare a series of guides to regional archival resources. Entitled *Ontario's Heritage: A Guide to Archival Resources*, the series now invludes volume I, *Peterborough Region* (1978); volume VII, *Peel Region* (1979); and volume XIII, *North-East Ontario* (1980). A large number of county and local histories have been written in Ontario, with the late nineteenth century and the recent centenary period representing the years of peak production. The most useful guides are William F.E. Morley, *Canadian Local Histories to 1950: A Bibliography – Ontario and the Canadian North* (T: UTP 1978); and Barbara B. Aitken's *Local Histories of Ontario Municipalities Published in the Years 1957-1972* (rev. and enlarged ed., Kingston: Public Library Board 1972). Also see the register of theses on microfilm published by the National Library. Finally, Hazel I. MacTaggart has provided two invaluable guides to government documents in her *Publications of the Government of Ontario 1901-1955* (T: UTP 1964) and *Publications of the Government of Ontario 1956-1971* (T: Ministry of Government Services 1975). Dr Olga Bishop's *Publications of the Government of Ontario 1867-1900* (T: Ministry of Government Services 1976) successfully completes the cycle. The *Directory and Guide to the Services of the Government of Ontario* and *The Ontario Government Directory and Guide* (various dates) contain useful information on government publications.

PERIODICALS

Ontario History, the quarterly journal of the Ontario Historical Society, recently added a book review section and has been publishing a good deal of interesting work by younger scholars and graduate students which reflects changing trends in research interests. An *Index to the Publications of the Ontario Historical Society, 1899-1972* was compiled by Hilary Bates and Robert Sherman and published by the society in 1974.

The publications of La Société Historique du Nouvel-Ontario include studies of community life, educational development, church history, ecoomic and mining affairs, folk music, biographical portraits, and other themes. Although the quality varies greatly, they are indispensable to the study of Northern Ontario in general and Franco-Ontarian history in particular, as is the *Laurentian University Review*.

An important source for ethnic history is *Polyphony*, the bulletin of the Multicultural History Society of Ontario. One recent edition, for example, fall 1981, offers a valuable collection of articles on the Finns in Ontario and Canada.

Several periodicals devoted to more local studies should also be noted, including *Wentworth Bygones*, *Historic Kingston*, and *Western Ontario Historical Notes* and *Western Ontario History Nuggets* started by Fred Landon of that university. A list of articles published in the latter two between 1942 and 1972 was prepared at the D.B. Weldon Library of the University of Western Ontario. Some of the province's local historical societies (their names and addresses are conveniently listed on the back cover of OH) from time to time publish notes and transactions but there is no general guide to these.

GENERAL WORKS

Only a few chapters of Alexander Fraser's *A History of Ontario*, 2 vols. (T: Canada History Company 1907) deal with the post-Confederation period and their approach is that of an uncritical political narrative. The series *Canada and its Provinces* recognized that there is more to history than past politics and the two volumes dealing with Ontario, prepared by such scholars as W.S. Wallace, James Mavor, Adam Shortt, and B.E. Fernow, include discussions of education, the municipal and judicial systems, and economic development. Although aimed at the general reader and somewhat lacking in original research and critical analysis, they often repay rereading today. In 1927 two distinguished students of Ontario history, Fred Landon of the University of Western Ontario and J.E. Middleton, whose particular interest was municipal history, published in four volumes their *Province of Ontario: A History* (T: Dominion Publishing Company). A well-balanced description of social, economic, and political developments organized thematically, it includes separate essays on the provincial Liberal and Conservative parties, on trade, education, banking, transportation, the churches, and even on journalism, the courts, and the medical profession. Some attention is paid to particular regions within the province and a large section, 'An Historical Gazetteer of the counties and Districts in the Province of Ontario,' uses census and assessment data plus many of the thirty-five-odd Ontario Atlases which appeared in the late nineteenth century to provide brief descriptions of Ontario municipalities. In common with Fraser's *History*, much space, in this case over two volumes, is devoted to brief biographical essays on prominent citizens. Since the pre-Confederation period is also dealt with, the time spent on the more recent years is cut down drastically. Still, there is much of value in Middleton and Landon and they do not hesitate to take a critical approach, as in their judgment that Mowat Liberalism gradually 'petrified into a complete Toryism.' There is also some discussion of post-Confederation developments in Professor Landon's fine volume on *Western Ontario and the American Frontier*, which was first published in 1941 by Ryerson Press and Yale University Press in the Carnegie Endowment Series and reprinted in paperback in 1967 in the Carleton Library. G.P. de T. Glazebrook, *Life in Ontario: A Social History* (T: UTP 1968), is a bland narrative which contains some interesting material but generally confirms the impression that much additional monograph research must be done before a successful synthesis can be achieved. The most recent general history, Joseph Schull's *Ontario since 1867* (T: M&S for the Ontario Historical Studies Series 1978), is a useful and workmanlike survey, but it fails to achieve for Ontario the kind of insights into the provincial character provided by Morton's *Manitoba*. Roger Hall and Gordon Dodds, *A Picture History of Ontario* (Edmonton: Hurtig 1978), is a fascinating introduction to the province's rich visual heritage.

There are several other items of a general nature that it would be useful to mention at this point. Since J.E. Hodgett's invaluable *Pioneer Public Service* (T: UTP 1955) stops with Confederation, there is no administrative study of the provincial government but F.F. Schindeler's *Responsible Government in Ontario* (T: UTP 1969), which carefully examines the executive and the legislative branches, concludes that executive encroachments have so transformed the province's governmental system that parliamentary government may remain only as a myth. Schindeler's indictment provides a carefully documented study of the evolution of government in terms of his central thesis, but a volume broader in scope, less polemical, and devoting more attention to the pre-1945 period is still very much needed. There is an important geographical study, *Ontario*, edited by Louis Gentilcore (T: UTP 1972).

Two collections of essays available in paperback provide an introduction to Ontario history and an indication of recent trends in research. *Profiles of a Province*, a centennial project commissioned by the Ontario Historical Society and which appeared in 1967, includes sections on the formative years, the political scene, the economy, and the Ontario outlook. Very much a mixed bag, the volume was a reflection of weakness rather than strength, relieved

principally by S.F. Wise's perceptive study of Upper Canadian Toryism, several suggestive essays on modern politicians, and W.H.
Magee's thoughts on the literary scene. *Oliver Mowat's Ontario* (T:
MAC 1972), edited by Donald Swainson and more restricted in its
chronological scope, showed a higher standard of scholarship; essays
by Graeme Decarie on prohibition, Michael Bliss on the collective
impulse in the business community, and H.V. Nelles on the political
economy of the resource sector are among the better contributions.
Aspects of Nineteenth-Century Ontario (T: UTP 1974), edited by F.H.
Armstrong, H.A. Stevenson, and J.D. Wilson, is a *festschrift* in honour of Dr J.J. Talman, one of the province's pioneer social historians.

Ontario governments have been as adept as any in Canada at the
art of Royal Commissioning, and some of the most important material relating to Ontario history is contained in the reports and in the
transcripts of evidence. The several guides to government publications conveniently list the Royal Commissions and commissions of
inquiry; and there is also an excellent unpublished preliminary
inventory, *Records of Commissions and Committees* (1969), which is
available for use at the Ontario Archives. McTaggart usefully indicates which of the reports in her period (1901-55) were published in
the Sessional Papers while Sessional Paper No 6, 1894, lists Royal
Commissions which appeared between 1867 and 1894. Another
guide is R.P. Smith, *Royal Commissions of the Province of Ontario,
1867 to 1950* (Kingston: Queen's UP 1950).

There are several other resources which might best be described
in this catch-all section. Every student of Ontario history soon dis-
covers to his regret that too often historical statistics are unavailable
on a provincial basis and even when Urquhart and Buckley's *Historical Statistics of Canada* does deal with provincial matters, it usually
presents them in terms of national aggregates. A guide to regional
sources of statistical information is Dean Tudor, *Sources of Statistical
Data for Ontario* (O: Canada Library Association 1972). The province has also produced a constituency-by-constituency history of
election results compiled by Roderick Lewis, the chief election
officer. The most recent edition is the *Centennial Edition of a History
of the Electoral Districts, Legislatures and Ministries of the Province of*

Ontario 1867-1968 (T: QP nd). Most provinces have not had Hansards until fairly recently and Ontario is no exception, with regular recording of debates beginning only during the Drew administration of the 1940s. Fortunately, except for two brief periods, newspaper clippings from the holdings of the Ontario Archives and the Legislative Library have been microfilmed and this *Newspaper Hansard*, drawn very largely from the Toronto *Globe*, is available from 1867 in the Provincial Archives and in some university libraries. Finally, the old *Canadian Annual Review of Public Affairs*, which appeared between 1901 and 1938, and the new version, which commenced publication in 1960, contain essays on Ontario affairs.

PROVINCIAL POLITICS, 1867-96

In provincial politics, as in all other aspects of Ontario history, the volume of published material is less than overwhelming, and it is frequently necessary to turn to MA and PHD theses which are usually available on interlibrary loan or on microfilm. For the same reason, it is perhaps premature to attempt to place what material does exist in any historiographical tradition and in most cases a brief assessment will suffice.

Only two chapters of Bruce W. Hodgins's study of *John Sandfield Macdonald* (T: UTP 1971) deal with the post-Confederation phase of the career of the man who was Ontario's first premier, but they are sufficient to demonstrate that several enduring themes in Ontario politics date from 1867. Sandfield's defence of an eastern Ontario point of view emphasizes the regional basis of Ontario politics while Professor Hodgins's discussion of his social and educational policies clearly demonstrates that enlightened programs did not begin with Mowat Liberalism. D.G. Kerr, 'The 1867 Elections in Ontario: The Rules of the Game,' CHR, 1970, provides a fascinating glimpse of the seamier side of public life, while Margaret Helen Small, 'A study of the Dominion and the Provincial Elections of 1867 in Ontario' (MA thesis, Queen's University 1968), is a careful piece of electoral analysis. For the electoral collapse of Sandfield's coalition see J.D. Livermore, 'The Ontario Election of 1871 ...' OH, 1979. Richard Splane's 1948 MA thesis for the University of Toronto, 'The Upper

Canada Reform Party 1867-1878,' is a thoughtful analysis of political ideas and practices, while the intimacy of the connections between provincial and federal Liberals renders W.R. Graham's 'The Alexander Mackenzie Administration, 1873-1878: A Study of Liberal Tenets and Tactics' (MA thesis, University of Toronto 1944) and Dale Thomson, *Alexander Mackenzie: Clear Grit* (T: MAC 1960), of interest to students of provincial politics.

A 1967 University of Toronto doctoral dissertation by Margaret Evans, 'Oliver Mowat and Ontario, 1872-1896: A Study in Political Success,' introduces Mowat, the consummate political leader, but in many respects is now dated. Of the several articles about Mowat published by Mrs Evans, the most useful is that which appeared in *Profiles of a Province*, briefly summarizing her dissertation. An earlier two-volume biography by C.R.W. Biggar which appeared in 1905 (reprinted NY: AMS 1971) was written in the old 'life and letters' style and, as its author put it, 'in a spirit of loyal and affectionate remembrance.' Carman Miller's article, 'Mowat, Laurier and the Federal Liberal Party, 1887-1897,' which appeared in Swainson, ed., *Oliver Mowat's Ontario*, is an adequate treatment of its subject. Peter Dembski's 1975 Guelph PHD thesis, 'William Ralph Meredith, Leader of the Conservative Opposition in Ontario, 1878-1894,' is a workmanlike study of an important political figure. Desmond Morton in 'The Globe and the Labour Question ... 1886,' OH, 1981, challenges earlier views about the relationship between trade unionists and Liberal politicians.

Late nineteenth-century religious tensions are examined in their political dimension in Peter Dembski, 'A Matter of Conscience: The Origins of W.R. Meredith's Conflict with Archbishop J.J. Lynch,' OH, 1981; Martin A. Galvin, 'The Jubilee Riots in Toronto, 1875,' CCHAR, 1959; J.R. Miller, '"Equal Rights For All"; The E.R.A. and the Ontario Election of 1890,' OH, 1973, and 'The Jesuit Estates Act Crisis,' JCS, 1974; James T. Watt, 'Anti-Catholicism in Ontario Politics: 1894,' OH, 1967, and 'Anti-Catholic Nativism in Canada: The Protestant Protective Association,' CHR, 1967; and Janet B. Kerr, 'Sir Oliver Mowat and the Campaign of 1894,' OH, 1963. Despite its tendency to read like a loosely-strung-together collection of documents, Franklin A. Walker's *Catholic Education and*

Politics in Ontario (T: UTP 1964), which draws upon a wide variety of Catholic archival material, is by far the most comprehensive study of both the separate schools and French-language education controversies for the years 1867 to the 1930s. Professor Miller's views are presented most fully in his valuable study *Equal Rights: The Jesuits' Estates Act Controversy* (M: MQUP 1979) which attempts, not always convincingly, to explain cultural tensions by reference to broader social and political processes. C.J. Houston and W.J. Smyth, *The Sash Canada Wore* (T: UTP 1980), by examining the historical geography of the Orange Order in Canada, emphasizes the extent of the Order's influence in Ontario and the variety of attractions it possessed in a new society which possessed few competing institutions. The agrarian unrest of the Mowat years is discussed in S.E.D. Shortt's essay 'Social Change and Political Crisis in Rural Ontario: The Patrons of Industry, 1889-1896,' which appeared in Swainson, ed., *Oliver Mowat's Ontario*, and in J.D. Smart, 'The Patrons of Industry in Ontario in the 1890's' (MA thesis, Carleton University 1970). Douglas O. Baldwin's 1973 York PHD thesis, 'Political and Social Behaviour in Ontario, 1879-1891: A Quantitative Approach,' attempts to apply a new methodology to the study of the Ontario political culture. Graham White's 1979 McMaster PHD thesis, 'Social Change and Political Stability in Ontario: Electoral Forces 1867-1977,' uses electoral statistics to test earlier generalizations about Ontario political behaviour, and suggests interesting new hypotheses; as does B.P.N. Beaven, 'The Last Hurrah: A Study of Liberal Party Development and Ideology in Ontario, 1878-1893' (PHD thesis, University of Toronto 1981). R. Peter Gillis, 'E.H. Bronson and Corporate Capitalism: A Study in Canadian Business Thought and Action, 1880-1910' (MA thesis, Queen's University 1975), which examines the role of a major businessman who served in Mowat's cabinet, argues that Bronson was an important leader of a conservative reform impulse in turn-of-the-century Ontario.

PROVINCIAL POLITICS, 1896-1923

Oliver Mowat's leaving the office of premier in 1896 ended an era, but the new age of Tory progressivism was delayed by the astute political opportunism and brilliant oratory of Sir George Ross. Educator, prohibitionist, businessman, imperialist, Ross played many roles but perhaps was most significant as a transitional figure in the province's shift from the agrarian-based, moralistic Liberalism of Mowat to the new style politics of Whitney and Adam Beck. Unfortunately, there is no good study of either Ross or his period and the absence of an adequate collection of Ross Papers poses perhaps insuperable difficulties. Two useful MA theses are Douglas Dart, 'George William Ross, Minister of Education for Ontario, 1883-1899' (University of Guelph 1971), and David O. Trevor, 'Arthur S. Hardy and Ontario Politics, 1896-1899' (University of Guelph 1973). Some light is thrown on the late 1890s and early 1900s by Charles W. Humphries's well-written PHD thesis, 'The Political Career of Sir James P. Whitney' (University of Toronto 1966), and his interpretation of Tory reformism, which he attributes very largely to pressures from the growing urban middle class reacting against traditional agrarian values, is convincingly summarized in 'The Sources of Ontario "Progressive Conservatism," 1900-1914,' CHAR, 1967. Unfortunately, Professor Humphries's work is overbalanced in the direction of Whitney's opposition years and he pays little attention to a number of important subjects. *Silent Frank Cochrane* by Scott and Astrid Young (T: MAC 1973) is a brief portrait of Whitney's powerful minister of lands, forests, and mines. Two essays, 'The Gamey Affair' by C.W. Humphries, and 'The Cruise of the Minnie M' by B.D. Tennyson, both in OH, 1967, describe the political corruption perpetrated by the dying Ross government. Michael Piva in 'Workers and Tories: The Collapse of the Conservative Party in Urban Ontario 1908-1919,' UHR, 1977, argues, not entirely convincingly, that class loyalties shaped urban voting patterns.

Newton Wesley Rowell, leader of the opposition between 1911 and 1917, had a career which reflected many of the central currents in Ontario's development. Leading Methodist layman, prohibitionist, social reformer, and corporation lawyer, he is the subject of a major biography by Margaret Prang, *N.W. Rowell: Ontario Nationalist* (T: UTP 1975), and his Ontario role is summarized by her essay in *Profiles of a Province*. Although almost nothing has been written on the major social policies of the Whitney period, the dramatic public power movement has attracted much attention. A. Brady, 'The Ontario Hydro-Electric Power Commission,' CJEPS, 1936, is a good introduction, while *Adam Beck and the Ontario Hydro* by W.R. Plewman (T: Ryerson 1947) is an informative, pungent, and gossipy account by one who knew the incredible Hydro czar well. Although Merrill Denison's *The People's Power: The History of Ontario Hydro* (T: M&S 1960) has the faults and many of the virtues of an official history, it does convey some of the excitement of the period and rightly emphasizes the role played in the Hydro movement by small businessmen and municipal reformers. Richard Lucas, 'The Conflict over Public Power in Hamilton, Ontario, 1906-1914,' OH 1976, demonstrates how the existence of a powerful labour movement affected adversely the struggle for public power in one community; and H.V. Nelles, 'Public Ownership of Electrical Utilities in Manitoba and Ontario,' CHR, 1976, introduces an important comparative dimension. *An Expensive Experiment* (NY: 1913) by R.P. Bolton and *Niagara in Politics* (NY: E.P. Dutton 1925) by James Mavor are examples of the literature produced by the enemies of Hydro. See too Kenneth C. Dewar's 1975 Toronto doctoral thesis, 'State Ownership in Canada: The Origins of Ontario Hydro.'

The thrust of H.V. Nelles's important volume, *The Politics of Development: Forests, Mines and Hydro-electric Power in Ontario, 1849-1941* (T: MAC 1974), is largely devoted to what might be described as the progressive period in Ontario politics from about the turn of the century to the early 1920s. It provides a fascinating study of the dynamics of the businessman-politician relationship in the exploitation of Ontario's incredibly rich natural resources and attempts to explain the development of indigenous traditions of resource exploitation rooted in Ontario history yet reflecting all the circumstances of the day. The idea of a public interest prior to and more important than mere private profit was asserted most successfuly in hydro-electric development and with least impact in the more individualistic mining industry. The limitations imposed by the power of private enterprise, the culpability of politicians, the reality of provincial status, and the circumstances of an international economy are effectively analyzed, and the consequences of the close relationship between powerful businessmen, often of American origin and with American backing, and provincial politicians on the province's democratic processes are assessed. Although some of Professor Nelles's judgments, particularly in his later chapters, are far too sweeping and his theory in places crowds unduly upon a reality both more complex and more trite than he would allow, this conceptually powerful volume is the best work on an Ontario subject in many a year. A strikingly different interpretation is argued convincingly in R. Peter Gillis's article, 'The Ottawa Lumber Barons and the Conservation Movement, 1880-1914,' JCS, 1974. The conservation movement for a later period, from the late 1930s on, is dealt with in Arthur Herbert Richardson's *Conservation by the People: The History of the Conservation Movement in Ontario to 1970*, ed. A.S.L. Barnes (T: UTP 1974), a study which is dry and official in its approach.

There are only fragmentary studies of the impact of World War I on Ontario life. *The Province of Ontario in the War* by J. Castell Hopkins (T: Warwick Bros. & Rutter 1919) provides an introduction in the manner befitting the editor of the *Canadian Annual Review*. Barbara M. Wilson, *Ontario and the First World War 1914-18* (T: UTP for the Champlain Society 1977), a collection of documents with a good introduction, focuses on elite opinion and omits important themes, such as Franco-Ontarian dissent. T. Gerald Stortz, 'Ontario Labour and the First World War' (MA thesis, University of Waterloo 1976), emphasizes the economic dimension of labour discontent and is a useful corrective to earlier accounts of labour's role in this era. B.D. Tennyson's 'The Political Career of Sir William H. Hearst' (MA thesis, University of Toronto 1963) and articles by the same author in OH, 1963, 1964, 1965, and 1966 provide an introduction to the issues of the Hearst years. F.J.K. Griezic in '"Power to the People" ... The Manitoulin By-Election, October 24, 1918,' OH, 1977, argues that rural depopulation and temperance did not figure prominently in the agrarian electoral success. In an article on 'The Ontario General Election of 1919: The Beginnings of Agrarian Revolt,' JCS, 1969, Professor Tennyson argues that the Hearst administration had governed progressively and that its defeat that year must be attributed to the general spirit of post-war unrest, while Peter Oliver in

'Sir William Hearst and the Collapse of the Ontario Conservative Party,' CHR, 1972, emphasizes internal decay and political mismanagement. Also concerned with the 1919 election is K.D. Wakefield's MA thesis (Queen's University 1973), 'Measuring One-Party Dominance: A study of Maurice Pinard's Theory of Third Party Emergence with reference to the Case of the UFO in the Ontario General Election of 1919.'

Wartime rural unrest is examined in R.W. Trowbridge, 'War-Time Discontent and the Rise of the United Farmers of Ontario' (MA thesis, University of Waterloo 1966), and by W.R. Young in 'Conscription, Rural Depopulation, and the Farmers of Ontario, 1917-1919,' CHR, 1972. The fascinating farmers' movement which took over the government in 1919 has been much studied but the results remain largely in thesis form. The best work is still Jean MacLeod, 'The United Farmer Movement in Ontario, 1914-1943' (MA thesis, Queen's University 1958), and her broader 'Agriculture and Politics in Ontario since 1867' (PHD thesis, University of London 1961). Russell Hann's pamphlet, *Some Historical Perspectives on Canadian Agrarian Political Movements: The Ontario Origins of Agrarian Criticism of Canadian Industrial Society* (T: New Hogtown Press 1973), is a thoughtful and provocative class analysis. John David Hoffman, 'Farmer-Labor Government in Ontario' (MA thesis, University of Toronto 1959), is an account by a political scientist which emphasizes intra-party relations as does an article by the same author (CJEPS, 1961). Martin Robin's volume, *Radical Politics and Canadian Labour 1880-1930* (Kingston: Queen's University 1968), is particularly useful on labour's involvement in the Drury administration and demonstrates how swiftly the spirit of co-operation collapsed. A more general discussion is J.F. Gahan, 'A Survey of the Political Activities of the Ontario Labour Movement, 1850-1935' (MA thesis, University of Toronto 1945). Accounts by contemporaries include L.A. Wood's 1924 volume, *A History of Farmers' Movements in Canada* (T: UTP 1975); *The Challenge of Agriculture* (T: Morang 1921), a study of the UFO by its educational secretary, M.H. Staples; and *Farmer Citizen* (T: Ryerson 1968), the memoirs of W.C. Good, the UFO's self-styled philosopher. *Farmer Premier: The Memoirs of E.C. Drury* (T: M&S 1966) is of considerable interest

but thoroughly unreliable as the old gentleman was not well served
by his editor. W.E. Raney, the Drury administration's attorney general, is the subject of an article by Peter Oliver entitled 'W.E. Raney
and the Politics of Uplift,' JCS, 1971, which relates the administration's moral reform policies to its rising political unpopularity.
The same author's *G. Howard Ferguson: Ontario Tory* (T: UTP for
the Ontario Historical Studies Series 1977) studies the life of the
Ontario premier of the 1920s in the context of evolving provincial
social and economic policy. Oliver has also published a collection of
essays, some old and some new, entitled *Public and Private Persons:
The Ontario Political Culture 1914-1934* (T: CI 1975), in which he
seeks to comprehend the relationship between particular figures and
the larger political culture.

PROVINCIAL POLITICS, 1923-73

Except for the Hepburn interlude, the Conservative party has been
in office in Ontario since 1923. The political history of that era
remains largely unwritten. Richard Alway's 'Mitchell F. Hepburn
and the Liberal Party in the Province of Ontario 1927-1943' (MA
thesis, University of Toronto 1965) was a sound beginning while
Neil F. McKenty's *Mitch Hepburn* (T: M&S 1967) is a racy account
which focuses on key issues as the liquor question, separate schools,
hydro-electric matters, and the Oshawa General Motors strike, but
falls short of being a full biography. McKenty emphasizes the rural
outlook which Hepburn imposed on the Liberal party but the conclusion both of the book and of an article, 'That Tory Hepburn,' in
Profiles of a Province that Hepburn was indeed a Tory fails to probe
the full extent of the premier's demagoguery or to take into account
the contrast in styles between him and such figures as Howard Ferguson and George Henry. One aspect of the 1937 election is discussed in 'A "Silent" Issue: Mitchell Hepburn, Separate-school
Taxation and the Ontario Election of 1937' by Richard Alway, which
appeared in M. Cross and R. Bothwell, eds., *Policy by Other Means*
(T: CI 1972). On the Conservative dynasty which started in 1943,
there is little of interest. The CCF, however, is better served, particularly by Gerald L. Caplan, who in *The Dilemma of Canadian Social-*

ism: The CCF in Ontario (T: M&S 1973), and in two articles (CHR, 1963, and CJEPS, 1964) presents a rise and fall theory of the CCF which demonstrates the extent of the party's weaknesses during the Depression and attempts an explanation of its striking success in 1943 and of the diastrous election of 1945. Ian MacPherson, 'The 1945 Collapse of the CCF in Windsor,' OH, 1969, throws further light on how internal divisions and external opposition resulted in the failure of that year. Leo Zakuta, *A Protest Movement Becalmed* (T: UTP 1964), should also be noted.

The essay by John Wilson and David Hoffman, 'Ontario: A Three-Party System in Transition,' which appeared in Martin Robin, ed., *Canadian Provincial Politics* (T: PH 1972), attempts an interpretation of the course of Ontario politics since Confederation but achieves success only for the more recent post-war period in which techniques of electoral and legislative analysis are brought to bear on the party structure. 'The Liberal Party in Contemporary Ontario Politics,' *Canadian Journal of Political Science, 1970*, is a model piece of analysis by the same authors. Ontario political history remains sadly deficient in work which goes beyond questions of leadership and results of individual elections, and not until more is done along the lines attempted by Professors Wilson and Hoffman will we begin to have a satisfactory understanding of the province's political structure. In the meantime, Donald C. MacDonald, one of the province's most distinguished politicians, has compiled a collection of essays, *Government and Politics of Ontario* (T: MAC 1975), and Jonathan Manthorpe has provided a journalistic account, *The Power and The Tories: Ontario Politics, 1943 to the Present* (T: MAC 1974).

FEDERAL-PROVINCIAL RELATIONS

For many years the major and almost the only work in the field was J.C. Morrison's 'Oliver Mowat and the Development of Provincial Rights in Ontario: A Study in Dominion-Provincial Relations, 1867-1896.' An MA thesis done at the University of Toronto under the supervision of D.G. Creighton, and published in *Three History Theses* (T: Ontario Department of Public Records and Archives 1961), it describes in ample detail if somewhat unsympathetically the classic episodes in Mowat's provincial rights struggle. The brief section of federal-provincial relations in Mrs Evan's Mowat suggests that not provincial rights but Mowat's 'domestic' policies were primarily responsible for his political success. Christopher Armstrong in *The Politics of Federalism: Ontario's Relations with the Federal Government, 1867-1942* (T: UTP 1981 for the Ontario Historical Studies Series) argues that increasing urbanization and industrialization by the late nineteenth century had transformed the relationship between federal and provincial governments and suggests that powerful business groups had become the most effective players in the federal-provincial 'game.' Although Armstrong tends to underestimate both the extent of Ontario's commitment to a powerful central government and the significance of political parties in the federal dynamic, this carefully researched effort adds a significant new dimension to our understanding of Canadian federalism. Another example of the approach is the essay by Professors Armstrong and H.V. Nelles, 'Private Property in Peril: Ontario Businessmen and the Federal System, 1898-1911,' in Glenn Porter and Robert Cuff, eds., *Enterprise and National Development* (T: Hakkert 1973). This is not the place to describe the standard accounts of federal-provincial relations written from a national perspective, but two of particular interest to Ontario are Ramsay Cook, *Provincial Autonomy, Minority Rights and the Compact Theory, 1867-1921* (O: OP 1969), which demonstrates the major role played by Ontario figures in the early enunciation of provincial rights theory, and Richard Simeon, *Federal-Provincial Diplomacy* (T: UTP 1972), which uses a case study approach to explore the dynamics of several recent issues. Richard Alway's 'Hepburn, King and the Rowell-Sirois Commission,' CHR, 1967, and the McKenty biography, which deals with the Hepburn-King feud in detail, leave the student puzzled as to whether personal animosities or long-standing provincial interests were more to the fore in provincial policy formation. Finally, the provincial government, believing its cause to be just and not blind to the uses of political propaganda, has always advanced its views in great detail in position papers, budget addresses, and elsewhere and these are readily available in most major libraries.

NORTHERN ONTARIO

Separate studies of *Settlement and the Forest Frontier in Eastern Canada*, by A.R.M. Lower, and *Settlement and the Mining Frontier*, by H.A. Innis, are printed together as vol. IX of the Canadian Frontiers of Settlement series (T: MAC 1936), and although the bulk of the Innis section is on Northwestern Canada, taken together they provide an invaluable beginning to scholarly analysis of Northern Ontario. Two chapters in Morris Zaslow, *The Opening of the Canadian North, 1870-1914* (T: M&S 1971), are a perceptive and well-balanced general account of settlement, the mining and forestry industries, transportation, and the role of government in Northern Ontario and Quebec. Not the least of the merits of Professor Zaslow's work is the useful comparative framework in which it studies the two areas. Nelles's *The Politics of Development* is a third indispensable source for Northern Ontario. Richard S. Lambert, with Paul Pross, *Renewing Nature's Wealth: A Centennial History of the Public Management of Lands, Forests & Wildlife in Ontario 1763-1967* (T: Department of Lands and Forests 1967), is a major effort dealing with much more than Northern Ontario.

The bibliographies in the above works, particularly Zaslow and Lambert, provide full assessments of additional literature which for reasons of space cannot be repeated here. Among the most useful works on mining are *Metals and Men: The Story of Canadian Mining* (T: M&S 1957) and *Sudbury Basin* (T: Ryerson 1953), both by D.M. LeBourdais, and *The Mineral Resources of Canada* (T: Ryerson 1933) and *The American Impact on Canadian Mining* (T: 1941), both by E.S. Moore. T.W. Gibson, *Mining in Ontario* (T: Department of Mines 1937), is a brief factual account by the long-time deputy minister of the Department of Mines. O.W. Main, *The Canadian Nickel Industry* (T: UTP 1955), is a judicious study of an industry of vital importance to the whole province. There are also a number of studies of particular mining camps such as S.A. Pain's study of Kirkland Lake, *Three Miles of Gold* (T: Ryerson 1960). Settlement studies include G.L. McDermott, 'Frontiers of Settlement in the Great Clay Belt of Ontario and Quebec,' *Annals of the Association of American Geographers*, 1961, and Benoît-Beaudry Gourd, 'La

Colonisation des Clay Belts du Nord-Quest québécois et du Nord-Est ontarien,' RHAF, 1973. Albert Tucker, *Steam into Wilderness: Ontario Northland Railway, 1902-1962*, is a balanced, scholarly study which places the institutional history of an important developmental project in its political context. O.S. Nock, *Algoma Central Railway* (T: Nelson 1975), is a popular study. A growing interest in labour relations and working-class culture in northern communities is manifested in such works as Jean Morrison, 'Ethnicity and Violence: The Lakehead Freight Handlers before World War I,' in G. Kealey and P. Warrion, eds., *Essays in Canadian Working Class History*; Brian Hogan's *Cobalt: Year of the Strike, 1919* (Cobalt: Highway Book Shop 1978); Doug Baldwin's 'A Study in Social Control: The Life of the Silver Miner in Northern Ontario,' *Labour*, 1977; and Laura Sefton MacDowell's 1979 University of Toronto PHD thesis on the Kirkland Lake goldminer's strike of 1941-2. Northern Ontario has also inspired a number of idiosyncratic yet colourful general accounts by interest parties which interpret development in terms of heroic deeds and individual enterprise. The best of these are O.T.G. Williamson, *The Northland Ontario* (T: Ryerson 1946), and S.A. Pain, *The Way North* (T: 1964). Denis M. Watson's 'Frontier Movement and Economic Development in Northeastern Ontario, 1850-1914' (MA thesis, University of British Columbia 1966) is a first-rate study by a geographer.

THE ECONOMY

Ontario, of course, is part of a larger regional economic system, perhaps best described as Laurentian, which in turn is as closely connected with the Northeastern United States as with the rest of Canada. What has been written to date on the Ontario economy has seldom coincided with the province's political boundaries and the student must turn to national and international studies described elsewhere for an understanding of the province's economic development. Nonetheless, with its own fiscal policies, its energy and industrial strategies, and, perhaps most important of all, control of its own natural resources, Ontario does constitute an economic region, one which has attracted remarkably little scholarly analysis. This is particularly surprising since the volume and quality of studies devoted to the Quebec economy have revealed how fruitful a provincial approach can be. At present, however, we are restricted to a few books, some published essays, and a considerable number of graduate dissertations. As a result we know a good deal about individual railways, about individual entrepreneurs and particular industries, but no one as yet has attempted to put it all together in a synthesis which would include as well an assessment of the impact of provincial fiscal and economic policies. Only when the three volumes on Ontario economic development commissioned by the Ontario Historical Studies Series and being written by Professors Douglas McCalla, Ian Drummond, and Kenneth Rea are in print we may expect to have a general overview comparable in quality to that available for other North American regions.

One first-rate study which provides a clear sense of the actual workings of the economy in an era when merchants operating primarily through partnership agreements played a leading developmental role in Douglas McCalla's revealing volume *The Upper Canada Trade, 1834-1872: A Study of the Buchanans' Business* (T: UTP 1979). In *A Canadian Millionaire: The Life and Business Times of Sir Joseph Flavelle, Bart. 1858-1939* (T: MAC 1978), Michael Bliss demonstrates how a small-town Ontario merchant buying directly from farmers and reselling at retail, wholesale, and for export became one of the dominant business figures of his day. Bliss's fine biography of Flavelle also includes much of value on the social values of Ontario businessmen as did his earlier work, *A Living Profit: Studies in the Social History of Canadian Business, 1883-1911* (T: M&S 1974).

Among the more useful published essays are W.M. Drummond, 'The Impact of the Post-War Industrial Expansion on Ontario's Agriculture,' CJEPS, 1958; K.A.J. Hay, 'Trends in the Location of Industry in Ontario, 1945-1959,' CJEPS, 1965; H.A. Innis, 'An Introduction to the Economic History of Ontario from Outpost to Empire,' in *Profiles of a Province*; J.E. MacNab, 'Toronto's Industrial Growth to 1891,' OH, 1955; J.T. Saywell, 'The Early History of Canadian Oil Companies: A Chapter in Canadian Business History,' OH, 1961; A.G. Talbot, 'Ontario Origins of the Canadian Explosives Industry,'

OH, 1964; Margaret Van Avery, 'Francis R. Clergue and the Rise of Sault Ste. Marie,' OH, 1964; R.G. Hoskins, 'Hiram Walker and the Origins and Development of Walkerville, Ontario,' OH, 1972; and David F. Walker's 'Transportation of Coal into Southern Ontario, 1871-1921,' OH, 1971, and 'The Energy Sources of Manufacturing in Southern Ontario, 1871-1921,' *Ontario Geography*, 1971. Recent studies of particular railway promotions include R.M. Stamp, 'J.D. Edgar and the Pacific Junction Railway,' OH, 1963; J. Konarek, 'Algoma Central and Hudson Bay Railway: The Beginnings,' OH, 1970; James Eadie, 'Edward Wilkes Rathbun and the Napanee Tamworth and Quebec Railway,' OH, 1971.

The more important theses are C.A. Hall, 'Electric Utilities in Ontario under Private Ownership, 1890-1914' (PHD, University of Toronto 1968); R. Sauvé, 'Economic Growth of Eastern Ontario – Trend and Structural Analysis' (MA, University of Ottawa 1961); and there are also several studies of economic growth at the county level such as D.J. Hall, 'Economic Development in Elgin County 1850-1880' (MA, University of Guelph 1971).

The classic treatise on agriculture is R.L. Jones, *History of Agriculture in Ontario, 1613-1880* (T: UTP 1946). The more recent *A History of Agriculture in Ontario* by G. Elmore Reaman, 2 vols. (T: Saunders 1970), while bringing the story up to the present, is an undistinguished effort. Related studies are D.A. Lawr, 'The Development of Ontario Farming, 1870-1914: Patterns of Growth and Change,' OH, 1972; P.M. Ennals, 'The Impact of the Penetration of American Agricultural Technology into Southern Ontario during the Nineteenth Century' (PHD thesis, University of Toronto 1970); and L. Reeds, 'The Agricultural Geography of Southern Ontario' (PHD thesis, University of Toronto 1956). Donald H. Akenson, ed., *Canadian Papers in Rural History*, 2 vols. (Gananoque: Langdale Press 1978, 1980) contains several important essays on farming in nineteenth-century Ontario.

The pulp and paper industry has long been of pivotal importance to the Ontario economy, and studies of its growth and difficulties include C.P. Fell, 'The Newsprint Industry,' in H.A. Innis and A.F.W. Plumptre, eds., *The Canadian Economy and its Problems* (T: CIIA 1934); E.A. Forsey, 'The Pulp and Paper Industry,' CJEPS,

1935; John A. Guthrie, *The Newsprint Paper Industry* (Cambridge: Harvard UP 1941); and chapter 7 in V.W. Bladen, *An Introduction to Political Economy* (London: OUP 1941).

Geographers continue to do much of the research and analysis which will necessarily precede any attempt to formulate a general interpretation, and James Gilmour, *Spatial Evolution of Manufacturing in Southern Ontario, 1851-1891* (T: UTP 1972), is a fine example of such efforts, as are D.M. Ray, *Market Potential and Economic Shadow: A Quantitative Analysis of Industrial Location in Southern Ontario* (Chicago: University of Chicago, Dept. of Geography Research Paper no 101 1965); N.C. Field and D.P. Kerr, *Geographical Aspects of Industrial Growth in the Metropolitan Toronto Region* (T: Regional Development Branch, Dept. of Treasury and Economics 1968); and John U. Marshall, *The Location of Service Towns* (T: UTP 1969). Geographers have also contributed the *Economic Atlas of Ontario* (T: UTP 1969), an internationally acclaimed contribution to economic geography. Alan Wilson's *John Northway: A Blue Serge Canadian* (T: Burns & MacEachern 1965) is a case study in entrepreneurship. T.W. Acheson's 'The Social Origins of Canadian Industrialism: A Study in the Structure of Entrepreneurship 1880-1910' (PHD thesis, University of Toronto 1971), while national in its scope, casts much light on Ontario traditions of business leadership. We are beginning as well to get some valuable comparative studies of a type which will be essential if we are to understand Ontario's role in a national and international perspective. See, for example, John McCallum, *Unequal Beginnings: Agriculture and Economic Development in Quebec and Ontario until 1870* (T: UTP 1980), which convincingly utilizes a staples approach to explain, among other things, varying rates of manufacturing development in the two provinces; and Roy E. George, *A Leader and a Laggard: Manufacturing Industry in Nova Scotia, Quebec and Ontario* (T: UTP 1970). Finally, there is a mass of material on economic development in provincial and federal government reports and studies, including some valuable studies published by the Ontario Economic Council.

The above items are far from being a comprehensive list, but it is evident that any effort to achieve an ordered regional analysis has been hindered on the one hand by the natural inclination to treat

Ontario as part of a larger economic entity and on the other hand by a tendency to write fragmented accounts without any attempt at comprehensiveness or synthesis.

URBAN, LOCAL, AND SOCIAL STRUCTURAL STUDIES

It is impossible here to mention, let alone assess, the multitude of studies of cities and towns or even the many county histories which the professional historian tends to underestimate and neglect. While a critical guide to such work is much needed, it is a project in itself and the bibliographies noted above must provide guidance. The leading example of the old metropolitan approach to urban history which examined the external relations and internal development of cities as they related to factors of growth is D.C. Masters's solid study, *The Rise of Toronto, 1850-1890* (T: UTP 1947). Jacob Spelt, *Urban Development in South-Central Ontario* (1955: T: M&S 1972), is a pioneering comparative study of urban growth in the context of general economic development. Donald Kerr and Jacob Spelt, *The Changing Face of Toronto: A Study in Urban Geography* (O: QP 1965), uses an historical approach to analyse the growth of a huge metropolitan configuration. Jacob Spelt's *Toronto* in the Canadian Cities series (T: Collier-Macmillan 1973) is an expanded version of the same book. More recently, of course, urbanologists have turned from studies of growth to attempts to write the internal history of the city in terms of its social development and the life patterns of its inhabitants. No greater contrast between the old and the new exists than in the extended narrative treatment G.P. de T. Glazebrook gives to *The Story of Toronto* (T: UTP 1971) and the largely quantitative analysis provided by a geographer, Peter G. Goheen, *Victorian Toronto 1850 to 1900* (Chicago: Unversity of Chicago, Dept. of Geography Research Paper no 127 1970). While Professor Glazebrook's approach may be deplorably unanalytic and incurably anecdotal, a reviewer suggested that in much of Goheen's book 'the city and its people seem to become incidental to the testing of techniques such as factor analysis, surface trend mapping, and regression analysis.' Nonetheless Goheen, who uses a sampling of assessment rolls to develop his conclusion that the largely pre-industrial city of 1870 had little in common with the Toronto of 1899, which by that date had become in many of its patterns more appropriately comparable to the city of recent years, undoubtedly is doing the kind of work which is essential if we ever hope to be able to offer generalizations about the historical experience of Ontario's cities based on valid and sufficient empirical data.

Not all quantitative work must be as difficult for the layman to comprehend as is Goheen, and the Hamilton project headed by Michael Katz and the Peel County project under David Gagan have successfully used routinely generated records such as census material, birth, death, and marriage certificates, land deeds, wills, assessment rolls, and city directories to attempt to reconstruct the life patterns of entire nineteenth-century populations. These are team projects investigating social structure and mobility and attempting to develop new analytic techniques for the social historian. Some of the results of their work is in M. Katz, 'Social Structure in Hamilton, Ontario,' which appeared in *Nineteenth-Century Cities: Essays in the New Urban History*, ed. Stephen Thernstrom and Richard Sennett (New Haven: Yale UP 1969), and Katz's 'The People of a Canadian City,' CHR, 1972; H.J. Graff, 'Literacy and Social Structure in Elgin County, Canada West, 1861,' SH, 1973; Herbert J. Mays, ' "A Place to Stand": Families, Land and Permanence in Toronto Gore Township, 1820-1890,' CHAR, 1980; David Gagan and Herbert Mays, 'Historical Demography and Canadian Social History: Families and Land in Peel County Ontario,' CHR, 1973; and David Gagan, 'Land, Population and Social Change: The "Critical Years" in Rural Canada West,' CHR, 1978. Gagan's major work, *Hopeful Travellers: Families, Land, and Social Change in Mid-Victorian Peel County, Canada West* (T: UTP for the Ontario Historical Studies Series 1981), takes a somewhat less cataclysmic approach to social change than do the earlier articles. For a spirited attack on Gagan's methodology and a convincing defence by Gagan, see CHR, June 1981. The most important work remains M.B. Katz, *The People of Hamilton, Canada West: Family and Class in a Mid-Nineteenth-Century City* (Cambridge: Harvard UP 1975), a fine study of an urban social structure and one emphasizing transiency and inequality as its primary characteristics.

Some of the most exciting work in urban history deals with urban reform movements in the late nineteenth century and in the 'progressive' era to 1914. Both Desmond Morton's biography, *Mayor Howland: The Citizens' Candidate* (T: Hakkert 1973), which deals with Toronto in the 1880s, and C. Armstrong and H.V. Nelles, *The Revenge of the Methodist Bicycle Company: Sunday Streetcars and Municipal Reform in Toronto, 1888-1897* (T: Peter Martin 1977), describe a reform impulse promulgated by loose coalitions of labour leaders, evangelicals, and middle-class professionals. John Weaver, on the other hand, in two articles, 'Order and Efficiency: S. Morley Wickett and the Urban Progressive Movement in Toronto 1900-1915,' OH, 1977, and 'The Meaning of Municipal Reform: Toronto, 1895,' OH, 1974, and Peter Gillis in 'Big Business and the Origins of the Conservative Reform Movement in Ottawa, 1890-1912' focus on the relationship between urban reform, middle-class values, and new forms of business organization. Paul Rutherford, ed., *Saving the Canadian City: The First Phase 1880-1920* (T: UTP 1974), is a superb anthology of early articles on urban issues which demonstrates the far-reaching impact of urbanization on most aspects of Canadian development. It may be supplemented as a general introduction to urban issues by John C. Weaver, *Shaping the Canadian City: Essays on Urban Politics and Policy, 1890-1920* (T: Institute of Public Administration of Canada 1977). Two books by Leo A. Johnson based primarily on traditional qualitative sources, *History of the County of Ontario, 1615-1875* (Oshawa: Corporation of the County of Ontario 1973) and *History of Guelph, 1827-1927* (Guelph: Guelph Historical Society 1977), are good examples of how an able professional historian uses local materials to address significant historical problems. Another important local essay is Gilbert A. Stelter, 'The Origins of a Company Town: Sudbury in the Nineteenth Century,' *Laurentian University Review*, 1971, while Albert Rose, *Governing Metropolitan Toronto: A Social and Political Analysis, 1953-1971* (Los Angeles: University of California Press 1973), is a brief but enlightening study of a governmental experiment which has attracted international attention. Harold Kaplan's *Urban Political Systems* (NY: Columbia UP 1967) applies structural-functional analysis to the study of Metropolitan Toronto in the period to 1966. Timothy J.

Colton's *Big Daddy: Frederick G. Gardiner and the Building of Metropolitan Toronto* (T: UTP 1980), while not entirely successful as biography, is an authoritative study of the blockbuster politician's role in establishing metropolitan government in Toronto.

SOCIAL HISTORY

In this field much of the best work necessarily is done within a local and regional framework. In labour history, for example, where the focus has shifted from labour unions to a broader interest in working-class culture, the important journal, *Labour/Le Travailleur*, founded in 1976, has numerous articles on Ontario subjects, much of it written from a neo-Marxist perspective by younger scholars dissatisfied with the political and institutional focus of earlier labour historians. Good examples of the newer approach are Bryan Palmer's *A Culture in Conflict: Skilled Workers and Industrial Capitalism in Hamilton, Ontario, 1860-1914* (M: MQUP 1979) and Gregory S. Kealey, *Toronto Workers Respond to Industrial Capitalism, 1867-1892* (T: UTP 1980). Although somewhat turgidly written and frequently discursive in organization, Palmer's study nonetheless is an important statement of the work of the cultural school. More technically competent, Kealey's volume, after demonstrating the extent of industrialization in Toronto in the 1860s and 70s and tracing the rise of protectionist sentiment, focuses on the impact of industrialization on shoemakers, coopers, metal-trade workers, and printers. Kealey argues that artisanal traditions substantially influenced the relationship among classes in these years of economic transformation. Less convincingly perhaps, he also examines the role of the working class in social organizations such as the Orange Order and in electoral politics. In fact, these two volumes are the culmination at least of the first stage of the program, announced in the 1973 volume *Primary Sources in Canadian Working-Class History*, ed. Russell G. Hann *et al.* (Kitchener: Dumont Press) and in the useful collection of essays edited by Kealey and Peter Warrian, *Essays in Canadian Working-Class History* (T: M&S 1976), to produce a new kind of labour history which would study workers 'in a totality that includes their cultural backgrounds and social relations, as well as their institutional memberships and economic and political behaviour ...' Because so much of this work is rooted in region and locality, it serves to demonstrate how important local influences have been in giving rise to distinctive labour traditions within Canada.

A more traditional study which also emphasizes regional distinctiveness and the impact of conservative and continental influences on Ontario's labour tradition is Robert H. Babcock's valuable *Gompers in Canada: A Study in American Continentalism before the First World War* (T: UTP 1974). More national in focus but including substantial material on Ontario are the well-known works by H.A. Logan, Charles Lipton, Gad Horowitz, Martin Robin, Irving Abella, and Stuart Jamieson (see Labour and working-class history section). Doris French, *Faith, Sweat and Politics* (T: M&S 1962), is a brief, colourful biography of D.J. O'Donoghue, a figure of importance in the labour movement in late nineteenth-century Ontario. In the periodical literature the more important work includes, in *Labour*: G.S. Kealey, '"The Honest Workingman" and Workers' Control: The Experience of Toronto Skilled Workers, 1860-1892' (1976); Wayne Roberts, 'Artisans, Aristocrats and Handymen: Politics and Unionism among Toronto Skilled Building Trades Workers, 1896-1914' (1976); Bruce Scott, 'A Place in the Sun: The Industrial Council at Massey-Harris, 1919-1929' (1976); Desmond Morton, 'Taking on the Grand Trunk: The Locomotive Engineers' Strike of 1876-7' (1977); Craig Heron, 'The Crisis of the Craftsman: Hamilton's Metal Workers in the Early Twentieth Century' (1980); Wayne Roberts, 'Toronto Metal Workers and the Second Industrial Revolution, 1889-1914' (1980); in CHR, Craig Heron and Bryon Palmer, 'Through the Prism of the Strike: Industrial Conflict in Southern Ontario' (1977); in CHAR, Gregory Kealey, 'Artisans Respond to Industrialism: Shoemakers, Shoe Factories and the Knights of St. Crispin in Toronto' (1973); in SH, G.S. Kealey and B. Palmer, 'The Boards of Unity: The Knights of Labour in Ontario, 1880-1900' (1981).

There are as yet few systematic studies of wage rates or working conditions. Gregory Kealey, who edited an abridged version of the Royal Commission on the Relations of Capital and Labour, 1889, under the title *Canada Investigates Industrialism* (T: UTP 1973), has offered a brief pamphlet which serves to introduce several themes, *Hogtown, Working Class Toronto at the Turn of the Century* (T: New Hogtown Press 1974). Michael J. Piva's *The Condition of the Working Class in Toronto, 1900-1921* (O: University of Ottawa Press 1979) is a more substantial study which argues that low wages, periods of unemployment, and weak trade unionism left most Toronto workers to live in conditions of poverty. Although Piva's work is a valuable contribution, it leaves many questions unanswered and must be regarded as merely an opening volley in what may become an ongoing historical debate. Several essays by Ramsay Cook, including 'Henry George and the Poverty of Canadian Progress,' CHAR, 1977, focus on the ideas of social critics in turn-of-the-century Ontario.

The 1974 volume *Women at Work: Ontario 1850-1930*, ed. Janice Acton *et al.* (T: Women's Educational Press), while flawed as professional history, is generally imaginative and useful. Other publications which are providing a foundation for women's history in Ontario and Canada include S. Trofimenkoff and A. Prentice, eds., *The Neglected Majority: Essays in Canadian Women's History* (T: M&S 1978); L. Kealey, ed., *A Not Unreasonable Claim: Women and Reform in Canada, 1880s-1920s* (T: Women's Educational Press 1979); R. Cook and W. Mitchinson, eds., *The Proper Sphere: Woman's Place in Canadian Society* (T: Oxford 1976); and V. Strong-Boag, *The Parliament of Women: The National Council of Women of Canada, 1893-1929* (O: Museum of Man 1976). V. Strong-Boag, ed., *A Woman with a Purpose: The Diaries of Elizabeth Smith 1872-1884* (T: UTP 1980), provides insights into the life and mentality of a middle-class professional woman in late nineteenth-century Ontario. The role of working-class women is studied by Marilyn Barber in 'The Women Ontario Welcomed: Immigrant Domestics for Ontario Homes, 1870-1930,' OH, 1980, and by Wayne Roberts in *'Honest Womanhood': Feminism, Femininity, and Class-consciousness among Toronto Working Women, 1892-1914* (T: New Hogtown Press 1976).

With respect to religion, most work to date has been national in approach and institutional in character. An important exception is William Magney's study of the Methodist church's response to social change, 'The Methodist Church and the National Gospel, 1884-1914,' which demonstrates the essentially conservative nature of the social gospel tradition in Ontario (*The Bulletin*, 1968, Ryerson Press for The United Church); while Richard Allen, *The Social Passion: Religion and Social Reform in Canada 1914-1928*, further emphasizes the different social messages of Christianity in Ontario and Western Canada. Generally, however, religious history remains the most neglected area of post-Confederation Ontario history.

The establishment in the 1970s of the Multicultural History Society of Ontario will have an important long-run effect on the writing of ethnic and multicultural history. To date, the society has focused its activities on the preservation and collection of archival materials, the recording of oral history, and the publication of its journal, *Polyphony*. Much of its work, such as the 1981 booklet edited by Donna Hill, *A Black Man's Toronto 1914-1980: The Reminiscences of Harry Gairey*, will be invaluable source material for generations of professional historians. One attractive effort dealing with Toronto which uses photographic evidence is Robert Harney and Harold Troper, *Immigrants: A Portrait of the Urban Experience, 1890-1930* (T: Van Nostrand 1975). There is a large amount of other material on ethnic groups, much of it published under the auspices of national organizations, which will prove useful to academic historians. One of the few recent works which fully meets professional standards is Stephen A. Speisman, *The Jews of Toronto: A History to 1937* (T: M&S 1980), although Speisman focuses on middle-class and elitist concerns and fails to do justice to the Jewish community's rich traditions of radical dissent and working-class culture. Several books, of mixed value, have been published to date in the Secretary of State's Multiculturalism Program. One of the series, *A Future to Inherit: Portuguese Communities in Canada* by Grace M. Anderson and David Higgs (T: M&S 1976), represents a useful collaboration between a sociologist and a social historian.

Rivalling the new working-class history in significance and volume are studies dealing with social welfare and social reform; in this area no single school or approach has emerged as dominant. Two of the most important works are unpublished Toronto doctoral theses: T.R. Morrison's 'The Child and Urban Social Reform in Late Nineteenth Century Ontario, 1875-1900' (1970) and Susan Houston's 'The Impetus to Reform: Urban Crime, Poverty and Ignorance in Ontario, 1850-1875,' (1974). Notwithstanding important differences in approach, both Morrison and Houston emphasize the middle-class and secular contribution to an emerging reform ethos, and each interprets reform movements in conservative terms as a mechanism of social cotrol. Published examples of Morrison's work include a somewhat diffuse article, '"Their Proper Sphere": Feminism, the Family and Child-Centred Social Reform in Ontario, 1875-1900,' OH, 1976, and 'Reform as Social Tracking: The Case of Industrial Education in Ontario, 1870-1900,' *Journal of Educational Thought*, 1974. The place to begin, however, is still Richard B. Splane's *Social Welfare in Ontario* (T: UTP 1965). Despite his institutional approach and the need to deal with the extended period from the 1790s to 1893, Splane succeeds in putting the legislative and structural framework in place for the study of crime, punishment, public health, care of the poor, and child welfare. Andrew Jones and Leonard Rutman, *In the Children's Aid: J.J. Kelso and Child Welfare in Ontario* (T: UTP 1981), is a straightforward, attractively written introduction to Kelso and his colleagues in the child-saving movement which clearly demonstrates the tension between those who emphasized institutional care and others who focused on family and foster care as the solution for social problems. See too the article in *Ontario History* (1978) by Andrew Jones on Kelso's role in the closing of Penetanguishene Reformatory in the early twentieth century. A major and ground-breaking work which deals with many aspects of social reform, including public health, educational change, and the evolving role of women and children, is Neil Sutherland, *Children in English-Canadian Society: Framing the Twentieth-Century Consensus* (T: UTP 1976). Professor Sutherland does not avoid the problems inherent in a pioneering effort, and some of his conclusions doubtless will be superseded, but he succeeds in providing a stimulating introduction to social issues of increasing concern to middle-class urban Canadians of the early twentieth century. A useful thesis which analyses the evolving attitudes and responses to poverty and traces the early origins of the social-work profession is James Pitsula, 'The Relief of Poverty in Toronto, 1880-1930' (PHD thesis, York University 1979). See also Pitsula's two published articles, 'The Treatment of Tramps in Late Nineteenth-Century Toronto,' CHAR, 1980, and 'The Emergence of Soicial Work in Toronto,' JCS, 1979. Prohibition, one of the great social movements of the past century, awaits its historian. In addition to the older work by Ruth Spence, *Prohibition in Canada* (T: 1919), there is Gerald A. Hallowell, *Prohibition in Ontario 1919-1923* (T: Ontario Historical Society 1972), a rather narrowly political study, and an essay which takes a more social approach by Graeme Decarie in Swainson, ed., *Oliver Mowat's Ontario*.

There is a glaring need for more work on immigration to Ontario in the post-Confederation period and for demographic studies. The movement of impoverished and orphaned British waifs into the provinces receives scholarly analysis in Joy Parr, *Labouring Children: British Immigrant Apprentices to Canada, 1869-1924* (M: MQUP 1980), and Wesley D. Turner, 'Miss Rye's Children and the Ontario Press, 1875,' OH, 1976, and Kenneth Bagnell, *The Little Immigrants* (T: MAC 1980), is a popular treatment. I.C. Taylor, 'Components of Population Change, Ontario 1850-1940' (MA thesis, University of Toronto 1967), is particularly useful for tracing rural out-migration. It should be supplemented by the contemporary account by John MacDougall, *Rural Life in Canada* (1913; T: UTP 1972). Other work of value includes S. Speisman, 'Munificent Parsons and Municipal Parsimony,' OH, 1973, a study of poor relief in Toronto, and M. Piva, 'The Workmen's Compensation Movement in Ontario,' OH, 1975.

If the general contours of Ontario's social development in the period to 1914 now are at least vaguely discernible, the period after World War I remains an historiographic desert. For an introduction to the later period the student should refer to two older books by Harry M. Cassidy, *Unemployment and Relief in Ontario, 1929-1932* (T: Dent 1932) and *Public Health and Welfare Organization in Canada* (T: Ryerson 1945). A recent overview is Dennis Guest, *The Emergence of Social Security in Canada* (V: UBCP 1980), and there is an important article by James Struthers, 'A Profession in Crisis: Charlotte Whitton and Canadian Social Work in the 1930s,' CHR, 1981.

The Franco-Ontarians, constituting about 10 per cent of the population and occupying a special position as representative of one of the two founding cultures, have attracted more attention. The more notable studies include Leopold Lamontagne's essay 'Ontario: The two Races,' in Mason Wade, ed., *Canadian Dualism* (T: UTP 1960). T.H.B. Symons, 'Ontario's Quiet Revolution: A Study of Change in the Position of the Franco-Ontarian Community,' in R.M. Burns, ed., *One Country or Two?* (M: MQUP 1971), a long essay focusing on educational matters but dealing also with federal-provincial and Ontario-Quebec relations, argues that the changes in Ontario in the 1960s in regard to Francophone citizens were so many and so profound as to constitute a revolution. A large proportion of works dealing with Franco-Ontarians describe their struggle for educational rights: Walker, *Catholic Education and Politics in Ontario*; C.B. Sissons, *Bi-lingual Schools in Canada* (T: Dent 1917); Marilyn Barber, 'The Ontario Bilingual Schools Issue: Sources of Conflict,' CHR, 1966; Margaret Prang, 'Clerics, Politicians, and the Bilingual Schools Issue in Ontario, 1910-1917,' CHR, 1960; Peter Oliver, 'The Resolution of the Ontario Bilingual Schools Crisis 1919-1929,' JCS, 1972; and André Lalonde, *Le Réglement XVII et ses répercussions sur le Nouvel Ontario* (Sudbury: La Sociétè historique du Nouvel-Ontario 1966). Victor Lapalme, 'Les Franco-Ontarians et la politique provinciale' (MA thesis, University of Ottawa 1968), is a political analysis, while M.J. Fitzpatrick, 'The Role of Bishop Francis Michael Fallon in the Conflict between the French Catholics and the Irish Catholics in the Ontario Bilingual Schools Question, 1910-1920' (MA thesis, University of Western Ontario 1969), is a revealing and able effort. D.G. Cartwright's 'French Canadian Colonization in Eastern Ontario to 1910' (PHD thesis, University of Western Ontario 1973) is indispendable. Robert Choquette, *Language and Religion: A History of English-French Conflict in Ontario* (O: University of Ottawa Press 1975) deals primarily with Franco-Ontarian and Irish-Catholic relations between 1900 and 1927. Although it contains much important new material, it retains most of the faults of a hastily published doctoral dissertation. Choquette's work on Catholic organizational change should be supplemented by D.G. Cartwright's careful articles 'Ecclesiastical Territorial Organization and Institutional Conflict in Eastern and Northern Ontario, 1840 to 1910,' CHAR, 1978, 'Institutions on the Frontier: French-Canadian Settlement in Eastern Ontario in the Nineteenth Century,' *Canadian Geographer*, 1977. Gail C. Brandt's ' "J'y suis, j'y rest": The French Canadians of Sudbury, 1883-1913' (PHD thesis, York University 1976) is a successful application of quantitative methodology.

In educational history the prominence of cultural-religious disputes has ensured that separate schools have been as much studied as French-language matters and among the leading efforts are Franklin Walker and C.B. Sissons, *Church and State in Canadian Education* (T: Ryerson 1959). As for general studies, some of the early attempts to write the province's educational history are valuable for their own sake and as a reflection of contemporary attitudes. These include Walter N. Bell, *The Development of the Ontario High School* (T: UTP 1918), and John McCutcheon, *John Seath and the School System of Ontario* (T: UTP 1920). Two general studies of Canadian education which include much Ontario material are C.E. Phillips, *The Development of Education in Canada* (T: Gage 1957), and J.D. Wilson, R.M. Stamp, and L.P. Audet, eds., *Canadian Education: A History* (T: PH 1970). Robin S. Harris, *Quiet Evolution: A Study of the Educational System of Ontario* (T: UTP 1967), is a brief introductory survey lacking in analytic rigour. Financial and administrative questions are examined in a political context in an able study by D.M. Cameron, *Schools for Ontario: Policy-making, Administration and Finance in the 1960s* (T: UTP 1972). In a category by itself is the eight-volume series by W.G. Fleming, *Ontario's Educative Society* (T: UTP 1971-2). This enormous chronicle of the education explosion which occurred largely when William Davis was minister is uncritical but indispensable, the obvious starting-point for anyone interested in the recent history of education in Ontario. The Ontario Institute for Studies in Education has published a series of guides to educational records available in the Ontario Archives and elsewhere which are of great assistance to the student of educational history. An example from the series is *Items Relating to Education in Private Papers in the Ontario Archives*, prepared by Roy Reynolds (T: OISE 1973).

Within the past few years educational historians have de-emphasized the older institutional approach with its focus on statutes, bureaucratic forms, and curriculum. The 'new educational history' represents a concerted effort to write educational history as a branch of social history and to take into account the social and economic context of educational change and to utilize all the tools of social scientific inquiry. An excellent example of the new approach is the collection of revisionist essays in Michael Katz and Paul Mattingly, eds., *Education and Social Change: Themes from Ontario's Past* (NY: New York UP 1975). Ian E. Davey, 'Educational Reform and the Working Class: School Attendance in Hamilton, Ontario, 1851-1891' (PHD thesis, University of Toronto 1975), is a valuable work of the same genre. Another good example, Alison Prentice's finely crafted monograph, *The School Promoters: Education and Social Class in Mid-Nineteenth Century Upper Canada* (T: M&S 1977), still focuses largely on a single individual, Egerton Ryerson. More traditional and narrative in approach is Robert Stamp's valuable survey, *The Schools of Ontario 1876-1976* (T: UTP for the Ontario Historical Studies Series 1982). N. McDonald and Alf Chaiton, eds., *Egerton Ryerson and his Times* (T: MAC 1978), is a pot-pourri with respect to method and quality. Despite a dubious methodology and a curious thesis, Harvey J. Graff, *The Literacy Myth: Literacy and Social Structure in the Nineteenth Century City* (NY: Academic Press 1979) makes a contribution to understanding educational attainments in mid-nineteenth-century Ontario cities.

For higher education there exists a substantial number of histories of particular institutions. Older works include W.S. Wallace, *A History of the University of Toronto 1827-1927* (T: UTP 1927); J.J. and R.D. Talman, *'Western' – 1878-1953* (L: University of Western Ontario 1953); and C.B. Sissons, *A History of Victoria University* (T: UTP 1952). Other colleges and universities have also been studied and there is much on Ontario institutions in the Studies in the History of Higher Education in Canada series, including Robin S. Harris's encyclopedic *A History of Higher Education in Canada, 1663-1960* (T: UTP 1976) and Laurence K. Shook's sensitive volume *Catholic Post-Secondary Education in English-speaking Canada* (T: UTP 1971). Charles M. Johnston's well-researched and informative two-

volume history of *McMaster University* (T: UTP 1976, 1981) is a
model institutional study which addresses a variety of significant
social and educational themes. Hilda Neatby's *Queen's University*, I:
1841-1917 (M: MQUP 1978) is an important study by a distinguished
historian of an institution that has played a role of importance in the
life of the province since the middle of the nineteenth century,
while John Gwynne-Timothy, *Western's First Century* (L: University
of Western Ontario 1978), is a competent study of the University of
Western Ontario. *Halfway up Parnassus* (T: UTP 1974) is a welcome
if somewhat anodyne memoir of life at the University of Toronto by
that institution's former president, Claude Bissell. E.E. Stewart,
'The Role of the Provincial Government in the Development of the
Universities of Ontario, 1791-1965' (PHD thesis, University of
Toronto 1970), is an indispensable study particularly valuable for
the more recent period. While there is room for much more by way
of administrative and institutional studies, what the field needs most
at the moment is a social approach which would cut across the story
of particular institutions to examine such questions as changing public perceptions of the role of higher education, the expanded function of the universities in an urban and industrial age, and the
impact of the local, national, and even international environment on
the Ontario university.

CONCLUSION

There has been no effort made in this bibliographic survey to deal
with cultural or intellectual history while a number of other important themes, including journalism, sports and recreation, and the
history of science have also been ignored. Two important con-
straints have been lack of space and a recognition that to some
extent these topics are treated elsewhere in this volume. More
important, however, is the absence of work on the above subjects
which is consciously and explicitly regional. That a book is written in
Ontario by an Ontario author and includes subject matter which in
part at least relates to Ontario must necessarily give that work a
certain regional quality, yet some subjects cannot and others simply
have not been effectively dealt with in the regional context. To the

extent that art, architecture, and perhaps even theatre and music have been affected by the Ontario environment and developed characteristics which could not have been gained elsewhere, an approach which seeks to define and explain those characteristics is not only justified but essential. One stimulating attempt to deal with the province's intellectual and cultural history is William Westfall's 'The Dominion of the Lord: An Introduction to the Cultural History of Protestant Ontario in the Victorian Period,' QQ, 1976. The many recent excellent coffee-table books on Ontario furniture, gravestones, art and architecture, barns, the rural countryside and small towns will one day be of immeasurable assistance to those attempting a cultural synthesis which will come to terms with the evolution of the Ontario mind. In a study of attitudes and ideologies such as Carl Berger's brilliant volume *The Sense of Power: Studies in the Ideas of Canadian Imperialism* (T: UTP 1970), which is devoted so largely to figures living in or nurtured by Ontario, a more explicit analysis of the impact of that particular environment might or might not have been helpful. It seems likely, however, that such will be the direction of future studies in these areas.

This, however, is not necessarily desirable and is far from inevitable. A major problem for the student of Ontario history will continue to be that of definition. The sheer bulk of the work cited above should not deceive anyone or lead to the conclusion that the past record in Ontario studies is one of impressive achievement. Too much of the work zone remains fragmented, incomplete, and even antiquarian; too little attains high standards of scholarship and almost none points in the direction of a convincing regional synthesis. The few exceptions have been pointed out in the above essay, but the absence of successful overviews and general interpretations of Ontario society must alert us to the difficulties involved. This goes beyond any mere preoccupation with national history and seems by a curious irony to reflect one of the conundrums faced for so long by national historians. If efforts to achieve a national synthesis have been defeated by Canada's stubbornly intractable regional realities, the very diversity, the size, and the lack of definition of Ontario society pose similar problems for provincial historians. Perhaps Arthur Lower was right after all in his puckish assertion that there is no such animal as the 'Ontarian.' Those who believe, however, that regionalism remains as an important approach to the study of this society must hope that they are not doomed to repeat in their work that search for an elusive provincial identity that proved so frustrating and stultifying when pursued on a national level.

RAMSAY COOK

French Canada

Historical writing in French Canada has undergone significant
changes in the past two decades, changes which in many ways reflect
and parallel the altered character of Quebec society since the 1950s.
French-speaking historians have been asking new questions about
their past just as many Quebeckers have been questioning their present and speculating about their future. Put rather simply, Quebec
in the years since the Second World War has become an increasingly
secular and urban French-speaking North American society. No
longer does the church play a major role in such social institutions as
the educational system, nor does Roman Catholicism define to any
great extent the cultural values of Quebec. Where once the leading
historians in Quebec were either clerics or trained by clerics, today's
historians with very few exceptions are secular in both background
and education. Where the role of the church and the survival of *la
nation canadienne-française* once preoccupied French-Canadian
historians almost exclusively, the new historians, while not uncon-
scious of the national question, are more likely to be engaged in
examining economic development, demographic patterns, urban
growth, ideological conflict, and working-class organization and life.
    To understand this development it is important to say something
about Quebec historical writing in general, and especially about
work on the period before Confederation. Indeed, it is useful to
observe that post-Confederation history in Quebec, while receiving

much more attention than at any time in the past, is still not the main field of interest, controversy, and innovation for French-speaking historians. It is the period between 1760 and 1850 that has been subject to the most thorough revision by recent writing and that, in turn, increasingly influences the manner in which the post-Confederation period is approached.

The impact and meaning of the British Conquest has long been the central historical question for Quebeckers (see the essay entitled 'Conquêtisme' in my book *The Maple Leaf Forever*, T: MAC 1971). But until the 1950s the economic impact of that momentous event had rarely been measured. Since the mid-fifties, however, the works of Michel Brunet and Fernand Ouellet have made economics the major concern in discussions of the Conquest.

Out of the controversy over the economic implications of the Conquest came the most important historical work published in Quebec since François-Xavier Garneau launched French Canadians on an unending quest for the true meaning of their past with his *Histoire du Canada* in 1845. Fernand Ouellet's brilliant and provocative *Histoire économique et sociale du Québec, 1760-1850* (M: Fides 1966; trans. T: Gage 1980) formulated the questions which have since dominated French-Canadian historical writing: the role of French Canadians in the Quebec economy and their attitude to economic matters, sources of capital investment, markets, the viability of the seigneurial system, and the adaptation of agricultural techniques, the growth of urban centres, and the relationship between economics, politics, religion, and nationalism. Ouellet's work examined in detail, for the first time, the mass of statistical evidence available to the historian with the skill and patience to use it. In a more recent work, *Le Bas Canada 1791-1840: Changements structuraux et crise* (O: Editions de l'Université d'Ottawa 1976; trans. T: M&S 1980), Ouellet has added a detailed political and religious dimension to his earlier study, thus providing a fresh understanding of the developments leading up to the Rebellion of 1837 and its aftermath.

Ouellet's interpretation of these tempestuous years has not gone unchallenged. Anyone interested in this fundamental controversy will find the essential issues clearly set out in T.J.A. LeGoff's article, 'Agricultural Crisis in Lower Canada, 1802-12: A Review of a Controversy,' CHR, 1974. Whatever the outcome, the socio-economic approach which Ouellet first developed is now as dominant in the interpretation of Quebec's past as the clerico-nationalist one once was. Such works as Louise Dechêne's *Habitants et marchands de Montréal aux XVIIe siècle* (M: Plon 1974), at one end of the time scale, and Jacques Rouillard's *Les travailleurs du coton au Québec, 1900-15* (M: PUQ 1974), at the other, both reflect this orientation. Moreover, most Quebec historians have descended from the nationalist pulpits occupied so frequently by their predecessors, leaving nationalist advocacy to such polemicists and simplifiers as Léandre Bérgeron whose popular *Petit manuel d'histoire du Québec* (M: Editions Québécoises 1969) displayed an almost total innocence of the new trends in French-Canadian historical writing.

HISTORIOGRAPHY, BIBLIOGRAPHY, JOURNALS,
AND RESEARCH GUIDES

Serge Gagnon's *Le Québec et ses historiens de 1840 à 1920* (Q: PUL 1978) is a thorough and convincing analysis of the traditional approach to historical writing in Quebec. Alfred Dubuc's 'L'influence de l'école des Annales au Québec,' RHAF, 1979, reveals something of the influences that have radically altered that approach. There are, in addition, many useful surveys of Quebec historiography. One of the most recent is contained in *Recherches sociographiques* (1974), an issue entirely devoted to historiographical essays. Of special interest for post-Confederation historians are Joseph Levitt's careful analysis of Robert Rumilly, the most prolific Quebec historian, and Pierre Savard's judicious 'Un quart de siècle d'historiographie québécoise, 1947-1972.' Fernand Ouellet's 'La recherche historique au Canada-français,' in Louis Baudouin, éd., *La recherche au Canada Français* (M: PUM 1968), is a clear expression of that seminal historian's viewpoint. My own essays on the subject, 'The Historian and Nationalism,' in *Canada and the French-Canadian Question* (T: MAC 1966), and '*La Survivance* French-Canadian Style,' in *The Maple Leaf Forever*, are chiefly concerned with an analysis of nationalism in historical writing. An informed outsider's judgments are found in Robert Mandrou, 'L'historiographie cana-dienne-française: Bilan et pérspective,' CHR, 1970. Very few of these essays deal exclusively with the post-Confederation period, but all contribute something towards an understanding of the recent evolution of French-Canadian attitudes and approaches to the past.

Most of the standard bibliographical aids to the history of French Canada are now slightly outdated. The most useful and exhaustive is Paul Aubin's *Bibliographie de l'histoire du Québec et du Canada, 1966-1975* (Q: Institut Québécois de recherche sur la culture 1981). Still valuable for history students is René Durocher and Paul-André Linteau, *Histoire du Québec: Bibliographie sélective, 1877-1970* (M: BE 1970). *Québec 1940-1969: Bibliographie* (M: PUM 1971), compiled by Robert Boily, is especially rich in social science references. Claude Thibault's *Bibliographia Canadiana* (T: Longman 1973), is quite complete but must be used with discrimination and patience. Jacques Cotnam's *Contemporary Quebec: An Analytical Bibliography* (T: M&S 1973) is useful for what it covers, while the *Guide d'histoire du Canada* (Q: PUL 1968), edited by André Beaulieu, Jean Hamelin, and Benoît Bernier, contains not only a fairly exhaustive list of books and articles but is introduced by a perceptive survey of Canadian historical writing contributed by Serge Gagnon. *Livres et auteurs québécois*, published annually, prints essays and book reviews concerned with history and is indispensible for anyone who wishes to keep abreast of recent writing.

There are several scholarly journals which regularly publish articles, book reviews, and bibliographies on French-Canadian topics. The most important of these is *Revue d'histoire de l'Amérique française*, founded in 1947 by chanoine Lionel Groulx as an outlet for his clerico-nationalist views. It has developed into a first-class professional journal, published four times a year. Its annual bibliographies are carefully compiled and highly inclusive. *Recherches sociographiques*, published at Laval University, is an interdisciplinary journal providing historians with an opportunity to publish their work alongside that of other social scientists. In Quebec, in contrast to the rest of Canada, sociology and political economy have maintained, to a substantial degree, a firm historical grounding. Consequently, the work of sociologists like Fernand Dumont, Jean-Charles Falardeau, and Marcel Rioux, economists like Albert Faucher and Gilles Paquet, and political scientists like Léon Dion, André-J. Belanger, and Vincent Lemieux, which appears in *Recherches sociographiques* and elsewhere, is of great value to historians. *Histoire sociale/Social History*, published twice yearly at the University of Ottawa, is perhaps the most interesting historical journal currently published in Canada, though it has not carried much material on post-1967 Quebec. The *Canadian Historical Review*, published quarterly by the University of Toronto Press, is open to historians of both official languages but recently has had few articles or book reviews in French. The *Annual Report of the Canadian Historical Association*, recently rechristened *Historical Papers*, also contains many important articles on French-Canadian history.

There are several valuable publications that research students will find it beneficial to consult. *The Union List of Manuscripts* (O: QP 1975), as its title suggests, attempts to include all manuscript collections in public depositories. *L'état général des archives publiques et privées du Québec* (Q: Ministère des affaires culturelles 1968), should also be consulted. *Répértoire des publications gouvernementales du Québec, 1867-1964* (Q: Imprimateur de la Reine 1968), compiled by André Beaulieu, Jean-Charles Bonenfant, and Jean Hamelin, and the supplements for 1965-8, provide careful guidance to the mass of published government documents. André Beaulieu and Jean Hamelin's *Les Journaux de Québec* (Q: PUL 1965), is an excellent analytical guide to Quebec newspapers, though it is occasionally incomplete in its details. *Annuaire de Québec/Québec Yearbook*, published regularly since 1914, is a rich store of information about most facets of Quebec life, while the *Canadian Annual Review*, particularly in the years since John T. Saywell revived it in 1960, regularly contains authoritative articles on Quebec politics, economics, and constitutional developments.

GENERAL STUDIES

Histoire du Québec contemporain: De la Confédération à la crise (1867-1929) (M: BE 1979; trans. T: Lorimer 1982), written by Paul-

André Linteau, René Durocher, and Jean-Claude Robert, has been greeted with widespread enthusiasm. It represents the first attempt by the younger generation of Quebec historians to draw together the research of French- and English-speaking historians on post-Confederation Quebec. Unlike most textbooks, this one approaches the subject in a thematic fashion dealing with social, economic, political, and ideological history in separate sections. For the most part, this innovative approach is successful and students of modern Quebec history now have a reliable synthesis with which to begin their studies.

Mason Wade's *The French Canadians*, 2 vols. (rev. ed., T: MAC 1968), remains useful though twenty-five years have passed since its original publication. Wade relies heavily on Robert Rumilly's forty-one volume *Histoire de la province de Québec* (M: Various publishers 1940-69) which, when read critically, remains a storehouse of valuable information. It must be used with some care not merely because of the author's strongly conservative-nationalist bias, but also because the sources of Rumilly's information are frequently not revealed. That reservation is counter-balanced, to some extent, by the recognition that Rumilly has had access to documents which, at least so far, have not been available to other researchers. Rumilly's numerous biographies, notably those of Mgr Laflèche, Honoré Mercier, Henri Bourassa, and Maurice Duplessis, for the most part simply rework the material contained in the *Histoire* and are subject to the same reservations.

There are several textbooks which contain valuable accounts of French-Canadian history. In English, *Canada: Unity in Diversity* (T: HRW 1967), by Jean Hamelin, Fernand Ouellet, and Paul Cornell, contains several excellent chapters on Quebec. Different in tone and content is Jean-Claude Robert's *Du Canada français au Québec libre: Histoire d'un mouvement indépendentiste* (M: Flammarion 1975), whose subtitle reveals its central interpretative theme. It places heavy emphasis on recent history. *Histoire des Canadas* (M: HMH 1975), by Rosario Bilodeau, Robert Comeau, André Gosselin, and Denise Julien, organizes the history of Canada within the framework of three colonialisms: French, British, and American. For a sound, thoroughly objective general account Jean Hamelin, *et al.*,

Histoire du Québec (Ste Hyacinthe: Edisom 1976), is the best of the textbooks.

CONFEDERATION, THE CONSTITUTION, AND MINORITY RIGHTS

Despite the interest of French Canadians in the real and imagined injustices of Confederation, not much has been written on this topic by their historians. Polemic rather than scholarship characterizes much that has been published. That is certainly the case with Lionel Groulx's *La Confédération canadienne* (M: *Le Devoir* 1918), though that is not surprising since it was written in the midst of the conscription crisis of the First World War. The same author's account of Francophone minority schools, *L'enseignement française au Canada*, 2 vols. (M: Granger Frères 1933), is more dispassionate, though now rather outdated. Jean-Charles Bonenfant's *La naissance de la Confédération* (M: Leméac 1969) and *The French Canadians and the Birth of Confederation* (O: CHA Booklet no 21 1966) present a balanced summary account. Andrée Desilet's *Hector Langevin* (Q: PUL 1969); Peter Waite's *The Life and Times of Confederation* (T: UTP 1962); and W.L. Morton's *The Critical Years* (T: M&S 1964) all include informative sections on Confederation. The articles by G.F.G. Stanley and Walter Ullmann, the first on the so-called compact theory of Confederation, and the second on the role of the Quebec bishops in Confederation, found in Ramsay Cook, ed., *Confederation* (T: UTP 1967), are important.

Professor Gil Rémillard's *Le fédéralisme canadien* (M: Québec/ Amérique 1980) is a thorough and impressive study of the legal and constitutional aspects of Confederation, past and present. Though its historical sections are somewhat superficial, its examination of judicial matters is exceptionally valuable. Père Richard Arès has analysed and expounded French-Canadian views of Confederation in two heavily documented books: *Dossier sur le pacte fédératif de 1867* (M: Bellarmin 1967) and *Nos grandes options politiques et constitutionnelles* (M: Bellarmin 1967). Ramsay Cook's *Provincial Autonomy, Minority Rights, and the Compact Theory 1867-1921* (O: Information Canada 1969) covers some of the same ground from a different perspective. Paul Gérin-Lajoie's *Constitutional Amendment in Canada* (T: UTP 1950) remains the standard study of this complex topic. The Carleton Library edition of the *Tremblay Report* (T: M&S 1973), ed. David Kwavnick, is a forceful statement of traditional French-Canadian nationalism and its constitutional implications. Claude Morin's *Quebec versus Ottawa* (T: UTP 1976) is a highly personal assessment of federal-provincial relations in the 1960s while Jean-Louis Roy presents a useful compilation and summary of Quebec's recent constitutional positions in *La choix d'un pays: le débat constitutionnel Québec-Canada, 1960-76* (M: Leméac 1978). These books should be supplemented by Donald Smiley's *Canada in Question* (T: MHR 1981) and by several essays in F.R. Scott's brilliant *Essays on the Constitution* (T: UTP 1977).

The history of the rights of the French-speaking minorities outside of Quebec has received a good deal of recent discussion. While dealing with a larger number of subjects than the minorities, Arthur Silver's *The French-Canadian Idea of Confederation, 1864-1900* (T: UTP 1982) presents a sharply revisionist interpretation of the French-Canadian nationalist elite's conception of the place of French and Catholic culture in North America. W.L. Morton's *Manitoba: A History* (T: UTP 1957), his introduction to *Alexander Begg's Red River Journal* (T: CS 1956), and the documents he edited, *Manitoba: The Birth of a Province* (Altona: Manitoba Records Society 1965), are fundamental to an understanding of the origins of cultural conflict in the West. Of similar importance is Marcel Giraud, *Le Métis canadien: Son rôle dans l'histoire de l'Ouest* (Paris: Universite de Paris, Institut d'Ethnologie 1945). Biographies of Louis Riel by G.F.G. Stanley (T: Ryerson 1963) and Hartwell Bowsfield (T: OUP 1971); *Gabrielle Dumont* (Edmonton: Hurtig 1975) by George Woodcock; and Thomas Flanagan's *Louis 'David' Riel: Prophet of the New World* (T: UTP 1979) are all valuable studies of the Métis and their leaders.

The conflict over minority schools in Ontario and Western Canada is dealt with in three well-documented volumes: Robert Choquette, *Language and Religion: The History of English-French Conflict in Ontario* (T: University of Ottawa Press 1975); Paul Crunican, *Priests and Politicians: Manitoba Schools and the Election of 1896* (T: UTP 1974); and M.R. Lupul, *The Roman Catholic Church and the*

North-West School Question (T: UTP 1974). A series of articles in R.C. Brown, ed., *Minority Schools and Politics* (T: UTP 1969), and 'Regulation 17: Resolution of the Ontario Bilingual Crisis, 1916-29,' in Peter Oliver's *Public and Private Persons* (T: CI 1975), offer additional, useful studies. To these should be added the work of two French-speaking westerners: A.N. Lalonde, 'L'intelligensia du Québec et la migration des Canadiens français vers l'Ouest canadien, 1970-1930,' RHAF, 1979, and two studies by Robert Painchaud, 'French-Canadian Historiography and Franco-Catholic Settlement in Western Canada, 1870-1915,' CHR, 1978, and 'The Franco-Canadian Communities in Western Canada since 1945,' in D.J. Bercuson and P.A. Buckner, eds., *Eastern and Western Perspectives* (T: UTP 1981).

Evidence of a revival of historical work on the Acadian communities in the Maritimes is witnessed by a variety of solid studies. Most important is the volume of essays, covering almost every facet of Acadian life and history, edited by Jean Daigle, *Les Acadiens de Maritimes* (Moncton: Centre des études acadiens 1980). A useful brief survey is G.F.G. Stanley, 'The Flowering of the Acadian Renaissance,' in Bercuson and Buckner, eds., *Eastern and Western Perspectives*. Two leaders of the late nineteenth-century Acadian Renaissance have been studied in the Rev. Camille Antonio Doucet, *Une étoile s'est levée en Acadie: Marcel-François Richard* (Rogersville: Author 1973), and Della M.M. Stanley, *Pierre-Armand Landry* (Moncton: Editions de l'Acadie 1977). George Rawlyk's *Acadian Education in Nova Scotia* (O: Information Canada 1970) and Alexandre J. Savoie, *Un siècle de révindications scolaires au Nouveau Brunswick* (Edmundston: 1980), are helpful accounts of the Francophone minority's apparently unending struggle for educational rights.

While somewhat dated now, *La dualité canadienne/Canadian Duality* (T: UTP 1960), ed. J.-C. Falardeau and Mason Wade, contains several excellent essays on French-English relations in education, politics, economics, and constitutional matters. Professor Falardeau's own contribution remains, after twenty years, extremely perceptive. Finally, since the matter of majorities and minorities is, at root, a matter of numbers, *La situation démolinguistique au Canada: Evolution passé et prospective* (M: Institut de recherches des politiques

1980) by Réjean Lachapelle and Jacques Henripin is of fundamental importance as an analysis of changing demographic and linguistic patterns in Canada.

POLITICS AND INSTITUTIONS

Much work remains to be done in the historical study of Quebec political parties. At present the most satisfactory way to approach the topic is through the biographies of leading political figures. Cartier, Laurier, Bourassa, St. Laurent, Duplessis, and Trudeau have all been studied and their biographies are cited in the chapter on National Politics. Similarly the memoirs of Raoul Dandurand, Chubby Power, Georges-Emile Lapalme, Pierre Sevigny, and Antonio Barrette are valuable, if read critically. Blair Neatby's *Laurier and the Liberal Party in Quebec: A Study in Political Management* (T: M&S 1973) is a carefully documented examination of the federal Liberals during a crucial period. Marc La Terreur's *Les Tribulations des conservateurs au Québec de Bennett à Diefenbaker* (Q: PUL 1973) helps to explain why Quebec has been so strongly Liberal during most of the twentieth century. H.F. Quinn's *The Union nationale* (rev. ed., T: UTP 1979), though based only on published sources and therefore somewhat limited, is the only available published study of the politics of the period between 1935 and 1960, except for Rumilly. Jean-Louis Roy's *La Marche des Québécois* (M: Leméac 1976) provides a wealth of economic, social, and institutional background to the Union nationale period, and argues that the reactionary character of the Duplessis administration has been exaggerated. The most thoroughly studied party in Quebec is the one of perhaps the least significance, Social Credit. That movement has been analysed in two exceptionally able works: Maurice Pinard, *The Rise of a Third Party* (rev. ed., T: PH 1975), and Michael B. Stein, *The Dynamics of Right-Wing Protest: A Political Analysis of Social Credit in Quebec* (T: UTP 1973). The latter contains an informative historical section on the origins of *créditisme*. A recent volume of essays entitled *Partis politiques au Québec* (M: HMH 1976), ed. Réjean Pelletier, presents some new research on Quebec political parties, including an analysis of some aspects of the Parti Québécois. For background to that party André D'Allemagne's partisan but informative *Le R.I.N. de 1960 à 1963* (M: Editions l'étincelle 1974) is useful. Vera Murray, *Le Parti Québécois* (M: HMH 1976), is the first of what will doubtless be a spate of books on the party. Jean Provencher's *René Lévesque: Portrait d'un Québécois* (M: *La Presse* 1973) is superior to Peter Desbarats's *René: A Canadian in Search of a Country* (T: M&S 1976), though both books contribute to an understanding of the PQ leader.

Electoral studies are increasingly numerous but are mainly concerned with recent elections. Two articles provide general surveys: Jean Hamelin, Jacques Letarte, and Marcel Hamelin, 'Les élections provinciales dans le Québec,' *Cahiers de géographie de Québec*, 1959-60, and Vincent Lemieux, 'Québec: Heaven is Blue and Hell is Red,' in Martin Robin, *Canadian Provincial Politics* (T: PH 1972). Important electoral studies include Marcel Caya, 'Aperçu sur les élections provinciales du Québec 1867 à 1886,' RHAF, 1975, and Ronald Rudin, 'Regional Complexity and Political Behavior in a Quebec County, 1867-1886,' SH, 1976. More recent elections are examined in Vincent Lemieux, *et al., Quatre elections provinciales au Québec: 1956 Duplessis; 1960 Lesage; 1962 Lesage; 1966 Johnson* (Q: PUL 1969). For the very important 1970 election, which saw the collapse of the Union nationale and the emergence of the Parti Québécois, there is a thorough analysis and interpretation in Vincent Lemieux, Marcel Gilbert, and André Blais, *Une Élection de réalignement* (M: Editions du Jour 1970). For details of election returns see Vincent Lemieux, *Le quotient politique vrai: Le vote provincial et fédéral au Québec* (Q: PUL 1969), and for party platforms consult Jean-Louis Roy, *Les programmes électoraux du Québec*, 2 vols. (M: Leméac 1970). André Bernard's collection of essays entitled *Québec: Elections 1976* (M: HMH 1976) is a preliminary contribution to an understanding of the critical election of 15 November 1976. 'The Parti Québécois comes to Power,' *Canadian Journal of Political Science*, 1978, by Maurice Pinard and Richard Hamilton, utilizes survey research and election returns to present a clear, convincing analysis of the sources of PQ strength and weakness.

General studies of Canadian government and federalism are valuable for an understanding of the institutional environment of Quebec public life. For more specific information on Quebec, Louis

Sabourin, ed., *Le système politique de Canada: Institutions fédérales et québécoise* (O: Editions de l'Université d'Ottawa 1968), contains a wide selection of informative essays. André Bernard's *Réflexions sur la politique au Québec* (M: Editions de Sainte Marie 1968) and Edmon Orban's *Le Conseil Législatif de Québec, 1867-1967* (M: Bellarmin 1967) are informative about special features of Quebec's public institutions. F.W. Gibson, ed., *Cabinet Formation and Bicultural Relations: Seven Case Studies* (O: Information Canada 1970), contains much material relating to Quebec and R. Desrosier's *Le personnel politique québécois* (M: BE 1972) includes two very useful articles, Jean Hamelin and Louis Baudouin, 'Les cabinets provinciaux, 1867-1967,' and Robert Boily, 'Les hommes politiques du Québec.' An extremely important work, which attempts to integrate institutions, politics, parties, and ideology, is Marcel Hamelin's *Les premieres années du parlementarisme québécoise, 1867-1878* (Q: PUL 1974). John T. Saywell's *The Office of Lieutenant-Governor* (T: UTP 1957) contains important material on this office in Quebec. There are several contributions to R.M. Burns, ed., *One Country or Two?* (M: MQUP 1971), that detail the integration of the institutions of Quebec and the rest of Canada, and discuss some of the difficulties that might result from an effort to separate them. Edmond Orban, ed., *La modernisation politique du Québec* (M: BE 1976), discusses some current institutional problems, including an essay by Claude Morin on what he sees as the confining effect that Canadian federalism has had on Quebec's 'modernization.'

ECONOMICS

Albert Faucher is the father of economic history in Quebec. His studies of the nineteenth century have examined broad questions of technological development, capital investments, the role of the French-Canadian entrepreneur, and the relationship of the Quebec economy to the rest of Canada and to the United States. His two most important books are *Histoire économique et unité canadienne* (M: Fides 1970) and *Québec en Amérique au XIXe siècle* (M: Fides 1973). Another study of very high quality, a successor to Ouellet's *Histoire économique et sociale du Québec*, is Jean Hamelin and Yves

Roby, *Histoire économique du Québec, 1851-96* (M: Fides 1971). W.F. Ryan's *The Clergy and Economic Growth, 1896-1914* (Q: PUL 1966) not only contains some fine economic history but also attempts to come to grips with one of the central controversies of Quebec economic studies: Did the church aid or retard industrialization? Ryan's answer, which is not based on an exhaustive study of all parts of Quebec, is affirmative for the areas that interested him, Three-Rivers and the Chicoutimi-Lac St Jean region. A solid, if somewhat technical and heavily statistical account of Quebec economic history is André Raynauld, *et al., Croissance et structures économiques de la Province de Québec* (Q: Ministère de l'industrie et commerce 1961). Maurice Saint-Germain's *Une économie à libérer: Le Québec analysé dans les structures économique* (M: BE 1973) is a provocative socio-economic analysis of Quebec development. Gilles Lebel, *Horizon 1980* (Q: Gouvernement du Québec, Ministere de l'industrie et du commerce 1970), offers a valuable study of the evolution of the Quebec economy between 1946 and 1968.

There is still much work to be done in writing the history of Quebec's resources and industrial development. John Dales's *Hydroelectricity and Industrial Development: Quebec 1898-1940* (Cambridge: Harvard UP 1957) is a first-class account of one major industry. Paul Sauriol, *The Nationalization of Electric Power* (M: Harvest House 1962), provides much useful information as background to the 1963 decision of the Lesage government to bring the last remaining private power companies under Quebec Hydro. Another important Quebec resource that has been studied in some historical detail is asbestos. Something of its history may be found in Pierre-E. Trudeau, ed., *The Asbestos Strike* (T: Lorimer 1974). Two older works which may still be read with profit are A.J. de Bray, *L'essor industriel et commercial du peuple canadien* (M: Beauchemin nd), and Errol Bouchette, *L'indépendance économique du Canada-français* (M: Wilson and Lafleur 1913). de Bray's book is useful mainly for statistical information, while Bouchette analyses the reasons for the apparent lack of French-Canadian entrepreneurship in Quebec's industrial development. Some of the essays in Robert Comeau, ed., *Economie québécoise* (M: PUQ 1969), deal with this latter topic, though many other subjects are examined, too. All of the essays in

René Durocher and Paul André Linteau, *Le 'Retard' économique et l'infériorité économique des Canadiens français* (M: BE 1971), are devoted to a discussion of the French Canadians' particular economic problems in an industrial economy. French-Canadian participation in the economic development of Quebec has become the subject of some of the liveliest debates in Quebec historical writing. To those who once insisted that French Canadians should remain pure and unadulterated by commerce, and also to those who have held that French Canadians have been excluded from major entrepreneural activity, some new responses have been provided. Paul-André Linteau, in 'Quelques réflexions autour de la bourgeoisie québecoise, 1850-1914,' RHAF, 1976, and in more detail in his splendid *Maisonneuve* (M: BE 1981), has demonstrated that, particularly in real estate development, Francophones have played a major economic role. Brian Young's two books, *Promoters and Politicians: The North Shore Railways in the History of Québec, 1854-85* (T: UTP 1978), and *George-Etienne Cartier: Montreal Bourgeois* (M: MQUP 1981), both reveal substantial French-Canadian participation in railway financing. Jean-Pierre Wallot's *Joseph-Edmund McComber: Mémoirs d'un bourgeois de Montréal, 1874-1949* (M: HMH 1980) demonstrates Francophone success in merchant activity. Two studies of more recent developments are also valuable: Jorge Niosi, *La bourgeoisie canadienne* (M: BE 1980), which, in chapter III, discusses the rise of a new group of Francophone businessmen, and Jean-Marie Rainville's *Hierarchie ethnique dans la grande entreprise* (M: Editions du Jour 1980), which gives some useful evidence about contemporary French-Canadian economic power. Finally, Yves Roby's careful study, *Les Québécois et les investissements américains, 1918-1929* (Q: PUL 1976), shows that Quebeckers have been as willingly dependant upon foreign investment as other Canadians.

Though the importance of agriculture in Quebec has long been recognized, its history is only just beginning to undergo detailed examination. The rural economy is considered in a general manner by Faucher, *Histoire économique*, and by Hamelin and Roby, *Histoire économique du Québec*. Useful background may also be found in chapter III of R. Cole Harris and John Warkentin, *Canada before*

Confederation (T: OUP 1974). Charles Lemelin's 'The State of Agriculture,' in Jean-Charles Falardeau's *Essays on Contemporary Quebec* (Q: PUL 1953), is still useful. A provocative comparison between Quebec and Ontario is offered in John McCallum, *Unequal Beginnings: Agriculture and Economic Development in Quebec and Ontario until 1870* (T: UTP 1980). But the most important new work in rural history is contained in local studies which may be sampled in Normand Seguin, ed., *Agriculture et colonisation au Québec* (M: BE 1980), or in Seguin's detailed monograph, *La conquête du sol au XIXe siècle* (M: BE 1977). An indication of the complexity and potential value of new, quantitative studies of rural change, this time in the Saguenay region, can be found in Gérard Bouchard, 'Family Structure and Geographic Mobility in La Terrière,' *Journal of Family History*, 1977, and 'Un essai d'Anthropologie régionale: l'histoire sociale au Saguenay aux XIXe et XXe siècles,' *Annales*, 1979.

Not much work has been done on farmers' organizations in Quebec but Firmin Létourneau's *l'U.C.C.* (M: Action nationale 1949), a highly sympathetic study of the Union Catholique des Cultivateurs, is useful. The co-operative movement, whose activities were both rural and urban, is discussed with care by Yves Roby, *Alphonse Desjardins et les caisses populaires*, (M: Fides 1964).

SOCIETY, RELIGION, AND EDUCATION

The social history of modern Quebec, like that of most of Canada, is still in its infancy. Some of the essays in Marcel Rioux and Yves Martin, eds., *French-Canadian Society* (T: M&S 1964), especially those by Jean-Charles Falardeau on the church, Jacques Brazeau on the problems of French Canadians in the public service, Norman Taylor on French-Canadian entrepreneurs, and Hubert Guindon's provocative study of Quebec's social evolution, are useful for historians. There is also some social history in almost every work of political and economic history and the study of labour also entails a look at the larger society. There is much about society in Jean-Louis Roy's book on the Duplessis years, and a collection like Hubert Charbonneau's *La Population du Québec: Etudes retrospectives* (M: BE

1973) contains much valuable information about population growth and movement. Though not strictly speaking works of history, and somewhat controversial in their conceptions, two sociological works are very important in understanding Quebec's transformation from a rural to an urban society. These are Horace Miner, *St Denis: A French-Canadian Parish* (Chicago: University of Chicago Press 1963), and E.C. Hughes, *French Canada in Transition* (Chicago: University of Chicago Press 1943).

Some Quebec social institutions have been studied. The history of the Roman Catholic church is briefly surveyed in Nive Voisin, André Beaulieu, and Jean Hamelin, *Histoire de l'Eglise Catholique au Canada* (M: Fides 1971), and more extensively in Herman Plante's *L'Eglise Catholique au Canada* (TR: Editions du Bien Publique 1970), though this book concludes in 1886. The many biographies of bishops and other churchmen are usually very pious, one of the more interesting being Rolland Litalien's study of Mgr Moreau of Ste Hyacinthe, *Le prêtre québécois à la fin du XIXe siècle* (M: Fides 1970). The first volume of a careful and fully documented biography of one of the most influential and intellectual of nineteenth-century bishops is Nive Voisin, *Louis-François LaFlèche*, (TR: Eaisem 1980). Less scholarly, but nevertheless perceptive, is Robert Migner's study of the famous colonization missionary, *Curé Labelle* (M: La Presse 1979).

Perhaps the best introduction to the role and importance of the church in Quebec can be gained by combining some quantitative material with a series of broad interpretive essays. The quantitative material is provided in two important articles by Louis Edmond Hamelin: 'Nombre annuel des nouveaux prêtres, Canada français (1600-1933),' *Bulletin des recherches historiques*, 1959, and 'Evolution numérique seculaire du clergé catholique dans le Québec,' *Recherches sociographiques*, 1961. Some further statistical information, and interpretation, can be found in Bernard Denault et Benoît Lévesque, *Eléments pour une sociologie des communautés réligieuses au Québec* (M: PUM 1975). Interpretive essays which touch sensitively on parish life, education, sacerdotalism, and journalism can be found in Pierre Savard, *Aspects du Catholicisme canadien-français au XIX siècle* (M: Fides 1980).

There are some special studies of the role of the church in society which are important. William Ryan's study of the church and economic development has already been noted. Jean Hulliger, in *L'enseignement social des evêques canadiens de 1891 à 1950* (M: Fides 1958), sets out, somewhat uncritically, the bishops' attempts to apply the teachings of the church to industrial society. Trudeau's *Asbestos Strike* contains some interesting material on this theme, especially in the contributions of abbé Gérard Dion and Fernand Dumont. P. Hurtubise *et al.* present a series of extremely interesting studies of the role of the layman in the Quebec church in *Le laïc dans l'Eglise canadienne-française de 1830 a nos jours* (M: Fides 1972). The essays by Pierre Savard and René Durocher are particularly rewarding. There is only one published study, based on modern research, of that important topic, the relations of church and state. Antonin Dupont's *Les relations entre l'Eglise et l'Etat sous L.-A Taschereau* (M: Guerin 1973) is strongly critical of Taschereau, and might be read in company with B.L. Vigod, 'Qu'on ne craigne pas l'encombrement des compétences: Le gouvernement Taschereau et l'éducation 1920-1929,' RHAF, 1974, which is more sympathetic to the Liberal premier. On the place of the church in contemporary Quebec the six-volume *Report* of the Commission d'Etude sur les Laïcs et l'Eglise (M: Fides 1972-4) contains a wealth of material. A thorough survey of recent writing on the history of the church in Quebec is found in Nive Voisine's 'La production des vingt dernières années en histoire de l'Eglise du Québec,' in *Recherches sociographiques*, 1974.

Historically, one of the principal responsibilities of the Quebec church lay in the field of education. This subject is surveyed in Louis-Phillipe Audet, *Histoire de l'enseignment au Québec*, 2 vols. (T: HRW 1971), and in the same author's contributions to J.D. Wilson, R.H. Stamp, and Audet, *Canadian Education: A History* (T: PH 1970). There are some informative essays in Marcel Lajeunesse, éd., *L'éducation au Québec: 19e et 20e siècles* (M: BE 1971). One of the most important studies in educational and social history in Quebec published recently is Claude Galarneau's *Les collèges classiques au Canada français* (M: HMH 1978). Galarneau provides, for the first time, a systematic analysis of these central educational institutions through the use of statistical material concerning college graduates and careful assessment of course content. It is a work of central significance for anyone who wants to understand Quebec society. Contemporary educational developments are best viewed through the various volumes of the *Royal Commission on Education*, or Parent Commission (Q: QP 1964-8). The establishment of a Ministry of Education, which was the first concrete result of that commission, is described by Léon Dion, *Le bill 60 et la société québécoise* (M: HMH 1967).

LABOUR HISTORY

Labour history is a relatively new field in French-Canadian history, and one that is growing in quality and quantity. General histories of Canadian labour, such as those by Logan and Lipton, include some material on the union movement in Quebec. *Le travailleur québécois et le syndicalisme* (M: PUQ 1971), by Richard Desrosiers and Denis Héroux, adds much additional detail. Trudeau's *The Asbestos Strike*, and Jean-Paul Lefebvre, éd., *En grève* (M: Editions de l'Homme 1963), together cover six major strikes since 1937. Jean Hamelin, éd., *Les travailleurs québécois, 1851-1896* (M: PUQ 1973), contains several excellent essays in labour history, some of which go beyond trade union history to examine the conditions of working-class life. Terry Copp's fine study, *The Anatomy of Poverty* (T: M&S 1974), examines Montreal working-class life and the government policies that were supposed to better that life. His conclusion is that the policies had little effect. Jean de Bonville's *Jean-Baptiste Gagnepetit: Les travailleurs Montréalais à la fin du XIX siècle* (M: Aurore 1975), though not as thorough as Copp, also merits attention. The essays in Fernand Harvey, éd., *Le mouvement ouvrier au Québec* (M: BE 1980), are sometimes rather overloaded with sociology but some, notably Harvey's own study of the Knights of Labour in Quebec, are of good quality. Harvey's *Révolution industrielle et travailleurs* (M: BE 1978) is an impressive analysis of the investigation of the Royal Commission on Capital and Labour (1888) as it related to the condition of the Quebec working class. Another excellent work is Jacques Rouillard, *Les syndicats nationaux au Québec de 1900-*

1930 (Q: PUL 1979). The same author's article, 'Mutations de la Confédération des travailleurs catholiques du Canada, 1940-1960,' RHAF, 1980, covers the important period during which the Catholic unions became deconfessionalized as the Confédération des Syndicats nationaux. Rouillard has also written an informative, popular *Histoire de la CSN, 1921-1981* (M: BE 1981). Taken together with his excellent early work, *Les travailleurs du coton au Québec, 1900-1915* (M: PUQ 1974), which places workers' history firmly in a socioeconomic context, Rouillard has established himself as Quebec's leading labour historian. Finally, mention should be made of Louis-M. Tremblay's study of the ideology of organized labour in Québec. While there is much more to unions than ideology, *Le syndicalisme québéçois: Idéologie de la CSN et de la FTQ, 1940-1970* (M: PUM 1972) is a useful discussion of the politicization of the trade union movement.

One of the main leaders of Quebec trade unionism in this century, Alfred Charpentier, has left a fascinating autobiography, *Cinquante ans d'action ouvrière: Les mémoires d'Alfred Charpentier* (Q: PUL 1974), though his earlier book, *Ma conversion au syndicalisme catholique* (M: Fides 1946), remains an extremely revealing document. Finally, on workers and politics there is a collection of documents edited by Stanley Ryerson *et al., L'action politique des ouvrières québécois (fin de XIXe siècle à 1919)* (M: PUQ 1976). These documents should be read in conjunction with Jacques Rouillard's 'L'action politique ouvrière, 1899-1915,' in Fernand Dumont *et al., Idéologies au Canada français* (Q: PUL 1974).

WOMEN

Since Quebec was slower than most parts of Canada to grant women the right to vote and to modify laws which discriminated against women, interest in women's history has only been stirred recently. Catherine Cleverdon's *The Woman Suffrage Movement in Canada* (T: UTP 1974) covers the subject adequately in a chapter entitled 'The First shall be Last.' Micheline D. Johnson covers the ground again in 'History of the Status of Women in the Province of Quebec,' in *Studies of the Royal Commission on the Status of Women* (O:

Information Canada 1971). A prominent leader of the Quebec feminist movement, Thérese Casgrain, has told her story with verve in *A Woman in a Man's World* (T: M&S 1974). Another autobiography which is essential to an understanding of woman's place in Quebec is Claire Martin's *In an Iron Glove* (T: Ryerson 1968). Also of interest is Jennifer Stoddard, 'The Woman Suffrage Bill in Quebec,' in Marylee Stephenson, ed., *Women in Canada* (T: New Press 1973).

The traditional view of women in Quebec is analysed by Susan Mann Trofimenkoff, 'Henri Bourassa and the Woman Question,' JCS, 1975, and in Laure Conan, *Si les canadiennes le voulaient* (M: Leméac 1974). The views of Mgr Paquet, Henri Bourassa, Olivar Asselin, Joséphine Dandurand, and Marie Gérin-Lajoie are represented in Ramsay Cook and Wendy Mitchison, eds., *The Proper Sphere: Woman's Place in Canadian Society* (T: OUP 1976). New research that is beginning to show the complexity of women's history in Quebec is contained in Marie Lavigne et Yolande Pinard, eds., *Les femmes dans la société québéçoise* (M: BE 1977), and in Marie Lavigne, Yolande Pinard, and Jennifer Stoddard, 'The Fédération nationale St Jean-Baptiste,' in Linda Kealey, ed., *'A Not Unreasonable Claim': Women and Reform in Canada, 1880-1920* (TD: Women's Educational Press 1980). But to these must be added three studies which deal with the relationship of women in the church to the feminist movement: Micheline Dumon-Johnson, 'Les communautés réligieuses et la condition féminine,' *Recherches sociographiques*, 1978; Danielle Juteau Lee, 'Les réligieuses du Québec: leur influence sur la vie professionelle des femmes, 1908-54,' *Atlantis*, 1980; and Marta Danylewyez, 'Changing Relationships: Nuns and Feminists in Montreal, 1890-1925,' SH, 1981. Suzanne Cross's 'The Neglected Majority: The Changing Role of Women in 19th-Century Montreal,' SH, 1973, was a pioneering work which demonstrated the need to approach women's history from a social perspective. Polemical, but still worth reading, is Mona-Josée Gagnon, *Le Québec des hommes* (M: Editions du Jour 1974).

IDEOLOGY

Denis Monière's *Ideologies in Quebec* (T: UTP 1981) is the first attempt to provide a synthesis of much new work that has been accomplished in the study of ideologies in Quebec. While useful and provocative, it is a book that must be used critically and cautiously. Its weakness is twofold. First, it is only as strong as the secondary works on which it is based, and there are many subjects which are not yet adequately covered in the published literature. Secondly, the author applies some rather rigid and essentially undemonstrated neo-Marxist categories to Quebec society and ideas. The reader should be mindful of the criticisms presented in Fernand Ouellet's review in *Social History*, 1979. Nadia Eid, *Le clergé et le pouvoir politique au Québec: une analyse de l'idéologie ultramontaine au milieu du XIXe siècle* (M: HMH 1978), presents a detailed account of ultramontaine doctrines and attempts to place them in a somewhat restrictive socio-economic framework. It is a valuable work, but one that is open to a variety of criticisms, many of which are stated by Phillippe Sylvain, RHAF, 1980. René Hardy's *Les Zouaves* (M: BE 1980) and Christian Morissonneau's *La terre promise: le myth du Nord québécois* (M: HMH 1978) offer interesting accounts of the 'imperialistic' implications of conservative nationalism in nineteenth-century Quebec. Jean de Bonville, 'La liberté de presse à la fin du XIXe siècle: le cas de *Canada Revue*,' RHAF, 1978, uses a little known case of clerical suppression of anti-clerical writing to reveal an important aspect of ultramontain power. Yvan Lamonde's fine study, *La philosophie et son enseignement au Québec, 1665-1920* (M: HMH 1980), probes the philosophic roots of the ideas that dominated Quebec for over two-and-a-half centuries.

Two collections of a rather uneven quality, relying primarily on newspapers and periodicals for ideas about nationalism, religion, politics, and society, are Fernand Dumont *et al.*, *Idéologies au Canada français 1850-1900* and *Idéologies au Canada français, 1900-1929* (Q: PUL 1971, 1974). Two other volumes in the same series cover more specialized but important problems. André-J. Bélanger's *L'apolitisme des idéologies québécoise: La grand tournant, 1934-36* (Q: PUL 1975) is an impressive effort to explain the persistent hostility to politics found in Quebec ideology, especially nationalist ideology. Geneviève Laloux-Jain's *Manuels d'histoire du Canada au Québec et en Ontario de 1867 à 1914* (Q: PUL 1974) analyses the way in which varying views of nationalism have shaped historical writing. The latter topic, dealing with more recent textbooks, is dealt with in Marcel Trudel and Geneviève Jain, *Canadian History Textbooks: A Comparative Study* (O: Information Canada 1969).

The predominant ideology in Quebec has been nationalism. For a selection of nationalist views see Ramsay Cook, ed., *French-Canadian Nationalism: An Anthology* (T: MAC 1970). Pierre-E. Trudeau's opening chapter in *The Asbestos Strike* remains a brilliant, if polemical, essay as does Michel Brunet's 'Les trois dominantes dans la pensée canadienne-française: l'agriculturisme, l'anti-étatisme et le messianisme,' in his *La présence anglaise et les canadiens* (M: Beauchemin 1958). Marcel Rioux, 'The Development of Ideologies in Quebec,' in G.L. Gold and M.A. Tremblay, eds., *Communities and Culture in French Canada* (M: HRW 1973), offers an overview from a nationalist viewpoint. A Marxian approach to ideology in Quebec is presented by Gilles Bourque and Nicle Laurin-Frenette, 'La structure nationale québécoise,' in *Socialisme québécoise 1971*, and in a rather unsatisfactory abridged version in Gary Teeple, ed., *Capitalism and the National Question in Canada* (T: UTP 1972).

Any student of modern Quebec nationalism would need to be familiar with the ideas of Henri Bourassa, chanoine Lionel Groulx, and André Laurendeau, who spent their lives writing and thinking about the nature of French Canada and its place in North America. While voluminous and sometimes pretentious, Lionel Groulx's *Mes mémoirs*, 4 vols. (M: Fides 1970-4) presents a quite extraordinary running commentary on Quebec nationalism and nationalists in this century. An excellent selection of this ideologue's writings has been brought together and translated by Susan Mann Trofimenkoff in *Abbé Groulx: Variations on a Nationalist Theme* (T: CC 1974). The same author's *Action française: French-Canadian Nationalism in the Twenties* (T: UTP 1975) is a thorough study of the organization which was the vehicle for Groulx's views. Some of Bourassa's writings in translation are found in Joseph Levitt, ed., *Henri Bourassa on Imperialism and Biculturalism* (T: CC 1970). Supplementary reading should include Levitt's excellent *Henri Bourassa and the Golden Calf* (O: University of Ottawa Press 1969), which goes beyond the usual discussions of Bourassa's nationalism and takes stock of his social ideas. There is as yet no full-scale study of Laurendeau, the pupil of both Bourassa and Groulx who became editor of *Le Devoir* and co-chairman of the Royal Commission on Bilingualism and Biculturalism. There is a short study of his career in Ramsay Cook, *Canada and the French-Canadian Question* (T: MAC 1966), and two very good selections of his writings which complement one another: Phillip Stratford's *André Laurendeau: Witness for Quebec* (T: MAC 1974) includes the whole of Laurendeau's important *The Conscription Crisis of 1942*, while Ramsay Cook and Michael Behiels, eds., *The Essential Laurendeau* (T: CC 1976), provides documents illustrating Laurendeau's intellectual evolution. Finally, attention should be drawn to the nineteenth-century nationalist writer, Jules-Paul Tardivel, whose ideas can be studied in his novel translated as *For my Country* (T: UTP 1975). That edition includes a brilliant introduction by A.I. Silver which is extremely important to an understanding of the dominant clerico-conservative nationalism of the late nineteenth and early twentieth century.

A rather different French-Canadian intellectual tradition, more liberal and less nationalist, can be discovered in Léopold Lamontagne's *Arthur Buies* (Q: PUL 1957), and Hervé Carrier, *Le sociologue canadien: Léon Gérin* (M: Bellarmin 1960), which deals with late nineteenth-century figures. Two works which analyse liberal thinkers of this century are Marcel-Aimé Gagnon's *Jean-Charles Harvey: Précurseur de la révolution tranquille* (M: Beauchemin 1970), which sets out the ideas of a non-conformist novelist and newspaperman, and Robert Parisé, *Georges-Henri Lévesque* (M: Alain Stanké 1976), which expounds the ideas of the founder of the important School of Social Sciences at Laval University. Finally, reference should be made to two collections of short studies of French-Canadian thinkers: Laurier Lapierre, ed., *The Four O'Clock Lectures: French-Canadian Thinkers of the Nineteenth and Twentieth Centuries* (M: McGill UP 1966), and Jean-Charles Falardeau, *L'essor des sciences sociales au Canada-Français* (Q: Ministère des affaires culturelles 1964).

CULTURE

There is no clear distinction between cultural and intellectual history, and in Quebec nationalism has played as significant a role in cultural as in intellectual life. Three useful studies of Quebec literature examine this aspect of French-Canadian culture. Jean-Charles Falardeau, *Notre société et son roman* (M: HMH 1967), attempts to discover what novels reveal about social evolution. Maurice Lemaire, *Les grande thèmes nationalistes du roman historique canadien-français* (Q: PUL 1970), explores the way in which the historical novel in Quebec has been nationalist in content. Jack Warwick's *The Long Journey: Literary Themes of French Canada* (T: UTP 1968) looks at the fashion in which French-Canadian fiction has persistently returned to the theme of the North, in the manner of the *coureur-des-bois*. There are many general surveys of French-Canadian literature. The most comprehensive is Pierre de Grandpré, éd., *Histoire de la littérature française du Québec*, 4 vols. (M: Beauchemin 1967-70), while Gérard Tougas, *The History of French Canadian Literature* (T: Ryerson 1967), is the most useful survey in English.

The history of French-Canadian painting is exceptionally well explained in Jean-René Ostiguy, *Une siècle de peinture canadienne 1870-1970* (Q: PUL 1971). The two most important artists of twentieth-century Quebec are the subjects of studies by Guy Robert. His *Jean-Paul Lemieux* (Q: Editions Garneau 1968) is a beautifully illustrated book accompanied by a brief but sound text. His *Borduas* (Q: PUL 1972) is a thorough and engrossing study of the cultural history, and even the intellectual history, of Quebec from the twenties to the fifties. François-Marc Gagnon's *Paul-Emile Borduas: Biographie critique et analyse de l'oeuvre* (M: Fides 1978), is another study of this great artist which, without superseding Robert's study, offers much that is new in information and especially interpretation.

For the popular arts, which have been extremely important in Quebec's culture, there are three especially valuable books: Jean Palardy, *The Early Furniture of French Canada* (T: MAC 1963), and two volumes by Michel Lessard and Hugette Marquis, *Encyclopédie des antiquités du Québec* and *Encyclopédie de la maison québécoise* (M: Les Editions de l'Homme 1971, 1972). Marius Barbeau's *J'ai vu Québec* (Q: Editions Garneau 1957) is still a beautiful reminder of the traditional society that modernization has gradually destroyed.

CONTEMPORARY HISTORY

Books dealing with contemporary Quebec, its socio-economic problems and the debate over its future relations with the rest of Canada, are not, strictly speaking, historical studies. Nevertheless, there are many books which those interested in the tumultuous developments in Quebec in the last twenty years will find rewarding. An excellent place to start is with a collection of essays that is now nearly thirty years old, *Essays on Contemporary Quebec* (Q: PUL 1953), ed. Jean-Charles Falardeau. It includes studies of industrial development, agriculture, religion, politics, and ideology which are not only very good in their own right, but which sum up the state of Quebec society on the eve of the Quiet Revolution. It is a book that can be fruitfully compared with a later collection of essays edited by J.-L. Migué, *Le Québec aujourd'hui: Régards universitaires* (M: HMH 1971), which covers much the same ground after twenty years of change.

In English the most recent summary and analysis of Quebec developments since 1945 is Dale Postgate and Kenneth McRoberts, *Quebec: Social Change and Political Crisis* (T: M&S 1981). It is thorough and balanced, and its footnotes provide an up-to-date list of books and articles on a wide variety of current topics in Quebec. A second study which concentrates on these years in Léon Dion's *Nationalismes et politique au Québec* (M: HMH 1975), which attempts to distinguish nationalisms according to traditional political categories of conservative, liberal, and socialist. Marcel Rioux's *Quebec in Question* (T: James Lewis and Samuel 1972), while clearly independentist in outlook, is full of provocative interpretations. *Politics in the New Quebec* (T: M&S 1978), by Henry Milner, is a Marxian account of recent Quebec history, more sophisticated than Léandre Bergeron's *Petit manuel d'histoire du Québec* (M: Edition Québécoise 1969), but nevertheless overly simple in its explanation of complex events.

The interpretation of the past on which the separatist understanding of the present rests is best stated in Maurice Séguin's *L'idée d'indépendance au Québec: Genèse et historique* (M: BE 1968). That interpretation is challenged by Fernand Ouellet in 'The Historical

Background of Separatism in Quebec,' in Cook, *French-Canadian Nationalism*. Though sometimes ignored, the writings of Pierre Vadeboncœur, particularly his *La ligne du risque* (M: HMH 1963) and *La dernière heure et la première* (M: l'Hexagone 1970), probe deeply into the Quebec psyche and society from a nationalist perspective. Though rather dated now, René Lévesque *et al.*, *Option Quebec* (T: M&S 1969), is a useful source of Parti Québécois ideas. 'For an Independent Quebec,' by René Lévesque, *Foreign Affairs*, 1976, is a remarkably revealing statement of that politician's intellectual and even emotional make-up. The collection of articles entitled *Les québécois* (M: Parti Pris 1971) presents the viewpoint of young writers in the sixties whose radicalism derived from Karl Marx, Jean-Paul Sartre, Jacques Berque, and Franz Fanon. Malcolm Reid's *The Shouting Sign Painters* (T: M&S 1972) is an uncritical celebration of that group. Pierre Vallières, *The White Niggers of America* (T: M&S 1971), is a very personal, radical assessment of Quebec. It is often moving in its autobiographical sections, though its analysis is heavily rhetorical. A good study of the verbal and sometimes physical violence of the left-wing fringe of Quebec nationalism is found in Marc Laurendeau, *Les Québécois violents* (M: BE 1974).

The literature on the FLQ crisis of October 1970 is extensive but far from satisfactory since most of the crucial government documents are still confidential. Gérard Pelletier's *The October Crisis* (T: M&S 1971) states the federal government's position, while Denis Smith's *Bleeding Hearts ... Bleeding Country* (Edmonton: Hurtig 1971) critically dissects that position. John T. Saywell's *Québec 70: A Documentary Narrative* (T: UTP 1971) is an indispensable narrative of the confused events of the autumn of 1970. Jacques Lacoursière, *Alarme citoyens* (M: *La Presse* 1972); Jean-Claude Trait, *FLQ 70: Offensive d'automne* (M: Les Editions de l'Homme 1970); and Gustaf Morf, *Terror in Quebec: Case Studies of the FLQ* (T: CI 1970) are among the better instant books of the period.

The most effectively argued French-Canadian defence of federalism is Pierre-E. Trudeau, *Federalism and the French Canadians* (T: MAC 1968), though Gilles Lalande, *Pourquoi le fédéralisme* (M: HMH 1972), looks at the system in more detail. David Cameron's *Nationalism, Self Determination and the Quebec Question* (T: MAC 1974) is one of the few books which attempts to set out Canadian controversies over nationalism and federalism in the context of modern European political and social theory. Even if it is somewhat brief in its discussion of Quebec, its early chapters are well worth serious attention. Léon Dion's *The Unfinished Revolution* (M: MQUP 1976) is a very thoughtful political scientist's reflections on two decades of rapid change in Quebec. *Le nationalisme québécois à la croisée des chemins* (Q: Centre québécois de rélations intérnationales, *La Collection Choix* 1975) provides a set of widely differing interpretations of the direction of Quebec nationalism. Dale C. Thomson, ed., *Quebec Society and Politics: Views from Inside* (T: M&S 1973), presents many of the same views, in English. The volumes of the *Report of the Royal Commission on Bilingualism and Biculturalism*, 5 vols. (O: QP 1965-70) and the many subsidiary studies published by the commission are all worth consulting, though special attention should be paid to volume III which deals with the place of French Canadians in the Canadian social structure.

With the election of the *indépendantiste* Parti Québécois government of René Lévesque and the return to power, federally, of Pierre-E. Trudeau, the debate over Quebec's place in Canada continues. Louis Balthazar and Ramsay Cook present somewhat different perspectives in R. Kenneth Carty and Peter Ward, eds., *Entering the Eighties* (T: OUP 1980). Two young philosophers, Michael Morin and Claude Bertrand, in their *Le territoire imaginaire de la culture* (M: HMH 1979), destructively criticize the whole concept of nationalism, while Gilles Bourque and Anne Legaré in *Le Québec: La quéstion nationale* (Paris: Maspero 1978) insist that the problem is one of classes, not of nations. Sheila Arnopoulos and Dominique Clift, in their important study *The English Fact in Quebec* (M: MQUP 1980), point to the important changes which have taken place in the once dominant Anglophone community in Quebec. More controversial are Clift's views of the changes that he perceives in the Francophone community which he dissects effectively in *The Decline of Nationalism in Quebec* (M: MQUP 1982). Some future historian will judge the ultimate value of works of this type.

Few of the books on contemporary events were written by historians. Today the nationalist front lines are more often occupied by sociologists and political scientists than historians, something of a change from the past. Whatever the explanation, it is certainly not that Quebec historians are completely detached from present controversies. Rather, it is more likely that, under the influence of new approaches to history, they are simply too excited by the prospect of re-examining their past.

WILLIAM B. HAMILTON

Atlantic Canada

Anyone interested in the history of the Atlantic provinces since 1867 soon realizes that the period has received relatively little attention. Preoccupied with what has been aptly described as the 'Golden Age' of Maritime historiography, historians have concentrated on the pre-Confederation years and the region awaits a latter day John Bartlet Brebner or Daniel Cobb Harvey to unravel its more recent history. The above comment, written for the first edition of this bibliography in 1974, is still largely valid. While significant strides have taken place in historical writing in Atlantic Canada over the past decade, an emphasis on the pre-Confederation period remains. Confirmation can be found in a count of papers presented before regional historical societies, in the articles published in both learned and popular journals, and in the lists of theses and dissertations completed. Three articles will serve to place the 'state of the art' in perspective: Delphin Muise – 'The Atlantic Region in Recent Canadian National Histories,' *Acadiensis*, 1975; Clarence G. Karr, 'The Atlantic Provinces and the Development of the Canadian Historiographical Tradition,' DR, 1977; and Ernest Forbes, 'In Search of a Post-Confederation Maritime Historiography,' *Acadiensis*, 1978. In his appraisal of the current scene, Forbes points to two failures: '... of mainstream Canadian historians to pursue themes which readily include the Maritimes, or to include the Maritimes in themes which they did pursue', and '... of academics residing in the region [failing] to respond effectively to the desperate search for an historical perspective ...'

Despite this gloomy assessment there are positive signs on the horizon. Writing in *Queen's Quarterly*, 1969, George Rawlyk pinned hopes for a 'New Golden Age of Maritime Historiography' on '... a shift in emphasis from the purely political to the social, to the intellectual [and] to the economic.' To a considerable extent this change has taken place. It is not without significance that the largest number of post-1974 entries in this bibliography fall in the socio-economic category. Three reasons loom in any explanation of this development. First, largely as a result of a recent emphasis on Atlantic Canada studies at the universities in the region, a new generation of historians has begun to tackle themes ranging from labour and working-class history to urban and industrial studies to the religious, social, and cultural heritage of the region. Secondly, to the forefront in this evolution has been the Maritime Studies Group at Memorial University. Any analysis of the recent historiography of Atlantic Canada must take into account the trail-blazing efforts of these historians. Finally, the flowering of a regional historical journal, *Acadiensis*, created an impetus. Not only is *Acadiensis* providing a forum for much of the research in the history of Atlantic Canada; it is seriously attempting to redress the balance in favour of the post-Confederation period. The number of citations from *Acadiensis* in this bibliography will bear witness to its success. While the time span covered by this bibliography has not always been emphasized, it should not be taken to mean that the student must start from scratch. There are significant books and monographs, key articles tucked away in scholarly journals, valuable material in Royal Commission reports, and informative studies in related fields – most notably political science and historical geography. Hopefully, the entries that follow will point the way to these sources and provide a coherent picture of what is available. In the context of this section of the book the phrase 'post-Confederation' has deliberately been given a broad interpretation to cover all four provinces since 1867. This approach permits a more balanced view of the subject and, aside from simple convenience, may help encourage investigation of common themes important in gaining an understanding of the entire region.

BIBLIOGRAPHIC AIDS AND REFERENCE MATERIALS

The student with limited background who approaches a research topic in the history of the Atlantic provinces may well begin with Douglas Lochhead, ed., *Bibliography of Canadian Bibliographies* (2nd ed., T: UTP 1972). If searching for general leads, the index in this volume will bear close study. W.F.E. Morley, *The Atlantic Provinces* (T: UTP 1967), another obvious starting-point, is an indispensable reference for both general studies and local history to 1950. William B. Hamilton, *Local History in Atlantic Canada* (T: MAC 1974), contains a capsule history of the region along with bibliographical suggestions on a wide range of topics. The most complete guide is Claude Thibault, *Bibliographia Canadiana* (T: Longman 1973). Be forewarned that references to Atlantic Canada are widely scattered in this massive volume. Use the general index and do not neglect entries in the Addenda. Norah Story, *The Oxford Companion to Canadian History and Literature* (T: OUP 1967), provides an annotated bibliography for each province. See also Norah Story, *Supplement to the Oxford Companion to Canadian History* (T: OUP 1973).

The provincial archives and university libraries of the region have, from time to time, produced bibliographic guides. By far the most useful, because of its complete coverage and excellent organization, is Hugh A. Taylor, ed., *New Brunswick History: A Checklist of Secondary Sources* (Fredericton: Public Archives of New Brunswick 1971). A first supplement to the *Checklist*, compiled by Eric L. Swanick, was issued in 1974. Another example, Alice R. Stewart's *The Atlantic Provinces of Canada* (2nd ed., Orono: University of Maine 1971), provides a comprehensive list of major secondary sources. A running watch should be kept on contemporary research by referring to the Atlantic provinces section in Recent Publications Relating to Canada in the *Canadian Historical Review*. Important bibliographies with entries listed by province will be found in *Acadiensis*. The *New England Quarterly* publishes occasional bibliographies on New England and many of the entries have significance for Atlantic Canada. Scholarly articles dealing with the history of the region find their way into a wide variety of journals. The most important ones directly bearing on the region are *Acadiensis, American Review of Canadian Studies*, *Bulletin Société Historique Acadienne*, New Brunswick Historical Society *Collections*, Nova Scotia Historical Society *Collections, Dalhousie Review, New England Quarterly, Newfoundland Quarterly*, and *Nova Scotia Historical Quarterly* (renamed in 1981 the *Nova Scotia Historical Review.*) Additional bibliographical information will be found in Brian Tennyson, *Cape Breton: A Bibliography* (H: Department of Education 1978); Robert Vaison, *Nova Scotia: Past and Present* (H: Department of Education 1976); F.H. Armstrong, A.F.J. Artibise, M. Baker, eds., *Bibliography of Canadian Urban History*, Part II: *Atlantic Provinces* (Monticello, Ill.: Vance Bibliographies 1980); Ian Ross Robertson, 'Recent Island History,' *Acadiensis*, 1975.

Olga Bishop, *Publications of the Governments of Nova Scotia, Prince Edward Island and New Brunswick* (O: National Library 1957), is an essential reference for government documents. Unfortunately, there is no comparable treatment for Newfoundland. John P. Greene, ed., *A Preliminary Inventory* (St John's: Public Archives of Newfoundland and Labrador 1970), lists current holdings of that institution.

Throughout this section reference will be made to several unpublished theses. Information concerning a number of theses relating to Nova Scotia may be found in Delphin Muise, 'Theses on Nova Scotian History,' *Education Office Gazette*, 1968. The basic reference for Nova Scotian political figures is C. Bruce Fergusson, *Nova Scotia M.L.A.'s 1758-1958* (H: Public Archives of Nova Scotia 1958). None of the other provinces have, as yet, produced like directories. Background on leading Newfoundland politicians may be found in R. Hibbs, ed., *Who's Who in and from Newfoundland* (2nd ed., St. John's, 1930), and James R. Thomas, ed., *Newfoundland and Labrador Who's Who* (Centennial Edition, St John's: E.C. Boone 1967). A source of contemporary information is *The Atlantic Yearbook*, an annual publication of Unipress, Fredericton, NB. For the newspapers of New Brunswick consult J. Russell Harper, *Historical Directory of New Brunswick Newspapers and Periodicals* (Fredericton:

University of New Brunswick 1961). An essential reference for Nova Scotian newspapers is Gertrude Tratt, *A Survey and Listing of Nova Scotia Newspapers 1752-1957* (H: Dalhousie University 1979).

GENERAL STUDIES

In the absence of a comprehensive scholarly history of Atlantic Canada since 1867 one must piece together the history of the region from a variety of sources. In a significant article, 'Economic Growth in the Atlantic Region,' *Acadiensis*, 1978, the late David Alexander encouraged regional historians 'to bridge the Cabot Strait.' An important step in this direction has been taken by the Maritime Studies Group at Memorial University. Their publications include Keith Matthews and Gerald Panting, eds., *Ships and Shipbuilding in the North Atlantic Region* (1977); David Alexander and Rosemary Ommer, eds., *Volumes not Values: Canadian Sailing Ships and World Trade* (1979); Lewis R. Fischer and Eric W. Sager, eds., *The Enterprising Canadians: Entrepreneurs and Economic Development in Canada 1820-1914* (1979); Rosemary Ommer and Gerald Panting, eds., *Workingmen Who Got Wet* (1980). Each volume contains a rich selection of papers presented at conferences sponsored by the Maritime History Group.

Most of the research in Acadian history has concentrated on the Expulsion and the years immediately following that unhappy event; however, Naomi Griffiths, *The Acadians: Creation of a People* (T: MHR 1973), devotes some attention to the evolution of a distinct Acadian nationalism. Much of the history and not a little of the political rhetoric of Atlantic Canada has concentrated on questions relating to regional identity and protest. For contrasting views see George Rawlyk, 'Nova Scotia's Regional Protest 1867-1967,' QQ, 1968; C.M. Wallace, 'The Nationalization of the Maritimes,' in J.M. Bumsted, ed., *Documentary Problems in Canadian History* (Georgetown: Irwin-Dorsey 1969); J. Murray Beck, 'The Maritimes: A Region or Three Provinces,' TRSC, 1977; David Alexander, 'New Notions of Happiness: Nationalism, Regionalism and Atlantic Canada,' JCS, 1980; and Ernest Forbes, 'The Origins of the Maritime Rights Movement,' *Acadiensis*, 1975. A more comprehensive treatment will be found in the same author's *The Maritime Rights Movement 1919-27* (M: MQUP 1979). The overall question of regional identity is surveyed in several essays in Mason Wade, ed., *Regionalism in the Canadian Community 1867-1967* (T: UTP 1969). Significantly, only two of the fourteen articles in George Rawlyk's *Historical Essays on the Atlantic Provinces* (T: M&S 1967) deal with the post-Confederation period. One of these, A.G. Bailey, 'Creative Moments in the Culture of the Maritime Provinces,' (originally published in DR, 1949), is a study of the late nineteenth-century milieu which produced the Fredericton school of poets. General historiographical information is in Carl Klinck, *Literary History of Canada* (2nd ed., T: UTP 1977). J.R. Smallwood, ed., *The Book of Newfoundland*, 6 vols. (St John's: Newfoundland Book Publishers 1937-75), provides a *potpourri* of Newfoundland history with considerable emphasis on the period since 1867. More interpretative are the articles in R.A. MacKay, ed., *Newfoundland Economic, Diplomatic, and Strategic Studies* (T: OUP 1946), and Peter Neary, ed., *The Political Economy of Newfoundland* (T: CC 1973). St John Chadwick, *Newfoundland: Island into Province* (L: Cambridge UP 1967), despite a promising title, is only marginally useful for general trends and developments.

POLITICAL HISTORY

Nova Scotia
The classic work on Nova Scotian politics is Murray Beck, *The Government of Nova Scotia* (T: UTP 1957). Two theses which survey political trends in nineteenth-century Nova Scotia are Delphin Muise, 'Elections and Party Development: Federal Politics in Nova Scotia 1867-87' (PHD University of Western Ontario 1971), and Phyllis Blakeley, 'Party Government in Nova Scotia 1878-97' (MA Dalhousie University 1945). In the same context K.G. Pryke, 'The Making of a Province: Nova Scotia and Confederation,' CHAR, 1968, may be cited. Additional insight can be gained by consulting Pryke's *Nova Scotia and Confederation 1864-74* (T: UTP 1979). The immediate post-Confederation repeal movement is covered in R.H. Campbell, 'The Repeat Agitation in Nova Scotia 1867-69,' NSHS, *Collections* 1942, and Donald Warner, 'The Post-Confederation Annexation

Movement in Nova Scotia,' CHR, 1947. Phyllis Blakeley, 'The Repeal Election of 1886,' NSHS, *Collections* 1945, carries the question down to 1890 when it temporarily faded from the scene. A systematic analysis of nineteenth-century federal elections in Nova Scotia may be found in Delphin A. Muise, 'Parties and Constituencies: Federal Elections in Nova Scotia 1867-1896,' CHAR, 1971. In this important article Muise puts forward the thesis that Nova Scotia was 'not a smouldering hot bed of anti-confederation sentiment.' That 'great fever in the lower provinces – the fisheries,' as John A. Macdonald put it, is discussed in R.S. Longley, 'The Fisheries in Nova Scotian Politics 1865-71,' NSHS, *Collections* 1942. Additional information is provided in Ronald Tallman, 'Peter Mitchell and the Genesis of a National Fisheries Policy,' *Acadiensis*, 1975. For the pivotal federal election of 1896 see Kenneth McLaughlin, 'The Canadian General Election of 1896 in Nova Scotia' (MA thesis, Dalhousie University 1967). More readily available is K.M. McLaughlin, 'W.S. Fielding and the Liberal Party in Nova Scotia 1891-96,' *Acadiensis*, 1974, and Colin D. Howell, 'W.S. Fielding and the Repeal Elections of 1886 and 1887,' *Acadiensis*, 1979. E.R. Forbes, 'The Rise and Fall of the Conservative Party in the Provincial Politics of Nova Scotia 1922-33' (MA thesis, Dalhousie University 1968), takes a look at one of the rare periods of Conservative rule in that province – the Rhodes-Harrington government of 1925-33. A succinct analysis of the more recent revival of the Progressive Conservative party in the province will be found in Peter Aucoin, 'The Conservative Leader in Nova Scotia' (MA thesis, Dalhousie University 1966). As well, the reminiscences of one of the leading 'players' in the unfolding story, Dalton Camp, are worth consulting. See *Gentlemen Players and Politicians* (T: M&S 1974). Nova Scotia has had a tradition of strong pockets of support for the political left. Recent skirmishes surrounding the New Democratic party are chronicled in Paul MacEwan, *The Akerman Years: Jeremy Akerman and the Nova Scotia New Democratic Party 1965-1980* (Antigonish: Formac 1980). Other than the entries listed below under the headings Biographical Studies and Economic History, there has been a paucity of research in twentieth-century Nova Scotian politics. Unfortunately, a similar gap exists in the political history of New Brunswick and Prince Edward Island.

New Brunswick
The standard treatment of political development in New Brunswick is Hugh G. Thorburn, *Politics in New Brunswick* (T: UTP 1961). The manoeuvring which surrounded the Smith-Wilmot government formed to oppose the inclusion of New Brunswick in Confederation and the anti-Confederation movement through to 1882 is treated in Carl Wallace, 'Albert Smith – Confederation and Reaction in New Brunswick,' CHR, 1963. For the role of Arthur Hamilton Gordon (lieutenant-governor, 1861-6) in the Confederation dilemma see J.K. Chapman, 'Arthur Gordon and Confederation,' CHR, 1956. Two articles by A.G. Bailey throw additional light on the Confederation question in the province: 'Railways and the Confederation Issue in New Brunswick,' CHR, 1940, and 'The Basis and Persistence of Opposition to Confederation in New Brunswick,' CHR, 1942. Further discussion of late nineteenth-century New Brunswick politics will be found in four MA theses: Esther Greaves, 'Peter Mitchell: A Father of Confederation' (University of New Brunswick 1958); D.L. Poynter 'The Economics and Politics of New Brunswick 1878-83' (University of New Brunswick 1961); M. Gordon, 'The Andrew G. Blair Administration and the Abolition of the Legislative Council of New Brunswick, 1882-92' (University of New Brunswick 1964); and J.I. Little, 'The Federal Election of 1896 in New Brunswick' (University of New Brunswick 1964). The downfall of the McNair administration in 1952 and the advent of a new era in New Brunswick politics is chronicled in Camp, *Gentlemen Players and Politicians*. For a discussion of bilingualism see Robert M. Gill, 'Bilingualism in New Brunswick and the Future of l'Acadie,' *American Review of Canadian Studies*, 1980.

Prince Edward Island
The centenary of Prince Edward Island's entry into Confederation inspired considerable research in political history; however, Frank MacKinnon, *The Government of Prince Edward Island* (T: UTP 1951), remains the best account of Island politics. A full and extremely informative study, Francis W.P. Bolger, *Prince Edward Island and Confederation* (Charlottetown: St Dunstan's UP 1964), surveys the crucial decade prior to 1873. For initial reading there is D.C. Har-

vey, 'Confederation in Prince Edward Island,' CHR, 1933. A fascinating account of an American mission to 'talk fish and trade' is unfolded in Ronald D. Tallman, 'Annexation in the Maritimes – The Butler Mission to Charlottetown,' DR, 1973. Lorne C. Callbeck, *The Cradle of Confederation* (Fredericton: Brunswick Press 1964), treats the full sweep of Island history. Three books inspired by the 1973 centennial are Francis W.P. Bolger, ed., *Canada's Smallest Province: A History of P.E.I.* (Charlottetown: PEI Heritage Foundation 1973), and David Weale and Harry Baglole, *The Island and Confederation: The End of an Era* (Summerside: Williams & Crue 1973). For a satirical look at the 1973 centennial along with a host of related topics see Harry Baglole and David Weale, *Cornelius Howatt: Superstar!* (Summerside: Williams & Crue 1974).

Newfoundland
References to late nineteenth-century Newfoundland politics are scattered; however, Frederic F. Thompson, *The French Shore Problem in Newfoundland* (T: UTP 1961), covering one of the most vexing diplomatic and political issues, touches on broader matters. The following articles provide wide-ranging analyses of some of the major events: Fred J. Newhook, 'Newfoundland's First Rejection of Confederation: The Election of 1869,' *Newfoundland Quarterly*, 1961; G.F.G. Stanley, 'Further Documents relating to the Union of Newfoundland and Canada,' CHR, 1948; Harvey Mitchell, 'Canada's Negotiations with Newfoundland 1887-95,' CHR, 1959; and Mitchell, 'Constitutional Crisis of 1889 in Newfoundland,' CJEPS, 1958. Two MA theses at Memorial University help in unravelling the intricacies of post-1867 Newfoundland politics: E.C. Moulton, 'The Political History of Newfoundland 1865-74' (1963), and Kenneth J. Kerr, 'A Social Analysis of the Members of the Newfoundland House of Assembly, Executive Council and Legislative Council for the period 1855-1914' (1973). In addition, J.K. Hiller, 'A History of Newfoundland 1874-1901' (PHD thesis, Cambridge University 1971), places the last quarter of the century in perspective. The twentieth century is well served by two important books. S.J.R. Noel, *Politics in Newfoundland* (T: UTP 1971) is a well-written, comprehensive, and informative study, while Peter Neary, *The Political*

Economy of Newfoundland (T: CC 1973), authoritatively documents the period 1929-72. Insight into particular issues is provided by G.O. Rothney, 'The Denominational Basis of Representation in the Newfoundland Assembly 1919-62,' CJEPS, 1962; G.E. Panting, 'The Fishermen's Protective Union of Newfoundland and the Farmers Organizations in Western Canada,' CHAR, 1963; Ian McDonald, 'W.F. Coaker and the Fishermen's Protective Union in Newfoundland Politics' (PHD thesis, University of London 1971); Henry B. Mayo, 'Newfoundland's Entry into Confederation,' CJEPS, 1949; and Parzival Copes, 'The Fishermen's Vote in Newfoundland,' *Canadian Journal of Political Science*, 1970. Not surprisingly, much emphasis has been placed on the fall of responsible government and the role of the Commission of Government. A concise introduction to the topic is G.E. Panting, 'Newfoundland's Loss of Responsible Government,' in Bumsted, ed., *Documentary Problems in Canadian History*. More detailed information is contained in two theses, H.A. Cuff, 'The Commission of Government in Newfoundland: A Preliminary Survey' (MA, Acadia University 1959), and R.A. Clarke, 'Newfoundland 1934-1949 – A Study of the Commission of Government' (PHD, University of California (Los Angeles) 1951). Volume III of J.R. Smallwood, ed., *The Book of Newfoundland*, outlines the events which culminated in Confederation in 1949 (see also references to Smallwood in Biographical Studies below). A provocative treatment of post-1949 Newfoundland politics is presented in four articles by Peter Neary: 'Democracy in Newfoundland: A Comment,' JCS, 1969; 'Party Politics in Newfoundland 1949-71: A Survey and Analysis,' JCS, 1971; 'Party Politics in Newfoundland: The End of the Smallwood Era,' JCS, 1972; and 'Changing Government: The 1971-72 Newfoundland Example,' *Dalhousie Law Journal*, 1979.

Local government and Maritime Union
The peculiarities of local government in the Atlantic provinces are discussed in C. Bruce Fergusson, *Local Government in Nova Scotia* (H: Public Archives of Nova Scotia 1961); J. Murray Beck, 'The Evolution of Municipal Government in Nova Scotia 1749-1973' (H: Royal Commission on Education, Public Services and Provincial-

Municipal Relations 1974); H.J. Whalen, *The Development of Local Government in New Brunswick*, (Fredericton: QP 1963); J.C. Crosbie, 'Local Government in Newfoundland,' CJEPS 1956); and H.J. Finnis, *Local Government in the Changing Economy of Cape Breton* (Antigonish: St Francis Xavier University 1968). Administrative changes in New Brunswick are examined in an excellent study by Ralph R. Krueger, 'The Provincial-Municipal Revolution in New Brunswick,' *Canadian Public Administration*, 1970. In 1864 the concept of Maritime Union lay behind the Charlottetown Conference; since that time it has periodically surfaced as a panacea for the political and economic ills of the area. For the historical background see J.M. Beck, *History of Maritime Union: A Study of Frustrations* (Fredericton: 1969), and C. Bruce Fergusson, 'Maritime Unions,' QQ, 1970. For the most recent scheme advocating Maritime Union see *Maritime Union Study* (Fredericton: QP 1970). The early years of the Maritime Council of Premiers are discussed by A.A. Lomas in *Canadian Public Administrator* (1977). A definitive study of the Maritime Rights movement is Forbes, *The Maritime Rights Movement 1919-27*.

BIOGRAPHICAL STUDIES

Despite an impressive roll call of prominent personalities, including four of Canada's sixteen prime ministers (Thompson, Tupper, Borden, and Bennett), scholarly biographical studies are conspicuous by their absence. A few of the early figures are covered in volume X of the *Dictionary of Canadian Biography* and subsequent volumes of this series will be awaited with interest. Joseph Howe belongs, in part, to the 'Golden Age'; however, for his participation in the Confederation debate see J.M. Beck, 'Joseph Howe and Confederation: Myth and Fact,' TRSC, 1964, and 'Howe and the Enactment of the BNA Act: Final Disillusionment of a Statesman of Empire,' NSHS, *Collections*, 1980. Balanced general accounts by the same author appear in *Our Living Tradition*, Fourth Series (T: UTP 1962), ed. R.L. McDougall, and 'Joseph Howe: Anti-Confederate' (O: CHA Booklet no 17 1965). Some of the conflicting views concerning Howe are surveyed in George Rawlyk, ed., *Joseph Howe: Opportunist? Man of Vision? Frustrated Politician?* (T: CC 1967).

Other leading personalities in the Confederation debate in Nova Scotia are analyzed in volume XXXVI of the Nova Scotia Historical Society *Collections* (A.G. Archibald, R.B. Dickey, P.S. Hamilton, W.A. Henry, Jonathan McCully, J.W. Ritchie, Charles Tupper, and M.I. Wilkins). Arthur Hamilton Gordon is the subject of a complete biography, J.K. Chapman's *The Career of Arthur Hamilton Gordon* (T: UTP 1964). James Hannay's *Sir Leonard Tilley* (T: Morang 1911) is worth consulting; however, a more objective treatment will be found in a thesis by Carl Wallace, 'The Career of Sir Samuel Leonard Tilley' (PHD, University of Alberta 1972). For references to Peter Mitchell see Political History above. The life of Timothy Warren Anglin, prominent New Brunswick journalist and politician, is well told in William M. Baker, *Timothy Warren Anglin: Irish Catholic Canadian* (T: UTP 1977). The best treatment of both Tupper and Thompson is found in two Toronto doctoral theses: A.W. MacIntosh, 'The Career of Sir Charles Tupper in Canada 1864-1900' (1960), and J.D. Heisler, 'Sir John S.D. Thompson 1844-94' (1955). An earlier biography of Thompson, J. Castell Hopkins, *Life and Work of Rt. Hon. Sir John Thompson* (Brantford: 1895), is unsatisfactory from the viewpoint of modern scholarship. A forthcoming biographical study of Thompson by Peter Waite is eagerly awaited; meanwhile we have to be content with the preview provided by Waite's articles: 'John Sparrow Thompson and Son: The Halifax Youth of a Prime Minister,' NSHS *Collections* 1980, and 'Annie and the Bishop: John S.D. Thompson goes to Ottawa,' DR, 1977-8. Be particularly wary of Sir Charles Tupper's carefully 'laundered' *Recollections of Sixty Years in Canada* (T: Cassell 1914). An important article on the political career of his son is Frank Patterson, 'Sir Charles Hibbert Tupper,' NSHS *Collections* 1977. W.S. Fielding, a leading political figure of the period, has attracted attention in C. Bruce Fergusson, *The Mantle of Howe* (Windsor: Lancelot Press 1970) and *Mr. Minister of Finance* (Windsor: Lancelot Press 1971). The life and times of Sir Robert Borden may be traced in his own *Memoirs*, published posthumously in 1938 and now available in a second edition in the Carleton Library series, 1969. R. Craig Brown's biography, *Robert Laird Borden*, 2 vols. (T: MAC 1975, 1980), although short on his early life, is, nonetheless, a full and complete study of the career of Canada's eighth prime minister. The human side of Borden is portrayed in Henry Borden, ed., *Letters from Limbo* (T: UTP 1971). Sir Frederick Borden, Sir Robert Borden's contemporary and relative, is examined in Carman Miller, 'The Public Life of Sir Frederick Borden' (MA thesis, Dalhousie University 1964). W. Stewart Wallace, *The Memoirs of Rt. Hon. Sir George Foster* (T: MAC 1933), provides some insight into a career which spanned the years from 1882 to the 1920s. E.M. Macdonald, *Recollections Political and Personal* (T: Ryerson 1935), is a gossipy though informed view of the politics of the 1920s and 30s. Insight into the career of Nova Scotian premier E.H. Armstrong is provided by A. Jeffrey Wright, 'The Hapless Politician: E.H. Armstrong of Nova Scotia,' *Nova Scotia Historical Quarterly*, 1976. Ernest Watkins, *R. B. Bennett* (L: Secker & Warburg 1963), surveys the life of Canada's eleventh prime minister. It should be used in conjunction with J.R.H. Wilbur, ed., *The Bennett New Deal: Fraud or Portent?* (T: CC 1968), which critically analyses Bennett's handling of the Depression.

Two books useful in charting the career of Angus L. Macdonald are *Speeches of Angus L. Macdonald* (T: Longmans Green 1960), and John Hawkins, *The Life and Times of Angus L.* (Windsor: Lancelot 1969). Macdonald, once described as a 'poet in politics,' is, perhaps, his own best interpreter. Hawkins's biography, although it verges on hagiography, nevertheless has some merit because of considerable research among Macdonald's close associates. The Nova Scotian trait of 'following the leader' is examined in Fulton Logan, 'Personality as an Issue in Nova Scotian Politics' (MA thesis, Dalhousie University 1972), which analyses this phenomenon through the careers of Fielding, Murray, Macdonald, and Stanfield. For Stanfield's provincial career see Peter Aucoin, 'The Stanfield Era: A Political Analysis,' DR, 1967, and E.D. Haliburton, *My Years with Stanfield* (Windsor: Lancelot 1972). A recent biography – pro Stanfield and generally quite fair – is Geoffrey Stevens, *Stanfield* (T: M&S 1973). The politician in Atlantic Canada whose career looms largest in recent history is J.R. Smallwood. We are too close in time to have an objective portrait of his remarkable life; however, the student is directed to Richard Gwyn, *Smallwood: The Unlikely Revolutionary*

(T: M&S 1968), and the subject's own *I Chose Canada* (T: MAC 1973). See also Peter Neary, 'Joey Smallwood: He's One of We,' *Canadian Forum*, 1973.

ECONOMIC AND SOCIAL HISTORY

T.N. Brewis, *Regional Economic Policies in Canada* (T: MAC 1969), is an important starting-point for research in the recent economic history of the region. Appropriate chapters in general texts such as W.T. Easterbrook and H.G.J. Aitken, *Canadian Economic History* (T: MAC 1961), or A.W. Currie, *Canadian Economic Development* (T: Nelson 1960), will help set the stage. Neary, *The Political Economy of Newfoundland*, is an important reference for economic matters in Newfoundland from the Depression years to the present. More specialized studies will be found in Stanley A. Saunders, *The Economic History of the Maritime Provinces* (O: KP 1939), issued as a study for the Royal Commission on Dominion-Provincial Relations; Stanley A. Saunders, *Studies in the Economy of the Maritime Provinces* (T: MAC 1939); B.S. Keirstead, *Economic Effects of the War on the Maritime Provinces* (H: Dalhousie University 1944); Alexander K. Cairncross, *Economic Development and the Atlantic Provinces* (Fredericton: Atlantic Provinces Research Board 1961); and J.F. Graham, *Fiscal Adjustment and Economic Development: A Case Study of Nova Scotia* (T: UTP 1963). An important commentary and critique of developments in New Brunswick is contained in Thomas J. Plunkett, 'The Report of the Royal Commission on Finance and Municipal Taxation in New Brunswick,' *Canadian Public Administration*, 1965. A reprint of the same article appears in D.C. Rowat, ed., *The Canadian Municipal System* (T: M&S 1969). Economic development in the Atlantic region has been greatly influenced by federal policies – perhaps to a greater extent than in other parts of the country. For a discussion of the impact of the National Policy see Stanley A. Saunders, 'The Maritime Provinces and the National Policy: Comments upon Economic Regionalism in Canada,' DR, 1937, and T.W. Acheson, 'The National Policy and the Industrialization of the Maritimes 1880-1910,' *Acadiensis*, 1972. Additional insight may be obtained from K.G. Pryke, 'Labour and Politics: Nova Scotia at Con-

federation,' SH, 1970, and Brian D. Tennyson, 'Economic Nationalism and Confederation: A Case Study in Cape Breton,' *Acadiensis*,
1972. Much of the significant interpretation and reinterpretation of
the economic history of Newfoundland is traceable to the prolific
pen of the late David Alexander. For example: 'Development and
Dependence in Newfoundland 1880-1970, *Acadiensis*, 1974; 'Newfoundland's Traditional Economy to 1934,' *Acadiensis*, 1976; 'Economic Growth in the Atlantic Region 1880-1940,' *Acadiensis*, 1978;
and 'Literacy and Economic Development in Nineteenth-Century
Newfoundland,' *Acadiensis*, 1980. An important case study of an
individual community may be found in Peter Neary's 'Traditional
and Modern Elements in the Social and Economic History of Bell
Island and Conception Bay,' CHAR, 1973. Alexander's 'A New Newfoundland: The Traditional Economy and Development to 1934,' a
paper presented to the Canadian Historical Association, Kingston,
1973, offers a fresh interpretation of the economic history of Newfoundland and is illustrative of the impressive research now being
undertaken by the Maritime History Group. An important study of
shipping, shipbuilding, and Maritime industrial history generally is
to be found in Basic Greenhill and Ann Giffard, *Westcountrymen in
Prince Edward's Isle* (T: UTP 1967). There are also a number of specialized studies touching on economic matters published by the
Queen's Printer, Fredericton, for the Maritime Union Study of
1970. Publications of the Institute of Social and Economic Research
at Memorial University have significance for any enquiry into the
socio-economic history of the region. In addition, publications of
the Maritime History Group cited in General Studies ought to be
consulted. A useful overview of one conference sponsored by this
group as well as a general commentary on the economic history of
the region is to be found in Alan Wilson, 'An Enterprising Conference,' *Acadiensis*, 1981.

Royal Commission reports
One of the most ready sources for the economic history of the
region is Royal Commission reports, as witnessed by the fact that
since 1867 Atlantic Canada has been subjected to over one hundred
federal investigations alone (see return tabled in the House of Com-

mons, 12 March 1969). Some of the most important are Industrial Unrest of Steelworkers at Sydney (O: 1924); Fisheries of the Atlantic Provinces (O: 1925); Maritime Claims (Duncan Report) (O: 1926); Newfoundland Royal Commission (Amulree Report) (O: 1933); Dominion-Provincial Relations (Rowell-Sirois Report) (O: 1939); Canada's Economic Prospects (Gordon Report) (O: 1957); Report of the Royal Commission for the Preparation of the Case of the Government of Newfoundland for the Revision of the Financial Terms of Union (St John's: 1957); Report of the Royal Commission on Newfoundland Finances (O: 1958); Coal Industry (Donald Report) (O: 1960); Report of the New Brunswick Royal Commission on Finance and Municipal Taxation (Byrne Report) (Fredericton: 1963); and Royal Commission on Education Public Services and Provincial-Municipal Relations (Graham Report) (H: 1974). A helpful guide to Royal Commission reports in Nova Scotia is the checklist *Nova Scotia Royal Commissions and Commissions of Enquiry 1877-1973* (H: Legislative Library 1973).

Industrial studies and labour history
Over the years the fishing industry has attracted the attention of both historians and economists. H.A. Innis's monumental *The Cod Fisheries: The History of an International Economy* (T: UTP 1954, 1978), especially chapters 11-14, is invaluable. The early international entanglements surrounding the industry are surveyed in Charles S. Campbell, 'American Tariff Interests and the Northeastern Fisheries,' CHR, 1964. Of particular concern to Newfoundland is Shannon Ryan, 'The Newfoundland Cod Fishery in the Nineteenth Century' (MA thesis, Memorial University 1971). An abridged version of the thesis was presented to the Canadian Historical Association in June 1973. Two articles by Parzival Copes, containing much useful material, are 'Community Resettlement and Rationalization of the Fishing Industry in Newfoundland,' paper presented to the Canadian Economics Association, June 1971, and *The Resettlement of Fishing Communities in Newfoundland* (O: Canadian Council on Rural Development 1972).

Not surprisingly, Atlantic Canada has become the focal point for a number of significant studies in labour history – much of it centred on decades of strife in the Cape Breton coal fields. Relevant sections of the following works ought to be consulted before going on to specialized studies: Michael S. Cross, *The Workingman in the Nineteenth Century* (T: OUP 1974); G. Kealey and P. Warren, *Essays in Working-Class History* (T: M&S 1976); I. Abella and D. Millar, eds., *The Canadian Worker in the Twentieth Century* (T: OUP 1978). A useful collection of articles (some reprints from other sources) is to be found in Don Macgillivray and Brian Tennyson, eds., *Cape Breton Historical Essays* (Sydney: College of Cape Breton Press 1980). Other important articles are: Don Macgillivray, 'Cape Breton in the 1920s: A Community Beseiged,' in Brian Tennyson, ed., *Essays in Cape Breton History* (Windsor: Lancelot 1973); Don Macgillivray, 'Henry Melville Whitney comes to Cape Breton: The Saga of a Gilded Age Entrepreneur,' *Acadiensis*, 1979; David Frank, 'The Cape Breton Coal Industry and the Rise and Fall of the British Empire Steel Corporation,' *Acadiensis*, 1977. In more popular vein is Paul MacEwan's *Miners and Steelworkers: Labour in Cape Breton* (T: Hakkert 1976); however, the latter chapters dealing with the contemporary political scene are less than objective. Silver Donald Cameron has contributed an intensive analysis of the fishermen's strike of the early 1970s in *The Education of Everett Richardson* (T: M&S 1977).

A good understanding of the impact of the co-operative movement may be obtained from *The Social Significance of the Cooperative Movement* (Antigonish: Extension Dept., St Francis Xavier University 1960), and Alexander Laidlaw, ed., *The Man from Margaree: Writings and Speeches of M.M. Coady* (T: M&S 1971). The Maritime co-operative movement in its national context is surveyed in Ian MacPherson, 'The Origins of the Canadian Cooperative Movement 1900-1914,' CHAR, 1972, and in 'Appropriate Forms of Enterprise: The Prairie and Maritime Cooperative Movements 1900-1955,' *Acadiensis*, 1978. See also Jim Lotz, 'The Historical and Social Setting of the Antigonish Movement,' *Nova Scotia Historical Quarterly*, 1975, and Daniel W. MacInnis, 'Clerics, Fishermen, Farmers and Workers: The Antigonish Movement and Identity in Eastern Nova Scotia' (PHD, MacMaster University 1975). Four books which take a critical look at trends in the economy of Nova Scotia are Roy E.

George, *A Leader and a Laggard: Manufacturing Industry in Nova Scotia, Quebec and Ontario* (T: UTP 1970); John T. Sears, *Institutional Financing of Small Business in Nova Scotia* (T: UTP 1972); Roy E. George, *The Life and Times of Industrial Estates Limited* (H: Dalhousie Institute of Public Affairs 1974); and Philip Mathias, *Forced Growth* (T: James Lewis & Samuel 1971).

Urban studies
Serious research in urban history is still in its infancy in the Atlantic provinces. An important introductory study of Saint John, Halifax, and St John's is J.M.S. Careless, 'Aspects of Metropolitanism in Atlantic Canada,' in *Regionalism in the Canadian Community* (T: UTP 1969). Also of significance are two articles: D.A. Sutherland, 'Halifax 1815-1914: Colony to Colony,' UHR, 1975, and Robert H. Babcock, 'Economic Development in Portland, Me., and Saint John, N.B. during the Age of Iron and Steam 1850-1914,' *American Review of Canadian Studies*, 1979. See also Fischer and Sager eds., *The Enterprising Canadians*. Halifax, the largest city in the region, has not been given the attention which its long and colourful history warrants. Thomas Raddall's oft quoted *Halifax: Warden of the North* (T: M&S 1965) suffers by comparison with his other works. Phyllis Blakeley, *Glimpses of Halifax* (Belleville: Mika 1973), covers the years 1867-1900, while Michael J. Bird, *The Town that Died* (T: Ryerson 1962), gives a popular treatment of the explosion of 1917. Another account of the same event is given in Graham Metson, ed., *The Halifax Explosion* (T: MHR 1978). Worth consulting are Parzival Copes, *St. John's and Newfoundland: An Economic Survey* (St John's: St John's Board of Trade 1961); E. Roy Harvey, *Sydney: An Urban Study* (T: CI 1971); and P. O'Neill, *The Oldest City: The Story of St. John's* 2 vols. (Erin, Ont.: Porcépic Press 1975). See also references mentioned in Armstrong, Artibise, and Baker, *Bibliography of Canadian Urban History*.

RELIGIOUS HISTORY

Most of the denominational histories concentrate upon the nineteenth century; however, relevant portions of Philip Carrington,

The Anglican Church in Canada (T: Collins 1963), and A.A. Johnston, *A History of the Catholic Church in Eastern Nova Scotia*, 2 vols. (Antigonish: St Francis Xavier UP 1960, 1972), summarize some of the more recent highlights. George E. Levy, *The Baptists of the Maritime Provinces* (Saint John: 1946), takes that denomination through to the twentieth century. The earlier D.W. Johnson, *History of Methodism in Eastern British America* (Sackville: Tribune Publishers nd), is of value for the pre-1925 years. A more recent survey of the Presbyterian church may be found in Archibald D. MacKinnon, *History of the Presbyterian Church in Cape Breton* (Antigonish: Formac 1975).

The influence of deep-rooted religious trends, particularly as they touch on educational matters, may be traced in chapters dealing with the Atlantic provinces in C.B. Sissons, *Church and State in Canadian Education* (T: Ryerson 1959). There are also a number of informative local church histories: R.V. Harris, *The Church of St. Paul* [Halifax] (T: Ryerson 1949), or G.M. Story, *George Street United Church: One Hundred Years of Service* (St John's: 1973). Because religious and educational questions are so completely entwined, note the entries which follow under Educational History. A significant article which covers a wide range of twentieth-century social and religious history is E.R. Forbes, 'Prohibition and the Social Gospel in Nova Scotia,' *Acadiensis*, 1971.

EDUCATIONAL HISTORY

G.A. Frecker, *Education in the Atlantic Provinces* (T: Gage 1956), provides a summary of general information. More helpful are two provincial studies: K.F.C. MacNaughton, *The Development of the Theory and Practice of Education in New Brunswick* (Fredericton: University of New Brunswick 1947), and F.W. Rowe, *The History of Education in Newfoundland* (T: Ryerson 1952). The relevant portions of A.L. Prentice and S.E. Houston, eds., *Family, School and Society in Nineteenth-Century Canada* (T: M&S 1975) are also of interest. Excellent coverage of mid-nineteenth-century developments in Prince Edward Island will be found in Sister Mary Olga McKenna, 'The Impact of Religion and Politics in the Structure of Education in

Prince Edward Island,' *Canadian Association Foundations of Education Annual Report*, 1967, and Ian Robertson, 'Education, Politics and Religion in Prince Edward Island' (MA thesis, McGill University 1968). In this context see also William B. Hamilton, 'Curriculum and Cultural Conflict in the Maritimes,' in 'The Curriculum in Canada in Historical Perspective,' *CSSE Yearbook*, 1979; Michael Hatfield, 'H.H. Pitts and Race and Religion in New Brunswick,' *Acadiensis*, 1975; Martin S. Spigelman, 'Des paroles en l'air: Quebec Minority Rights and the New Brunswick School Question,' DR, 1978; and Nanciellen Sealy, 'Language Conflict and Schools in New Brunswick,' in M.L. Kovacs, ed., *Ethnic Canadians: Culture and Education* (Regina: 1978). General trends in the educational history of all four Atlantic provinces may be traced in chapters 5, 6, and 7 by William B. Hamilton in *Canadian Education: A History* (T: PH 1970), ed. J.D. Wilson, R.M. Stamp, and L.-P. Audet. George Rawlyk and Ruth Hafter, *Acadian Education in Nova Scotia* (O: Information Canada 1970), a study prepared for the Royal Commission on Bilingualism and Biculturalism, is a comprehensive survey of Acadian education down to 1965. Of significance because of an institutional impact on generations of Canadian jurists and politicians is John Willis, *A History of Dalhousie Law School* (T: UTP 1979).

HISTORICAL GEOGRAPHY – DEMOGRAPHIC STUDIES

An excellent overview of the historical geography of the region is contained in Alan Macpherson, ed., *The Atlantic Provinces* (T: UTP 1972). Pertinent chapters in L.D. McCann, ed., *Heartland and Hinterland: Canadian Regions in Evolution* (T: PH 1982), ought also to be consulted. A full and extremely informative analysis of the geography and agricultural history of Prince Edward Island is contained in Andrew Hill Clark, *Three Centuries and the Island* (T: UTP 1959). One ethnic minority which has received considerable scholarly attention is the black population of the region. Much of Robin W. Winks's *The Blacks in Canada: A History* (New Haven: Yale UP 1971) deals with Atlantic Canada. Other sources of information are Winks, 'Negroes in the Maritimes: An Introductory Survey,' DR, 1968-9, and 'Negro School Segregation in Ontario and Nova Scotia,'

CHR, 1969. See also George Rawlyk, 'The Guysboro Negroes: A Study in Isolation,' DR, 1968, and D.H. Hill, 'Negro Settlement in Canada' (a report presented to the Royal Commission on Bilingualism and Biculturalism, 1966). W.A. Spray, *The Blacks in New Brunswick* (Fredericton: Brunswick Press 1972), is a well-researched history of black settlement in that province. Frances Henry's ethnographic analysis, *The Blacks of Nova Scotia* (T: Longman 1973); suffers by comparison with Professor Spray's book. See also D.H.J. Clairmont, *Nova Scotia Blacks: An Historical and Structural Overview* (H: Dalhousie University 1970), and John N. Grant, *Black Nova Scotians* (H: Nova Scotia Museum 1980). Charles W. Dunn, *Highland Settler: A Portrait of the Scottish Gael in Nova Scotia* (T: UTP 1953), is a penetrating study of the impact of emigration on a folk culture. Raymond MacLean, *Beyond the Atlantic Roar* (T: M&S 1974), takes a cross-disciplinary approach in tracing the evolution of Scottish settlement in Nova Scotia. John J. Mannion, *Irish Settlement in Eastern Canada* (T: UTP 1974), examines Irish settlement patterns in the Avalon Peninsula (Newfoundland), Miramichi Valley (New Brunswick), and Peterborough (Ontario) areas. It is a classic study of cultural transfer and may well serve as a model for further research in Atlantic Canada. Additional information may be gleaned from John Mannion, ed., *The Peopling of Newfoundland: Essays in Historical Geography* (St John's: 1977). The impact of the Irish on another section of Atlantic Canada is traced in A.A. MacKenzie, *The Irish in Cape Breton* (Antigonish: Formac 1979). Finally, the perennial problem of 'Going Down the Road' is placed in historical perspective in Alan A. Brookes, 'Out-Migration from the Maritimes 1860-1900,' *Acadiensis*, 1976.

MORRIS ZASLOW

The North

REFERENCE MATERIALS

Preparation of a bibliography of works bearing on the history of the
Canadian North faces two sorts of difficulties – defining 'the North,'
and choosing among a very broad spectrum of relevant but not primarily historical writings. Defining the North is mainly the task of
geographers, who have used physical criteria such as latitude and
climate modified by practical considerations like political or statistical boundaries. In recent times, however, they have begun incorpo-
rating human and developmental factors into their definitions of the
North and its various sectors. Thus the distinguished geographer
L.-E. Hamelin, who has made northern Canada his lifelong interest,
devised a system of rating northern locations according to six physical and four human categories, from which he derives a VAPO index
that assigns the localities to 'Base Canada' or to the 'Middle,' 'Far,'
or 'Extreme' Norths. A simpler approach, which relies entirely on
human factors, is that of R.T. Gajda, 'The Canadian ecumene –
inhabited and uninhabited areas,' *Geographical Bulletin*, 1960, who
used population density (as F.J. Turner had done for his frontier
hypothesis) to sketch a frontier line that divided Canada in two
uneven parts, the southern one of which embraced only one-
seventh of the land area but contained over 98 per cent of the
nation's population. He defined that region (which corresponds

quite closely to Hamelin's 'Base Canada') as 'the ecumene' – the permanently settled, developed part of Canada, as distinct from the partly-developed or undeveloped North. Pierre Biays, in his valuable *Les Marges de l'Oekoumene dans l'Est du Canada* (Q: PUL 1964), concluded that the different resource industries affected the expansion (or recession) of the ecumene, and that each industry had an appropriate ecumene of its own. The Abitibi region, for instance, experienced a series of advances in line with the industrial and transportational development of the district, with mining being the principal dynamic for expansion during the latest period. Hamelin also attempted to define the northward advance of the boundaries of his 'Norths' by applying the VAPO criteria to communities in earlier times.

Geographers have tried in these ways to define the advance of Canada's northern frontiers during the past century; M. Zaslow, *The Opening of the Canadian North, 1870-1914* (T: M&S 1971) is an historian's effort to illustrate the processes and course of the northward expansion since Confederation. A bibliography covering the period since 1867 should properly include works that study the development of practically the entire four western provinces and the largest parts of Quebec and Ontario during their early 'pre-ecumene' period. Such works fall within the purlieu of the other chapters of this book and, besides, are discussed at some length in the Bibliographic Essay of *The Opening of the Canadian North*. This chapter, accordingly, will adopt as its subject-area the North as defined (for Canada) by *The Arctic Bibliography*, the massive compilation prepared by the Arctic Institute of North America [AINA] – that is, the Yukon and Northwest Territories, Nouveau-Québec and Labrador, plus the Arctic parts of the provinces surrounding Hudson Bay.

The major difficulty with preparing a northern bibliography for historians is the sparseness of writings by authors trained in historical methods or who approached their subjects from a historical perspective, coupled with the enormous numbers of writings by scientists and scholars from every academic discipline on the aspects of the North with which they are concerned, or observer accounts (narrative, descriptive, analytical) by residents or travellers dealing with facets of the northern scene at a given time or times. Both sorts of writings have their limitations but also their value, and the task of the historian of the North – which becomes progressively easier with greater experience and knowledge – is to gain as much benefit as he can from them. The number of potentially useful pieces is staggering. *The Arctic Bibliography*, published between 1947 and 1975 by the AINA in sixteen mainly biennial large volumes, listed works from every conceivable field of study, over 20,000 items of which (of a total in excess of 108,000) relate to northern Canada as defined here. The number swells with every passing day; since 1975 the bibliography has been continued as a computerized data storage and a retrieval system, ASTIS, that can be consulted for specific topics.

Another comprehensive multi-disciplinary bibliography (classified as to subjects) is provided in the Recent Polar Literature section carried in *The Polar Record*, the thrice-yearly periodical of the Scott Polar Research Institute at Cambridge University, though the bibliography has been published separately since 1972. Similar regional bibliographies of value are A. Cooke and F. Caron, comps., *Bibliography of the Quebec-Labrador Peninsula*, 2 vols. (Boston: G.K. Hall; Q: Centre d'Etudes Nordiques 1968), and on a smaller scale, J.R. Lotz, comp., *A Yukon Bibliography* (O: Dept. of Northern Affairs and National Resources 1964). Bibliographies on special topics can also be consulted where appropriate. Examples include T. Abler, D. Sanders, and S. Weaver, comps., *A Canadian Indian Bibliography, 1960-1970* (T: UTP 1974); the convenient (and free) Indian Claims Commission, *Indian Claims in Canada: An Essay and Bibliography* (O: Information Canada 1975); and the University of Manitoba Center for Settlement Studies, *Bibliography – Resource Frontier Communities*, 2 vols. (Winnipeg: the Center 1969). The catalogues of some prominent northern or Arctic libraries (eg, Arctic Institute, Scott Polar, Stefansson Library at Dartmouth College) have been published, chiefly by the G.K. Hall Company, and should be available in major Canadian libraries.

The vast majority of published works relating to the history of the North are found in periodical literature, and in government reports and special publications. Journals that are especially North-oriented include *Arctic*, the quarterly of the Arctic Institute, which concentrates mainly on papers presenting the results of scientific researches; *Polar Record*, previously mentioned, which devotes some space to the Antarctic but offers more historical pieces than does *Arctic*, in addition to well-chosen news items and major documents; *The Musk Ox*, an excellent publication of the Institute for Northern Studies, University of Saskatchewan; and the Department of Indian Affairs and Northern Development [DIAND] bimonthly *North/Nord*. *The Beaver* is well-edited and illustrated, and is especially strong in coverage of Indian and Inuit arts, and reminiscences of, or pieces on, HBC and other northern personnel. *Canadian Geographic* is less helpful in these regards, and the *National Geographic* has printed a fair number of pieces over the years on the Canadian North. The federal government agencies are also responsible for many important studies. Of particular note are those of the Northwest Territories and Yukon Branch of the Department of the Interior between 1920 and 1935 by W.C. Bethune, F.H. Kitto, L.T. Burwash, and others, and since 1960 by DIAND's Northern Co-ordination and Research Centre [NCRC] and its successor, the Northern Scientific Research Group [NSRG]. Many other northern studies are published by the Geographical, Mines, Geological Survey, National Museums branches, and by the Departments of Transport, Marine, etc. Useful reports and research papers are also published by provincial government agencies, university-based northern research institutes, and companies interested in the North. The fact that this chapter concentrates on printed books should not cause readers to forget that periodical articles and government publications are just as important sources as are the monographs listed below.

An additional source of articles on the Canadian North is the multi-disciplinary co-operative book of essays that contains historical pieces and others that may also be useful. One such collection, made with university students in mind, is W.C. Wonders, ed., *Canada's Changing North* (T: M&S 1971). Regionally-oriented works include C.A. Dawson, ed., *Canada's New North-West* (T: UTP 1947); J. Malaurie and J. Rousseau, eds., *Nouveau-Québec: Contribution à l'étude de l'occupation humaine* (Paris: Mouton 1964); C.S. Beals and D.A. Shenstone, eds., *Science, History and Hudson Bay*, 2 vols. (O: Dept. of Energy, Mines and Resources 1968); and M. Zaslow, ed.,

A Century of Canada's Arctic Islands, 1880-1980 (O: Royal Society of Canada 1981). Published reports of several conferences on northern matters also may be of value, particularly the reports of the six or seven National Northern Development Conferences held in Edmonton at intervals since 1958. Another type of co-operative book, that deals with the Arctic as a whole, may be relevant. Examples include W.L.G. Joerg, ed., *Problems of Polar Research* (NY: American Geographical Society 1928); the especially helpful R. St J. Macdonald, ed., *The Arctic Frontier* (T: UTP 1966); and T.E. Armstrong, G.W. Rowley, and G. Rogers, *The Circumpolar North* (L: Methuen 1978), with Graham Rowley's important updating survey of the Canadian North. The growing number of collaborative works on particular topics includes some that are also very pertinent, among them being N.H.R. Graburn and B.S. Strong, eds., *Circumpolar Peoples: An Anthropological Perspective* (Pacific Palisades: Goodyear Publishing 1973); W.A. Fuller and P.G. Kevan, eds., *Productivity and Conservatism in Northern Lands* (Morges, Switz.: International Union for Conservation of Nature and Natural Resources 1970); and B.F. Sater, ed., *Arctic and Middle North Transportation* (Washington: AINA 1970).

EXPLORATION AND TRAVEL

A basic tool for the history of Arctic exploration is A. Cooke and C. Holland, comps., *The Exploration of Northern Canada, 500 to 1920* (T: Arctic History Press 1978), which meticulously calenders every known voyage to the Canadian Arctic, giving details and bibliographic notes for each trip. A convenient review of the explorations in the High Arctic is A. Taylor, *Geographical Exploration in the Queen Elizabeth Islands* (O: QP 1955). Useful histories of Arctic exploration include J. Mirsky, *To the Arctic!* (NY: Knopf 1948); L.P. Kirwan, *The White Road* (L: Hollis & Carter 1959); and for the period 1905-34, J.G. Hayes, *The Conquest of the North Pole* (L: Thornton Butterworth 1934). The celebrated individual explorations and explorers are represented by official accounts by the participants, and numerous popular ones based largely or wholly on those accounts. Among the most important are A.W. Greely, *Three Years of Arctic*

Service, 2 vols. (NY: Charles Scribner's Sons 1885), retold by T. Powell in *The Long Rescue* (L: W.H. Allen 1961); Otto N. Sverdrup, *New Land*, 2 vols. (L and NY: Longmans 1904), the basis for T.C. Fairley, *Sverdrup's Arctic Adventure* (T: Longmans Green 1959); Roald Amundsen, *The Northwest Passage*, 2 vols. (L: A. Constable 1908); L.H. Neatby, ed., *My Life among the Eskimos: The Baffinland Journals of Bernhard Adolph Hantzsch, 1909-1911* (Saskatoon: University of Saskatchewan 1977); D.B. MacMillan, *Four Years in the White North* (NY: Harper 1918); R.A. Peary, *The North Pole: Its Discovery in 1909* (NY: Frederick A. Stokes; (L: Hodder & Stoughton 1910) and *Secrets of Polar Travel* (NY: Century 1917); F.A. Cook, *My Attainment of the Pole* (NY: Polar Publishing 1911); and J.E. Weems, *Race for the Pole* (NY: Henry Holt 1960).

The main Canadian Arctic voyages are described in A.P. Low, *Cruise of the 'Neptune' 1903-04* (O: Government Printing Bureau 1906); the three Bernier voyages, 1906-11, in corresponding government reports and the posthumous autobiography, J.E. Bernier, *Master Mariner and Arctic Explorer* (O: Le Droit 1939); and the Canadian Arctic Expedition of 1913-18, in V. Stefansson, *The Friendly Arctic* (NY: MAC 1921). Stefansson's Canadian career is also treated in his *My Life with the Eskimo* (NY: Harper 1913); *The Adventure of Wrangel Island* (L: Jonathan Cape 1926); and the autobiographical *Discovery* (NY: McGraw-Hill 1964). His career is examined critically in W.L. McKinley, *Karluk* (L: Weidenfeld & Nicolson 1976), an account by one of the last survivors of the wreck of that expedition ship in 1913, and especially in R.J. Diubaldo, *Stefansson and the Canadian Arctic* (M: MQUP 1978), a revisionist work based on official and archival sources.

The fifty-year period after 1867 was also a classical period of overland exploration and travel in remote parts of the Arctic mainland that eventuated in numerous participants' accounts. The most important of these include E.F.S.J. Petitot, *Les grandes Esquimaux* (Paris: E. Plon, Nourrit 1887), *Quinze ans sous le Cercle Polaire* (Paris: E. Dentu 1889), and other works; F. Schwatka, *Nimrod in the North* (NY: Cassell 1885) and *Along Alaska's Great River* (NY: Cassell 1885); Warburton Pike, *The Barren Ground of Northern Canada* (L and NY: MAC 1892) and *Through the Sub-Arctic Forest* (L and NY:

E. Arnold 1896); J.W. Tyrrell, *Across the Sub-Arctics of Canada* (T: William Briggs 1897); Frank Russell, *Explorations in the Far North* (Iowa City: University of Iowa 1898); D.T. Hanbury, *Sport and Travel in the Northland of Canada* (NY: MAC; L: E. Arnold 1904); E. Thompson Seton, *The Arctic Prairies* (NY: Charles Scribner's Sons 1911); G.M. Douglas, *Lands Forlorn* (NY: G.P. Putnam's Sons 1914); also D. Wallace, *The Lure of the Labrador Wild* (NY: Fleming H. Revell 1905), and W.B. Cabot, *In Northern Labrador* (L: J. Murray 1912).

WHALERS, FUR TRADERS, AND TRAPPERS

The half-century after Confederation also saw the ending of the British- and American-operated whaling industries in the Canadian Arctic. The impact of the industry on the native people and the wildlife in the eastern Arctic is treated in thorough, informative fashion by W.G. Ross in his *Whaling and Eskimos: Hudson Bay, 1860-1915* (O: National Museum of Man 1975), based on careful analysis of dozens of whalers' logs. A.B. Lubbock, *The Arctic Whalers* (Glasgow: Brown, Son & Ferguson 1937), a survey of the British-based industry, is particularly informative for the final stages in the eastern Arctic. A.H. Markham, *A Whaling Cruise to Baffin's Bay* (L: Sampson Low, Marston, Low & Searle 1875), and R. Ferguson, *Arctic Harpooner* (Philadelphia: University of Pennsylvania Press 1938), are vivid personal accounts. Two similarly autobiographical accounts by leading ship captains in the western Arctic also are available: J.A. Cook, *Pursuing the Whale* (NY: Houghton Mifflin 1926), and H.H. Bodfish, *Chasing the Bowhead* (Cambridge: Harvard UP 1936); also a general treatment, J.R. Bockstoce, *Steam Whaling in the Western Arctic* (New Bedford: Old Dartmouth Historical Society 1977). Canadian eyewitness accounts may be found in the RNWMP *Reports* for the years 1903-16, also in Low's *Cruise of the 'Neptune.'*
    The fur trade, an early and still-continuing industry in the Canadian North, has produced a very large complement of northern books. Standard histories of the fur trade that carry the industry beyond 1867 – such as H.A. Innis, *The Fur Trade of Canada* (1927; rev. ed., T: UTP 1956), and the updated edition of D. MacKay, *The*

Honourable Company (T: M&S 1949) – may be consulted with profit. a convenient reference work for the northern trade is Peter Usher, *Fur Trade Posts of the Northwest Territories, 1870-1970* (O: NSRG 1971). Biographical accounts that deal with aspects of the industry abound. For the HBC they include P.A. Godsell's informative, useful *Arctic Trader* (NY: Putnam 1932) and his *The Vanishing Frontier* (T: Ryerson 1939); J.W. Anderson, *Fur Trader's Story* (T: Ryerson 1961), a straightforward account of thirty-two years' service in the eastern Arctic; E. Lyall, *An Arctic Man: Sixty-Five Years in Canada's North* (Edmonton: Hurtig 1979), whose career spanned the development of the eastern Arctic from 1914 almost to the present; J. Milne, *Trading for Milady's Furs* (Saskatoon: Western Producer Prairie Books 1975), good on the trials of a young recruit of the early 1920s; J.N.S. Buchan, *Hudson Bay Trader* (L: Clerke & Cockeram 1951), the account of Governor General Lord Tweedsmuir's son's year at Cape Dorset, 1938-9; and D. Pryde, *Nunaga* (L: MacGibbon & Kee 1971), a surprisingly frank, revealing account of the author's exploits and prowess in the Central Arctic during the 1960s.

Other companies are represented by such books as Lowell Thomas, *Kabluk of the Eskimos* (Boston: Little, Brown 1932), a romanticized account of L.A. Romanet's years as a Revillon trader in Ungava prior to 1914; H.S.M. Kemp, *Northern Trader* (NY: Bouregy & Curl 1956), the story of a trader for the Lamson-Hubbard and Northern Trading Companies; Peter Baker, *Memoirs of an Arctic Arab* (Saskatoon: Yellowknife Publishing 1976), the autobiography of a free-trader active in the Mackenzie District, particularly during the early 1920s; T. McInnes, *Klengenberg of the Arctic* (L: Jonathan Cape 1932), a very interesting, informative, somewhat whitewashed account of the first white trader to settle among the Inuit of Victoria Island, 1905-30; and Richard Finnie, *Lure of the North* (Philadelphia: David McKay 1940), a fine description of the ex-whaler fur-trading society growing up along the Arctic coast in 1930-1. Two HBC traders' wives also wrote useful books about conditions in the Mackenzie basin area during the 1920s: Louise Rourke, *Land of the Frozen Tide* (L: Hutchinson 1928), and Jean Godsell, *I was No Lady* (T: Ryerson 1959). Another group of autobiographical books depict the free, outdoors, adventurous life of the northern trapper: Helge

Ingstad, *The Land of Feast and Famine* (NY: Knopf 1933); E. Munsterhjelm, *The Wind and the Caribou* (T: MAC 1953) and follow-up book, *Fool's Gold* (T: MAC 1957); and A.L. Karras, *North to Cree Lake* (NY: Trident Press 1970). For a change of pace, there is the story of the methodical, industrious, fine-fur trapper Chick Ferguson, *Mink, Mary and Me* (NY: M.S. Mill 1946). Finally, a pair of accounts describe the arduous task of driving a large reindeer herd from Alaska to the Mackenzie delta during the 1930s to assist the Inuit of that region: A.R. Evans, *Reindeer Trek* (T: M&S 1935), and Max Miller, *The Great Trek* (Garden City, NY: Doubleday Doran 1936).

MISSIONARIES, POLICEMEN, GOVERNMENT SCIENTISTS, AND OTHERS

A basic work for the Anglican missions in the North is T.C.B. Boon, *The Anglican Church from the Bay to the Rockies* (T: Ryerson 1962), the history of the ecclesiastical province of Rupert's Land that includes Northern Canada, or did until recently. Accounts of missionaries noted for their Arctic service include H.A. Cody, *An Apostle of the North* (L: Seeley 1908), the life of Bishop W.C. Bompas; F.A. Peake, *The Bishop who ate his Boots* (T: Anglican Church of Canada 1967), a biography of Bishop I.O. Stringer; Arthur Lewis, *The Life and Work of E.J. Peck amongst the Eskimo* (NY: A.C. Armstrong 1904); and Bishop A.L. Fleming, *Archibald the Arctic* (NY: Appleton-Century-Crofts 1956), and his earlier *Perils of the Polar Pack* (T: Missionary Society of the Church of England 1932), on the Rev. E.W.T. Greenshield.

Roman Catholic mission work is presented in three hagiographic books by R.P. Duchaussois, translated as *Mid Snow and Ice* (L: Burns, Oates & Washbourne 1923), *The Grey Nuns in the Far North* (T: M&S 1919), and *Modern Apostles: Our Lay Brother Missionaries* (Buffalo: Missionary Oblates of Mary Immaculate 1937). The best work on a northern religious figure is the highly informative, accurate, sometimes unusually frank autobiography of Bishop Gabriel Breynat, *Cinquante ans au pays des neiges*, 3 vols. (M: Fides 1945-8), of which there is an abbreviated and expurgated one-volume translation, *The Flying Bishop* (L: Burns & Oates 1955). The bishop's educational policies are criticized in an excellent PHD thesis by R.J. Carney, 'Relations in Education between the Federal and Territorial Governments and the Roman Catholic Church in the Mackenzie District, N.W.T., 1867-1965' (University of Alberta 1974). G. Carrière's many writings on the Oblate missions include a life of Breynat's eastern contemporary, *Le père du Keewatin: Mgr. Ovide Charlebois, O.M.I.* (M: Rayonnement 1962). Worthy of note is a trio of autobiographies of priests who served in the Central Arctic around the late 1930s – G. de Poncin's introspective *Kabloona* (NY: Reynal & Hitchcock 1941); R. de Coccola, *Ayorama* (T: OUP 1955); and the critical, bitter *Inuk* by R.P. Buliard (L: MAC 1953); also the autobiography of W.A. Leising, *Arctic Wings* (Garden City, NY: Doubleday 1959), the better of two accounts of missionary-pilots' work on behalf of their church. The history of the Moravian missions to the Labrador Inuit is treated in an old work, J.W. Davey, *The Fall of Torngak* (L: Partridge 1905), and in modern anthropological works by Jenness and Zimmerly (see below).

RCMP activities in the North received surprisingly full treatment in the official reports between 1903 and 1940, which have been reworked in 'true detective' style by Godsell and others, notably in Harwood Steele, *Policing the Arctic* (T: Ryerson 1935). The best survey and analysis is W.R. Morrison, 'The Royal Canadian Mounted Police on Canada's Northern Frontier, 1895-1940' (PHD thesis, University of Western Ontario 1973). So many policemen wrote about their northern experience that H.A. Innis quipped, 'The Mounted Police are now intent, it appears, on getting their book as well as their man.' The most important of these are V.A.M. Kemp, *Without Fear, Favour or Affection* (T: Longmans Green 1958); H.P. Lee, *Policing the Top of the World* (L: John Lane 1928); S.R. Montague, *North to Adventure* (NY: Robert M. McBride 1939); C. Rivett-Carnac, *Pursuit in the Wilderness* (Boston: Little, Brown 1967); and on the distaff side, Luta Munday, *A Mounty's Wife* (L: Sheldon 1930). A celebrated case, the first murder trials of two Inuit, is treated in R.G. Moyles, *British Law and Arctic Men* (Saskatoon: Western Producer Prairie Books 1979), the most valuable feature of which are copious extracts from the proceedings of the trials.

Another celebrated case, that of 'Albert Johnson,' seems to be developing a literature of its own: Dick North, *The Mad Trapper of Rat River* (T: MAC 1972); the fictionalized *The Mad Trapper: A Novel* (T: M&S 1980) by Rudy Wiebe; and a recently-completed movie. J.H. Sissons, the first full-time NWT justice, left a justificatory review of his career, *Judge of the Far North* (T: M&S 1968).

Some federal government agencies have been active in the North even longer than the police, in particular those concerned with surveying, mapping, and assessing the resources of Canada's vast territory. These are treated in two major works, which also describe the northern careers of scores of northern scientists. D.W. Thomson, *Men and Meridians*, 3 vols. (O: QP 1966-8) deals with the several surveying organizations of the Canadian government, and M. Zaslow, *Reading the Rocks: The Story of the Geological Survey of Canada, 1842-1972* (T: MAC 1975), describes the work of an organization that mapped the terrain as well as the geology, collected specimens for the National Museum (which it administered), and carried on research in all those fields. Brief reviews of the accomplishments to date of these and the other scientific disciplines (such as oceanography, climatology, biology, archeology, and anthropology) active in the High Arctic, especially since 1945, are given in Zaslow, ed., *A Century of Canada's Arctic Islands*.

A number of books describe the work of individual civil servants in the North. A geologist and leading administrator, Charles Camsell, described his early career in the factual, unadorned *Son of the North* (T: Ryerson 1954); the ornithologist J. Dewey Soper drew on previous articles and reports for his *Canadian Arctic Recollections: Baffin Island 1923-31* (Saskatoon: University of Saskatchewan 1981); and A.D. Copland wrote a helpful biography of the important doctor and medical administrator, *Livingstone of the Arctic* (O: Author 1967). An Indian agent, Dr C. Bourget, reviewed his career in *Douze ans chez les sauvages au Grand Lac des Esclaves, 1923-35* (Ste Anne de Beaupré: Author 1938). Later medical service is represented by J.P. Moody, *Arctic Doctor* (NY: Dodd, Mead 1955); G. Howerd, *Dew-Line Doctor* (L: Robert Hale 1960); and D.M. Copeland, *Remember Nurse* (T: Ryerson 1960). Two schoolteachers also have written about their northern work: Margery Hinds, *School-*

House in the Arctic (L: Geoffrey Bles 1958), and Phyllis M. Taylor, *Dog Team and School-Desk* (L: Herbert Jenkins 1960), while northern education was made the subject of an important special volume of *The Canadian Superintendent: Education North of 60* (T: Ryerson 1965). Scientists, federal employees, and others have published popular accounts about their northern experiences while in the field. Some examples of these are J.D. Leechman, *Eskimo Summer* (T: Ryerson 1945); Mrs T.H. Manning, *Igloo for the Night* (L: Hodder & Stoughton 1943); N. Polunin, *Isle of Auks* (L: E. Arnold 1932); and A.C. Twomey and N. Herrick, *Needle to the North* (Boston: Houghton Mifflin 1942).

Biographical accounts by a variety of travellers and 'rolling stones' form another group of potentially useful writings. Pre-eminent examples of the latter are H.T. Munn, *Prairie Trails and Arctic Byways* (L: Hurst & Blackett 1932); C.D. Brower, *Fifty Years below Zero* (NY: Dodd, Mead 1942); and especially the excellent biography of a recluse, *The Legend of John Hornby* (T: MAC 1962), by G. Whalley, whose subject's tragic end is described in Edgar Christian's brave diary, *Unflinching* (L: John Murray 1937). Travel accounts can sometimes gain added value because they retrace earlier routes and thereby reveal changes over time; a good example is the successive accounts of travel along the Mackenzie waterway, including Elihu Stewart, *Down the Mackenzie and Up the Yukon in 1906* (L and NY: John Lane 1913); Agnes D. Cameron, *The New North* (NY and L: D. Appleton 1910); F. Waldo, *Down the Mackenzie* (NY: MAC 1923); and L.R. Freeman, *The Nearing North* (NY: Dodd, Mead 1928). M.H. Mason, *The Arctic Forests* (L: Hodder & Stoughton 1924), and R.M. Patterson, *The Dangerous River* (L: George Allen & Unwin 1954), describe remoter parts of the Mackenzie basin. Accounts of oceanic voyages during the interwar years include D.W. Gillingham, *Umiak!* (L: Museum Press 1955), of a voyage to the Western Arctic on the HBC ship *Baychimo*, and D.S. Robertson, *To the Arctic with the Mounties* (T: MAC 1934), of a voyage on the annual eastern Arctic Patrol. Air travel in the 30s occasioned Edgar Laytha's *North Again for Gold* (NY: Frederick A. Stokes 1939), with useful descriptions of the mining booms of the 1930s at Great Bear Lake and Yellowknife, the former of which is also the subject of F.B.

Watt, *Great Bear: A Journey Remembered* (Yellowknife: Outcrop 1980).

TRANSPORTATION

The relationship between improvements in transportation and economic advances, and the inter-relationships among the different media of transportation within the northern context are explored in such works as M. Zaslow, 'The Development of the Mackenzie Basin, 1920-1940' (PHD thesis, University of Toronto 1957), and his MA thesis on the earlier period 1871-1921 (Toronto 1948); in C.A. Dawson, ed., *The New North-West*; in Gordon Bennett: *Yukon Transportation: A History* (O: DIAND 1978); in K.J. Rea, *The Political Economy of the Canadian North* (T: UTP 1968); and in B.F. Sater, ed., *Arctic and Middle North Transportation*. Railways, which furnish the underpinning for many-sided economic development, have not played a very important role in the past history of the North since only three or four lines have extended north far enough to affect northern development directly. Much of that construction occurred only in the past thirty years, too late to be noticed in most railway histories. An exception is R.F. Leggett, *Railroads of Canada* (V: Douglas, David & Charles 1973), which includes a concise outline of the post-World War II northward construction. As for the individual railways, there are the previously-mentioned Zaslow theses (for the Northern Alberta Railways); a good recent history of the Ontario Northland, A.V. Tucker, *Steam into Wilderness* (T: Fitzhenry & Whiteside 1978); of the Algoma Central (if that is relevant) by O.S. Nock, *The Algoma Central Railway* (T: Nelson 1975). For the Hudson Bay Railway there is only the dated, disappointing H.A. Fleming, *Canada's Arctic Outlet* (Berkeley: University of California Press 1957); and for the unique White Pass and Yukon, and early history by its president, S.H. Graves, *On the 'White Pass' Pay-Roll* (Chicago: Lakeside Press 1908), and the modern Cy Martin, *Gold Rush Narrow Gauge* (Los Angeles: Trans-Anglo Books 1969).

Water transportation, which has been a significant element to the present, is represented in the Rivers of America series by volumes on the Yukon and the Mackenzie, the previously mentioned works by Dawson and by Zaslow, and a good but dated MA thesis, G.B. Theissen, 'Transportation on the Mackenzie River System' (University of Saskatchewan 1962). Arctic navigation is reviewed in Beals and Shenstone, eds., *Science, History and Hudson Bay*, and T. Appleton, *'Usque Ad Mare': A History of the Canadian Coast Guard and Marine Services* (O: Dept. of Transport 1968). For specific ships and voyages there are R. Wild, *Arctic Command: The Story of Smellie of the 'Nascopie'* (T: Ryerson 1955), an inadequate account of that important HBC ship's role; R.A. Irvine, *The Ice Was All Between* (T: Longmans Green 1959), on the new HMCS *Labrador* historic traverse of the Northwest Passage in 1954; and H.A. Larsen *et al.*, *The Big Ship* (T: M&S 1967), on the career of the historic RCMP patrol ship *St Roch*. For overland travel since 1945 there are Frank Illingworth, *Highway to the North* (L: Ernest Benn 1955); Jim Christy, *Rough Road to the North: Travels along the Alaska Highway* (T: Doubleday 1980); and the American journalist Edith Iglauer's *Denison's Ice Road* (T: CI 1974), stories of the tractor-train operations of John Denison.

Aviation holds a special place, particularly during the 1920s and 1930s, in pushing back the northern frontiers of Canada. J.R.K. Main, *Voyageurs of the Air: A History of Civil Aviation in Canada* (O: Dept. of Transport 1967), offers a comprehensive survey of the entire industry, including northern operations from the beginning. The bush-pilot era is described by several participants, especially F.H. Ellis, an early air mechanic who wrote profusely, if uncritically, about that epoch, particularly in two books: *Canada's Flying Heritage* (T: UTP 1954) and *In Canadian Skies* (T: Ryerson 1959). The best autobiographical account, by a pilot involved in many notable firsts, is W.E. Gilbert and K. Shackleton, *Arctic Pilot* (L: Nelson 1940). Guy Blanchet, *Search in the North* (T: MAC 1960), relates the disappearance and safe return of the Macalpine party of touring mining executives in 1929, while E.L. Myles, *Airborne from Edmonton* (T: Ryerson 1959), reviews the main early aviation developments in teh northwest. A different sort of aeronautical pioneering, the effort to develop a transatlantic northern air route in 1933-4, is treated in J. Grierson, *High Failure* (L: William Hodge 1936), while Basil Clarke, *Polar Flight* (L: Ian Allen 1964), affords a general treatment of modern-day aviation in Arctic regions.

WORLD WAR AND POST-WAR DEFENCE

Two great dramatic events punctuate the otherwise fairly regular development of the North – the Klondike gold discovery and rush in the 1890s (treated in detail in the bibliographic essay of Zaslow, *The Opening of the Canadian North* and not repeated here for reasons of space), and the Second World War. The impact of that war in northern Canada has still not received a proper measure of historical research and publication. The main exception is the distinguished C.P. Stacey's *Arms, Men and Governments: The War Policies of Canada, 1939-1945* (O: Minister of National Defence 1971), an excellent, meticulously researched work based on top-level sources. By relating the wartime developments in the North to Canada's total World War II experience, Stacey helps offset the perspective of the most detailed American sources, chief of which is S.W. Dziuban, *Military Relations between the United States and Canada, 1939-1945* (Washington: Dept. of the Army 1959). This full account of American wartime activities in northern Canada, a volume in the official military history, *The United States Army in World War Two*, unfortunately is based completely on American materials without benefit of the sometimes counterbalancing Canadian sources. Another volume in the same series, S. Conn and B. Fairchild, *The Framework of Hemisphere Defence* (Washington: Dept. of the Army 1960), has some value in that it places the activities in Canada in the larger American perspective. Certain other volumes in this series review the Canadian operations of the corps or units with which they are concerned. The prime contractor for the Canol Project commissioned a sumptuous book by R.S. Finnie, *Canol* (San Francisco: Ryder & Ingram 1945), on that dramatic, controversial enterprise. For the other great construction project, the Alaska Highway, there are the early-day descriptions of H.C. Lanks, *Highway to Alaska* (NY: D. Appleton-Century 1944), and Gertrude Baskine, *Hitch-Hiking the Alaska Highway* (T: MAC 1944).

Most chapters in C.A. Dawson, ed., *The New North-West*, describe the impact of the American presence in that region, for the authors toured the region in 1943, 1944 or 1945 during the course of their researches. Another visitor of 1942, British High Commissioner

Malcolm MacDonald, whose observations greatly influenced Canadians' attitudes towards the massive US presence in the region, set down his impressions in a book, *Down North* (L: OUP 1945). The Canada-United States wartime co-operation is treated in H. Griffin, *Alaska and the Canadian Northwest* (NY: W.W. Norton 1944), and B. Kizer, *The U.S.-Canadian Northwest: A Demonstration Area for International Postwar Development* (Princeton: Princeton UP; L: OUP 1943); this co-operation led to the publication of *Canada's New Northwest* (O: KP 1947), the product of the researches of the Canadian section of the North Pacific Planning Project. All in all, however, Canadian historians have largely overlooked this very important episode in the development of the North.

Much the same can be said of the post-war role of the Canadian North in defence. For the most part readers still must rely on the appropriate chapters of the mainly biennial volumes of *Canada in World Affairs*, published by the Canadian Institute for International Affairs CIIA; articles in that society's quarterly *International Journal*; official reports and publications of the Departments of External Affairs and National Defence; government white papers on these two subjects; occasional articles in *Foreign Affairs*; and pieces in *National Geographic*, particularly describing the continuing US military presence in Northern Canada, such as the DEW Line or nuclear submarine voyages. These last are the subject of W.R. Anderson, *Nautilus 90 North* (Cleveland: World Publishing; L: Hodder & Stoughton 1959); J. Calvert, *Surface at the Pole* (L: Hutchinson 1961); and G.P. Steele, *Seadragon: Northward under the Ice* (NY: E.P. Dutton 1962). For air operations during the war and in the 1950s there is W.S. Carlson, *Lifelines through the Arctic* (NY: Duell, Sloan, Pearce 1962). The Cold War and the long-standing debate over nuclear weapons in the North inspired innumerable pieces in newspapers, newsmagazines, and mass-circulation monthlies; also such books as M. Conant, *The Long Polar Watch* (NY: Council on Foreign Relations 1962), and the pair by the Canadian-born American journalist J.M. Minifie, *Peacemaker or Powder-Monkey?* (T: M&S 1980) and *Open at the Top* (T: M&S 1964). The associated Canadian sensitivities over Arctic sovereignty account for numerous publications on that subject since the wartime Yvon Bériault, *Les pro-*

blèmes politiques du Nord Canadien (M: B. Valiquette 1942), which dealt with the island land masses. Recent concern for sovereignty over the waters surrounding those islands has inspired semi-official articles by J. Allen Beesley, Gordon W. Smith, and by the academician Donat Pharand, whose writings include the book *The Law of the Sea of the Arctic* (O: University of Ottawa Press 1973). The heightened attention that followed SS *Manhattan*'s attempts to transit the Northwest Passage inspired the co-operative work, E.J. Dosman, ed., *The Arctic in Question* (T: OUP 1976), in addition to a call for a north-oriented foreign policy in F. Griffiths: *A Northern Foreign Policy* (T: CIIA 1979).

NORTHERNERS – NATIVE PEOPLES AND WHITE SETTLERS

Prior to the Second World War the northern native peoples figured mostly in biographies, travel narratives, or anthropological studies, the last group beginning in the 1880s with Abbé Petitot and Franz Boas, and the principal Canadian government work being done by the Canadian Arctic Expedition of 1913-18. Possibly the most important such studies of the Inuit were made by the Fifth Thule Expedition, led by Knud Rasmussen, who wrote an informative popular account of its work, *Across Arctic America* (NY and L: G.P. Putnam's Sons 1927). Two of his colleagues also produced popular accounts: K. Birket-Smith, *The Eskimos* (L: Methuen 1936), and P. Freuchen, *The Book of the Eskimo* (Cleveland: World Publishing 1961). A Canadian classic from the same period of early contact is Diamond Jenness, *People of the Twilight* (NY: MAC 1928). Many of the previously mentioned books by missionaries, traders, officials, and travellers devote considerable attention to the northern Indians or Inuit.

Since 1945 emphasis seems to have shifted to the acculturation, and even the survival, of the modern-day Inuit. The mood was initiated by two influential books by Farley Mowat, *People of the Deer* (Boston: Little, Brown 1951) and *The Desperate People* (Boston: Little, Brown 1959), based on summer field trips to Keewatin in 1948 and 1949 as a naturalist for the federal government. These sensationalized, accusative books were widely criticized by northerners then and afterwards, among them by Lyall, *An Arctic Man*, who knew the situations and the persons about whom Mowat wrote. At any rate, the Mowat books were followed by such a torrent of writing that the Inuit soon became one of the most studied and written-about peoples on earth. The most important work on the Inuit for historians is D. Jenness's 5-volume study, *Eskimo Administration*, particularly vol II: *Canada*, vol. III: *Labrador*, and vol. V: *Analysis and Reflections* (M: AINA 1962-8), the product of the author's experience with, and thoughts about, the Inuit situation, re-enforced by examinations of relevant government records. Many of the studies on Inuit economy and society were commissioned and published by the NCRC and NSRG. A useful collection of articles dealing with the Inuit is V.F. Valentine and F.G. Vallee, eds., *Eskimos of the Canadian Arctic* (T: M&S 1965).

Some recent works on contemporary Inuit acculturation are J.J. and I. Honigmann, *Eskimo Townsmen* (O: University of Ottawa 1965), on the situation at Frobisher Bay, and *Arctic Townsmen* (O: St Paul University 1970), based on that at Inuvik; H.W. Finkler, *Inuit and the Administration of Criminal Justice in the N.W.T.: The Case of Frobisher Bay* (M: PUM 1975); the recent D.F. Raine, *Pitseolak – A Canadian Tragedy* (Edmonton: Hurtig 1980), an unfortunate story of a talented misfit; and M.A. Freeman, *Life among the Quallumaat* (Edmonton: Hurtig 1978), on the successful integration of a remarkable Inuk woman into white society. The acculturation of the Labrador Inuit is the subject of D.W. Zimmerly, *Cain's Land Revisited: Culture Change in Central Labrador, 1775-1972* (St John's: Memorial University 1975).

Books that deal specifically with the northern Indian and Métis are relative few. Here again one must look mainly to the publications of the NCRC and NSRG, notably the multi-volume Mackenzie Delta Research Project, or the academic journals. An important sociological work in the field is R. Slobodin, *Métis of the Mackenzie District* (O: St Paul University 1966). A first textbook history of the native peoples of the North was prepared for the NWT administration by K.J. Crowe, *A History of the Original Peoples of Northern Canada* (M: MQUP 1974). An interesting experiment, it is an elementary treatment, aimed perhaps at grade 6 level pupils. The current era of northern native land claims has inspired, and been greatly helped by, R. Fumoleau, *As Long As This Land Shall Last* (T: M&S 1976), a carefully partisan review of the negotiating and administering of Indian Treaties 8 and 11, based mainly on Bishop Breynat's Papers; and the openly polemical Mel Watkins, ed., *Dene Nation: The Colony Within* (T: UTP 1977).

An encouraging recent trend is the appearance of books by native authors. Those by northerners include the autobiographical M. Metayer, trans., *I. Nuligak* (T: Peter Martin 1966); J. Tetso *Trapping is my Life* (T: Peter Martin 1970); P. Pitseolak, *Pictures out of my Life*, ed. Dorothy Eber (M: Design Collaborative Books; T: OUP 1972); and the very different Edith Josie, *Here are the News* (T: CI 1966), a collection of the author's news despatches of occurrences at Old Crow, YT, to the Whitehorse *Star*. Inuit art has generated numerous books, such as G. Swinton, *Eskimo Sculpture* (T: M&S 1965), or H. Goetz, *The Inuit Print* (O: National Museum of Man 1977), and several volumes also present and discuss Inuit poetry, legends, reminiscences, and jokes.

The native and the northern scenery have also inspired many southern Canadian artists, poets, and novelists. Painters are represented by the indefatigable A.Y. Jackson, *The Far North: A Book of Drawings* (T: Rous & Mann 1927), and his autobiographical *A Painter's Country* (T: CI 1958), and W. Kurelek, *The Last of the Arctic* (T: MHR 1976); and poetry by Al Purdy, *North of Summer: Poems from Baffin Island* (T: M&S 1967). Novelists, inspired by the lives and characters of northern natives, have sought to portray them in such works as John Houston, *The White Dawn* (NY: Harcourt, Brace, Jovanovich 1971), who utilized his insight into Inuit character and knowledge of regional history, and the novels of Yves Theriault, *Ashini* and *N'Tsuk* (both M: Harvest House 1972), fine character studies of northern Indians, and his *Agaguk* (T: Ryerson 1963) and *Agoak* (T: MHR 1979), two Inuit stories that show his grasp of native character but rely as much on exciting adventure, violence, and a touch of prurience. Such realistic novels may help readers gain truer understanding of the North and its people, but it is otherwise with efforts like that of M. Richler, *The Incomparable Atuk* (L: A. Deutsch 1963), which make no effort to understand the native but use him simply as a foil to satirize whatever it is that the author wishes to attack. Northern wildlife is another source of inspiration, such as K. Conibear, *North Land Footprints* (L: Lovat Dickson 1936), as are the northern white settlers. Two examples of this last are Elliott Merrick, *Frost and Fire* (NY: Charles Scribner's Sons 1939), a novel about life in Labrador; and John Buchan, *Sick Heart River* (T: Musson 1940), in which the governor general used the knowledge he had gained of the lower Mackenzie River area during a visit in 1937. Finally, there are innumerable photographic books, with accompanying texts by Fred Bruemmer, Richard Harrington, and others, that portray the Inuit, the Indian, the northern scenery, and the native life. One fine book of photographs, with an excellent, scientifically literate text, is George Calef's *Caribou and the Barren Lands* (O: Canadian Arctic Resources Committee 1981).

The white community has also become a subject for study in the past generation, mainly by geographers and sociologists. One good history thesis, by Ethel G. Stewart, 'Fort McPherson and the Peel River Area' (MA, Queen's University 1955), shows the gradual evolution of a northern centre and its rapid transformation in the decade 1945-55. The great sociological work by Rex Lucas, *Minetown, Milltown, Railtown: Life in Communities of Single Industry* (T: UTP 1971), analyzes northern industrial centres in a general way that is pertinent to such communities as Yellowknife, Tungsten, or Norman Wells. *Yellowknife* (T: Peter Martin 1967) is mainly a collection of adventure tales, while P. Koroscil, *Whitehorse* (T: Lorimer 1979), is more of a standard urban history. Marginal people and groups are examined by several works, notably J.R. Lotz, ed., *The People Outside* (O: St Paul University 1971). Books dealing with the relations between the white settlers and their native neighbours, and equally critical of 'welfare colonialism,' include the popularly-written Hugh Brody, *The People's Land: Eskimos and Whites in the Eastern Arctic* (Harmondsworth: Penguin Books 1975), and the academic study, R. Paine, ed., *The White Arctic: Anthropological Essays on Tutelage and Ethnicity* (St John's: Memorial University 1976), one of several volumes on like topics from the Institute of Social and Economic Research. Finally, there is a book expressing the white settlers' anxieties and frustrations over current issues: Colin Alexander, *The Angry Society* (Yellowknife: Yellowknife Publishing 1976), a parting shot, as it were, from the longtime publisher of the Yellowknife newspaper, *News of the North*.

THE SEVENTIES: PROBLEM DECADE

A key issue of concern, that of environmental control, has been in and out of Canadians' attention for about a century but has grown increasingly important since 1945, and has been given a northern focus since 1970 by massive resource development projects such as the James Bay hydro project or the Mackenzie valley pipeline. A book that touches on early concerns for the northern environment is Janet Foster, *Working for Wildlife* (T: UTP 1978), which treats early federal government efforts to preserve the wood bison, caribou, and muskox in the NWT. The conservation movement is outlined in concise form by T.L. Burton, *Natural Resource Policy in Canada* (T: M&S 1972), and the Arctic oceanographer Max Dunbar's *Environment and Common Sense* (M: MQUP 1971); also in many of the papers in the four volumes of *Background Papers* (O: QP 1962) of the Resources for Tomorrow Conference, Montreal 1961. The James Bay project is attacked in Boyce Richardson, *James Bay: The Plot to Drown the North Woods* (NY: Sierra Club; T: CI 1972) and *Strangers devour the Land* (T: MAC 1975), while the preliminary oil searches in the NWT inspired such works as J.K. Naysmith, *Canada's North – Man and the Land* (O: DIANR 1971), a report on government policy; J. Woodford, *The Violated Vision: The Rape of Canada's North* (T: M&S 1972); and one of the earliest of many publications by the Canadian Arctic Resources Committee [CARC], *Arctic Alternatives* (O: CARC 1973), ed. D.H. Pimlott, K.M. Vincent, and C.E. McKnight. The debate over the Mackenzie valley pipeline reached its climax with the highly-visible Berger Commission, whose far-flung hearings and mountains of testimony (available in some major libraries) culminated in the report, T.L. Berger, *Northern Frontier, Northern Homeland*, 2 vols. (O: Ministry of Supply and Services 1977-8). Arising from the discussions and hearings are H. and K. McCullum, *This Land is not for Sale* (T: Anglican Book Centre 1975); H. and K. McCullum and J. Olthuis, *Moratorium* (T: Anglican Book Centre 1977); and M. O'Malley, *The Past and Future Land* (T: Peter Martin

1976), emotional works by supporters of the Berger Inquiry; also the scholarly, more dispassionate P. Pearse, ed., *The Mackenzie Pipeline* (T: M&S 1974). The debate continues following the withdrawal of the Mackenzie valley proposal as new developmental issues arise, for example, in F. Bregha's detailed account and critique of the Alaska Highway gas pipeline project, *Bob Blair's Pipeline* (T: Lorimer 1979). The recent literature is epitomized by the pro-development D. Peacock, *People, Peregrines and Arctic Pipelines* (V: J.J. Douglas 1977); the technical study, P. Williams, *Pipelines and Permafrost* (L: Longman 1979); and the concerned naturalist John Livingston, *Arctic Oil: The Destruction of the North?* (T: CBC 1981), the text of a lecture series in the program The Nature of Things. The issue of preserving the environment seems to have unlimited staying power, in southern Canada at least.

The uncertain, questioning mood of the 1970s is also caught by the last category of books about the Canadian North discussed in this article – monographs that attempt to deal generally with the whole North, with the territories north of 60, or with either the Yukon or the NWT. The earliest such works were prepared and published by the Department of the Interior and were factual, descriptive accounts that mainly stressed economic resources and current or prospective developments. They include the series, *The Yukon Territory*, the first of which was published in 1907, and for the NWT two compilations by W.C. Bethune, *Canada's Eastern Arctic* (1935) and *Canada's Western Northland* (1937). An important survey written outside government that reflected North Americans' growing interest in the Canadian North during the Second World War is R.S. Finnie, *Canada moves North* (NY: MAC 1942), reissued in expanded, updated form (T: MAC 1948). After the war the North became far more accessible to air travellers, thanks to expanded services and facilities plus a great amount of free military flights made available to properly-accredited civilians. N. Polunin, *Arctic Unfolding* (L: Hutchinson 1949), described one such broad-ranging scientific survey based on air travel. Pierre Berton combined his northern experience with observations during a series of air flights to produce a comprehensive, largely descriptive and narrative review, *The Mysterious North* (NY: Knopf 1956). The noted world traveller and journalist Ritchie Calder made a similar series of sweeps across the North, then published his *Men against the Frozen North* (L: George Allen & Unwin; T: Nelson 1957) as a companion-piece to his earlier *Men against the Jungle* and *Men against the Desert*. Based largely on interviews with local residents, the book is informative but nowadays seems highly opinionated and needlessly pretentious.

The mid-60s brought greater interest in the northern territories, with attention shifting perceptibly away from economic development to the questions of past federal administration and devolving greater autonomy upon the resident population, questions that paralleled contemporary discussions over the boundaries of the NWT and transferring the government to a northern centre. The years brought the *Report* and accompanying studies of the Carrothers Commission on NWT government (1966); the starting of an annual chapter, 'The Yukon and Northwest Territories,' in the *Canadian Annual Review* (from 1963); and the publication of such books as R.A.J. Phillips, *Canada's North* (T: MAC 1967), which offers readable but rather sketchy reviews of major topics, mainly administrative and social, by a senior civil servant previously involved in the federal administration of the North; K.J. Rea, *The Political Economy of the Canadian North* (T: UTP 1968), a thorough review of the economic history of the territories with particular emphasis on government roles in development; and J.R. Lotz, *Northern Realities: The Future of Northern Development in Canada* (T: New Press 1970), a somewhat disorganized, emotional critique of the management of the northern territories by the federal government.

The clouded, troubled 70s, with their complex economic, political, social, ethnic, environmental, and native rights issues, have produced a new group of books that tend to be interpretive and problem-oriented rather than descriptive and factual. Northern development was the subject of a Science Council of Canada study program that concentrated on the decision-making process and how it might be applied in varying circumstances and in the light of many differing considerations. A number of special studies were commissioned, one of which (Background Study no 36) was K.J. Rea, *The Political Economy of Northern Development* (O: Science Council of Canada 1976), a survey of past approaches to policy-making in Canada and abroad. The Science Council's Report 26, *Northward Looking: A Strategy and a Science Policy for Northern Development*, appeared in 1977. *The National Interest: The Politics of Northern Development, 1968-75* (T: M&S 1975), ed. E.J. Dosman, addressed itself to the same question – the problems that anticipated oil and gas production posed for the Canadian-American relationship, and the process of federal government decision-making on complex northern issues. The geographer L.-E. Hamelin, in his highly acclaimed (Governor General's award) book, *Canadian Nordicity: It's Your North Too*, transl. William Barr (M: Harvest House 1979), reviewed northern geography and regional zonation, then turned to discuss and analyze political factors – the federal government's position in the North and its relationship with the territorial and Quebec governments – and the various issues relating to, and arising out of, economic development. The book offers a wealth of stimulating ideas and forthright opinions, the fruits of the author's observations of Canada's North over the past generation. A recent book, Gurston Dacks, *A Choice of Futures: Politics in the Canadian North* (Agincourt: Methuen 1981), brings the problem aspects centre-stage, discussing native claims, self-government, and economic questions associated with resource development. Relying almost entirely on post-1960 writings, his book is uninhibited by historical considerations in reaching its conclusions. Nonetheless, it gives readers the most comprehensive, convenient account of the myriad events and changes of this last bewildering decade that they are likely to encounter. Even the footnotes constitute a valuable listing of the most recent writings on, or pertaining to, the Canadian North. So long as the current difficulties continue, what new crops of northern books will we encounter during the coming few years?

Index

This index should be used in conjunction with the Contents pages, not as a substitute for them.